Brown: GCSE Law

AUSTRALIA
Law Book Co.
Sydney

CANADA and USA
Carswell
Toronto

HONG KONG
Sweet & Maxwell Asia

NEW ZEALAND
Brookers
Wellington

SINGAPORE and MALAYSIA
Sweet & Maxwell Asia
Singapore and Kuala Lumpur

Brown: GCSE Law

John Wilman

Ninth Edition

LONDON
SWEET & MAXWELL
2005

First Edition 1978
Second Edition 1982
Third Edition 1986
Fourth Edition 1989
Fifth Edition 1993
Sixth Edition 1996
Seventh Edition 1999
Eighth Edition 2002
Ninth Edition 2005

Published in 2005 by
Sweet & Maxwell Ltd of
100 Avenue Road,
London NW3 3PF
Typeset by Servis Filmsetting Ltd, Manchester
Printed in England by Ashford Colour Printers

No natural forests were destroyed to make this product;
only farmed timber was used and replanted

A CIP catalogue
record for this book is available from
the British Library

ISBN 0-421-897902

Preface

The aim of this book is to prepare students for the higher and foundation tiers of the GCSE examination in law. It is also a valuable source of information for law elements in GCSE Citizenship courses. Major changes from the eighth edition include developments following the Anti-Terrorism Crime and Security Act 2001, and further consideration of the effects of the Human Rights Act 1998. A large number of changes effected by the Criminal Justice Act 2003, including the selection of juries, sentencing and many other important measures are also covered in the ninth edition. Actual and proposed constitutional changes are also discussed, and many new cases and statutes have been added.

There has been a re-ordering of the text since the eighth edition and the inclusion of a new chapter, *Enforcing the Law*. A number of up-to-date specimen examination questions appear at the end of, and occasionally in the body of, each chapter, as are useful websites for further information. Features retained from the eighth edition are the *'talking points'*, suggested coursework titles and a chapter containing hints for revision, examination technique and advice on the presentation of coursework. In the Appendix there is a glossary containing an explanation of the more common legal terms and phrases. Words explained in the glossary are in many cases printed in italic type in the body of the text when they first appear.

Acknowledgements

I would like to thank the Assessment and Qualifications Alliance for permission to reproduce past examination questions. Thank are also due to the Football Association for providing a copy of the FA Premier League and Football League players' contract.

The Christmas Day (Trading) Act 2004 and the Department of Constitutional Affairs form N201 dealing with small claims in the county court are Crown copyright. They and the jury service form are reproduced with the permission of the Control of Her Majesty's Stationery Office.

I would once again like to thank friends and colleagues, in particular Mr Alan Jones JP, for their helpful comments and advice. Thanks again are due to my wife Sarah for her support and encouragement, and for help in bolstering my rudimentary computing skills.

The staff of Sweet and Maxwell have shown their usual courteous attention and friendly assistance, for which I am again grateful. I would also like to thank them for checking the page proofs and preparing the tables and index.

March 2005   JFW

Contents

Table of Cases

Table of Statutes

1 | The Nature and Sources of Law

WHAT IS MEANT BY "LAW"?

What is the precise meaning of the word "law"? For our purposes it might be defined as

- a code of conduct for people in a particular community, which
- controls their relationship with the state, and which
- controls their activities towards each other concerning their private and business lives.

To be effective, law must be binding upon the whole community, and every person in that community must obey the law. It follows, therefore, that the law must be enforceable. A law which cannot, or will not, be enforced is no law at all.

In many respects, laws are accepted by most people in a community. The majority of road users, for example, would accept the necessity for all drivers to travel on the same side of the road, or to stop at a red light. Nevertheless, people who do not obey these rules are subject to *sanctions*, that is to say penalties by way of punishment. This is the way that the law is enforced. The same applies to all kinds of breaches of the law, from the most minor of motoring offences to murder. In that branch of the law which controls people's private or business activities, sanctions may take the form of paying sums of money by way of compensation, or some other form of remedy.

The "law" which we are concerned with here must be distinguished from other kinds of laws. The laws of cricket, for example, are observed by cricketers all over the world, but they are not "law" in the context we are discussing. Members of the community do not have to play cricket, and if they do, are free to alter or adapt the laws for their own convenience. An example might be when playing beach cricket while on holiday. The kind of law we are dealing with, on the other hand, cannot be ignored or changed for the convenience of individuals or groups within a community. Two men cannot, for example, ignore the criminal law and decide to have a western-style gunfight, as in the case of *R. v Maloney* (1985), where the survivor was found guilty of manslaughter. You will find details of this case in Chapter 9.

The difficulty in defining law, and the nature of law, is that it concerns cultural, moral, religious and egalitarian values, together with political policy and philosophy. Whatever the nature of law, if it is to be effective, it must encompass and bind the whole community, and it must be enforceable.

Religion and morality

Moral and religious attitudes still have a fundamental effect on our law. "Thou shalt not kill" and "thou shalt not steal" are not only religious commandments, but are enshrined within our law. This is because the community as a whole considers it to be wrong to kill, or to steal. It would still be against the law for a starving person to steal food or to kill for food, as in *R. v Dudley and Stephens* (1884), a case in which shipwrecked sailors killed and ate the cabin boy (see Chapter 10).

In a more general sense, the law frequently reflects a community's moral values. Such values are often difficult to define, since what might be moral to one person might be immoral to another. One person, for example, might consider the National Lottery to be a form of gambling, and therefore immoral, whereas another might considerate to be a justifiable form of excitement with the additional worthy aim of benefiting charities.

Because the public's moral values tend to change with the passing of time, the law frequently has to alter and adapt to accommodate these changes. Over the last few decades, attitudes to homosexuality, prostitution, suicide, pornography, the censorship of films, plays and so on have all altered considerably. As a result, the law has changed accordingly. Although many people still consider certain areas of human behaviour to be immoral, Parliament has reflected the attitudes of the majority of the community by passing laws to make certain conduct lawful which was previously against the law. Other notable changes in the public's attitudes have resulted in the widespread opening of shops, public houses (in Wales), and the playing of professional sport on Sundays. Recent changes have further relaxed the laws relating to gambling and the drinking of alcohol.

The law and us

Since the end of the Second World War, laws dealing with the welfare of the community have been introduced on a huge scale. The State has recognised the need to help the less fortunate members of society, and Parliament has passed laws to benefit those who are in the greatest need. The benefit of this *legislation* (law making) is available to all who qualify. In some cases all people qualify, regardless of their means. The lowest-paid worker and the millionaire are both entitled to the same state pension on reaching the age of 60 years for women and 65 for men, and everybody over 60 is entitled to the same winter fuel allowance.

The law affects every one of us from the cradle (and before) to the grave (and beyond). In addition to the obvious restrictions on anti-social behaviour, some element or other of the law affects nearly everything we do. A person who attends school, college or workplace is affected by laws which govern the condition of the building, health and safety, hours of attendance, and many other things. Law affects you when you travel, use your computer, enter a football ground, buy a chocolate bar, go to a club, and so on. It is important, therefore, that we should have some knowledge of our law and how it is administered.

The law and justice

The main aim of the law should be to provide justice. How good or effective then is English law? In the vast majority of cases, justice is undoubtedly done and good order maintained. On the other hand, as law is a human institution, and therefore can be fallible, mistakes sometimes occur. High-profile cases like those of the Birmingham Six, or the Guildford Four show us that in the area of criminal justice, important reforms needed to be made to try to guard against such miscarriages of justice.

As a legal system becomes more advanced and sophisticated, it is possible that the *letter of the law* might become more important than the *spirit of the law*. When that happens, a court might come to a decision which is legally correct, but does not provide justice. An example of such a case is that of *LNER v Berriman* (1946) where compensation was denied after a railway worker was killed by a train while he was maintaining the track (see page 29). Often Parliament may act to prevent future instances of injustice, as happened in the case of *Re Bravda* (1968). Details of this case will be found in Chapter 11.

The state and the community

In the foregoing paragraphs, we have encountered frequent use of the words *community* and *state*. These terms sometimes cause confusion, and indeed there are many interpretations of what they actually mean. For our purposes, put simply, by "the state" we mean the United Kingdom of which the Queen is the constitutional head. The United Kingdom in its turn comprises England, Wales, Scotland and Northern Ireland. This book however is concerned only with English law, which applies to the communities of England and Wales. "The community" therefore in this case can be said to be that group of people bound by a common system of law. Scotland has its own distinctive system.

THE NECESSITY FOR LAW

Crime

Man admits killing sisters and elderly couple

TEENAGERS THREW PUPIL TO HIS DEATH IN RIVER, COURT TOLD

Drink driver crashed

Police hunt killer of girl, 18

Prisoner freed in armed raid

"Drunken father killed ailing son"

These headlines appeared in one national newspaper over the course of a few days in early 2005. Similar ones can be seen in newspapers on most days of the week. If there was no system of law, the persons responsible for the above events would be under no fear of punishment or sanction by the state, which represents the community. Murder has always been considered to be a particularly terrible offence. It is therefore essential that there is an established procedure for providing that murder is a serious crime, and that murderers will be punished. The same is true for all other offences, ranging from rape, robbery, burglary and theft to the most trivial of motoring offences. In a civilised community there must be a clearly defined body of criminal law which can be enforced.

Rights and freedoms

If a community did not have a system of law capable of being enforced, the result might well be anarchy. The strongest individuals or groups could dominate with arbitrary and unfair rules to suit their own purposes, regardless of the well-being of the majority. People could do as they liked, with no fear of the consequences. If a community is to develop as a fair and free society, laws must be in place to ensure that an individual's rights and freedoms are protected. This is a very important area of our law, and one which in recent years has achieved a high profile.

Business and family

As a country develops its industry and business, its law must similarly develop and create a system which will ensure that business deals and transactions may take place with reasonable certainty, that disputes can be settled and that breaches of law will be enforced and compensated. As business throughout the world has grown and developed over the last hundred years, so have mercantile and company law, the law dealing with insurance, revenue and taxation, consumer protection, industrial relations and similar matters. Disputes between individuals in a family context, such as those involving marriage and divorce, and wills and succession are also covered by a highly developed body of law.

Responsibilities

Law is not only needed to ensure that offenders will be punished, or that civil disputes will be settled. It also creates a code of conduct which the community wishes to follow. A community has its own values, and its law should reflect these values. The Factories Acts and the Health and Safety at Work Act 1974 created laws to protect workers from injury by placing a duty on an employer to provide a safe place of work. Drivers of motor vehicles are required to be insured so that a third party injured in an accident will be compensated for any loss suffered. Shopkeepers have to refund the cost of goods of an unsatisfactory quality returned by a customer, and manufacturers may be liable for damage caused by defective products.

It should be noted that not all breaches of criminal or civil law are necessarily deliberate. In the examples mentioned above, breaches of the law could occur which were not intentional. An employer could accidentally and unintentionally create a danger in the workplace. A motor accident could be the result of a momentary lack of attention, or a shopkeeper may not have known that goods were unsatisfactory, yet all three may have committed an offence or a breach of the law. There have been breaches of law because the community created the law. Individuals are required to conduct themselves for the benefit of the community as a whole.

DIVISIONS OF LAW

English law is usually classified as being either **public law** or **private law**.

Public law

Public law is the law which governs the relationship between the State and individual members within the State, and between one State and another. This division of law comprises several specialist classes of law.

Criminal law

Crime affects the whole community, and as criminal offences are considered to be committed against the State, they are tried and punished by a system laid down by the State. When an action is started, it is usually in the name of the monarch as Head of State, whether it is a Queen (*Regina*) or a King (*Rex*). Thus criminal cases are usually referred to as, for example, *R. v Brown*. Sometimes, for legal reasons, initials only are used, as in the case of *R. v R.* (1991) (see page 254).

Criminal law is designed to protect the public from attacks on their individual property or person, and to enable any individual or group of individuals to perform their rights and duties under the law. Although a crime is against the State, an individual may suffer from the offence, so, as will be seen below in "Private law", in addition to the punishment laid down by the State, the individual will be able to obtain compensation for personal loss.

Constitutional law

This branch of law deals with the method of government within the State. Constitutional law affects the general public, in that it provides for the structure of the legislature (in this country the Houses of Parliament), the formation of the Executive (the Cabinet), the courts and legal system (the Judiciary) and the system of administration for both local and central government. The laws created and administered by these bodies affect the rights, duties and freedoms of each individual within the State. Ideally, there should be a separation of the powers of executive, legislature and judiciary, but in this country only the latter exercises a separate power.

Administrative law

As the Government has legislated for the provision of a large number of benefits for individual members of the State (*e.g.* welfare benefits), the courts and administrative tribunals (usually set up by the Government) have developed a body of laws and principles to regulate and control the agencies which administer the legislative provisions.

Administrative law is usually concerned with appeals and complaints from individuals against the ministerial agencies.

Private law

This branch of the law is usually called **civil law**. Unlike the criminal law, which deals with offences against the state, representing the community as a whole, civil or private law concerns dealings and disputes between individual members of the community.

When civil cases are referred to, the names of the individual parties are used: *Smith v Jones*. The first named is usually called the *claimant*. (**Note**: until recently, the claimant was called the *plaintiff*, and you will still find this word frequently used. The two words refer to the same party, and in reports of past civil cases described in this book, the term *plaintiff* will commonly be retained). The claimant is the person bringing the action. The person against whom the action is being brought is the second named, and is called the *defendant*. Occasionally you might see a case with a name like this: *Re Bravda* (referred to above). The Latin word *re* means "in the matter of" or "concerning", and is often used in, for example, cases which involve wills.

Although civil law only affects the individuals concerned, it does not mean that the state is in no way involved. In many instances the state will have created the law which regulates the conduct between the individuals, and will also administer the courts to hear and decide upon disputes which have arisen. The main distinction is that in a criminal case the state brings the action, and stipulates and administers any punishment. In civil cases, on the other hand, the individual starts the action and the courts award the wronged party the remedy best suited to the situation. For example in negligence (Chapter 9) or a breach of contract (Chapter 6), a sum of money, called *damages* may be sufficient compensation. If however a trespasser refuses to leave another person's land, an *injunction* may be needed to ensure that the trespasser leaves the land. Civil remedies are discussed in Chapter 3.

Classes of civil law:

Law of contract

This branch of law deals with agreements which are intended to be legally binding.

Law of tort

Torts are civil wrongs other than breaches of contract or trust. They include such wrongs as trespass, negligence, nuisance and defamation.

Law of property

The rights of individuals to ownership and possession of their property, both land and personal property (chattels). The law of succession deals with wills and how property is distributed after death.

Family law

The law concerning marriage, divorce and separation, and the responsibilities, and duties of parents towards each other and to their children.

Welfare law

As administrative law (see above) deals with disputes arising from the provision of State benefits, welfare law is concerned with the rights of individuals to obtain State benefits, and the rights and duties of parties with respect to housing and employment.

Note

A wrongful action can often give rise to both a prosecution in the criminal court, and an action in the civil court. A person who is prosecuted for dangerous driving, for example, as well as being punished in the criminal court, may be sued for damages in the civil courts by an individual who is injured by his actions. A crime may also be a tort. An assault, for example, is a crime for which a person may be prosecuted and punished. It is also a tort (trespass to the person), for which a victim may sue the assailant for damages in the civil courts. Certain kinds of defamation, nuisance and trespass to land are also crimes.

HOW THE LAW HAS GROWN

It was the Norman conquest of 1066 which established the basis of English law. Before William the Conqueror arrived, laws and the courts which administered them varied from area to area. There was no system which applied to the country as a whole. The Normans established a common law system by adapting the best existing laws and applying them to the whole country, but it was in the reign of Henry II (1154–1189) that the greatest steps were taken to develop the common law.

As the common law evolved, it developed a certain degree of formality and rigidity. The effects of this were mitigated by the system known as *equity*, where decisions and remedies tended to ignore the formal rules of law and were based on conscience and natural justice. Inevitably there was occasional conflict between law and equity, and in the early 17th century it was decreed that in such a conflict, equity should prevail.

By the 19th century, law and equity were administered by many different courts, often in competition with one another. The Judicature Acts 1873–1875 created a unified court structure in which both law and equity were administered, and further reforms were enacted in 1880 and 1970 to give us substantially the system we have today.

The structure and function of the courts, both civil and criminal, will be examined in Chapter 2.

TALKING POINT

"A law that cannot be enforced is no law at all". Do you think that this is true? In what ways do you think that law is enforced?

SUGGESTED COURSEWORK TITLES

What is meant by "law"? Why is it necessary for a community to have a settled system of law?

Describe the main differences between public and private law. In what ways do our laws protect the interests of the community?

SOURCES OF LAW

Where do our laws come from? Where do they start? In English law there are two main sources: *legislation* (Acts of Parliament, often called statutes), and *judicial precedent* (the decisions of judges). There are also subsidiary sources such as *custom* and books of authority, although in modern times only very occasionally has law arisen in these ways.

If a person is accused of breaking the criminal law, it is essential that all interested parties are aware of the source of that law which is involved. If, for example, a person deliberately removes goods from a shop without paying, the shopkeeper, the police, the shopper, the judge and any lawyers involved will need to know the law which applies if the case is to come before the court. This particular offence arises from legislation passed by Parliament in the Theft Act 1968, later added to and amended by the Theft Act of 1978. The sources of the law concerning theft or stealing are these two acts of Parliament, together with decisions made in court on the interpretation of them, as for example, in *R v Morris* (1983).

The same is true in a civil case. If, for example, a person says something untrue and damaging about someone else, all parties concerned will need to know the sources of relevant law in a potential action for defamation.

There is a well-known maxim in law that "ignorance of the law is no excuse". It is no defence to say that you did not know that what you were doing was against the law. Although it is presumed that everyone knows the law, obviously no single person knows all the laws of the land. Even judges, barristers and solicitors have to look up the law, but because of their training they are aware of where the law originated, and are able to go to the relevant source.

Details of the various sources of the law are dealt with below.

JUDICIAL PRECEDENT

Judicial precedent, or case law as it is often called, is the source of a large part of common law and equity. The law is "judge-made", in that when a judge makes a decision in a court case on a particular aspect of law, other judges may be bound to follow this decision in subsequent similar cases. Once the law has been established, the example or the precedent is *binding* on other judges, who must make a similar decision in cases concerning this aspect of law.

The doctrine of judicial precedent became firmly established by the late nineteenth century, although a system of precedent existed for hundreds of years before that. It was not until a reliable system of law reporting was started in 1866, and the administration of the courts was reorganised by the Judicature Acts 1873–1875, that judicial precedent became an established source of law.

STARE DECISIS (THE STANDING OF DECISIONS)

Not all decisions of judges create a precedent. Some courts are more important than others. The higher the court which creates a precedent, the greater the authority the decision will have.

A general rule is that lower courts are bound by decisions of higher courts, and some courts are bound by their own previous decisions. The hierarchy or standing of the courts is as follows.

The House of Lords

This court should not be confused with the House of Lords as part of Parliament, where it has a legislative function. The House of Lords, as a judicial court, is the highest appeal court in civil and criminal matters, and decisions of this Court are binding on all lower courts. Unlike most other courts, the House of Lords is not bound by precedent and may depart from its own previous decisions if it wishes to do so, but if a precedent is to be reversed consideration should be given to the effect it would have, particularly on criminal law and commercial and business transactions.

In 1966 the House of Lords issued a Practice Statement, in which it declared that it was no longer necessarily bound by its own previous decisions. There have been several occasions in recent years when the court has overruled its previous decisions. For example, in *R. v Shivpuri* (1986), a criminal case, the Court overruled its previous decision in *Anderton v Ryan* (1985) made only a year before, and in *Murphy v Brentwood District Council* (1990), a claim for negligence, the Court overruled a 1978 decision.

In *R. v R.* (1991), the House of Lords overturned a principle which had stood for hundreds of years, and declared that a husband who rapes his wife can be prosecuted.

In a more recent case, *R. v G. and Another* (2003), the House of Lords reversed a long-established principle concerning the nature of recklessness as laid down in *R. v Caldwell* (1981).

If there appear to be two previous conflicting House of Lords' decisions, the lower courts must follow the later decision.

The Court of Appeal (Civil Division)

The Court is bound by decisions from the House of Lords and, although it has been suggested in court that the position should be otherwise, the Court is bound by its own previous decisions. This principle was established by the Court of Appeal in *Young v Bristol Aeroplane Co* (1944), although it was laid down that the Court may depart from its previous decisions under certain circumstances:

- where it considers that a decision was made "*per incuriam*", that is, in error;
- where there are two previous conflicting decisions, the Court may choose which decision is correct and overrule the other decision;
- when a later House of Lords decision applies, this must be followed:
- where a previous court presumed that a particular aspect of law existed, but did not properly consider it (*R. (Khadim) v Brent LBC Housing Benefit Review Board (2001)*).

Decisions of the Court of Appeal (Civil Division) are binding on all other lower courts, but do not bind the Criminal Division of the Court of Appeal.

However, in *Derby & Co Ltd v Weldon (No. 3)* (1989) the judge held that a court at first instance is not bound in every case to follow a Court of Appeal decision, but may take into consideration the possibility that the decision may be reversed in the House of Lords.

The Court of Appeal (Criminal Division)

Decisions of the House of Lords are binding on the Criminal Division, but (unlike the Civil Division of the Court of Appeal) this court is not always bound to follow its own previous decisions. The Court will probably follow decisions of its predecessor, the Court of Criminal Appeal, unless that would cause an injustice.

The decisions of this court bind all lower criminal courts and may bind inferior courts hearing civil cases. Decisions of this court are not binding on the Civil Division of the Court of Appeal nor is it bound by decisions of the Civil Division.

The Divisional Courts of the High Court

These courts are bound by the decisions of the House of Lords and Courts of Appeal. The civil divisional courts are bound by their own previous decisions, but the Divisional Court of the Queen's Bench Division (which deals with criminal matters) is not so strictly held to its previous decisions. Decisions of the Divisional Court are binding on judges of the same division of the High Court sitting alone, and on the inferior courts.

The High Court

Decisions of cases of *first instance*, where the judge sits alone, are binding on the inferior courts but are not binding on other High Court judges. A previous decision of a High Court judge may be treated as a *persuasive* precedent but will not be binding in other High Court cases. It is suggested that this also applies to High Court judges sitting in the Crown Court, but does not apply to Circuit judges or recorders, and they would be bound by previous decisions of a High Court judge. Decisions of the House of Lords, Courts of Appeal and Divisional Courts of the High Court are generally binding on these courts.

The inferior courts

The county courts and the magistrates' courts are bound by decisions of the superior courts. The inferior courts are not bound by their own decisions as they cannot create precedents.

The European Court of Justice

For most cases involving domestic law, the House of Lords remains the supreme court. However, it should be noted that for matters concerning points of European law, decisions of the European Court of Justice are binding on all courts in England and Wales, including the House of Lords.

European Community law will be dealt with later in this chapter.

BINDING AND PERSUASIVE PRECEDENTS

It is not the entire decision of a judge which creates a binding precedent. When a judgment is delivered the judge will give the reason for his decision (*ratio decidendi*), and it is this principle which is binding and must be followed in future cases.

On occasions, judges make general comments in the course of their judgment to explain a particular point. Remarks made "by the way" are known as *obiter dicta* and are persuasive authority, not binding precedent. If, however, the judge is well known and respected for previous judicial decisions, such comments may be followed as persuasive authority in cases where there appears to be no existing binding precedent. Other sources of persuasive authority are writers of outstanding legal works and decisions from courts of other countries such as the United States, Australia and New Zealand.

Ratio decidendi

Ratio decidendi is the vital part of case law. It is the principle upon which a decision is reached, and it is this principle which is binding on subsequent cases which have similar facts in the same branch of law.

Obiter dicta

The second element of a judgment, *obiter dicta*, are things said "by the way", and do not have to be followed.

Court of Appeal cases have three or more judges and the result is given on the decisions of the majority. A judge who disagrees with the decision of the other judges gives a dissenting judgment, which is *obiter dictum* and never binding. If the judge who dissented is respected, the dissenting judgment might be used as a persuasive authority if the case proceeds to the House of Lords. There have been instances of judges giving a dissenting judgment in the Court of Appeal, and later, when sitting as Law Lords in the House of Lords, hearing a completely different case, overruling the precedent created in the earlier Court of Appeal case. In these instances the Law Lords have been "persuaded" by the dissenting judgment to overrule an existing precedent.

Decisions of the Judicial Committee of the Privy Council are only persuasive authority because the Council is not part of the English legal system. However, because the Privy Council is mainly composed of the Law Lords, its decisions have great influence on subsequent cases with similar facts.

Distinguishing

Although the facts of a case appear similar to a binding precedent, a judge may consider that there is some aspect or fact which is not covered by the *ratio decidendi* of the earlier case. The judge will "distinguish" the present case from the earlier one which created the precedent.

Overruling

A higher court may consider that the *ratio decidendi* set by a lower court is not the correct law, so when another case is argued on similar facts, the higher court will overrule the previous precedent and set a new precedent to be followed in future cases.

Note that in such cases the decision does not affect the parties in the earlier case, unlike a decision which has been reversed on appeal (see below).

Reversal

When a court is hearing an appeal, it may uphold or "reverse" the decision of the lower court. For example, the High Court may give judgment to the claimant, and on appeal the Court of Appeal may "reverse" the decision and give judgment to the defendant.

Disapproval

A superior court may consider that there is some doubt as to the standing of a previous principle, and it may "disapprove", but not expressly overrule, the earlier precedent.

ADVANTAGES AND DISADVANTAGES OF PRECEDENT

Advantages

Certainty

When a precedent has been established the law becomes settled. Lawyers and laymen know and recognise the law and can act accordingly.

The existence of a wealth of detailed, practical knowledge

All case law arises from practical situations, and the law reports give detailed information of actual cases. In English law there are never "theoretical cases". The case before the court must be on facts in which one party claims a legal right from the other party.

Flexibility

We live in a changing world, and a law which was relevant 50 years ago may not be suitable now. The doctrine of precedent allows the law to grow according to the needs of the community and move with the times. For example, as we shall see later a person under 18 is known as a minor. A minor is bound by contracts for goods which are necessaries. Fifty years ago a motor car or motorcycle would certainly have been considered a luxury, but today the court would probably take the opposite view, particularly if a student or young employee lived a long distance from college or work.

Flexibility is probably the most important advantage.

Disadvantages

Rigidity

Although it is considered an advantage for law to be certain, a binding precedent may mean that the law is difficult to change. The House of Lords, however, may change a precedent by overruling a previous decision, and Parliament can legislate for a change of the law. Unfortunately, either method may take some considerable time to effect the change.

Danger of illogical distinctions

Judges may look for a justification for not following a precedent, particularly if it is considered to be a bad decision. A case may be distinguished from another for illogical reasons so that a different decision may be given.

The complexity and volume of the law reports

Law reports date back many hundreds of years and it may be difficult to find an appropriate case, as there are more than 400,000 reported cases.

THE LAW REPORTS

The basis of judicial precedent is reliable law reporting, the accurate recording of proceedings in court and the reasons for verdicts being reached. Without this, case law could not be a reliable source of law.

Cases have been reported from the thirteenth century onwards, with various degrees of accuracy and reliability. Some are held in high regard, and are still considered to be sound authority. Others are of more dubious reputation and are never followed. It has been said of one reporter of many years ago, named Bernardiston, that he often slept through cases, and that other reporters would write nonsense in his notebook, which he later printed.

Modern law reporting

Modern law reporting started when the Inns of Court created the Council of Law Reporting in 1865 to ensure a satisfactory standard of reporting of cases of legal significance. In 1870 the Incorporated Council of Law Reporting was established. The reporters, who are barristers, must present the report which is to be published to the judge of the case, who may revise the wording before publication.

[1994]

[COURT OF APPEAL]

A

RANTZEN V. MIRROR GROUP NEWSPAPERS (1986) LTD. AND OTHERS

1993   March 2, 3, 4; 31   Neill, Roch and Staughton L. JJ.

Defamation—Damages for libel—Assessment by jury—Jury's award of £250,000—Whether
"excessive"—Whether Court of Appeal to substitute lower award—Courts and Legal   B
Services Act 1990 (c. 41), s. 8(l)—Convention for the Protection of Human Rights and
Fundamental Freedoms (1953) (Cmd. 8969), art. 10

The plaintiff, a successful television presenter and the founder and chairman of the
"ChildLine" charitable service for sexually abused children, brought a libel action against
the defendants in respect of four articles published in "The People" newspaper on 3
February 1991. She claimed they bore the meanings (a) that the plaintiff had protected a
teacher who had helped her to expose sexual abuse at a boys' school by keeping secret   C
the fact that he was himself an abuser, thereby abandoning all her moral standards and in
particular her publicly professed concern for abused children; (b) that the plaintiff,
notwithstanding her position as founder of ChildLine, had taken no action in respect of
what she knew thus putting at risk the children at the school where the alleged abuser
was still teaching; (c) that the plaintiff's public statements and activities on behalf of
sexually abused children, given her misconduct and culpable omissions, were insincere
and hypocritical; and (d) that the plaintiff had untruthfully told the editor of "The
People" that publication of the story would hamper police inquiries into the matter   D
whereas the reason was to avoid publication of the facts of her misconduct and culpable
omissions. The defendants pleaded justification and fair comment. The jury found for the
plaintiff and awarded her damages of £250,000. The defendants appealed, seeking a
reduction of the damages in accordance with section 8 of the Courts and Legal Services
Act 1990[1] and article 10 of the Convention for the Protection of Human Rights and
Fundamental Freedoms.[2]
On the defendants' appeal:—
Held, allowing the appeal, that the court's power under section 8 of the Courts and   E
Legal Services Act 1990 to order a new trial or to substitute another award in any case
where the damages awarded by a jury were "excessive" should be construed in a manner
which was not inconsistent with article 10 of the European Convention for the Protection
of Human Rights and Fundamental Freedoms; that an almost unlimited discretion in a
jury to award damages for defamation did not provide a satisfactory measurement for
deciding what was a necessary restriction in a democratic society on the exercise of the
right to freedom of expression under article 10 to protect the reputation of others and the
common law therefore required that large awards of damages by a jury should be more   F
closely scrutinised by the Court of Appeal than hitherto: and that, in the circumstances,
the sum of £250,000 awarded by the jury was excessive because it was not proportionate
to the damage suffered by the plaintiff and would be reduced to £110,000 (post,
pp. 696C-H, 696B-C).
Dictum of Lord Goff of Chieveley in *Attorney-General v. Guardian Newspapers Ltd*
(No. 2) [1990] 1 A.C. 109, 283–285, HL(E.) applied.
Dicta of Lord Templeman in *Attorney-General v. Guardian Newspapers Ltd* [1987] 1
W.L.R. 1248, 1296, HL (E.) and of Lord Keith of Kinkel in *Derbyshire County Council v.*   G
Times Newspapers Ltd [1993] A.C. 534, 551, HL (E.) considered.
Per curiam. (i) At the present time it would not be right to allow references to be
made to awards by juries in previous cases. Awards substituted by the Court of Appeal in
the exercise of its powers under section 8(2) of the Act of 1990 stand on a different
footing and could be relied on as establishing the prescribed norm. There is no
satisfactory way in which conventional awards of damages for personal injuries can be
used to provide guidance for an award of damages for defamation and juries should not
be referred to them (post, pp. 694A-B, C, 695F-H).   H

[1] Courts and Legal Services Act 1990, s. 8(1)(2): see post, p. 685E-F.
[2] Convention for the Protection of Human Rights and Fundamental Freedoms, art. 10: see post,
pp. 685G-686A.

Rantzen v. Mirror Group Newspapers Ltd. (C.A.)   **[1994]**

A

(ii) The jury in a defamation action should be invited to consider the purchasing power of any award they may make and to ensure that it is proportionate to the damage which the plaintiff has suffered and necessary to provide adequate compensation and to re-establish his reputation (post, p. 696A).

Decision of Otton J. varied.

The following cases are referred to in the judgment of the court:

B

Attorney-General v. Guardian Newspapers Ltd [1987] 1 W.L.R. 1248; [1987] 3 All E.R. 316, HL (E.)

Attorney-General v. Guardian Newspapers Ltd (No. 2) [1990] 1 A.C. 109; [1988] 3 W.L.R. 776; [1988] 3 All E.R. 545, HL (E.)

Bird v. Cocking & Sons Ltd [1951] 2 T.L.R. 1260, CA

Broome v. Cassell & Co. Ltd [1972] A.C. 1027; [1972] 2 W.L.R. 645; [1972] 1 All E.R. 801, HL (E.)

C

Chicago (City of) v. Tribune Co. (1923) 139 N.E. 86

Coyne v. Citizen Finance Ltd (1991) 172 C.L.R. 211

Curtis Publishing Co. v. Butts (1967) 388 U.S. 130

Derbyshire County Council v. Times Newspapers Ltd [1993] A.C. 534; [1993] 2 W.L.R. 449; [1993] 1 All E.R. 1011, HL (E.)

Gertz v. Robert Welch Inc. (1974) 418 U.S. 323

Gorman v. Mudd (unreported), 15 October 1992; Court of Appeal (Civil Division) Transcript No. 1076 of 1992, CA

D

Greenlands Ltd v. Wilmshurst and The London Association for Protection of Trade [1913] 3 K.B. 507, CA

Lewis v. Daily Telegraph Ltd [1963] 1 Q.B. 340; [1962] 3 W.L.R. 50; [1962] 2 All E.R. 698, CA

Lingens v. Austria (1986) 8 E.H.R.R. 407

McCarey v. Associated Newspapers Ltd (No. 2) [1965] 2 Q.B. 86; [1965] 2 W.L.R. 45; [1964] 3 All E.R. 947, CA

Morgan v. Odhams Press Ltd [1971] 1 W.L.R. 1239; [1971] 2 All E.R. 1156, HL (E.)

E

New York Times Co. v. Sullivan (1964) 376 U.S. 254

Pamplin v. Express Newspapers Ltd (Note) [1988] 1 W.L.R. 116; [1988] 1 All E.R. 282, CA

Philadelphia Newspapers Inc. v. Hepps (1986) 475 U.S. 767

Praed v. Graham (1889) 24 Q.B.D. 53, CA

Reg. v. Secretary of State for the Home Department, Ex parte Brind [1991] 1 A.C. 696; [1991] 2 W.L.R. 588; [1991] 1 All E.R. 720, HL (E.)

Reg. v. Wells Street Stipendiary Magistrate, Ex parte Deakin [1980] A.C. 477; [1979] 2 W.L.R. 665; [1979] 2 All E.R. 497, HL (E.)

F

Rushton v. National Coal Board [1953] 1 Q.B. 495; [1953] 1 W.L.R. 292; [1953] 1 All E.R. 314, CA

Savalas v. Associated Newspapers Ltd (unreported), 15 June 1976, Melford Stevenson J.

Scott v. Musial [1959] 2 Q.B. 429; [1959] 3 W.L.R. 437; [1959] 3 All E.R. 193, CA

Sunday Times, The v. United Kingdom (1979) 2 E.H.R.R. 245

Sunday Times, The v. United Kingdom (No. 2) (1991) 14 E.H.R.R. 229

Sutcliffe v. Pressdram Ltd [1991] 1 Q.B. 153; [1990] 2 W.L.R. 271; [1990] 1 All E.R. 269, CA

G

Uren v. John Fairfax & Sons Pty Ltd (1966) 117 C.L.R. 118

Ward v. James [1966] 1 Q.B. 273; [1965] 2 W.L.R. 455; [1965] 1 All E.R. 563, CA

Wright v. British Railways Board [1983] 2 A.C. 773; [1983] 3 W.L.R. 211; [1983] 2 All E.R. 698, HL (E.)

The following additional cases were cited in argument:

Abbassy v. Commissioner of Police of the Metropolis [1990] 1 W.L.R. 385; [1990] 1 All E.R. 193, CA

H

Autronic A.G. v. Switzerland (1990) 12 E.H.R.R. 485

Blackshaw v. Lord [1984] Q.B. 1; [1983] 3 W.L.R. 283; [1983] 2 All E.R. 311, CA

Cornwell v. Myskow [1987] 1 W.L.R. 630; [1987] 2 All E.R. 504, CA

Hayward v. Thompson [1982] Q.B. 47; [1981] 3 W.L.R. 470; [1981] 3 All E.R. 450, CA; (pet. dis.) [1981] 1 W.L.R. 1309, HL (E.)

Rantzen v. Mirror Group Newspapers Ltd. (C.A.)   [1994]

Reg. v. Chief Metropolitan Stipendiary Magistrate, Ex parte Choudhury [1991] 1 Q.B.
    429; [1990] 3 W.L.R. 986; [1991] 1 All E.R. 306, DC
Winyard v. Tatler Publishing Co. Ltd (unreported), 16 July 1991; Court of Appeal (Civil
    Division) Transcript No. 707 of 1991, CA
Youssoupoff v. Metro-Goldwyn-Mayer Pictures Ltd (1934) 50 T.L.R. 581, CA

APPEAL from Otton J. and a jury.

By a writ issued on 8 February 1991 and reissued on 16 December 1991 the plaintiff, Esther Louise Rantzen, claimed damages against the defendants, Mirror Group Newspapers (1986) Ltd., Brian Radford, Richard Stott and Mirror Group Newspapers Plc., for libel in respect of four articles published in "The People" newspaper on 3 February 1991. By their defence dated 27 March 1991, as amended on 19 July 1991 and 29 November 1991, the defendants pleaded justification and fair comment. On 16 December 1991 the jury found in favour of the plaintiff and awarded her the sum of £250,000.

By a notice of appeal dated 15 January 1992 and amended on 20 March 1992 the defendants appealed on the grounds that (1) the judge had misdirected the jury on the issue of damages in that (a) he had given no proper guidance to assist the jury to "weight", or to consider the financial implications of, any sum which they might award; (b) he had given no proper direction as to the relevance and importance of a defence of partial justification to mitigation of damages; (c) he had invited the jury to take into account in assessing damages the fact that the defendants had not apologised to the plaintiff: he had not put the failure to apologise into its proper or any context, nor had he reminded the jury of the defendants' reasons for making no apology; (d) he had failed to give any proper direction as to the defendants' case on damages; (2) in any event, the sum in damages awarded by the jury was excessive and unreasonable, being a sum which no jury properly directed could have arrived at as appropriate compensatory damages for the plaintiff, and the jury must have applied a wrong measure of damages; and (3) the award was so high as to amount to a restriction or penalty upon the right to freedom of expression which was not prescribed by law and/or which was not necessary in a democratic society, and accordingly, the award was a violation of the defendants' rights under article 10 of the Convention for the Protection of Human Rights and Fundamental Freedoms, to which the court should have regard.

The facts are stated in the judgment.

Charles Gray Q.C. and *Heather Rogers* for the defendants. The judge misdirected the jury on the issue of damages in that he gave no proper guidance to assist the jury in weighing the financial implications of the amount of an award. [Reference was made to *Winyard v. Tatler Publishing Co. Ltd* (unreported), 16 July 1991; Court of Appeal (Civil Division) Transcript No. 707 of 1991; *Sutcliffe v. Pressdram Ltd* [1991] 1 Q.B. 153; *Abbassy v. Commissioner of Police of the Metropolis* [1990] 1 W.L.R. 385; *Pamplin v. Express Newspapers Ltd (Note)* [1988] 1 W.L.R. 116; *Morgan v. Odhams Press Ltd* [1971] 1 W.L.R. 1239; *Coyne v. Citizen Finance Ltd* (1991) 172 C.L.R. 211 and *McCarey v. Associated Newspapers Ltd (No. 2)* [1965] 2 Q.B. 86.]

The award of £250,000 was excessive and unreasonable. The jury must have applied the wrong measure of damages. The purpose of an award in libel is to compensate the plaintiff for the damage to his reputation: see *McCarey's* case [1965] 2 Q.B. 86. Until the enactment of section 8 of the Court and Legal Services Act 1990, which empowers the Court of Appeal to order a new trial or to substitute another award where damages awarded by a jury were excessive, the Court of Appeal did not interfere merely because the damages were high. It did so only if the amount was out of all proportion to the facts: see *Lewis v. Daily Telegraph Ltd* [1963] 1 Q.B. 340; *Greenlands Ltd v. Wilmshurst and The London Association for Protection of Trade* [1913] 3 K.B. 507; *McCarey* [1965] 2 Q.B. 86; *Sutcliffe v. Pressdram Ltd* [1991] 1 Q.B. 153 and *Cornwell v. Myskow* [1987] 1 W.L.R. 630.

In considering whether the court should interfere with the jury's award it is relevant to take account of the concerns expressed by the United States Supreme Court in *New York Times Co. v. Sullivan* (1964) 376 U.S. 254; *Curtis Publishing Co. v. Betts* (1967) 388 U.S. 130; *Gertz v. Robert Welch Inc.* (1974) 418 U.S. 323 and *Philadelphia Newspapers Inc. v. Hepps* (1986) 475 U.S. 767. Those decisions establish that where a newspaper article is of public interest it is for the plaintiff to prove not only falsity.

The Council publishes the Law Reports and Weekly Law Reports. The latter were first published in 1953 and replaced the "Weekly Notes". The Weekly Law Reports are consolidated for each year and issued in volumes, so that at the end of a year, there are usually about three or four volumes of the reports.

Reporting cases is not the monopoly of the Council and other companies and private organisations publish reports which have equal authority. The best known are the All England Law Reports, started in 1936, while reports from *The Times* are frequently cited in court.

Referring to the reports

Students should know how to refer to a law report. Cases are quoted, for example, as *Rapley v Rapley* [1983] 1 W.L.R. 1069. The reference after the names of the parties means that a student must consult the first volume of the Weekly Law Reports of 1983 and at page 1069 details of the case are reported. It would be an interesting exercise for students to look up some of the cases quoted and listed in this book. If your college or school does not have law reports in the library, you may find them in the nearest large public library. *Rapley v Rapley* is referred to in this book on p. 291.

Useful websites

For recent judgements of the House of Lords: *www.publications.parliament.uk/pa/ld/ ldjudinf.htm*.

For judgements in various courts: *www.lawreports.co.uk/index.htm* and *www.courtservice. gov.uk*.

LEGISLATION

Parliamentary supremacy

Legislation is law enacted by Parliament. When passed, an Act of Parliament, alternatively known as a *statute*, becomes the law of the land. A statute is superior to all other sources of law and judges must enforce this law in the courts, even if it is contrary to an existing binding precedent. This supremacy of Parliament over all other sources of law—the *sovereignty of Parliament*—means that Parliament makes laws which have to be enforced. They cannot be ignored, or changed, or challenged on the grounds that they are not legal. By way of contrast, the Supreme Court of the United States may rule that a law passed by the Senate is unconstitutional and illegal. In the English courts, it is not possible to challenge Parliament in this way. It is however possible for an English court to rule that a piece of legislation is, for example, contrary to the European Convention on Human Rights. Such an instance occurred in 2004 (see Chapter 5).

Parliament consists of two assemblies, the House of Commons and the House of Lords.

The House of Commons

The House of Commons is a wholly elected body of over 650 Members of Parliament. Members are elected to serve as MPs for their particular parliamentary constituencies on the "first past the post" basis. All members of the public who are on the register of electors are entitled to vote, although a sizeable minority chooses not to. The life of a Parliament is five years, though in practice a general election is called before that time, and all MPs from the Prime Minister downwards must stand for re-election. The leader of the political party which obtains a majority of MPs after a general election is invited to form the next Government, and becomes its Prime Minister.

The House of Lords

The House of Lords is an unelected body. Most of its members are appointed as life peers, some others are hereditary peers, and some are bishops. In 2002 there were attempts to reform the House of Lords to include a proportion of elected members, but owing to disagreement as to what this proportion should be, these attempts for the time being have come to nothing.

The process of a statute

A statute has to pass through a series of debates in both Houses before becoming law. Approval of the House of Lords is not essential for measures dealing with finance. There is a set procedure which has to be followed and until this has been finally completed the "statute" is called a bill (see below). The procedure which follows usually starts in the House of Commons before going to the Lords, but it may be reversed. For example, the Cheques Act 1992 was introduced in the House of Lords as a private bill by Lord Harmer-Nicholls.

First reading

The bill is formally presented and there is little debate. The purpose is to inform members of the bill's existence and to indicate that printed copies will be available.

Second reading

There is usually a debate on the general principles of the bill. If the vote is in favour, the bill goes to the next stage. It is not necessary to vote at this reading unless 20 members object.

The committee stage

The bill is examined in detail. Each clause is debated and may be amended or even excluded. As the name suggests, the examination may be by a "select" or "standing" committee, or it may be discussed by the entire House acting as a committee. The examination at this stage is very important. Select committees and standing committees (20–50 members) are appointed on the basis of the political parties' numerical strength in the House of Commons.

The report stage

Its purpose is to inform the House of changes that have been made to the bill and to give an opportunity for further discussion. The House may make additional amendments.

Third reading

Generally only verbal amendments to the bill may be made at this stage. It now passes to the other House.

The House of Lords

The above procedure is repeated in the House of Lords, unless it started in this House, when it would pass to the Commons.

The Royal Assent

After a bill has passed through Parliament, it does not become law until it has been signed or authorised by the Queen. The Assent is a formality and, by convention, cannot be refused. Immediately the Royal Assent is given, the Act of Parliament becomes law, unless another starting date has been provided for in the Act.

A bill lapses if it has not completed all the above stages by the time a session of Parliament has been ended by Prorogation, or when Parliament is dissolved for a general election. It may be introduced in another session of Parliament but the bill must pass through all the stages once again.

An Act of Parliament is printed and may be purchased by the general public from Her Majesty's Stationery Office, or its agents.

On p. 21 is a reproduction of the Christmas Day (Trading) Act 2004.

Bills

Provisions which are proposed to become law are presented to Parliament in draft form. At this stage they are called *bills*. There are three different types: public bills, private member's bills and private bills.

Public bill

Public Bills are usually drafted by civil servant lawyers under the control of the Prime Minister. They may be introduced by the Government or by a private member, and they alter or amend the law for the country at large.

Private member's bill

A private member may introduce a bill, although it is not likely to be successful in passing through the necessary stages unless it is adopted by the Government. The opportunity to present a Private Member's Bill is limited and a ballot is held early in the session to decide the order in which members may introduce a bill.

In February 1992 Andrew Hunter, M.P. for Basingstoke, introduced a Private Member's Bill which required sellers of timeshares to allow buyers a "cooling-off" period of 14 days, in case the buyers wish to change their minds. The Timeshare Act 1992, received the Royal Assent on March 16, 1992.

Private bill

These are bills for special interest or benefit of a person or persons. The most common presenters of these bills are local authorities wishing to widen the scope of their activities or powers.

Codification and Consolidation

Codification entails bringing together all the existing legislation and case law into a restatement of the law. Codification may be of either the complete law of a country or a particular branch of law. The law of most continental countries is codified, but in this country and other common law countries (mainly the United States and Commonwealth countries) there is little codification. At the end of the nineteenth century there was an attempt to codify commercial law, and as a result there were enacted the Partnership Act 1890, the Sale of Goods Act 1893 and the Bills of Exchange Act 1882. It has been suggested that the law of contract would be a suitable area for codification, but it is unlikely to be so affected in the near future.

Consolidation occurs when all the provisions of several Acts of Parliament, dealing with a common topic, are brought together into one Act. It is becoming very popular because, although it does not alter the law, it makes it easier for lawyers and laymen to find. Areas of law which have recently been consolidated include company law, marriage, taxation and employment protection.

Christmas Day (Trading) Act 2004

2004 CHAPTER 26

An Act to prohibit the opening of large shops on Christmas Day and to restrict the loading or unloading of goods at such shops on Christmas Day.

[28th October 2004]

BE IT ENACTED by the Queen's most Excellent Majesty, by and with the advice and consent of the Lords Spiritual and Temporal, and Commons, in this present Parliament assembled, and by the authority of the same, as follows:-

1. Prohibition of opening of large shops on Christmas Day

(1) A large shop must not be open on Christmas Day for the serving of retail customers.

(2) Subsection (1) does not apply to any of the shops mentioned in paragraph 3(1) of Schedule 1 to the 1994 Act (shops exempt from restrictions on Sunday trading).

(3) If subsection (1) is contravened in relation to a shop, the occupier of the shop is liable on summary conviction to a fine not exceeding £50,000.

(4) In its application for the purposes of subsection (2), paragraph 3(2) of Schedule 1 to the 1994 Act (which relates to the interpretation of paragraph 3(1) of that Schedule) has effect as if—

    (a)   the reference to weekdays were a reference to days of the year other than Christmas Day, and

    (b)   the reference to Sunday were a reference to Christmas Day.

(5) In this section—

"large shop" has the same meaning as in Schedule 1 to the 1994 Act, except that for the purposes of this section the definition of "relevant floor area" in paragraph 1 of that Schedule is to be read as if the reference to the week ending with the Sunday in question were a reference to the period of seven days ending with the Christmas Day in question;

"retail customer" and "shop" have the same meaning as in that Schedule.

2. Loading and unloading early on Christmas Day

(1) Where a shop which is prohibited by section 1 from opening on Christmas Day is located in a loading control area, the occupier of the shop must not load or unload, or permit any other person to load or unload, goods from a vehicle at the shop before 9 a.m. on Christmas Day in connection with the trade or business carried on in the shop, unless the loading or unloading is carried on—

    (a)   with the consent of the local authority for the area in which the shop is situated, granted in accordance with this section, and

(b)   in accordance with any conditions subject to which that consent is granted.

(2) The provisions of paragraphs 3 to 8 of Schedule 3 to the 1994 Act shall apply in relation to consent under subsection (1) as they apply in relation to consent under that Schedule, but as if-

(a)   the reference in paragraph 6(1) to Sunday were a reference to Christmas Day, and

(b)   the reference in paragraph 7(a) to an offence under paragraph 9 of that Schedule were a reference to an offence under subsection (3).

(3) A person who contravenes subsection (1) is liable on summary conviction to a fine not exceeding level 3 on the standard scale.

(4) In this section, "loading control area" means any area designated by a local authority as a loading control area in accordance with section 2 of the 1994 Act.

3. Enforcement

(1) It is the duty of every local authority to enforce within their area the provisions of sections 1 and 2.

(2) For the purposes of their duties under subsection (1), it is the duty of every local authority to appoint inspectors, who may be the same persons as those appointed as inspectors by the local authority under paragraph 2 of Schedule 2 to the 1994 Act.

(3) Paragraphs 3 and 4 of Schedule 2 to the 1994 Act (powers of entry and obstruction of inspectors) apply in respect of inspectors appointed under subsection (2) as they apply to inspectors appointed under paragraph 2 of that Schedule and, for the purposes of paragraph 3 of that Schedule as so applied, the reference in that paragraph to the provisions of Schedules 1 and 3 to the 1994 Act is to be taken to be a reference to the provisions of sections 1 and 2 of this Act.

(4) Paragraphs 5, 6 and 7 of Schedule 2 to the 1994 Act (offences due to fault of other person, offences by body corporate and defence of due diligence) apply in respect of the offences under sections 1 and 2 as they apply in respect of offences under the 1994 Act.

(5) In this section "local authority" has the meaning given by section 8 of the 1994 Act.

4. Consequential amendments

(1) The 1994 Act is amended as follows.

(2) In Schedule 1 (restrictions on Sunday opening of large shops)—

(a)   in sub-paragraph (4) of paragraph 2, omit "or Christmas Day", and

(b)   after that sub-paragraph insert—

"(5) Nothing in this paragraph applies where the Sunday is Christmas Day (the opening of large shops on

Christmas Day being prohibited by section 1 of the Christmas Day (Trading) Act 2004."

(3) In Schedule 3 (loading and unloading at large shops on Sunday morning), after paragraph 9 insert-
"Christmas Day
10. Paragraph 2 does not apply where the Sunday is Christmas Day (loading and unloading at large shops on Christmas Day being regulated by section 2 of the Christmas Day (Trading) Act 2004)."

5. Expenses
There is to be paid out of money provided by Parliament any increase attributable to this Act in the sums which under any other Act are payable out of money so provided.

6. Short title, interpretation, commencement and extent
(1) This Act may be cited as the Christmas Day (Trading) Act
(2) In this Act "the 1994 Act" means the Sunday Trading Act 1994 (c. 20).
(3) This Act comes into force on such day as the Secretary of State may by order made by statutory instrument appoint.
(4) This Act extends to England and Wales only.

Useful websites

For information about and texts of Acts of Parliament: *www.hmso.gov.uk*

For new law and the stages of Government bills: *www.parliament.uk*

Interpretation of a statute

It has been explained that Parliament is supreme, and that the courts cannot challenge the legality of a statute. The courts, however, do have some effect on the law created by legislation. An Act of Parliament may have been drafted badly, in that the words used may be ambiguous, or not clear in meaning or may not provide for every eventuality.

For example, if an Act was passed ordering "every dog to be destroyed" by a certain date, what would be the law relating to hounds or bitches? An owner of a bitch may contend that the law only concerns male animals of the canine species, and does not affect bitches. In such an event the dispute would go to the courts for the "legal" interpretation of the word "dog", as used in the Act.

It must be noted that it is the courts which usually interpret the meaning of statutes, not Parliament, although many Acts include an interpretation section on words and phrases used in the particular Act. In addition, the Interpretation Acts interpret many general words and terms that are used in Acts, unless a contrary intention appears. One example provides that "words in the singular shall include the plural and words in the plural shall include the singular".

In *Pepper (Inspector of Taxes) v Hart* (1993), it was held by the House of Lords that the courts could refer to Hansard (the reports of Parliamentary speeches), as a help to statutory interpretation, where the law was ambiguous or unclear. *Three Rivers DC v Bank of England No.2* (1996), confirmed this decision and held that it also applied when trying to interpret a statute which was introducing European materials, such as Directives. It was considered important to look at ministerial statements to ascertain the true purpose of the Act.

When the courts have to interpret the wording of an Act, there are certain approaches which can be adopted. It is left to the judge in a particular case to decide which approach is appropriate to it. These methods of approach are often called the "rules" of interpretation, and are as follows:

The Literal Rule

If the words of an Act are clear and unambiguous, the judge will interpret them in their ordinary, plain grammatical meaning. If hardship should result, then it is for Parliament subsequently to amend the Act to avoid potential injustice. In *LNER v Berriman* (1946), a man was killed by a train while *maintaining* the railway track. The Act provided for a lookout to be on duty to protect those engaged upon "*relaying or repairing*" the track, and so the Company escaped liability.

The Golden Rule

This principle follows on from the literal rule, in that the plain, ordinary meaning of the words is taken unless it would be absurd or repugnant to the law. Section 57 of the Offences Against the Person Act 1861, for example, provides that the offence of bigamy is committed by any person who "being married shall marry". Since by legal definition a marriage can only take place when both parties are single, the courts have interpreted "marry" to mean "go through a ceremony of marriage".

The Mischief Rule (The rule in Heydon's Case (1584))

In this rule, the courts try to discover the reason for the Act. The courts look for the defect, or the mischief which the Act was trying to remedy, and they then interpret the words accordingly.

Gardiner v Sevenoaks DC (1950). An Act required film to be stored in premises under certain conditions. G. kept his film in a cave and claimed that as a cave was not "premises" he was not bound by the requirements of the Act. The court held that the purpose of the Act was the safety of workers or other persons and therefore the cave was "premises" for the requirements of the Act. The court looked for the mischief the Act was designed to protect.

> *In DPP v Bell* (1994), a male prostitute was charged under the Street Offences Act 1959, of being a "common prostitute". The court held that on a true construction of the Act, the term "common prostitute" was limited to female prostitutes, because a report which resulted in the creation of the Act, clearly showed that the "mischief" the Act intended to remedy was the "mischief" created by women.

The ejusdem generis Rule

It is a principle of interpretation that where general words follow specific words, the general words must be applied to the meaning of the specific things. If an Act was worded "dogs, cats and other animals", the general words (and other animals) would have to be interpreted in the light of the specific words (dogs and cats). It would be obvious that the Act referred to domestic and not to wild animals.

> *Evans v Cross* (1938). The appellant was charged with ignoring a traffic sign. He claimed that a white line on the road was not a traffic sign for the purposes of the Act, which read, ". . . warning signposts, direction posts, signs or other devices". The court held that the general words (or other devices) must relate to the preceding words and in this case they did not.

The express mention of one thing implies the exclusion of another

If specific things are mentioned and not followed by general words, only these specific things are affected by the Act. A statute referred to "quarries and coal mines", and it was held that as there were no general words, the Act did not cover any kind of mine other than a coal mine.

If we look back at our hypothetical case of the dogs (see above), it can be seen that the literal rule and the golden rule would be unsuitable as the word "dog" has an ambiguous meaning.

If the mischief rule was applied, and it was shown that the reason for the Act was to stop dogs fouling the footpaths or pavements, or to stop the spread of rabies, then the interpretation might be all animals of that species, whether they be dogs or bitches.

In addition to the rules of interpretation, the courts may use external aids such as:

* the Oxford English Dictionary;
* textbooks;
* Law Commission Reports;
* guidelines in the Act (but not margin notes);
* delegated legislation; and
* Hansard. It was a rule that judges may not refer to Hansard (a publication which records the debates in Parliament) to help interpret a statute. However, the House of Lords in *Pepper v Hart* (1993), reversing a decision of the Court of Appeal which dealt with a tax

dispute with the Inland Revenue, referred to Hansard before reaching their decision. The House of Lords considered that reference to Hansard was permitted where:

the legislation is ambiguous or the literal meaning leads to an absurdity;

the material relied upon consists of statements by a minister or other promoter of a bill; and,

the statements relied on are clear.

DELEGATED LEGISLATION

What is delegated legislation?

Parliament may give Ministers, Government departments and other bodies the power to make laws which are binding on the community and the courts. Generally, Parliament lays down the framework of the law in an *enabling Act*, and then delegates to subordinates the authority to make laws and rules for specific purposes within the Act. This form of legislation is increasing every year and has become a very important source of law.

Why is there a need for delegated legislation?

- Because of the increasing volume of legislation, Parliament does not have the time to consider and debate every small detail needed for the routine administration of an Act.

- In an emergency, Parliament may not have the time to deal with the situation, or in fact may not be in session.

- Although Parliament has passed a statute, the members may not have the technical expertise or local knowledge to deal with the necessary details, so they are delegated to experts.

- It is a difficult procedure for Parliament to amend a statute. Delegated legislation is more flexible and elastic, and if experience shows that a regulation or procedure is not achieving its purpose, or is inappropriate to the aims of the statute, it can easily be amended or revoked.

How delegated legislation is made

Orders in Council

The Government, usually in times of emergency, may be given the power to make laws in this way. Such an Order requires a meeting of the Privy Council and the signature of the Queen.

Ministers of the Crown

Ministers are given the power to make rules and Orders under statutes which affect their own departments. For example, the Minister responsible for transport has the power to change the maximum speeds allowed on motorways and roads.

Notice also S.6(3) of the Christmas Day (Trading) Act 2004, reproduced on page 21.

Bye-laws

Parliament gives power to local authorities and certain other public bodies to make laws within the scope of their own areas of activity. These laws have to be approved by central government.

Publication

All delegated legislation is technically made public by "statutory instrument", but this term usually refers to rules and Orders made by Ministers of the Crown.

Control of delegated legislation

There are certain safeguards which ensure that delegated legislation is controlled.

- Parliament has the right to inspect every statutory instrument, and has a select committee to scrutinise certain legislation considered likely to be oppressive. Parliament also has the ultimate safeguard, in that it may revoke or rescind the delegated power.

- The courts may declare a statutory instrument to be *ultra vires* and void. *Ultra vires* means "beyond the powers", and if a court considers that the statutory instrument has gone outside the scope of the Act under which it was issued, it may make such a declaration. In *Att-Gen v Fulham Corp* (1921) an Act allowed the Corporation to build a wash-house, but the Corporation decided to open a laundry. The court held that it was "*ultra vires*" the Act, and issued an injunction restraining the Corporation.

> In *Bromley LBC v Greater London Council* (1982), the Transport (London) Act 1969 provided that the GLC had a general duty for the provision of integrated, efficient and economic transport facilities and services for Greater London. The GLC reduced fares by 25 per cent and required London boroughs to increase rates to pay for the cost. Bromley LBC claimed that this was invalid and the House of Lords agreed that the action of the GLC was *ultra vires* the 1969 Act.

- Before certain delegated legislation may be put into effect, it is necessary to have a public inquiry, so that public opinion may be tested, and an opportunity given to those who wish to object to the proposed legislation to air their misgivings.

EUROPEAN COMMUNITY LAW

European treaties

The Treaty of Paris, signed after the Second World War, was intended to create political unity within Europe, and prevent further wars. The Treaty of Rome, 1957, created the European Economic Community (EEC), and the United Kingdom became a member on January 1, 1973. The Maastricht Treaty of 1993 created the European Union (EU). The Treaty of Nice, 2003, gave wider powers to the European Court of Justice.

The membership of the EU was further extended in 2004, and now stands at 25 nation states.

European law

A completely new source of English law was created when Parliament passed the European Communities Act 1972. Section 2(1) of the Act provides that:

"All such rights, powers, liabilities, obligations and restrictions from time to time created or arising by or under the Treaties, and all such remedies and procedures from time to time provided for by or under the Treaties, as in accordance with the treaties are without further enactment to be given legal effect or used in the United Kingdom shall be recognised and available in law, and be enforced, allowed and followed accordingly . . ."

The effect of this section is that English courts (and all United Kingdom courts) have to recognise EC law, whether it comes directly from treaties or other Community legislation.

As soon as the 1972 Act became law, some aspects of English law were changed to bring them into line with European Community law. For example, certain principles of our company law were immediately amended, and certain sections of the Companies Act 1980 were the direct result of an EC directive (see below).

There are several institutions to implement the work of the European Community.

The European Parliament

The Parliament consists of representatives (Members of the European Parliament) from all the Member States, but the number of MEPs from each State varies; for example, Germany, France, Italy and the United Kingdom have more MEPs than some of the smaller countries. Elections for the Parliament are held simultaneously every five years in the individual States to appoint their representatives.

The Parliament has some control over the Community's budget and some administrative powers, but mainly it has an advisory function. It may, for example, advise the Commission (see below) on important policy matters. It does, however, have the power to demand the resignation of the Commission.

In 2004, the European Parliament refused to accept the appointment of a particular commissioner, (see below), which enforced the temporary withdrawal of the entire list. This was the first time that the body had shown such a degree of power and influence.

The Council of Ministers

This consists of one member from each Member State, although again the voting rights are not equal for each State. The political interests of the Member States are represented in the Council. Many of the laws produced by the Commission may only be executed with the consent of the Council.

The Commission

This has 20 members representing all Member States, who are appointed by the Council for their independence and competence. A President of the Commission is elected by the Member States. The commissioners work full-time to ensure the provisions of the Community are carried out and to exercise powers given to it by the Council. It is the Commission alone which instigates and proposes Community legislation.

In 1999 the Commission suffered a serious, if temporary, setback to its reputation when the entire membership was forced to resign following evidence of corruption.

The European Court of Justice

The Court consists of one judge from each State and a second judge from another State on a rotating basis.

The main functions of the Court are:

- to ensure that the law of the Treaty is followed;
- to decide cases which allege breaches of the Treaty by Member States. For example, the UK in breach of a Directive on equal pay;
- to rule on the interpretation of Community law, when asked to do so by a Member State.

Community legislation is enacted in the form of regulations, decisions and directives.

Regulations

A regulation is of general application in all Member States and, in theory, it is binding in this country without reference to Parliament. It is usual, however, for there to be some legislative action, if only to repeal law which is contrary to the regulation.

> In *Re Tachographs: EC Commission v United Kingdom* (1979), a Council Regulation provided that tachography (mechanical recording equipment) should be installed in all road vehicles used for the carriage of goods. The United Kingdom Government decided not to implement the regulation but left the road haulage industry to introduce the equipment on a voluntary basis only. The Commission referred the matter to the European Court of Justice and it was held that:
>
> * the Regulation provided that the Member States shall adopt the law, and
>
> * the Treaty provides that a regulation shall be binding in its entirety on the Member States.

Decisions

A decision has a more specific application, in that it may be addressed to a State or corporation, and is binding only on that State or corporation. It comes into effect immediately, but may need legislative action by the Member State.

Directives

A directive is binding on all Member States, but the States must bring it into being by whatever means they wish within a set time limit. In the United Kingdom it is usually issued by statutory instrument.

A 1975 Directive prescribed that States define how equal pay for equal work could be achieved. The UK omitted to do this within the time limit and the European Court of Justice held the UK Government to be in breach of the Treaty (*European Commission v United Kingdom* (1982)).

The Consumer Protection Act 1987 implemented an EC Directive of July 1985 (see p. 185).

On July 1, 1995, The Unfair Terms in Consumer Contracts Regulations were implemented into English Law to comply with the requirements of the EC Council Directive 93/13/ EEC, dated April 5, 1993, on unfair terms in consumer contracts. This directive gives consumers far greater protection than the Unfair Contracts Terms Act 1977. See page 190 for details of the new law.

The effect on the courts of EU law

European Community law has also had an effect on the courts and on case law. Any court from which there is no appeal (House of Lords) dealing with a case requiring an interpretation of a European treaty must suspend the case and submit it to the European Court for a ruling. Decisions of the European Court must be accepted, but it is the Member States' courts which must enforce them.

It is also probable that European law affects precedent in that, if the law is contrary to a binding precedent of English law, a lower court may ignore precedent and give a decision based on the Community law. In a Court of Appeal case Lord Denning discussed the effect of the Treaty of Rome upon English law.

"The Treaty does not touch any of the matters which concern solely England and the people in it. They are not affected by the Treaty. But when we come to matters with a European element the Treaty is like an incoming tide. It flows into the estuaries and up the rivers. It cannot be held back. Parliament has declared that the Treaty is henceforward to be part of our law. It is equal in force to any statute . . . ."

In *Factortame v Secretary for State for Transport* (1990), involving a dispute between British and Spanish fishing quotas, the Government, in an attempt to stop Spanish fishermen from fishing in British waters, passed an Act which made it very difficult for the Spanish to carry on as before. The Spaniards started a series of actions which eventually ended at the European Court of Justice. The Court ruled that the Treaty of Rome required national courts to ignore their own law when there was a conflict with European law, and to follow Community law. It must be pointed out that European Community law has also benefited UK citizens as the English courts have to follow Community law, for example, in areas of employment law, where a lady worker was able to receive benefits on retirement which had previously only been available to male employees (*Garland v BR Engineering Ltd* (1983)).

Useful website

For information on the EU: *www.europa.eu.int/inst-en.htm*

SUBSIDIARY SOURCES OF LAW

As was explained earlier, the following sources have little impact in modern times, but are still, technically, sources of law.

Local Customs

Custom is the origin of common law. From the earliest days of William the Conqueror's reign, judges have tried to discover existing customs and absorb them into the common system of law. Although custom has now become part of the formal legal system, in certain areas of England customs are still recognised and enforced by the courts. Although they are very rare, cases concerning the proof of a custom do occur from time to time. In *New Windsor Corporation v Mellor* (1975), for example, the Court of Appeal held that, by custom, local inhabitants had the right to use a green, "Bachelor's Acre", for sports and pastimes.

These exceptional cases only apply to the particular local area in which the custom exists. In addition, the person claiming the right of custom will have to prove that certain other specific conditions apply, (*Mercer v Denne* (1905))

Books of Authority

If a precedent cannot be found to cover an aspect of law, judges may refer to legal textbooks for help. In the past, only works of dead writers carried the requisite authority but in recent years judges have taken notice of the opinions of living writers.

SPECIMEN QUESTIONS

(a) In the context of European Union Law,

    (i) explain, in outline, the functions of the European Commission and the Council of Ministers;   (4 marks)

    (ii) briefly explain the key difference(s) between a Regulation and a Directive;

    (3 marks)

    (iii) name a European Union Treaty which is binding on the member states of the European Union.   (1 mark)

(b) In the context of the legislative process,

    (i) identify **four** stages in the passing of an Act of Parliament;   (4 marks)
    (ii) briefly explain what is meant by a Private Member's Bill;   (2 marks)
    (iii) discuss what is meant by "Parliamentary supremacy".   (4 marks)

(c) In the context of delegated legislation,

    (i) explain **two** different forms of delegated legislation;   (4 marks)
    (ii) identifying at least **one advantage** and **one disadvantage**, comment on how well the system of delegated legislation operates.   (6 marks)

(d) In the context of case-law and the doctrine of precedent,

    (i) explain, with examples, the principle that higher courts bind lower courts;

    (4 marks)

    (ii) briefly explain the terms *ratio decidendi* and *obiter dicta;*   (3 marks)
    (iii) identify **one** example of a Law Report;   (1 mark)
    (iv) comment on the **advantages** and **disadvantages** of the system of judicial precedent.   (4 marks)

(AQA, Higher Tier, June 2003)

TALKING POINTS

Most countries of the world have a written constitution and a codified legal system. The English legal system is a complicated mixture of custom, common law, judicial precedent and legislation. Should the whole lot be tidied up and re-written in a code of law?

Each Member of Parliament represents on average 65,000 people, for whom some voted in favour, and others against. A significant minority did not bother to vote at all. How representative is the House of Commons?

SUGGESTED COURSEWORK TITLES

Describe how the system of judicial precedent (case law) operates. Discuss the advantages and disadvantages of the system.

What is meant by delegated legislation? Discuss the advantages and disadvantages of such legislation. Do you think the controls on delegated legislation are effective?

2 | The Administration of the Law

THE COURTS

In this section we shall examine:

- the **structure** of the courts;

- their **constitution** (how they are made up; what types of judge hear the cases), and

- their **jurisdiction** (which areas of law they deal with).

Courts of first instance are courts in which cases are first heard. **Courts of appeal** (often called *appellate courts*), hear appeals against judgments given in the courts of first instance.

THE CIVIL COURTS

These courts hear any disputes which may arise in the area of civil law (see Chapter 1). Of these, only the county court is exclusively a court of first instance. The High Court, though mainly a court of first instance, also hears appeals from lower courts. The Court of Appeal and the House of Lords are exclusively courts of appeal.

The magistrates' courts and the Crown Court, which are mainly criminal courts, also have some civil jurisdiction. This will be dealt with later when discussing these courts.

The House of Lords

As a court of law, the House of Lords is the highest, and the final court of appeal, in the whole of the United Kingdom. In theory, an appeal is to the whole House, but in practice it is only the **Law Lords** (see below) who hear appeals. Other members of the House of Lords do not take any part in this process of the law.

Constitution

Appeals are heard by a committee of no fewer than three from the following:

- The Lords of Appeal in Ordinary—the "Law Lords". They are life peers who have been barristers for at least 15 years. They are usually appointed after sitting as Lords Justices of Appeal in the Court of Appeal.

- Peers who have held high judicial office.

In October 2004, a special panel of nine law lords heard a case involving powers to detain foreigners indefinitely under the Anti-Terrorism, Crime and Security Act 2001 (see Chapter 5). This is only the second time since the last world war that this number of judges has been used.

Proposed new Supreme Court

In June 2003, it was announced that the House of Lords as a court of law would be abolished and replaced by a new Supreme Court. The reasoning behind this is to separate the judicial process from the business of legislation. As the House of Lords is also part of Parliament, as discussed in Chapter 1, law lords may be seen as not being independent of the legislature. The Supreme Court would be completely separate from Parliament and from the Government. After the passing of the Human Rights Act in 1998 and the growth of judicial review cases (see Chapter 5), this is seen as being increasingly desirable.

The abolition of the House of Lords as a court of law would have the additional benefit of removing the court from the Palace of Westminster, where there is an acute shortage of space. The new Supreme Court would of course need spacious new premises suitable for its importance, with all the facilities necessary for its efficient working. Several existing buildings have been considered for this purpose, but no decision had been taken by the end of 2004.

The law lords themselves seem divided on the desirability of a new Supreme Court. Those in favour say that the separation of the judiciary from Government and Parliament is "a cardinal feature of a modern, liberal, democratic state". Those against the change maintain that the present system works very well, and that money would be better spent on other urgent needs, such as a new Commercial Court, and on improving the lower courts.

A consultation paper, *Constitutional Reform: a Supreme Court for the United Kingdom*, has been issued. This considers what form the court should take, what its constitution should be, and so on.

Jurisdiction

The House of Lords hears appeals from the Court of Appeal and, in certain cases direct from the High Court. Appeals from the Court of Appeal may only be made by leave of either that court or the House of Lords. The Administration of Justice Act 1970 provided that, if all parties agree, in cases concerning the interpretation of a statute (or on a point of law) which was subject to a binding precedent, the appeal could go direct from the High Court to the House of Lords. In this process, there is a "leapfrogging" of the Court of Appeal.

The Court of Appeal (Civil Division)

Jurisdiction

The court may hear appeals from the county court and the High Court on matters of law or fact. Appeals may also be heard on questions of law from the many administrative tribunals, such as the Restrictive Practices Court and the Lands Tribunal.

Appeals may be allowed or dismissed, or the court may order a new trial. The majority of appeals are on points of law, but appeals may dispute the judges' awards of damages or costs.

Constitution

Appeals are heard by a court consisting of no fewer than three of the following.

- The Lord Chief Justice.
- The President of the Family Division of the High Court.
- The Lords of Appeal in Ordinary (the Law Lords).
- The Master of the Rolls.
- The Lords Justices of Appeal.

As a general rule the appeals are only heard by a court consisting of the Master of the Rolls and the Lords Justices of Appeal. The usual number of judges for each case is three, but several divisions of the court may sit at the same time. In cases of great legal importance, five or more judges may sit in what is called a full court.

A Lord Justice of Appeal is appointed by the Queen on the advice of the Prime Minister. He must have been a barrister for 15 years, and usually a High Court judge for many years.

High Court of Justice

This court has unlimited civil jurisdiction and hears appeals from inferior courts (civil and criminal) and tribunals. The work of the High Court is divided amongst the following three divisions:

- The Queen's Bench Division.
- The Chancery Division.
- The Family Division.

Each division has jurisdiction to hear any High Court action, but for administrative convenience the divisions specialise in specific areas of work.

Constitution

The divisions consist of a head or president and High Court judges or *puisne* judges (pronounced pewny). In addition, cases may be heard before a judge or former judge of the Court of Appeal, a circuit judge, a recorder or a former High Court judge. The judges usually sit alone but in the divisional courts there must be at least two judges. The usual or ordinary High Court cases have original jurisdiction, which means that it is the first time the case has appeared before the courts. The divisional courts, in the main, have *appellate* jurisdiction and hear appeals from inferior or lower courts.

The Queen's Bench Division

Jurisdiction

Ordinary Court

As a court of first instance, this division hears more cases than either of the other divisions. It has the widest jurisdiction, and deals with all matters not covered by the other divisions. A great part of its jurisdiction is concerned with actions in tort and contract.

The Administration of Justice Act 1970 created two courts as part of the Queen's Bench Division.

- The Admiralty Court hears cases concerned with the Admiralty, and acts as a Prize Court.

- The Commercial Court hears cases on commercial matters, such as banking and insurance.

Appellate Court

The divisional court of the Queen's Bench Division hears appeals from certain administrative tribunals, and from solicitors on appeal from the Disciplinary Committee of the Law Society.

It also has jurisdiction to hear applications for the writ of *habeas corpus*, and the orders of *certiorari, mandamus* and prohibition (see p.134).

It may be noted here that the divisional court of the Queen's Bench Division also has criminal jurisdiction, in that it hears certain appeals from the magistrates' courts and (since the Access to Justice Act 1999), from the Crown Court by way of "case stated" (see p.54).

Constitution

The head of the Queen's Bench Division is the Lord Chief Justice, although his work is mostly concerned with hearing criminal appeals. The greater part of the work is heard by approximately 50 *puisne* judges.

The Chancery Division

Jurisdiction

Ordinary Court

Hears cases concerning trusts, property, company law, partnerships, winding up of companies and bankruptcy, mortgages, taxation, administration of estates of deceased persons and contentious probate cases.

Appellate Court

Appeals from the Commissioners of Inland Revenue are heard by a single judge.

The divisional court of the Chancery Division may hear appeals from the county court on certain bankruptcy and land registration matters.

Constitution

The nominal head of the Chancery Division is the Lord Chancellor, but he never sits. The Vice-Chancellor is the working head of the division and there are usually 12 puisne judges.

The Family Division

Jurisdiction

Ordinary Court

Hears cases dealing with:

- the validity and the breakdown of marriage and all relevant matters, such as the custody of children and the distribution of property.
- non-contentious probate matters.
- applications in respect of guardianship and wardship of minors, legitimation, adoption and disputes between spouses over title to property.

Appellate Court

The divisional court of the Family Division hears appeals on matrimonial and family matters from the country court and the magistrates' courts.

Constitution

The Family Division is headed by a president, and there are approximately 16 puisne judges.

The County Court

The county courts were set up in 1846 to provide the opportunity for claims to be settled cheaply, although it is still likely to prove expensive if a person engages the help of lawyers. County courts in England and Wales can be found in most sizeable towns.

Each court has a **district judge** responsible for the administration and day-to-day running of the court and its office. In addition to this administrative function, the district judge may hear small claims (see below).

Jurisdiction

The county courts deal with most civil matters. The most important are claims in contract and tort, and undefended divorce petitions. The courts also deal with certain other matters, such as recovery of land, disputes concerning partnerships, trusts and inheritance. Other areas of jurisdiction include matters concerning the adoption, guardianship and legitimacy of children, probate disputes where the estate is not very large, and the winding up of companies.

Case management

Among the reforms following the report by Lord Justice Woolf in to the civil justice system, was the management of cases by the court. Previously the parties' lawyers managed the cases, but now, as soon as the defence has been filed, the court takes over. The judge is the facilitator who enables a settlement to take place, and takes a robust interventionist approach to case management. The purpose of this reform was to speed up the process of civil justice by discouraging delaying tactics, and thus cutting down on costs. Once the judge takes over the management of the case, the process is set in train, dates are set for the hearing, and postponement is difficult.

Defended cases are allocated according to which "track", or method of dealing with the case, is the most suitable. The task of allocating claims to the right track falls to the district judge. These tracks are:

- the small claims track, for claims up to £5,000 (except for claims for possession of land or personal injury, where the limit is usually £1,000);

- the fast track for straightforward cases involving claims between £5,000 and £15,000;

- the multi-track, where the amount is over £15,000, or for complex claims for less than this amount.

The purpose of the fast track procedure is to reduce the time taken in bringing the case to court, and to bring about a consequent reduction in costs. A strict timetable is laid down by the court for dealing with pre-trial matters to prevent time-wasting by one or both of the parties to the action.

Although decisions may be made to transfer cases from the county court to the High Court, or the other way round, the general situation is that:

- claims between £15,000 and £25,000 will be tried by the county court multi-track procedure;

- claims for between £25,000 and £50,000 will be tried by either the High Court or county court multi-track procedure, depending on where proceedings are started; and

- claims over £50,000 will be tried by the High Court multi-track procedure.

Personal injury cases for less than £50,000 must be started in the county court, and defamation actions must be started in the High Court, but otherwise most actions for over £15,000 can be started in whichever court is the more convenient. The actual trial, however, may be transferred from one court to the other if this is deemed to be necessary.

Constitution

Judges of the county court are circuit judges who are appointed by the Queen on the recommendations of the Lord Chancellor. The country is divided into circuits in which there are approximately 270 county courts. Each circuit has one or more judges. The circuit judge travels around hearing cases in the county courts in the circuit or district. A circuit judge also hears criminal cases in the Crown Court (see page 51).

In addition to the circuit judges, recorders, district judges and judges of the High Court and Court of Appeal, if they agree, may sit in any circuit as directed by the Lord Chancellor.

District judges

There are 433 district judges in England, Wales and Northern Ireland. They are appointed from the ranks of solicitors or barristers, and have been described as "the backbone of the civil justice system". They replaced the former registrars of the county court, and the reforms of the Woolf report radically transformed their work, so that they now are the lynchpin of the system. In the county court, nearly 80 per cent of all claims fall within the jurisdiction of the district judges. Much of their work involves settling cases before trial, but of those cases which do go to court over 75 per cent are small claims (see below). District judges handle all the cases in the small claims track.

Small Claims

The small claims procedure was set up in 1973 in order to make it easier to recover relatively small amounts of money quickly and more cheaply than in the ordinary county court. The action was to be heard by way of arbitration, informally, usually in private, and without the need for legal representation. The limit for such claims has been successively raised over the years, and now stands at £5,000.

Following the recommendations of the Woolf report, small claims are now heard in the ordinary court rather than in private, and are rather less informal than previously. The district judge is trained to take a more inquisitorial and active part in the proceedings. This means asking questions and generally taking charge, instead of acting as a referee. The use of lawyers is discouraged. They may be engaged, but a successful claimant cannot recover the cost of their use from the unsuccessful one.

Claim Form

In the
Claim No.	

Claimant

SEAL

Defendant(s)

Brief details of claim

Value

Defendant's name and address

	£
Amount claimed	
Court fee	
Solicitor's costs	
Total amount	
Issue date	

The court office at

is open between 10 am and 4 pm Monday to Friday. When corresponding with the court, please address forms or letters to the Court Manager and quote the claim number.

N1-w3 Claim form (CPR Part 7) (4.99)   *Printed on behalf of The Court Service*

Notes for claimant on completing a claim form

Further information may be obtained from the court in a series of free leaflets.

- Please read all of these guidance notes before you begin completing the claim form. The notes follow the order in which information is required on the form.
- Court staff can help you fill in the claim form and give information about procedure once it has been issued. But they cannot give legal advice. If you need legal advice, for example, about the likely success of your claim or the evidence you need to prove it, you should contact a solicitor or a Citizens Advice Bureau.
- If you are filling in the claim form by hand, please use black ink and write in block capitals.
- Copy the completed claim form and the defendant's notes for guidance so that you have one copy for yourself, one copy for the court and one copy for each defendant. Send or take the forms to the court office with the appropriate fee. The court will tell you how much this is.

Notes on completing the claim form

Heading

You must fill in the heading of the form to indicate whether you want the claim to be issued in a county court or in the High Court (The High Court means either a District Registry (attached to a county court) or the Royal Courts of Justice in London). There are restrictions on claims which may be issued in the High Court (see 'Value' overleaf).

Use whichever of the following is appropriate:

'In the ....County Court'
(inserting the name of the court)

or

'In the High Court of Justice........................Division'
(inserting eg. 'Queen's Bench' or 'Chancery' as appropriate)
'..............................District Registry'
(inserting the name of the District Registry)

or

'In the High Court of Justice.......................Division,
(inserting eg. 'Queen's Bench' or 'Chancery' as appropriate)
Royal Courts of Justice'

Claimant and defendant details

As the person issuing the claim, you are called the 'claimant'; the person you are suing is called the 'defendant'. Claimants who are under 18 years old (unless otherwise permitted by the court) and patients within the meaning of the Mental Health Act 1983, must have a litigation friend to issue and conduct court proceedings on their behalf. Court staff will tell you more about what you need to do if this applies to you.

You must provide the following information about yourself **and** the defendant according to the capacity in which you are suing and in which the defendant is being sued. When suing or being sued as:-

an individual:

All known forenames and surname, whether Mr, Mrs, Miss, Ms or Other (e.g. Dr) and residential address **(including** postcode and telephone number) in England and Wales. Where the defendant is a proprietor of a business, a partner in a firm or an individual sued in the name of a club or other unincorporated association, the address for service should be the usual or last known place of residence **or** principal place of business of the company, firm or club or other unincorporated association.

Where the individual is:

under 18 write '(a child by Mr Joe Bloggs his litigation friend)' after the name. If the child is conducting proceedings on their own behalf write '(a child)' after the child's name.

a patient within the meaning of the Mental Health Act 1983 write '(by Mr Joe Bloggs his litigation friend)' after the patient's name.

trading under another name

you must add the words 'trading as' and the trading name e.g. 'Mr John Smith trading as Smith's Groceries'.

suing or being sued in a representative capacity

you must say what that capacity is e.g. 'Mr Joe Bloggs as the representative of Mrs Sharon Bloggs (deceased)'.

suing or being sued in the name of a club or other unincorporated association

add the words 'suing/sued on behalf of' followed by the name of the club or other unincorporated association.

a firm

enter the name of the firm followed by the words 'a firm' e.g. 'Bandbox - a firm' and an address for service which is either a partner's residential address or the principal or last known place of business.

a corporation (other than a company)

enter the full name of the corporation and the address which is either its principal office **or** any other place where the corporation carries on activities and which has a real connection with the claim.

a company registered in England and Wales

enter the name of the company and an address which is either the company's registered office **or** any place of business that has a real, or the most, connection with the claim e.g. the shop where the goods were bought.

an overseas company (defined by s744 of the Companies Act 1985)

enter the name of the company and either the address registered under s691 of the Act **or** the address of the place of business having a real, or the most, connection with the claim.

Brief details of claim

Note: The facts and full details about your claim and whether or not you are claiming interest, should be set out in the 'particulars of claim' *(see note under 'Particulars of Claim').*

You must set out under **this** heading:

- a concise statement of the nature of your claim
- the remedy you are seeking e.g. payment of money; an order for return of goods or their value; an order to prevent a person doing an act; damages for personal injuries.

Value

If you are claiming a **fixed amount of money** (a 'specified amount') write the amount in the box at the bottom right-hand corner of the claim form against 'amount claimed'.

If you are not claiming a fixed amount of money (an 'unspecified amount') under 'Value' write "I expect to recover" followed by whichever of the following applies to your claim:

- "not more than £5,000" **or**
- "more than £5,000 but not more than £15,000"**or**
- "more than £15,000"

If you are **not able** to put a value on your claim, write "I cannot say how much I expect to recover".

Personal injuries

If your claim is for 'not more than £5,000' and includes a claim for personal injuries, you must also write "My claim includes a claim for personal injuries and the amount I expect to recover as damages for pain, suffering and loss of amenity is" followed by either:

- "not more than £1,000" **or**
- "more than £1,000"

Housing disrepair

If your claim is for 'not more than £5,000' and includes a claim for housing disrepair relating to residential premises, you must also write "My claim includes a claim against my landlord for housing disrepair relating to residential premises. The cost of the repairs or other work is estimated to be" followed by either:

- "not more than £1,000" **or**
- "more than £1,000"

If within this claim, you are making a claim for other damages, you must also write:

"I expect to recover as damages" followed by either:

- "not more than £1,000" **or**
- "more than £1,000"

Issuing in the High Court

You may only issue in the High Court if one of the following statements applies to your claim:-

"By law, my claim must be issued in the High Court. The Act which provides this is ....(specify Act)"

or

"I expect to recover more than £15,000"

or

"My claim includes a claim for personal injuries and the value of the claim is £50,000 or more"

or

"My claim needs to be in a specialist High Court list, namely.................................(state which list)".

If one of the statements does apply and you wish to, or must by law, issue your claim in the High Court, write the words "I wish my claim to issue in the High Court because" followed by the relevant statement e.g. "I wish my claim to issue in the High Court because my claim includes a claim for personal injuries and the value of my claim is £50,000 or more."

Defendant's name and address

Enter in this box the full names and address of the defendant receiving the claim form (ie. one claim form for each defendant). If the defendant is to be served outside England and Wales, you may need to obtain the court's permission.

Particulars of claim

You may include your particulars of claim on the claim form in the space provided or in a separate document which you should head 'Particulars of Claim'. It should include the names of the parties, the court, the claim number and your address for service and also contain a statement of truth. You should keep a copy for yourself, provide one for the court and one for each defendant. Separate particulars of claim can either be served

- with the claim form **or**
- within 14 days after the date on which the claim form was served.

If your particulars of claim are served separately from the claim form, they must be served with the forms on which the defendant may reply to your claim.

Your particulars of claim must include

- a concise statement of the facts on which you rely
- a statement (if applicable) to the effect that you are seeking aggravated damages or exemplary damages
- details of any interest which you are claiming
- any other matters required for your type of claim as set out in the relevant practice direction

Address for documents

Insert in this box the address at which you wish to receive documents and/or payments, if different from the address you have already given under the heading 'Claimant'. The address must be in England or Wales. If you are willing to accept service by DX, fax or e-mail, add details.

Statement of truth

This must be signed by you, by your solicitor or your litigation friend, as appropriate.

Where the claimant is a registered company or a corporation the claim must be signed by either the director, treasurer, secretary, chief executive, manager or other officer of the company or (in the case of a corporation) the mayor, chairman, president or town clerk.

Advantages and disadvantages

The small claims procedure remains a relatively quick and cheap way of pursuing minor civil actions, and there are many excellent and clearly-written pamphlets available from the county court offices which help the ordinary person to make such claims.

There are, however, some drawbacks to the small claims procedure. Legal aid for representation is not available, a fact which may be relevant if one party without representation finds that the other—often a company or business—has instructed a lawyer. This situation would mean an unfair advantage to one side.

Another disadvantage is that the right of appeal is very limited, and only exists if the district judge has made a mistake of law. Even then, the cost of an appeal would probably be out of proportion to the amount of the original claim.

A further problem is enforcing the judgement. Even if a claimant wins the case, it is not always possible to recover the amount owing. Statistics show that only just over half of successful claimants actually manage to get their money back from the defendant.

System of Appeal through the Civil Courts

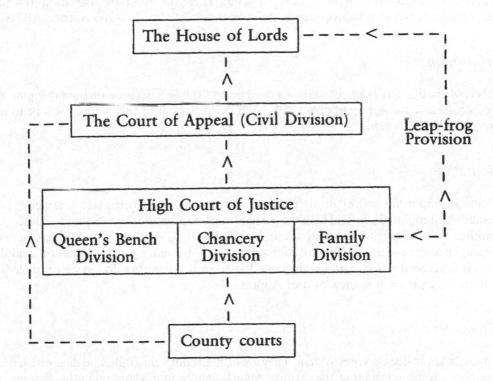

ALTERNATIVE DISPUTE RESOLUTION

Resolving civil disputes by going to court can often be a long, acrimonious and expensive business. There will be many occasions where a court hearing may be the least suitable way of dealing with disputes. An example might be where detailed scientific or medical points are involved (rather than legal ones), which a judge might not easily understand. As a result, alternative methods have become increasingly popular in recent years. ADR can take several forms: below are listed some of them.

Informal negotiation

This is the simplest and most common form of ADR. The parties will meet, with or without legal representatives, and attempt to sort out their problems by means of discussion and compromise. In this way, many civil disputes are "settled out of court".

Formal schemes of conciliation

The Advisory, Conciliation and Arbitration Service (ACAS), mediates in many industrial disputes and cases of unfair dismissal. The Parliamentary Commissioner for Administration (the Ombudsman), also investigates grievances against local and central government, as well as insurance and banking matters, (see Chapter 5). There are also trade organisations which deal with customer complaints, such as the Association of British Travel Agents (ABTA).

Arbitration

This is where the parties agree to allow a third party to make a decision on their dispute, and is controlled by the Arbitration Act 1996. A fuller treatment of this method will be found later on in this chapter.

Mediation

This is an important way of resolving some disputes in divorce cases (see Chapter 11). A mediator is appointed who will help the parties to come to a mutually acceptable agreement. Another mediation scheme is that set up by the Court of Appeal in 1996. The Court of Appeal arranges mediation if the parties agree to it. If they do agree to mediation, and the process is successful, the matter ends there. If not, or if the parties do not agree to mediation, the case proceeds to the Court of Appeal.

Tribunals

Tribunals lie outside the court system. They are of many different kinds, and deal with a wide variety of disputes. Details of the various tribunals can be found later on in this chapter.

Useful website

Advisory, Conciliation and Arbitration Service (ACAS): *www.acas.org.uk*

THE CRIMINAL COURTS

The House of Lords

The court hears appeals from the Court of Appeal (Criminal Division) and the divisional court of the Queen's Bench provided that these courts certify that a point of law of general public importance is involved, and leave to appeal has been granted by these courts or by the House of Lords.

The Court of Appeal (Criminal Division)

Jurisdiction

The Court hears appeals against decisions of the Crown Court by persons convicted on indictment, or by persons convicted by a magistrates' court but sentenced by the Crown Court. Appeals against conviction on matters of law may be made as of right, but only with leave of the court for other reasons.

Appeals against sentence may only be made by leave of the court. Should the Court of Appeal refuse to grant leave to hear an appeal, the convicted person may appeal to the Home Secretary, who has the power to refer the case back to the Court of Appeal.

The Court has the power to:

- dismiss ("quash") the decision,

- vary the sentence by making it longer or shorter (for example, the court has in recent years increased an over-lenient sentence in a case of incest from three years to six years imprisonment, and varied an 18-month suspended sentence to one of three years probation),

- order a new trial.

Constitution

The Lord Chief Justice is the head of this court, and in addition to the Lords Justices of Appeal, judges of the High Court (in practice, judges of the Queen's Bench Division) may sit if asked by the Lord Chief Justice. Circuit judges approved by the Lord Chancellor and nominated by the Lord Chief Justice may sit in the court.

The court must consist of at least three judges, but may consist of higher odd numbers (e.g. five or seven).

The Crown Court

The Courts Act 1971 abolished the courts of assize and quarter sessions, the Crown Courts at Liverpool and Manchester, and the Central Criminal Court in London, and established the Crown Court as a single court to carry out the work previously administered by these courts. The Act, however, provided that when the Crown Court sits in London, it shall be named the Central Criminal Court, or as it is traditionally called, "The Old Bailey".

The old courts, in the main, heard cases which were committed in the towns or districts in which the courts were situated, but the jurisdiction of the Crown Court is not so limited and its business may be carried out anywhere.

Jurisdiction

The Courts Act 1971, which created the Crown Court, provided that it shall be a superior court of record and will deal with:

- all cases on *indictment*, wherever committed,
- hear appeals from the magistrates' court against conviction or sentence,
- pass sentence on cases where the accused has been found guilty by the magistrates, but the lower court considers that it does not have the jurisdiction to pass the appropriate sentence,
- conduct certain civil work, previously carried out by the quarter sessions, such as dealing with appeals over licensing.

Note

An *indictment* is a written statement accusing a person of having committed a crime. Offences triable upon indictment are called *indictable offences*, and are generally the more serious crimes, like murder, manslaughter and rape.

Constitution

Judges of the Crown Court are as follows:

All Judges of the High Court

The Lord Chancellor may request a judge of the Court of Appeal to sit in the court, when he shall be regarded as a judge of the High Court.

Circuit Judges

They are appointed by the Queen, on the recommendation of the Lord Chancellor. The latter may remove them from office on grounds of incapacity or misbehaviour. Circuit judges are appointed from recorders of at least five years' standing, or from barristers of at least 10 years' standing. It should be noted that solicitors may be appointed as recorders and therefore this Act provides for the appointment of solicitors as High Court judges.

In addition to the above appointments, many persons holding judicial offices, such as all county court judges, recorders and chairmen of certain quarter sessions, became circuit judges when the Act came into operation on January 1, 1972. Circuit judges are full-time appointees, but they must retire at the age of 72, although the Lord Chancellor may allow them to continue in office until the age of 75. The jurisdiction of circuit judges is both criminal and civil (see the county courts, p. 39).

Circuit judges approved by the Lord Chancellor and nominated by the Lord Chief Justice may sit in the Court of Appeal (Criminal Division).

Recorders

They are appointed by the Queen on the recommendation of the Lord Chancellor, who may remove them from office on grounds of incapacity, misbehaviour or failure to satisfy the requirements of the terms of appointment. Recorders must retire at the age of 72.

Recorders, who are part-time judges, must be barristers or solicitors of 10 years' standing. Their appointment, which is on a temporary basis, states the period and frequency of their duties. Although recorders are primarily concerned with criminal cases, they have authority to sit as county court judges.

Justices of the Peace

Not less than two, and not more than four justices of the peace (lay magistrates), must sit with the judge when hearing appeals, or when a convicted person has been committed to the Crown Court for sentence. The same constitution of judge and justices has jurisdiction to hear any case before the Crown Court.

The distribution of Crown Court business

Cities and towns (known as court centres) in which the High Court and Crown Court sit are divided into three tiers.

First Tier

There are 24 court centres which deal with criminal and civil work, and the cases are tried by High Court judges and circuit judges.

Second Tier

There are 19 court centres which deal with criminal work only, and the cases are tried by High Court judges and circuit judges.

Third Tier

There are 46 court centres which deal with criminal work only, and the cases are tried by circuit judges.

The work of the Court is distributed amongst the various judges on the basis of the class of offence. For the purpose of the trial, offences are divided into four classes.

Class 1 contains serious offences, tried by a High Court judge, and includes treason, murder, genocide, and offences against the Official Secrets Act 1911, s.1. Murder may, however, be tried before a circuit judge.

Class 2 offences are tried by a High Court judge, unless the case is released by the authority of a presiding judge for trial by a circuit judge. A presiding judge is a High Court judge who has the responsibility for the distribution of the judges in a given circuit. The offences in this class include manslaughter, rape and sexual intercourse with a girl under 13.

Class 3 offences may be tried by a High Court judge, a circuit judge or recorder. The class includes all indictable offences, other than those allocated as Class 1, 2 or 4.

Class 4 offences may be tried by a High Court judge, circuit judge or a recorder, but cases are usually listed for trial by a recorder. Offences in this class include causing death by dangerous driving, causing grievous bodily harm, robbery and burglary, as well as all offences which may be tried either way, that is summarily or on indictment.

All cases in the crown court, with the exception of appeals and persons committed for sentence, are tried by a judge sitting alone, and before a jury.

The Criminal Appeal Act 1995 created the Criminal Cases Review Commission, to investigate possible miscarriages of justice.

Where a person has been convicted of an offence on indictment, and the Commission considers that there is a danger that, because of circumstances in the trial, there could be a miscarriage of justice and the verdict or sentence could not be upheld, the Commission:

- may refer the conviction to the Court of Appeal, and/or

- may refer to the Court of Appeal any sentence (not one fixed by law) imposed on the conviction.

- may be asked by the Court of Appeal to investigate any matter in a case it is dealing with in order to help the court in its deliberations.

With cases dealt summarily in the magistrates' court a similar procedure applies. Where a person has been convicted of an offence by a magistrates' court in England and Wales the Commission may at any time:

- refer the conviction to the Crown Court, and/or

- refer the sentence to the Crown Court.

The Crown Court, under this Act, may not award any punishment more severe than that awarded by the court whose decision is referred. The Crown Court may grant bail to the person whose conviction or detention has been referred to under the Act. A reference under the Act may only be made if the Commission consider there to be a real possibility that the conviction or sentence would not be upheld if the reference is made.

Community courts

In December 2004 the first experimental community court was established. The North Liverpool Community Justice Centre is a joint pilot project of the Home Office, the

Department for Constitutional Affairs and the Attorney General's office. The judge assigned to this court is a circuit judge who was appointed by a panel of five people, two of whom were community representatives. After being appointed, the judge had several meetings with residents in north Liverpool in order to get to know their problems and grievances.

The court has jurisdiction over civil and criminal matters, and has in-house police, crown prosecutors, probation officers and youth offending teams. The court is based on a similar successful scheme in New York, and is aimed at reducing the problems of anti-social behaviour which beset particular communities. The judge tries and sentences offenders who commit low-level crimes such as prostitution, vandalism, petty theft and drunk and disorderly behaviour. When sentencing, the judge will take into account the opinions of local people, particularly the victims of the crime, who have the opportunity of facing the offender. Convicted offenders may be ordered to write letters of apology to their victims, perform community service, attend anger-management counselling and so on. Any breach of such orders results in detention. The judge is responsible for monitoring treatment programmes and community punishments for all the cases before that court.

The centre is a two-year pilot programme which it is intended to be expanded throughout Britain.

The Magistrates' Court

The magistrates' courts deal with about 99 per cent of all criminal cases. This percentage gives an indication of the volume of work of the court and its importance in the legal system. There is a magistrates' court in every county and in most boroughs.

Magistrates also undertake duties on special panels, separate from their work in the adult magistrates' court. These include the Family Panel, the Youth Court Panel and the Licensing Committee.

Jurisdiction

The court has three main criminal functions:

A Court of Petty Sessions

This deals with minor offences that may be tried summarily, and carry a maximum penalty of not more than six months' imprisonment and/or a fine. Offences of criminal damage are tried in the magistrates' court unless the property destroyed or damaged is valued over £5,000. If over this amount, cases are tried in the Crown Court. With offences that may be triable either way (summarily or on indictment) the limit is £5,000. A summary offence means that the magistrates have power to hear the case without sending it for trial to the Crown Court. Examples of summary offences are drunkenness, minor motoring offences such as speeding, not obeying road signs and unauthorised parking, and riding a bicycle without lights after dark. A defendant in such cases may plead guilty by post, and need not attend the court.

Transfer for Trial Procedure

This procedure, introduced by the Criminal Justice and Public Order Act 1994, replaces the committal proceedings. The defence may apply to the court for the charge to be dropped on the grounds that there is insufficient evidence to put the accused on trial for the offence. The applications of the defence will be judged on the papers submitted, but the court may allow oral representations in difficult cases or if the accused is unrepresented.

Where the defence does not challenge the prosecution evidence, the case is transferred to the Crown Court without a hearing.

The Youth Court

When children (10–14 years) and young persons (14–17 years) are charged with a crime (other than homicide) they are brought before this special magistrates' court. The procedure is not as formal as in the usual court, and the purpose is to keep the young offender away from ordinary criminal proceedings. A youth court must not take place in a court where other sittings have taken place, or will take place within one hour. The court is not open to the public and the press may not publish the names of the charged persons or witnesses aged 10 to 17, unless a juvenile is charged with a serious offence and is unlawfully at large (has evaded capture). In such a case the courts may allow the name to be published so that the offender may be caught and brought before the court.

The sentences available to magistrates in the Youth Court are aimed primarily at the welfare and rehabilitation of the offender. They are dealt with in detail in Chapter 3.

Increase in sentencing powers

Before the Criminal Justice Act 2003, magistrates could only sentence an offender to six months' imprisonment for a single offence. Under provisions of the 2003 Act, due to take effect in late 2005, magistrates can sentence a person to up to 12 months' imprisonment for a single offence. There is further provision for increasing this by delegated legislation to 18 months. It is hoped that theses greater sentencing powers will result in more either-way cases being tried in the magistrates' court rather than being committed to the Crown Court for the more expensive and time-consuming trial by jury.

Civil Jurisdiction

The magistrates' court does have some civil jurisdiction. This may be summarised as follows:

- recovery of civil debts, such as income tax, rates, gas and electricity charges;

- family and matrimonial matters, such as applications for separation and custody of a child, maintenance and affiliation orders, and adoption;

- granting licences for premises for showing films, for the sale of alcohol or for gambling.

Constitution

A magistrates' court is presided over by at least two and not more than seven justices of the peace (magistrates). In England and Wales there are approximately 30,000 lay magistrates.

There are also over 120 District Judges (Magistrates' Courts), formerly known as *stipendiary magistrates*. They are full-time paid magistrates, appointed from the ranks of solicitors and barristers of seven years' standing, and are found mainly in the larger towns and cities.

A single magistrate may sit alone:

- in minor cases involving very small fines or periods of imprisonment, or

- when sitting as a District Judge

but generally, there must be two or more magistrates.

There is no jury in a magistrates' court. When a youth court is in session there must be a quorum of at least three magistrates, comprising women and men (*i.e.* there must be at least one woman or one man in the quorum).

Every magistrates' court has a justices' clerk, who is paid, usually legally qualified, and helps the justices on matters of law and procedure. Although they may only preside in the magistrates' court in the area of their commission, justices may sit in any Crown Court when required. Appeals from the magistrates' court go to:

Crown Court

The defendant may appeal against the sentence.

Divisional Court of the Queen's Bench Division

The prosecutor or defendant may appeal on points of law by means of "a case stated".

Appointment of Magistrates

Magistrates are appointed by the Lord Chancellor on the recommendations made to him by the local advisory committee for a particular area. These committees, which have up to twelve members, are made up of magistrates and non-magistrates. The names of those serving on such committees must be made public.

The aim in appointing magistrates is to achieve as wide a social, political and ethnic mix as possible, and to that end advertisements are often placed in the local press inviting applications. Individuals can also put forward their names to be considered, and names can also be submitted by local groups such as chambers of commerce or trade unions. Candidates should be of good character, have good understanding, communication and social awareness, be mature and of sound temperament, possess sound judgement and be committed and reliable.

When appointed, magistrates must undergo initial training. This is followed by subsequent periods of further training and refresher courses during the course of their appointment. Magistrates must between the ages of 21 and 65 when appointed, and retire at 70.

Despite the best of intentions, magistrates tend still to be predominantly middle aged and middle class. Ethnic minorities still comprise a very small proportion of appointees, and the requirements of careers and jobs usually deter younger applicants. However, it can at least be said that there is equality between the sexes, and there are now as many female magistrates as male.

As a result of the Courts Act 2003, magistrates are now appointed nationally, rather than locally. The Criminal Justice Act 2003 provides that the Lord Chancellor can remove lay magistrates from office on the grounds of incapacity, misbehaviour, incompetence, or neglecting their duties. Magistrates who suffer from incapacity may also be prevented from functioning.

It may be noted that in Lancashire, magistrates are appointed by the Chancellor for the Duchy of Lancaster on behalf of the Queen.

System of Appeal through the Criminal Courts

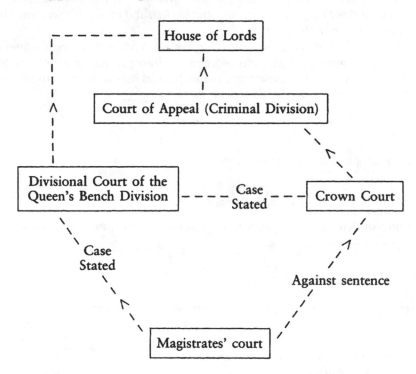

Criminal Justice Review

In December 1999, the Lord Chancellor asked Sir Robin Auld, an appeal court judge, to carry out a review of the criminal courts. His report, 700 pages long and making over 300 proposals for change, was published in October 2001.

One important recommendation was the establishment of a three-division criminal court. As the result of much criticism, mainly concerned with the erosion of the right to trial by jury and the increase in bureaucracy, the proposal was dropped.

Some of these reforms however have been the subject of legislation in the Criminal Justice Act 2003. They will be dealt with in succeeding chapters as they arise.

OTHER COURTS

The Judicial Committee of the Privy Council

The Committee does not make a decision but advises the Queen of its opinion, which is then implemented by an Order in Council. This Committee is outside the court system and its findings are not binding precedent on a lower court (see p. 9). However, because of the constitution of the Committee, it has immense persuasive authority. See the *Wagon Mound Case* (1961), p. 213.

Jurisdiction

The main work of the Committee is to hear appeals as set out below, but it is sometimes required to advise on other matters of law, such as the validity of certain legislation.
   The Committee hears appeals from:

- *Outside the United Kingdom*

   The Privy Council may hear appeals from the Channel Islands, the Isle of Man and certain Commonwealth countries.

- *Ecclesiastical Courts*

   It is the final court of appeal on ecclesiastical matters. Appeals are heard on matters concerning church buildings or the clergy.

- *Queen's Bench Division of the High Court*

   Appeals are heard from the Admiralty Court when acting as a Prize Court.

- *Medical Tribunals*

   Appeals are heard from doctors who have had their names removed from the medical register for disciplinary reasons.

Constitution

The Committee consists of no fewer than three, but usually five members from the following:

- The present and previous Lord President of the Council;
- Privy Councillors who hold or have held a high judicial office;
- The Lords of Appeal in Ordinary (the Law Lords);
- Persons who hold high judicial office in Commonwealth countries.

The Committee is usually formed from the Law Lords and, therefore, the constitution in practice is similar to the House of Lords.

Coroners' Courts

Jurisdiction

The main work of the court is concerned with inquests on persons who died a violent or unnatural death, or died from an unknown cause, or died in prison. A coroner may only inquire into deaths that occur in the district for which he is appointed.

If the verdict of the court is murder by a named person, the coroner may commit that person for trial. In this respect the court is similar to the preliminary hearing of the magistrates' court.

The court also has jurisdiction for disputes over treasure trove. Treasure trove is gold, silver or coins, etc., which have been deliberately hidden and the owner of which is unknown. If the coroner finds that the property was not hidden, but lost or misplaced for some reason, the finder acquires a good title, next to the real owner.

In 1992, an inquest jury decided that 14 silver coins, dating back from 1296 to 1582, and other items found in a field near Chester were not treasure trove but that they were probably lost or misplaced and were not hidden as a hoard. The coroner ordered the items to be returned to the finders.

Treasure trove belongs to the Crown, but it is often the practice for the Crown to pay a reward, based on the value of the property, to those who have not concealed the find.

Constitution

A coroner must be either a barrister, solicitor or medical practitioner of five years' standing, and is appointed by county, and certain borough councils to act within the district of the county or borough, but may be removed from office for misbehaviour. The coroner may, and sometimes must, summon a jury of between seven to 11 members. The jury's verdict need not be unanimous.

The Court of Justice of the European Communities

The Court of Justice of the European Communities which sits in Luxembourg ensures the observance and recognition of Community rules with regard to legal interpretation and application. It is concerned with disputes between Member States over Community matters. It hears appeals from Member States, individuals and the Community institutions on matters relating to the treaties, and its rulings are binding. The court is the final arbiter in all matters of law that lie within the scope of the treaties. It has an important function in creating Community case law and its decisions can have an effect on case law in the English courts (see p. 28).

The court is assisted by a Court of First Instance, which can hear applications for preliminary rulings. The European Court of Justice comprises judges nominated by the 25 member states. In addition there are advocates-general who give advisory opinion to the Court.

Useful website

For courts generally: *www.courtservice.gov.uk*

TRIBUNALS

Administrative tribunals

For a long period of time Parliament has delegated a judicial function to bodies or boards outside the usual system of the courts. Since 1945 this practice has grown, in the main due to the advent of nationalisation and the increase in social and welfare services provided by the state.

Instead of disputes being settled in court, certain Acts of Parliament have provided for the creation of tribunals to decide problems that have arisen within the particular scope of those Acts. In 1957, the Franks Committee (which reported on tribunals) estimated that there were over 2,000 tribunals, and it can be expected that this has increased. It is therefore impossible to give a complete list of the tribunals in existence, but the following will give some indication of their nature:

- Social Security Tribunals which hear disputes on such matters as claims for unemployment and sickness benefits;

- Rent Tribunals which hear disputes between landlords and tenants;

- Employment Tribunals which hear matters concerning unfair dismissal, redundancy payments and the like;

- Immigration tribunals, which hear appeals on the right to enter or remain in the United Kingdom;

- The Mental Health Review Tribunal, which considers the continued detention of mental patients in hospital; and

- Land Tribunals which hear disputes over the amount of compensation to be paid when land is compulsorily purchased by the local authority.

The main benefit of tribunals is that they help in administering Acts quickly and inexpensively. Procedure is less formal than in court and in many instances there is no need for the parties to be legally represented. In some tribunals, lawyers are not allowed. The constitutions of tribunals vary, but certain tribunals must have members who are lawyers, and the chairman of some tribunals may only be appointed by the Minister of the department concerned, from a list of persons nominated by the Lord Chancellor. Generally, a tribunal will have several members, usually a lawyer will be chairman, with the other members representing organisations likely to be affected by the dispute. There are certain cases in which tribunal chairmen may sit alone.

Domestic tribunals

Certain professional organisations have their own tribunals to settle disputes between members of their organisations. Conditions of membership will usually stipulate that disputes between members, and between members and the organisation, will be governed by a tribunal, and therefore members have mutually agreed beforehand how their differences will be settled.

In some cases Parliament has created a tribunal for a particular organisation. For example, the Medical Act 1956 created the Disciplinary Committee of the General Medical Council. Tribunals set up by statute are usually subject to a right of appeal, and provided that the tribunals do not go beyond the agreed powers, and follow the rules of natural justice, the courts have no jurisdiction.

Means of control

By the courts

- Making *prerogative orders* of *mandamus*, *certiorari* or prohibition (see p. 134). This method of control only applies against tribunals created by statute.

- By awarding an injunction to prevent a tribunal (statutory or domestic) performing against the rules of natural justice, or acting *"ultra vires"* (beyond its powers).

- Decisions from tribunals created by statute may be subject to appeals as provided by the statute.

By the Council of Tribunals

The Council was established by the Tribunals and Inquiries Act 1958.

It has an advisory function to review the working of statutory tribunals and makes reports when necessary to the Lord Chancellor who has the responsibility of appointing the members of the Council.

Useful website

For information on tribunals: *www.council-on-tribunals.gov.uk*

ARBITRATION

It is often the practice in commercial contracts to refer disputes to arbitration, instead of starting court actions. This form of arbitration is governed by the Arbitration Act 1996. If you look at the booking conditions in some holiday brochures, you will find that disputes are referred to arbitration. Therefore, if there is a dispute between a holidaymaker and the travel company, the parties will not go to court, but to arbitration.

Arbitration means that the two parties agree to allow a third party to decide the dispute. The arbitrator does this by making an "award", and giving the reasons for doing so. When an award has been made, neither party may start a court action in relation to the same dispute. The courts will not interfere with the decision unless the arbitrator acted improperly, or unless fresh evidence is introduced.

A different form of arbitration was established when the Advisory Conciliation and Arbitration Service (ACAS) was created by the Employment Protection Act 1975, to help in trade disputes and to improve industrial relations.

Arbitration is also available in the county court, under the small claims procedure (see p. 40).

SPECIMEN EXAMINATION QUESTIONS

1. (a) Under the Civil Procedure Act 1997, explain what is meant by the following:

    (i)   the "three track" procedure: (4 marks)
    (ii) "case management" by the judiciary.   (3 marks)

    (b) Identify and briefly discuss **one** form of "ADR".   (3 marks)

AQA, Higher Tier, June 2002

2. Cases within the English legal system can be heard before different courts and other bodies. These include the Magistrates'. Youth and Crown Courts, the County and High Courts, both divisions of the Court of Appeal, the House of Lords and a range of specialist tribunals.

In **each** of the following situations, **identify** which court or other body would hear the case and **briefly explain** why.

(a) Henry broke into Igor's house in the middle of the night and stole £10,000 worth of Igor's property. At an initial hearing, the magistrates have refused to try the case.   (2 marks)

(b) Javed, aged 17, approached Kieran in the street, grabbed his mobile phone and ran away. Javed has since been charged with theft.   (2 marks)

(c) Linus, an Irishman, applied for a job in a wood yard but was told that the job had already gone. Linus, who had previous experience as a wood worker, saw the same job advertised in the local paper the following week.   (2 marks)

(d) Martin was involved in a serious road traffic accident, as a result of Nathan's negligent driving. Martin expected to receive over £200,000 in damages, but the High Court only awarded half that sum. Martin is keen to pursue the matter further.   (2 marks)

AQA Foundation Tier, June 2004

TALKING POINTS

Why are the Law lords divided on the desirability of a new Supreme Court?

The small claims procedure has been described as "the jewel in the crown of the civil justice system". Do you agree?

SUGGESTED COURSEWORK TITLES

Describe the ways in which disputes can be resolved without going to court. Discuss how effective these various methods are in achieving their object.

Describe how lay people are used in the criminal justice system. Discuss the advantages and disadvantages of using ordinary people for this purpose.

THE JUDICIARY AND THE LEGAL PROFESSION

Appointment of Judges

High Court judges, circuit judges and recorders are appointed by the Queen on the recommendation of the Minister for Constitutional Affairs, formerly the Lord Chancellor, (see below). Law Lords and Appeal Court judges are appointed by the Queen on the advice of the Prime Minister, who is advised by the Minister for Constitutional Affairs.

Prospective junior and High Court judges are now invited to apply for these vacancies, which are publicly advertised. Those who are best qualified for particular positions are appointed, regardless of gender, race, religion, political affinity, sexual orientation or disability, except where a disability might prevent the candidate from fulfilling the physical requirements of the office. Those who are selected are interviewed by a panel, and the decision to appoint him or her is taken by the Minister for Constitutional Affairs. Applicants for junior judicial posts have to attend assessment days, which include written law exams and role play. Some may still be invited to become judges without having to apply in this way, and judges of the Court of Appeal and Law Lords are still created by invitation only.

When assuming office, all judges take an oath ". . .to do right to all manner of people after the laws and usages of this realm without fear or favour, affection or ill-will". In his review of the criminal justice system, Sir Robin Auld called for consultation on an appraisal system for all full-time judges. There would be a panel of three appraisers, one of which would be a lay person.

A Government consultation paper, *Constitutional Reform: a New Way of Appointing Judges*, has been issued to consider details of the operation of a new Judicial Appointments Commission. It is intended that this commission should make recommendations to the Minister of Constitutional Affairs, who would then either make the appointment, or reject the recommendation. This is currently the form of commission preferred by the Government. Other forms could be a commission which appoints all judges without reference to the Minister, or one which appoints junior judges in this way, but merely recommends the appointment of senior judges.

The Judicial Appointments Commission would be made up of equal numbers of judges, other legally qualified people (including academics) and lay people.

Criticism of the Judiciary

The background of the judiciary continues to attract criticism. It is said that judges are predominantly white, male, middle class, public school and Oxbridge, thus representing a rather narrow section of society. For this reason, they are sometimes thought to be out of touch with the public at large. Many judges strenuously deny this, and maintain that their day-to-day experiences in the courts give them a view of society which is broader than most other people's.

It remains true that there are very few judges from minority ethnic backgrounds, and only a relatively small number of women judges. This situation is gradually improving with the recruitment of junior judges being now more representative of society. However it was only in January 2004 that the very first woman Law Lord was appointed. She is Dame Brenda Hale, and it is also significant that her background is that of a legal academic, unlike her colleagues, who had long careers at the bar.

The way judges were appointed also attracted much criticism. Until the mid-1990s, becoming a judge was by invitation only. The then Lord Chancellor (see below), kept a confidential file on potential candidates, and as a result of secret soundings and consultations, would invite a person to become a judge. As mentioned above, this situation has now changed, and an even more radical reform is likely to take place soon.

Judicial Officers

The Lord Chancellor

In June 2003, the Government announced that the 1400-year-old office of the Lord Chancellor would be abolished. In its place, a Minister for Constitutional Affairs was appointed to assume some of the roles of the Lord Chancellor. In order to understand these changes, it is necessary to examine the previous traditional functions of the Lord Chancellor. His functions were as follows:

- Speaker of the House of Lords;
- a member of the Cabinet, as a Government Minister, chosen by the Prime Minister, and holding office only as long as the Government held power;
- a judge in the House of Lords and the Privy Council, and President of the Supreme Court and of the Chancery Division of the High Court.

It can be seen that the Lord Chancellor's roles embraced respectively the legislature (as Speaker of the House of Lords), the executive (as a member of the Government) and of the judiciary (as a senior judge). Clearly this ran contrary to the doctrine of the separation of powers, and was long considered to be an undesirable state of affairs.

The new Minister for Constitutional Affairs (in 2005 Lord Falconer), has far fewer powers than former Lord Chancellors had. He does not, for example, sit as a judge or as Speaker of the House of Lords. At the same time, many of the functions of the Lord Chancellor still needed to be carried out, and therefore Lord Falconer was also appointed Lord Chancellor in order to be responsible for such matters as the appointment of the judiciary.

As things stand (2005), one person occupies the positions of both the Minister for Constitutional Affairs and Lord Chancellor. It was intended that the office of Lord Chancellor would eventually be abolished when the new rules and procedures had become established. In December 2004 however it was announced that the office would continue, with the scope of its duties considerably reduced. Students will have to bear in mind the transitional nature of this situation when references are made to the Lord Chancellor or the Lord Chancellor's Department.

The Lord Chief Justice

This appointment is also made by the Queen on the advice of the Prime Minister. The Lord Chief Justice is head of the Queen's Bench Division of the High Court, but his principal duties are as head of the Court of Appeal (Criminal Division) and the Queen's Bench Divisional Court. On appointment he is made a peer, but, although entitled to hear House of Lords cases, in practice he rarely does.

The Master of the Rolls

The Master of the Rolls is appointed by the Queen, on the advice of the Prime Minister, and is made a peer on appointment. The holder of this office is the virtual head of the Court of Appeal (Civil Division); organising the work of the court, and deciding the composition of the divisions to hear appeals. As Master of the Rolls he supervises the admission of qualified solicitors to the rolls of the court, which then allows them to practise.

President of the Family Division of the High Court

This appointment is made by the Queen on the advice of the Prime Minister. The president is head of the Family Division and, in addition to organising the work of the Division, sits in the High Court and in the Divisional Court.

The Law Officers

The Attorney-General and Solicitor-General are usually members of the House of Commons, and their appointment, by the Queen on the advice of the Prime Minister, is political. In addition to being Members of Parliament, they are also experienced barristers.

The Attorney-General

The Attorney-General has the following duties:

- advising the Government on legal matters;
- representing the Crown in civil cases and acting as prosecutor in important criminal cases;
- certain prosecutions may only take place with the authority of the Attorney-General. The House of Lords recently upheld this right, after a private person had sought an injunction against postal workers;
- is head of the English Bar;
- supervises the work of the Director of Public Prosecutions.

The Solicitor-General

The Solicitor-General is the deputy of the Attorney-General, and has similar duties. Any act or function that may be discharged by the Attorney-General may also be carried out by the Solicitor-General, when the former has so authorised, or is ill or absent, or the office of Attorney-General is vacant.

The Director of Public Prosecutions

The holder of this post is appointed by the Attorney-General, but is a civil servant, not a politician. The DPP, who must be a barrister or solicitor of 10 years' standing, is head of a department responsible for starting most criminal prosecutions, although mostly through the Crown Prosecution Service (see Chapter 3).

Useful websites

Department of Constitutional Affairs: *www.dca.gov.uk*
For the judiciary: *www.dca.gov.uk/judicial/judgesfr.htm*

The Legal Profession

The legal profession in England and Wales, unlike in most other countries, is divided into two separate branches. These two bodies of lawyers have different functions in the legal system **Barristers** are mainly concerned with *advocacy* before the courts. This means pleading on behalf of their clients in the courts, and by using their skills, persuading the judge, jury or whoever of the rightness of their client's cause. **Solicitors**, although they also practise a certain amount of advocacy, generally work in offices, carrying out many and varied aspects of legal work, including the instruction of barristers.

Not all lawyers publicly practise law. Many are employed by companies or the Civil Service as legal advisers. Others, known as academic lawyers, teach or lecture in schools, colleges and universities. Many Members of Parliament are either barristers or solicitors.

Solicitors

Organisation

There are some 80,000 qualified solicitors in England and Wales, and their governing body is called **The Law Society**. Solicitors carry out a wide variety of work in all aspects of the law. They give advice on a wide range of legal matters, draw up wills, and act in the conveyancing (transferring) the ownership of houses and other premises. Other areas of their work include drafting partnership agreements, forming companies, preparing court cases, instructing barristers, interviewing witnesses, and acting for clients in divorce and other matrimonial disputes. Although most solicitors practise most aspects of law, individual partners in large firms may often specialise in particular branches of the law.

Solicitors can practise on their own, or, more usually in partnership with others. Some large city firms might have dozens of partners, whereas small country practices might have only two or three. Over 80 per cent of solicitors work in private practice. Subject to certain rules, solicitors are able to advertise their services, and such advertisements are now commonly to be seen in the press and other areas of the media.

Work

Solicitors lost their monopoly on conveyancing some time ago. Licensed Conveyancers, who must hold certain qualifications, and be experienced in the work of conveyancing, are allowed to practise in this field of law. In addition, probate business (dealing with wills) can now be done by such organisations as banks and building societies. On the other hand, in recent years, solicitors have gained widespread rights of audience in the courts. They were always traditionally able to act as advocates in the magistrates' courts and county courts, but now they have audience in the Crown Court and the High Court. The granting of audience to solicitors to the higher courts began with the passing of the Courts and Legal Services Act 1990, and the Access to Justice Act 1999 provides that all solicitors have an automatic right to audience in all courts so long as they have undergone the necessary training requirements. Solicitors who are advocates can now be appointed as Queen's Counsel (see below), and can also become judges. Many solicitors however still concentrate on traditional office work, and rarely appear in court. Nevertheless, there are now some 1000 solicitor-advocates.

Liability for negligence

Clients may sue solicitors for negligence in carrying out their professional functions. A solicitor's professional duty is to exercise reasonable skill and care in giving legal advice.

In *County Personnel Ltd v Pulver & Co* (1987), the Court of Appeal considered the case a firm of solicitors which failed to ascertain the rent payable on a headlease, and failed to explain the effect of a rent review clause to the client before entering into the underlease agreement. The court held the firm to be negligent, and liable for damages. In *Smith v Claremont Haynes & Co* (1991), it was held that a solicitor was negligent when failing to act promptly when preparing a will. The testator died before the will was completed for signing, with the result that the intended beneficiaries did not inherit their gifts. In *White v Jones* (1995) the House of Lords confirmed that intended beneficiaries are entitled to damages for professional negligence by a solicitor who delays the drawing up of a will, the testator dying before the will is executed.

In *Arthur JS Hall & Co v Simons* (2000), the House of Lords departed from the principle laid down in *Rondel v Worsley* (1969) (see p. 67). As a result, solicitors are no longer immune from actions for negligence while acting as advocates in court.

Under an ordinary partnership a solicitor may be personally liable for a claim for negligence against the firm of which he or she is a partner, even if that partner had nothing to do with the matter involved. However, it is now possible for solicitors since 2001 to form Limited Liability Partnerships. Under such arrangements, partners will be only liable for work for which they are personally responsible.

Solicitors can sue clients for non-payment of fees.

Training

There are three routes by which a person can qualify as a solicitor.

As a law graduate. This is the quickest route, and nearly two-thirds of solicitors qualify in this way. A law graduate proceeds to the, **Legal Practice Course** (LPC), usually a one-year full-time course which provides the practical skills required to be a solicitor. After successfully completing this course, it is usual to undertake **a two-year training contract** with a firm of solicitors in private practice. In recent years there has been considerable competition for these traineeships, with fewer vacancies than there are LPC students wanting them. This training contract builds upon areas studied in the LPC, with further emphasis on practical skills and advocacy. Training can also take place in other organisations such as the Crown Prosecution Service and local and central government.

As a non-law graduate. It is necessary for a non-law graduate to complete a one year full-time course leading to the **Common Professional Examination** (CPE). This examination covers essential core subjects, and is then followed by a similar period of training to that of a law graduate. About 20 per cent of all entrants qualify in this way.

As a non-graduate. It is possible to enter the profession as a non-graduate, although only a small minority of solicitors qualify in this way. A Solicitors First Examination Course is followed by the LPC, and a five-year training contract. Legal Executives (see below), sometimes take this route in qualifying as solicitors.

Enrolment

The name of a solicitor who qualifies is entered on the Roll of Solicitors, maintained by the Master of the Rolls. The solicitors' governing body, the Law Society, issues a certificate to practise which certifies that the requirements of examinations and training have been successfully met, and that the solicitor is fit to be an officer of the Supreme Court of Judicature.

Qualified solicitors must take part in a continuing professional development scheme, depending upon the individual's particular specialisation or requirements. Records must be kept of courses attended.

It is worthy of note that fifty years ago the solicitors' profession was almost entirely a male preserve. Now, half of those qualifying are women, and the proportion is gradually increasing.

Legal Executives

The Institute of Legal Executives holds examinations for staff who work in a solicitor's office but do not hold a legal qualification. A Fellow of the Institute may later qualify as a solicitor, and the Law Society makes provision for this category of entrant, similar to the requirements for a non-law graduate.

Barristers

Organisation

There are approximately 9000 qualified barristers. Their governing body is the **Bar Council**, which safeguards their interests and controls their activities. The barristers' branch of the legal profession is often referred to collectively as the Bar. Barristers are not allowed to form partnerships. They are self-employed and act alone, although in practice they share premises, known as chambers, with other barristers. They also share the services of a "barristers' clerk", who acts as secretary, allocates the work, organises meetings between barristers, solicitors and clients, and negotiates fees. The majority of barristers operate from chambers in London, though some are based in other major cities. Barristers are usually instructed by solicitors, who prepare a file with all the relevant details of a case. These files are known as *briefs*, and are allocated to barristers by the clerk. Since 2003 it has been possible for a client to approach a barrister directly, instead of through a solicitor, for advisory and advocacy work. However for a variety of practical reasons it will still generally be necessary to instruct a barrister through a solicitor.

Work

A barrister's main function is to act as advocate in cases before the court. Until provisions made in the Courts and Legal Services Act 1990 and the Access to Justice Act 1999, only barristers had audience in the higher courts. As was explained above, solicitors also can now appear as advocates in these courts, and barristers no longer enjoy this monopoly. Barristers still, however, carry out by far the greater share of advocacy in the higher courts. Besides their advocacy work, barristers also draft documents, such as pleadings and "counsel's opinion" on legal problems submitted by solicitors. Barristers often tend to specialise in a particular branch of law, and become known for that area of expertise.

Some barristers do not work as advocates. Like solicitors, they can also be employed by the Government, the Civil Service, private companies, colleges and universities as lecturers, and so on.

Many Members of Parliament, including the present Prime Minister and the Leader of the Opposition, are qualified barristers.

The "cab rank" rule

Barristers work to what is commonly known as the "cab rank" rule. This means that a barrister must accept a brief within his or her area of expertise, if not already committed to a case at the time, and provided that the fee is adequate (it has been said that in practice, this rule may sometimes be open to manipulation by the barristers' clerk).

Liability for negligence

Traditionally, barristers have not been liable for negligence for their advocacy in court. This principle was laid down in *Rondel v Worsley* (1969), where it was decided that as a matter of public policy, barristers should be immune from such actions. The public policy in question was that if barristers could be sued in these cases, then the floodgates would be open for any disgruntled litigant who lost a case to bring an action against the barrister involved. It would also result in the case having to be re-tried.

In *Saif Ali v Sydney Mitchell & Co* (1978), the House of Lords held that in certain circumstances a barrister could be liable in negligence in matters not connected with advocacy, or anything intimately connected with how the case would be conducted and managed in court.

The case of *Arthur JS Hall & Co v Simons* (2000) completely changed the situation. In this case, the House of Lords departed from the decision in *Rondel v Worsley*, and now there is no reason why a barrister should not be sued for negligence in the same way as a member of any other profession.

Training

To start training as a barrister, it is generally necessary to obtain an upper second class honours degree. This will more often than not be a law degree. If, however, it is in a subject other than law, the student must attend the one-year course leading to the Common Professional Examination, the same as an aspiring solicitor. All student barristers must join one of the four **Inns of Court** in London. These are Gray's Inn, Lincoln's Inn, Inner Temple and Middle Temple, and have a collegiate history going back many hundreds of years. Students must keep "terms", which means attending the Inn and dining the required number of times. This is currently twelve, and the dinners are now usually combined with some other training activity.

The next step in becoming a barrister is to take the **Bar Vocational Course**. This course is designed to provide

- practical training in specialist skills such as legal research, opinion writing, drafting, interviewing, negotiation and advocacy; and

- knowledge of legal principles of evidence, litigation and the rules of professional conduct.

Previously only available in London, the Bar Vocational Course can now be taken at any one of eight centres round the country.

Following the vocational examinations, successful students are "called to the Bar". However, before they may practise, a further year of training, known as **pupillage**, must follow. This is a period of practical training with an experienced barrister, known as the pupil-master. This is usually done in two six-month periods, with a different pupil-master in different chambers. In the later stages of pupillage, a student may take cases in court and accept fees. Finding a pupillage place can be very difficult, as there are far fewer places available than there are students wanting them.

After pupillage, the newly-qualified barrister must find a permanent place in chambers, known as a **tenancy**. This too is a difficult hurdle, as demand far outstrips supply.

As is the case with solicitors, barristers are required to follow a continuing professional development scheme, as well as further training in their first three years.

Queen's Counsel

A barrister of ten years' standing could in the past apply to be a **Queen's Counsel** (QC). A successful applicant is said to have "taken silk", owing to the tradition of a QC's wearing a gown of silk. The process of becoming a QC was similar to that of appointing senior judges, that is to say, by secret soundings, and not all applicants succeeded. Those who have been appointed QC however, can command higher fees, and be assisted by a junior barrister in court (a "junior" is any barrister who is not a QC, regardless of age or experience). The additional engagement of a junior in cases conducted by as QC was at one time mandatory, but is now discretionary. It is has in recent years been possible for solicitors to become QCs, but at the moment they form a tiny minority.

There has been much criticism in recent years of the QC system. The Bar sees it as a necessary bench-mark of excellence in the profession, which creates an elite of the most experienced and specialised advocates available. Others see the system as an artificial way of raising barristers' fees at a time when litigation is already extremely expensive. The Glidewell Report (2003) suggested changes in the appointment of QCs, but others think that the system should be abolished altogether. In 2004, the (then) Lord Chancellor suspended the appointment of QCs, and the matter was made subject to consultation and discussion.

In November 2004 it was announced that, from 2005, QCs would be selected by an independent panel, which would include non-lawyers. The scheme will provide for accreditation in criminal, civil and family work. Is it expected that the selection process may allow references from clients to play a part in the decision.

Complaints against the legal profession

As shown above, solicitors may be sued for negligence when their conduct is not of a reasonable minimum standard. This may be difficult, however, as other solicitors, particularly those practising in the same locality, are often reluctant to take such an action.

In 1986, the High Court held that a Welsh businessman had been overcharged by his solicitors, and reduced the solicitor's fees by nearly 50 per cent, and the solicitor was struck off. The businessman also claimed that the Law Society had failed in its duty to investigate his complaint against the solicitor.

As a result of this case the Law Society set up the Solicitors Complaints Bureau. The bureau dealt with such matters as negligence, delay, unprofessional conduct, unanswered letters, breakdown in communication, etc. Most complaints received by the bureau were settled by conciliation between its staff and the solicitors concerned.

In 1996, the Law Society abolished the Solicitors Complaints Bureau as a result of criticism concerning its inefficiency in dealing with complaints. It its place it set up the Office for the Supervision of Solicitors.

In matters concerning barristers, clients were able to complain by writing to the General Council of the Bar. If the complaint was upheld, it usually resulted in disciplinary action being taken against the barrister concerned, but did not directly help the client. In 1997, a Complaints Commissioner who is a non-lawyer and independent of the Bar Council, assumed oversight of the complaints procedure. The Commissioner refers any justified complaints to the Professional Conduct and Complaints Committee of the Bar Council. If a complaint is upheld, the barrister complained against may have to apologise, repay fees or pay compensation, and may be disciplined by the Bar Council.

Where the professions' own regulatory bodies are unable to deal satisfactorily with complaints, the matter can be referred to the Legal Services Ombudsman. This post was set up by the Courts and Legal Services Act 1990 to investigate complaints against not only solicitors and barristers, but also licensed conveyancers and legal executives. The Ombudsman has power under the Access to Justice Act 1999 to order a solicitor or the Law Society to pay compensation to a client where necessary.

A single legal profession?

Many countries do not have two professional legal bodies. The United States of America, for example, has a single legal profession in which lawyers or attorneys, as they are called, may deal with all legal matters. There are no restrictions on the tasks they may perform.

In English law, recent years have seen an increasing overlap between the work of solicitors and barristers. Solicitors have now the right of audience in the higher courts, and barristers may be hired directly by their clients instead of through the intermediary of solicitors. It is possible now for solicitors to become QCs and judges of the higher courts.

Nevertheless there is still a clear distinction between much of the work carried out by the two branches of the profession. It is still often necessary to hire both a solicitor and a barrister in many court cases. It is also true that on some occasions only a solicitor may be suitable for a particular legal task. On other occasions it may be considered desirable to engage a barrister. It is therefore still possible to argue the case for or against combining the two braches of the legal profession into one, a process generally referred to as **fusion**.

The disadvantages of two professions

* Where it is still necessary to employ both a solicitor and a barrister, a client has to pay two fees. It would save money if only one lawyer was needed to do both the preparatory work and also appear as advocate in court.

- Clients and solicitors are often well known to each other, or have built up a relationship of trust during the preparation of a case. A client might well be apprehensive about handing the case over in court to a barrister who may be a complete stranger.

- Employing two lawyers results in a duplication of paperwork, which is wasteful and increases costs.

- Having two professions may cause inefficiency because of the physical difficulty of two offices dealing with the paperwork. This could possibly result in a breakdown of communications.

- There is always the possibility of briefs being returned if a barrister is double booked. This results in further delay.

- There are two separate systems of legal education and training. If all lawyers followed the same basic training, a student could then make a decision at a later stage to specialise in a particular area and train accordingly.

Arguments against fusion

- Barristers are a specialist body of expert advocates. Being self-employed, they are able to go anywhere necessary to represent a client and are not tied to the requirements of office work.

- With a divided profession, a solicitor can call upon the expertise of an independent barrister who specialises in a particular area of law. If the professions were fused, solicitors in small country practices would possibly have to consult a rival firm, with the consequent risk of losing a client.

- The handing over of a case to a barrister at the trial stage may well bring a fresh mind to the case. Having not been so closely involved with the client during the preparatory stage, a barrister may well be more detached and objective.

- Many solicitors, especially in smaller firms, prefer the present system because they cannot afford the time away from their offices to conduct cases in court.

- Barristers have to take on work on the "cab rank" principle. They must accept a brief when offered provided that they are not already briefed for that day. This means that representation is assured, even in unpopular or potentially hopeless cases. A fused profession would make this system more difficult to operate.

- In countries where there is a fused legal profession, lawyers tend to divide into two branches anyway: advocates and "office" lawyers.

Useful websites

Law Society: *www.lawsociety.org.uk*
Bar Council: *www.barcouncil.org.uk*
Legal Services Ombudsman: *www.olso.org.uk*

SPECIMEN EXAMINATION QUESTION

(a) **Not including training**, describe **three** of the differences between solicitors and barristers.

(6 marks)

(b) Describe the specialist training required to be undertaken by a person who intends to become

   (i)   a solicitor;

   (ii) a barrister.   (6 marks)

(c) With reference to the legal profession, outline what is meant by

   (i)   a QC;

   (ii) the "cab rank" rule.   (5 marks)

(d) Briefly comment on whether or not the public would be better served by a single legal profession.   (3 marks)

AQA (Higher Tier), June 2004

TALKING POINTS

How representative of society are our judges?

Does the QC system still have a valuable place in our legal structure?

SUGGESTED COURSEWORK TITLE

Describe the training and work of barristers and solicitors. Discuss the arguments for and against the legal profession being fused into a single profession.

LEGAL AID AND ADVICE

People who are faced with legal problems usually need advice in dealing with them. The obvious solution is to seek the help of a solicitor. However, very many people do not know where to find one, especially one who is a specialist in the law relating to their particular case. It is true to say also that many people feel that visiting a solicitor is a rather daunting and intimidating experience. They are also of course frequently apprehensive about the cost involved. Solicitors' costs are high, even for routine advice, and if representation in court is required, fees will escalate further.

In order to afford access to legal advice for the ordinary person, various schemes have been devised over the years. Citizens Advice Bureaux, Law Centres and other agencies have provided access to help for a large number of people who would otherwise have been denied it. The funding of this advice and assistance has always been, and remains, a problem.

Citizens Advice Bureaux

CABx were introduced in 1938, and can be found in most towns. They depend very much on trained volunteers, as the funding of them is uncertain. Many are able to open only for a few hours per week. However, they provide a very valuable service, and under the Access to Justice Act 1999 their role may be further enhanced and their funding made more secure.

CABx offer free advice and help on a wide range of matters. Much of their work concerns social security and related problems, as well as such services as providing lists of solicitors' firms which deal with particular legal matters. A CAB will also be able to give information as to which solicitors provide free or fixed-fee interviews. Although the volunteers who staff the CABx are lay people, they are often experts in the field of law with which they most frequently deal. Some bureaux employ solicitors where professional help is needed, and some have help from volunteer solicitors.

Law Centres

Law Centres can be found in some of the larger towns. Their purpose is to provide free professional advice, and sometimes representation, in areas where people are most needful of it. They are to be found in districts where few or no solicitors are situated, and in communities which need their services the most. Law Centres are staffed by volunteer solicitors and lay people, and deal primarily with such problems as social security, housing, immigration and employment.

As Law Centres are funded for the most part by local authorities, their existence is often precarious. In times of financial cutbacks, several have had to close. However, the government has recently (2001) made it clear that Law Centres have an important role in the provision of legal services.

Free and Fixed-fee Interviews and Other Schemes

Many solicitors take part in a scheme which offers interviews which are free or for up to a maximum of £25. They are non-means tested, and usually are for a period of half an hour.

In recent years, the Law Society has allowed solicitors to advertise. This has meant that such services as free legal "surgeries", which people can attend without an appointment, can be brought to the attention of a wide section of the public. Solicitors also now advertise a wide range of services, particularly ones in which they specialise, such as divorce.

Pro bono work

The provision of services free of charge, *pro bono* work, is promoted by both braches of the legal profession. In addition to the Free Representation Unit, the Bar Pro Bono Unit and the Solicitors' Pro Bono Group are keen to establish this kind of work, now known as "law for free".

Other Agencies

In addition to the above, there are many other places where the public can obtain legal advice and assistance. These include:

- Trade unions
- Professional associations
- Motoring organisations, such as the RAC and AA
- Consumer protection groups
- Welfare associations.

These organisations often have their own legal departments, which provide advice and assistance for their members.

FUNDING LEGAL SERVICES

Going to law has always been an expensive undertaking. Solicitors usually charge a minimum of £120 per hour for routine interviews, and advice from a partner in a large City firm could cost three times this amount an hour and more. Paying for representation in court adds substantially to the costs, and in large and complex civil cases the costs can amount to many hundreds of thousands of pounds. For large companies or wealthy individuals, these expenses perhaps might not pose too insuperable a problem. A person of very limited means, on the other hand, could not possibly afford to pay for even the most modest of cases without some financial help. Clearly, unless this help is forthcoming, justice could be denied to such people. In criminal cases, where the liberty and livelihood of a person is at risk, this need for financial help becomes even more pressing.

Legal aid and advice in the past

Over the years there have been many schemes aimed at helping the less well off to meet the cost of legal advice and representation in court.

After the second world war, 1939–1945, there were proposals for a sort of legal NHS, under which legal services would be free, like medical treatment, on payment of national insurance contributions. The scheme came to nothing, although it continued to be mooted for several years.

The modern system of legal funding was the result of various Acts of Parliament, eventually consolidated in the Legal Aid Act 1988.

In civil cases, responsibility for the granting of legal aid had been transferred from the Law Society to the Legal Aid Board. The criteria for granting legal aid in civil cases depended on the application of a means test and a "merits" test. Legal aid in criminal cases was granted by the courts on the application of a means test and an "interests of justice" test, often referred to as the "Widgery Criteria", after a former Lord Chief Justice. These tests will be explained in more detail later.

In recent years, the national bill for legal aid has increased enormously. In order to bring it under control, the financial limits for qualifying have been increasingly raised, so that the proportion of those eligible has greatly declined. This has led to the criticism that the law was available only to the very rich or the very poor, and those in the middle income bracket were largely excluded.

The funding of legal aid by the old system was replaced by the Access to Justice Act 1999.

THE ACCESS TO JUSTICE ACT 1999

This act replaces the old legal aid system by establishing two new schemes, which came into effect from October 2000. They are:

- **The Community Legal Service**, which deals with civil matters, and

- **The Criminal Defence Service**, which covers criminal cases.

Section 1 of the act establishes the **Legal Services Commission**, which oversees the funding of these services. Members of this Commission, between seven and twelve in number, are appointed by the Lord Chancellor. They include people who have experience in or knowledge of such matters as funding legal services, the work of the courts, consumer affairs, social conditions and management.

The Commission has power to enter into contracts with suppliers of legal services. It also can make grants, loans and investments, promote publicity for its services, and undertake any inquiries or investigations as may be necessary for its operation.

The Commission replaces the Legal Aid Board in the funding of civil cases, and also is responsible for the Criminal Defence Service in the funding of criminal legal aid.

The Community Legal Service

The Community Legal Service deals with civil law matters, and is responsible for providing:

- general information about the law and legal system and the availability of legal services,

- legal advice,

- help in preventing, settling or otherwise resolving legal disputes,

- help in enforcing decisions, and

- help for legal proceedings not relating to disputes.

Money for providing these services comes from the **Community Legal Service Fund**. Such services includes advice assistance and representation by lawyers, the services of lay people, and other services like mediation.

The Community Legal Service Fund is maintained by the Legal Services Commission. The money is provided by the Lord Chancellor in accordance with the Government's overall budget. This means that there is a finite amount available and consequently a risk that when the money runs out, help may have to be refused. There is a certain amount of flexibility however, in that money can be switched as necessary between that available for family and that for other civil matters. In addition, very expensive cases can be funded by negotiating contracts on an individual basis from a central fund.

Section 5 of the act stipulates that in funding services as part of the Community Legal Service, the Commission shall "aim to obtain the best possible value for money".

Excluded Matters

There are some civil matters which cannot be funded by the Community Legal Service Fund. Conveyancing, the making of wills, matters involving trusts, boundary disputes, partnership law and other business disputes are not eligible for legal aid.

Before the 1999 Act, defamation cases were wholly ineligible for legal aid. After the Act, it is available only in exceptional cases, where there is a wider public interest. Up to 2005, only one defamation case had qualified for legal aid. The position might well change as a result of *Steel and Morris v United Kingdom* (2005). This case, heard in the European Court of Human Rights in Strasbourg, was the culmination of the long drawn-out 'McLibel' defamation case brought by McDonald's against two penniless environmental campaigners. It will be more fully dealt with in Chapter 5.

An important new exclusion from funding is that of negligence cases. A person who suffers loss or damage as the result of another person's negligence (see Chapter 9), except in the case of clinical negligence, is not now eligible for legal aid. Negligence cases are now to be funded by means of conditional fees (see below).

Cases where the amount in dispute is under £5000 also cannot be funded from the Community Legal Service Fund, nor can most tribunal hearings.

Criteria for Funding

Section 7 of the act states that funding is to be available only to those whose financial circumstances warrant it. This is known as a **means test**, and takes into account a person's

- **disposable income**—income available to a person after essential living expenses have been met, and

- **disposable capital**—assets available, such as bank and building society accounts, investments and other savings, jewellery and other valuables, and the value of a house over a certain amount after the outstanding sum owing on a mortgage has been deducted.

Maximum and minimum amounts for disposable income and capital are laid down by regulations issued by the Lord Chancellor. A person whose disposable income and capital are below the minimum amount stipulated will qualify for free legal aid. Those who are above the maximum limit will not qualify at all. Between the two, contributions are paid on a sliding scale, so that a person just above the minimum will pay a much smaller contribution than a person just below the maximum.

In addition to the means test, other criteria are taken onto account. These are:

- the likely cost, and the benefit which may be obtained,
- the availability of money in the Fund,
- the importance to the individual of the matter concerned,
- the availability of other services which could be used,
- the prospects of success in a dispute, (this is the former **merits test** under the old system),
- the public interest, and
- any other factors which the Lord Chancellor may order the Commission to consider.

It can be seen from the above that a person who qualifies financially for legal aid might not necessarily obtain it if the application of other criteria shows that it is not to be granted.

Providers of Legal Services

Solicitors have traditionally been the main providers of legal services, and this remains the case. In the past, the great majority of solicitors' firms undertook legal aid work, and the familiar "Legal Aid" logo was a feature of many a high street office. In 1994 the franchising scheme was introduced, whereby after fairly stringent criteria for qualifying, firms were awarded franchises, or contracts, to perform legally aided work. The idea was to provide value for taxpayers' money, while providing work of an assured standard. Those solicitors' firms which did not have such franchises were still able to carry out their previous legally aided services.

The Access to Justice Act integrates this franchising with a scheme involving specially approved providers of legal services. Those solicitors without such a contract are not able to provide services funded from public money.

Law Centres and Citizens Advice Bureaux (see above), are also eligible to be given contracts by the Legal Services Commission to provide publicly-funded help where other adequate facilities are lacking.

Conditional Fees

Conditional fees—no win, no fee—have been a feature of other legal systems, notably in the USA, for many years. There was a time when such arrangements were illegal under English law (indeed they constituted the crime of *champerty*). However, in 1995, this system became part of English law, and now forms an important element in the funding of civil disputes. As stated above, actions in the tort of negligence, for example, are excluded from public funding and are to be financed by the conditional fee system.

By this scheme, the client and solicitor agree on the fee which would normally be charged for the particular case in hand. On top of this fee, there is an "uplift" of up to 100 per cent of the original amount. This is the *success fee*. If the client wins the case, the solicitor receives the original fee plus the amount of the "uplift".

The success fee element payable by a successful client will come from the damages received. In practice, most solicitors place a "cap" on the success fee of 25 per cent of any damages awarded. The amount of the "uplift" cannot be claimed as part of the normal costs in a civil case, although the Access to Justice Act does allow the court to order the losing party to pay the amount of the success fee.

Insurance

The rule that a losing party will also pay the winning party's costs means that a client in a conditional fee arrangement will take out insurance against this. Where a party has taken this step and has gone on to win the case, the court can order the losing party to repay the winning party's insurance premium. This means that the cost of insurance has increased, and may sometimes even be hard to get. The Law Society has an affordable insurance scheme for personal injury actions, but in other areas, litigants must rely on private companies.

The Criminal Defence Service

Section 12 of the Access to Justice Act establishes the Criminal Defence Service for the purpose of "securing that individuals involved in criminal investigations or. . .proceedings have access to such advice, assistance and representation as the interests of justice require".

The Police and Criminal Evidence Act 1984 gave all suspects held at a police station the right to have access to legal advice. A solicitor or accredited representative is available day or night to offer any help that may be needed. The service is free and non-means tested, although suspects may of course engage and pay for their own solicitors if they prefer to do so. The Access to Justice Act states that such advice and assistance shall continue to be funded by the Legal Services Commission.

The Legal Aid Act 1988 brought in a scheme where local solicitors working on a rota basis are available at the magistrates' court. They give advice to any person who is unrepresented, and may also in certain circumstances, for example if the person is in danger of being held in custody, represent that person in court. The service is free and non-means tested.

Criteria for Funding Criminal Cases

Under the previous system for funding criminal cases, the courts would grant legal aid depending on the application of a **means** test and an **interests of justice** test. The Access to Justice Act provides that in deciding whether representation should be paid for from public funds, the same interests of justice are to be considered. They are similar to the old Widgery Criteria, namely:

• if the person is in danger of losing his liberty, livelihood or reputation;

• if a substantial point of law is involved;

• if an individual is unable to understand the proceedings or state his own case;

- if the tracing, interviewing or expert cross-examination of a witness on behalf of the person is involved, and

- if it is in the interests of another person that the individual is represented.

Unlike the funding of civil cases, where a finite budget is available, the funding of criminal cases will continue to be according to demand.

Useful websites

Citizens Advice Bureaux: *www.citizensadvice.org.uk*
Law Centres: *www.lawcentres.org.uk*
The Legal Services Commission: *www.legalservices.gov.uk*
The Community Legal Service: *www.justask.org.uk*

SPECIMEN EXAMINATION QUESTIONS

(a) Explain how a client in a civil case will qualify for the following:

   (i) Legal Help;
  (ii) Legal Representation.   (6 marks)

(b) Explain what is meant by "a conditional fee arrangement" and "appropriate insurance", in the context of a civil claim. Explain why a person in the middle income bracket may welcome such a development in the law.   (6 marks)

AQA, Higher Tier, June 2002

TALKING POINT

"The law, like the Ritz Hotel, is open to all". How far has the law become more accessible since the Access to Justice Act 1999?

SUGGESTED COURSEWORK TITLE

Describe how legal aid and advice is available in civil and criminal cases. Have the changes brought about by the Access to Justice Act 1999 fulfilled their purpose?

THE JURY

A jury is a group of men and women legally chosen to hear a case and to decide the facts from the evidence presented.

Juries are used in civil and criminal cases. Trial by jury in civil cases is not common and is usually restricted to actions involving defamation, malicious prosecution, fraud, and false imprisonment. Any party to one of these actions has the right to trial by jury. A jury will be ordered for other cases when the court considers it necessary, which it rarely does. A county court jury consists of eight jurors and a High Court jury has 12.

In criminal cases, juries of 12 persons are used in all trials in the Crown Court. There are seven to 11 jurors in a coroner's court. It is the duty of the judge to decide all matters of law, while the duty of the jury is to decide matters of fact.

Qualifications of Jurors

Although all trials are normally heard in the Crown Court before a judge and jury, the Criminal Justice Act 2003 provides for two exceptions. Trial by judge alone may take place in the Crown Court where:

- there is a serious risk that the jury will be subject to tampering; or

- the case is one of great financial or commercial length or complexity.

Until the passing of the Criminal Justice Act 2003, it was possible for many people in the community to evade jury service. Those connected with the law or the administration of justice, for example judges, barristers, solicitors, the police, and so on, were ineligible to serve on juries. So were the clergy (of whatever denomination), the mentally sick and those currently on bail in criminal proceedings. Other members for the community were excused as of right. These included those in the medical profession, the armed forces, Members of Parliament and people over 65. It was also possible to be released from jury service at the discretion of the judge if good reason could be shown. Such reasons could include problems with child care, examinations, holidays, etc.

New rules for qualification

In his report on criminal justice in 2001, Sir Robin Auld recommended that juries should reflect a much wider section of society. To this end, professional people previously ineligible or excused as of right should be included on juries. All but the mentally ill should be eligible for jury service.

These recommendations were accepted. The Juries Act 1974 was accordingly amended by the Criminal Justice Act 2003, which provides that to qualify for jury service a person must be:

- aged between 18 and 70;

- on the electoral register;

- resident in the United Kingdom, Channel Islands or the Isle of Man for at least five years from the age of 13;

- not mentally ill; and

- not disqualified.

The only people now *excused* jury service are full-time serving members of the Armed Forces. The only people who are *ineligible* are the mentally ill.

Disqualified people are those who:

- at any time in the previous ten tears have served any part of a prison sentence, youth custody or detention; or

- at any time in the last five years have been placed on probation.

As a result of the reforms introduced by the 2003 Act, members of professions previously ineligible now serve on juries. Some people have questioned whether it is a good idea for judges to do jury service on the grounds that they would naturally tend to dominate discussions in the jury room and – though not necessarily intentionally – unduly influence the other jurors. One judge has had to stand down as a juror on the grounds that he was acquainted with counsel involved in the case.

Summoning a jury

A list of all persons qualified for jury service is produced from the electoral register. The Central Juror Summoning Bureau, set up in 2001, uses computers to select at random a series of names from this list. Summonses to attend for jury service are then sent out to those who are selected. This group of people is known as the **jury panel**. Unless a person is disqualified, ineligible or excused, he or she must attend for jury service or risk a penalty, usually a fine.

Jury vetting

There are some cases where a person who holds extremist views may not be a suitable juror. It is the practice in such situations to "vet" the list of potential jurors by checking police, security and Special Branch records. Vetting takes place after the jury panel has been selected, as described above. In a case involving terrorism, for example, it may be undesirable to have on the jury someone who is known to have extreme political beliefs. The reason for this is that such a person might try to influence the other jurors unduly, or make public sensitive information in a case held *in camera* (not open to the public).

In order to vet a jury in these circumstances, the permission of the Attorney General, acting on the advice of the Director of Public Prosecutions, is required

JURY
SERVICE

YOUR JUROR'S NUMBER

You have been chosen for Jury Service. Your name was randomly chosen from the list of people who are registered to vote in elections.

Jury Service is an important public duty. You will be asked to consider the outcome of a criminal trial in the Crown Court. You will be among many people chosen each year for Jury Service and you will have an opportunity to be involved in the legal system.

Jurors may also be needed to serve in a civil case though this does not happen often. When it does, the trial will usually take place in the High Court or a county court. Jurors might also be needed to serve in a coroner's court.

Pages 1 and 2 of this form are your Jury Summons. It tells you where and when to start your Jury Service.

Pages 3 and 4 of this form are the reply to your Summons for Jury Service. The information you provide there will assist the jury summoning bureau when processing your form.

Important

- *You should detach pages 1 and 2 of this form and keep them in a safe place as you need to bring them with you on your first day of service.*

- *You will need to complete, detach and return pages 3 and 4, the reply to your Summons for Jury Service, to the jury summoning bureau (details shown on page 2), within 7 days of receiving this Summons.*

- *We will send you additional information once we have processed your reply.*

WARNING

You may have to pay a fine of up to £1,000 if:
- *you do not reply to this Summons; or*
- *you do not attend Court for Jury Service without a good reason; or*
- *you are not available to be a juror when your name is called at Court by the Jury Bailiff; or*
- *you are not fit to be a juror because of drink or drugs.*

THE BOOKLET ENCLOSED WITH THIS SUMMONS

The enclosed booklet explains who, by law, can and cannot be a juror and contains information that will help you complete the reply to your Summons for Jury Service form.

Please read the booklet thoroughly before completing the reply to your Summons for Jury Service on pages 3 and 4.

The information which you give on pages 3 and 4 will help the jury summoning bureau to process your Summons more efficiently.

Once your form has been processed, the jury summoning bureau will write to you confirming the date and time of your first day of attendance.

If the jury summoning bureau decides that you will not be a juror on this occasion, they will also write and tell you.

IF YOU NEED ADDITIONAL HELP OR INFORMATION

If, after reading the booklet, you need further help to fill in your reply to the Jury Summons, the jury summoning bureau will be pleased to help you. Their address, telephone number, e-mail address and fax number are shown below.

Further information is also available on the Court Service website at *www.courtservice.gov.uk*

If you would like a virtual tour of the jury system, featuring photographs, spoken commentary and comprehensive text in an interactive environment, then visit *www.juror.cjsonline.org*

If you need to contact the jury summoning bureau, please have your juror's number ready in case they need it. This appears underneath your name and address on page 1 of the Summons.

WHERE AND WHEN TO START YOUR JURY SERVICE

You must go to:

During your Jury Service you may be asked to go to another court nearby.

on:

at:

After your first day a court official will tell you when to arrive.

THE JURY SUMMONING BUREAU IS LOCATED AT:

JURY CENTRAL SUMMONING BUREAU
THE COURT SERVICE
FREEPOST LON 19669
POCOCK STREET
LONDON SE1 0YG

Telephone: 0845 355 5567 Office Hours 9 am - 5 pm, Monday to Friday
Fax: 020 7202 6812 E-mail: *jurysummoning@gtnet.gov.uk*

Issued on

by the Jury Summoning Officer with the authority of the Lord Chancellor.

You must fill in the second part of this form, the reply to your Summons for Jury Service, and send it to the jury summoning bureau *within seven days from the day on which you received this Jury Summons.* Please detach the reply to the Jury Summons at the perforation and return in the enclosed envelope.

REPLY TO YOUR SUMMONS FOR JURY SERVICE

Warning   *Please read this form and the accompanying booklet carefully before completing it. You may have to pay a fine if you refuse to give the information required, or you give false information, or cause or permit, someone else to give false information.*

HOW TO FILL IN THIS SECTION

Please use a blue or black pen only, and use BLOCK CAPITALS.

Where you are asked for information please do not write outside of the area given.

Tick boxes as appropriate. If you make a mistake, shade in that box, initial it, and tick the correct box.

PART 1   About you

A   Juror Number

B   *This section should only be completed if your name and address details are different from those printed on page 1.*
If you have changed address you will be moved to a nearer court.

Title   Mr ☐   Mrs ☐   Miss ☐   Ms ☐   Other ☐   *(please specify)*
Full Name *Please put all your names*
Address *Please include your post code.* *This will make sure that letters* *from the court reach you quickly*
Post code: ☐☐☐ ☐☐☐   Email address:

C   *This section asks for further information which you should give.*

Telephone number *Please give any telephone numbers* *where we can contact you between* *9.00 am and 5.00 pm*	Home	Work
		Mobile
Date of birth **Day** ☐ **Month** ☐ **Year** ☐☐☐		

PART 2   Are you qualified for Jury Service? *Please read Note 1 on page 2 of the booklet*

A   Will you be under 18 on the date
you are due to start your Jury Service?   No ☐   Yes ☐   If *Yes go to* **Part 5**

B   Will you have reached the age of 70 on
the date you are due to start your Jury Service?   No ☐   Yes ☐   If *Yes go to* **Part 5**

C   Have you lived in the United Kingdom, the Channel Islands or
the Isle of Man for any period of at least 5 years,   No ☐   Yes ☐   If *No go to* **Part 5**
since you were 13 years old?

D   *Please read the list in Box A in the booklet*
Are you on bail?   No ☐   Yes ☐

E   *Please read the list in Box A in the booklet*
Have you been convicted of an offence, and been given a   No ☐   Yes ☐
sentence in this list

F   *Please read the list in Box B in the booklet*
Do you suffer from a mental disorder in this list?   No ☐   Yes ☐

   If you have answered Yes to any of the questions D, E or F above please give details in the box below and then go to the declaration in Part 5.

PART 3   Deferral and Excusal   *Please read Note 2 on page 3 and 4 of the booklet*

Would you like to make an application to have your Jury Service deferred to a later date, or an application to be excused from Jury Service?

Important - your Jury Service can be deferred for up to 12 months, but can only be deferred once. You must therefore supply us with all dates to avoid now. You will only be excused from Jury Service if you cannot do it at any time during the next 12 months.

☐ No *Go to Part 4*
☐ Yes, I would like to be deferred
☐ Yes, I would like to be excused
(if you have already served within the last 2 years and wish to be excused as of right, please state details and Court attended below)

Please provide as much information as possible in the box below to support your application. If necessary, please enclose supporting evidence. We are unable to deal with correspondence sent direct by a third party, such as an employer.

I would like to be deferred / excused because

Please give ALL dates when you will not be available for Jury Service during the next 12 months, and give reasons

Go to Part 4

PART 4   Disability   *Please read Note 3 on page 4 of the booklet*

Do you have a disability for which the court will need to make special arrangements?   No ☐ *Go to Part 5*   Yes ☐ *Please mark one of these boxes if appropriate. If you do, please give details in the large box below.*

Visual impairment ☐   Wheelchair access ☐   Hard of hearing ☐   Other ☐

The special arrangements are

Go to Part 5

PART 5   Declaration   *Please read the Warning on page 2 of the booklet*

I have read the Jury Summons and booklet, including the Warnings on pages 1, 2 and 7 of the booklet. The information I have given is true to the best of my knowledge.

I understand that the answers I have given may be checked and that I may be prosecuted if I have deliberately given false information.

Signed	Date

FOR OFFICE USE ONLY	Excusal / deferral	granted ☐ not granted ☐	ineligible yes ☐ no ☐	Initial: Date:

4

Datasupplies (Stat) Limited 0191-4135936

The jury ballot

The jury for a particular case is selected publicly in court by ballot. The names of all the potential jurors on the panel are written on cards. These are shuffled and the names of the first twelve are called by the clerk to the court. Unless there are any challenges (see below), these twelve people will serve as the jury in the case about to begin.

Challenging

Either party in a trial may challenge any juror and request a replacement provided that an explanation is given in each case. The Criminal Justice Act 1988 abolished the right of peremptory challenge, but the defence and prosecution are allowed to challenge jurors on the ground of "cause". This may happen if the jurors have some connection to the accused. An example might be if the case is of a company accused of fraud, and a director of that company is a member of the jury.

In *R. v Ford* (1989), the Court of Appeal held that, in the absence of specific bias, ethnic origin cannot be a valid ground for challenging a juror, because juries are picked at random.

Discharging a jury

A judge may discharge an individual juror during the course of a trial in the interests of justice. It may become known that a juror has some personal connection to the accused, for example. It is also possible for a judge to discharge an entire jury, if it becomes obvious that a fair trial might be compromised.

Secrecy

Once jurors have retired to consider their verdict, they are forbidden from communicating with anyone but the trial judge or a specific court official until after the verdict has been given. The Contempt of Court Act 1981 forbids them from afterwards divulging anything of their deliberations.

Although there are many good reasons for maintaining this secrecy, it has been criticised on the grounds that it inhibits research into juries. Also, in the case of an appeal, the reasoning is "interred with the verdict".

Verdicts

The verdict of a jury in criminal cases does not have to be unanimous. The Juries Act 1974 provides that majority verdicts are acceptable:

- where the jury consists of 11 or 12 jurors and a majority of 10 jurors are in agreement.
- where the jury consists of 10 jurors, nine must agree, and

- the jury have deliberated for what the court considers to be a reasonable length of time. In the Crown Court, the period must be at least two hours, usually two hours and ten minutes.

- the foreman of the jury in the Crown Court states the number of the jurors who agreed and disagreed with the verdict.

In *R. v Pigg* (1983), the foreman only stated the number of jurors agreeing with the verdict, and did not state the number dissenting. The House of Lords held that it was sufficient if the words used by the foreman of the jury made it clear to ordinary persons how the jury was divided.

If it is necessary for a jury to stay in a hotel overnight, the trial judge should direct the jury that they should not continue their deliberations at the hotel, but should wait until the following day when they are back in the courtroom. In *R. v Tharakan* (1994), this direction was not given by the judge, and the defendant's appeal was upheld on the grounds that there was a risk that the jury's deliberations could have continued in the hotel.

Advantages and Disadvantages of Trial by Jury

Advantages

- A verdict from a jury of ordinary lay persons appears to be more acceptable to the public than if it came from a single judge.

- Ordinary lay people take part in the administration of law.

- A jury is impartial and has no direct interest in the result. In *R. v Gough* (1992), after the jury's verdict of guilty, it was discovered that a juror knew a close relative of the defendant, who later appealed on the grounds that this constituted a serious irregularity in the conduct of the trial. The Court of Appeal held that it would not interfere with a jury's verdict unless it could be shown that the defendant (a) did not have a fair trial or (b) was likely to have been prejudiced. In this case the Court considered that if there was any bias it was likely to be in favour of the defendant.

- There is an impression that not only has justice been done, it has been seen to be done.

- A jury will sometimes come to a verdict which is *just* rather than legally correct. In recent years juries, in cases with exceptional circumstances, have refused to follow the letter of the law and considered that only an acquittal would be a just verdict. Clive Ponting was acquitted of a charge under the Official Secrets Act, although the judge informed the jury that the accused had no defence in law. In 1992, Stephen Owen shot a man who, by reckless driving, had killed his son. The jury acquitted Mr Owen, while it was almost certain that a judge sitting alone would have held him to be guilty. The juries in these cases must have considered that justice was best served with an acquittal.

However, it should be noted that such "perverse" verdicts may be subject to appeal by either prosecution or defence lawyers.

Disadvantages

- Jurors may not be competent to understand the evidence presented and the issues involved. Cases involving fraud, which may last for many months, may involve the use of technical terms beyond the grasp of many jurors. In libel cases, for example, an average juror may not be able to appreciate the subtle meanings of the offending words—are they statements of fact or merely comments? In addition to reaching a decision, a libel jury has to decide the amount of damages which a successful plaintiff should receive, although they have no training in this aspect and the judge is only allowed to give advice or guidance in general terms. The courts, however, do have power to substitute the sum awarded, if it appears to the court that the jury's award is excessive or inadequate.

- Jurors may be easily convinced by the manner and presentation of the barristers during the trial, or be persuaded by a forceful or belligerent foreman when locked in the jury room.

- In some trials, for example motoring offences, juries have a sympathy with the accused. They may be fellow motorists and think, "There, but for the grace of God, go I".

- Although jurors receive payment for travelling expenses, etc., and an allowance for loss of earnings, it is probable that many people suffer financial loss.

- The period of jury service may take many weeks and this may place a strain on certain jurors, such as mothers with very young children or the more elderly. There is a danger that jurors may "agree" with a verdict to bring a quicker end to the trial.

- Jurors may experience frustration in having to wait in a court building for many days before being called to serve, and possibly never being called during the period of their service.

- Cover by television and newspapers of important or controversial trials may influence jurors. Although jurors should not discuss the case during the course of the trial, it is practically impossible to avoid the opinions of reporters and newsreaders.

- Jurors may suffer from post-traumatic stress disorder in the period after trials which involve horrific crimes, such as murder and rape, and in which the jury is exposed to graphic, gruesome details and photographs of the crime. In America jurors can receive psychiatric counselling directly after the trial is over, but in Britain this facility is not generally available and disturbed jurors have to cope as best as they can. Following the Rosemary West murder trial in 1995, jury members were offered counselling.

- It is possible for a black person to be tried by a wholly white jury. There has been a move to abate this possible disadvantage by ensuring that a certain number of non-white jurors are selected for a panel, although the actual selection for a particular case is still by ballot from the total jurors on the panel.

There is a suggestion that trials by judges alone would probably produce more correct decisions than trials before juries. This would eliminate any fear that members of the jury are in the pay or under the influence of the accused, and it may also solve many of the disadvantages mentioned above. It is an offence to do anything to harm or intimidate a juror or witness in criminal proceedings. This offence incurs a maximum penalty of five years' imprisonment or an unlimited fine or both.

"Jury nobbling"

It should be noted that the Criminal Procedure and Investigations Act 1996 provides that if a person has been aquitted of an offence by a jury, and a witness or juror has been intimidated during the proceedings of the case, the High Court has power to quash the aquittal, if it appears to the court that, but for the intimidation, the aquittal would not have taken place.

Useful website

For jury service leaflets: *www.courtservice.gov.uk*

LAY ASSESSORS

Lay assessors are qualified persons with expert knowledge, who are called to help or assist a judge in a case which needs special technical knowledge or expertise. They are mainly employed in the Admiralty Court and are known as nautical assessors.

SPECIMEN EXAMINATION QUESTIONS

(a) (i)   Identify **three** basic qualifications for jury service.   (3 marks)
     (ii) Name an Act which sets out these qualifications.   (1 mark)

(b) In the context of jury **selection**, explain what is meant by

     (i)   the jury ballot;
     (ii)   jury vetting;
     (iii) challenging.   (6 marks)

(c) Jury verdicts can be **unanimous** or by **majority**. Explain what is meant by these **two** terms.   (4 marks)

(d) Juries are occasionally used in **civil** cases.

     Identify a civil case where a jury may be used and explain any problem a civil jury might have to deal with.   (4 marks)

(e) Identifying **at least one advantage** and **one disadvantage**, comment on how well the system of trial by jury works.   (6 marks)

AQA Higher Tier, June 2003

TALKING POINTS

Should judges be obliged to serve on juries?

How many reasons can you think of for maintaining the secrecy of a jury's deliberations?

A distinguished former judge, Lord Devlin, said that a jury's ability to see things differently from judges was what made them worthwhile. Do you agree?

SUGGESTED COURSEWORK TITLE

Explain how a jury is selected and describe its function in relation to the judge. Discuss the advantages and disadvantages of the jury system, and consider the effects of trial by a judge alone.

3 | Enforcing the Law

SANCTIONS AND REMEDIES

As we have noted, law which cannot be enforced is no law at all. In order that people obey the criminal law, punishment should follow if they fail to do so. In the same way, people who disregard the civil law should be made to pay compensation to an injured party, or make up for the situation in some other way.

Sanction is the word used to indicate a sentence passed by way of punishment when an offender is found guilty in the criminal courts.

Remedies are awards in the civil courts to remedy a cause of complaint or compensate for an injury.

These ways of enforcing the law will be dealt with at greater length later in this chapter. First it is necessary to investigate the ways in which a person can be brought before the court to face criminal charges. We shall also see what powers exist to arrest individuals, and what arrangements can be made to release them while they are awaiting trial. This process is called granting *bail*.

THE CROWN PROSECUTION SERVICE

A person who has broken the criminal law must be *prosecuted*, brought before the court, tried and found guilty (*convicted*) before he or she can be punished. The **Prosecution of Offences Act 1985** established the Crown Prosecution Service (CPS), for England and Wales. The effect of the Act was to separate the prosecution of offenders from the investigation and detection by the police of criminal offences. Previously, it was the police who decided whether a person should be charged.

The CPS is headed by the Director of Public Prosecutions (DPP), who in turn reports to the Attorney-General. It is divided up into 42 areas in England and Wales, and staffed by qualified solicitors and barristers.

In deciding whether to bring a prosecution, the CPS must decide if there is enough evidence for **a realistic prospect of conviction**. In other words, it has to decide whether a court is *more likely than not* to find the defendant guilty. If this first test is not passed, then no prosecution will follow. If the CPS does conclude that there of enough evidence for a probable conviction, then it must decide whether or not the prosecution would be **in the public interest**.

Prosecutions in the public interest would be **likely** where:

- a conviction is likely to result in a significant sentence; or
- a weapon was used, or violence threatened during the offence; or
- the offence was committed against a public servant, such as a police officer or a nurse; or
- such offences are persistently committed in a particular locality.

Prosecutions are **less likely** to proceed where:

- the offender is elderly, or suffering from mental or physical ill-health; or
- the court is likely to impose a small penalty; or
- the offence was committed as the result of a genuine mistake; or
- the harm or loss is minor and was the result of a single incident.

As a result of the Criminal Justice Act 2003, the decision to charge offenders has moved from the police to the CPS, except in the case of certain minor offences. As a consequence of this, instances of charges being reduced or dropped altogether have more than halved.

Useful website

Crown Prosecution Service: *www.cps.gov.uk*

POWERS OF ARREST

How are persons who are accused of a criminal offence brought to court? There are three ways in which this can be done:

- by summons;
- by warrant for arrest;
- by arrest without a warrant.

The first two methods are known as "process".

Summons

A summons is a document which orders the accused to attend court. It is issued and signed by a magistrate, and states the nature of the offence and the time and place at which the accused should attend court. The summons is served or sent to the accused, who remains at liberty until the court hearing. A summons must be issued unless the offence is an indictable one, or subject to punishment by imprisonment.

Warrant

This document is an order for the arrest of a particular person and is addressed to police officers in the area concerned. The person suspected of an offence must be named or described in sufficient detail to be recognised as that person. It is unlawful to issue warrants that do not state the name or description of a person.

The warrant contains a statement of the offence and is signed by a magistrate. It empowers the police to arrest the suspected person and to bring him or her before the court. It is not strictly necessary for a police officer to possess the warrant at the time of the arrest but, if the accused demands, it must be shown as soon as is practicable.

A person arrested by warrant is not automatically at liberty until the time of trial, as would be the case with a summons. However, the magistrate may endorse the warrant at the time of issue so that the person named may be released on bail (see below), on an undertaking that the accused will appear in court at the specified time and place. Such a warrant is described as being "backed for bail" and the accused is released as soon as the conditions of the undertaking are complied with.

Generally, a warrant may only be issued for offences which are indictable or punishable by imprisonment. In addition, however, warrants may be issued if a person does not appear in court to answer a summons, or if the address of the accused is not sufficiently established for a summons to be served.

Arrest without a warrant

The **Police and Criminal Evidence Act 1984** provides for powers of arrest by the police and lessens the powers of arrest by private citizens.

Police officers

Police officers may arrest without a warrant, when they have reasonable grounds for suspicion, any person who

- has committed an arrestable offence,
- is committing an arrestable offence, or
- is about to commit an arrestable offence.

Arrestable offences are defined below. If there are no reasonable grounds for the above suspicion, the arrest is unlawful. The arrest would also be unlawful if the person arrested is not informed of the reason for the arrest at the time, or as soon as is practical afterwards.

A police officer may also arrest a person who has committed, or who is committing, any offence which is not an arrestable offence, and the police officer has reasonable grounds for suspecting that the service of a summons is impracticable or inappropriate because:

- the person arrested is unknown to the police, or

- is likely to cause injury or damage to other persons or property, or
- a child or other vulnerable person needs protection from the person being arrested.

As a general rule, a person can be detained by the police for up to 36 hours (Criminal Justice Act 2003). After this time, the person must be either released or charged with an offence. This period can be extended under certain circumstances up to a further 12 hours by the police themselves, and thereafter to a maximum of 96 hours after application to the magistrates. After this time, a suspect must be released or charged.

Private citizens

A private citizen may arrest a person when:

- an arrestable offence is being committed, or
- an arrestable offence has been committed, and the private citizen suspects the other person of having committed the offence.

Notice that the essential difference between powers of arrest by the police and that of private citizens is that a private citizen may only arrest a person who is **in the act of committing**, or **has committed** an arrestable offence, whereas a police officer can *in addition* arrest a person whom he or she reasonably suspects is **about to commit** such an offence.

Arrestable offences

An arrestable offence is:

- one which carries a penalty **fixed by law** (*e.g.* murder, where the sentence has to be life imprisonment);
- one for which a person aged 21 or over, not being previously convicted, may be sentenced to imprisonment of **five years or more**;
- one committed under certain Custom and Excise legislation, the Official Secrets Act, Sexual Offences Act, Theft Acts, and corruption in office, or attempting, inciting, or procuring the commission of any of these offences.

Stop and search

Section 1 of the **Police and Criminal Evidence Act 1984** provides that the police may detain a person or vehicle to carry out a search if they reasonably suspect that stolen or prohibited articles may be on or in the vehicle. Such articles would include things like burglary tools, offensive weapons, etc. The search must take place in a public place. The **Criminal Justice Act 2003** extended this power to persons suspected of carrying articles which are intended to be used for causing criminal damage, for example paint spray cans for graffiti.

A person also may be searched, although the police may only request the removal of a coat or jacket. Before making the search, the police officer must show identification, or if in plain clothes, show a warrant card. As soon as practical after the search, the police officer must make a written report of the time, place and date of the search, and any information regarding articles found, injuries to persons or damage to property as a result of the search.

The **Criminal Justice and Public Order Act 1994** provides that uniformed police officers may be authorised to stop and search pedestrians or vehicles, and their occupants, for offensive weapons. A senior police officer who reasonably believes that serious incidents of violence may take place, and that a stop and search operation may prevent such acts, may authorise a stop and search within a specified area for a period not exceeding 24 hours. Officers will not need grounds for suspicion against an individual, and any weapons seized may be retained by the police. A person who refuses to stop is liable to a maximum of three months' imprisonment and/or a level three fine (see Sentencing, later in this chapter).

Entry and search

Police officers may enter private premises to search for evidence and seize items connected with an arrestable offence. The Code of Practice provides that the search should be at a reasonable hour, and with due consideration for property and the occupants' privacy. A police officer may enter and search, with the occupier's written permission, to

- execute a warrant; or

- arrest for an arrestable offence (without a warrant); or

- arrest a person unlawfully at large.

In addition, when a person has been arrested for an arrestable offence, a police officer may search that person's premises provided the police officer has reasonable grounds for suspecting that evidence of that, or some other offence, will be discovered.

Seizure

In addition to all the powers described above, a police officer who is lawfully on premises may seize any item or article which is reasonably believed to be evidence of an offence, and if not seized would be lost, destroyed, concealed or damaged.

ASSAULTS ON THE POLICE

The **Police Act 1996** provides that

- any person who assaults a police officer while on duty shall be guilty of an offence, and shall be liable to imprisonment for a term not exceeding six months or a fine, or both;

- any person who resists or wilfully obstructs a constable in the execution of his or her duty shall be liable to imprisonment for one month or to a fine, or both.

COMPLAINTS AGAINST THE POLICE

The Police Act set up the Police Complaints Authority, which had the power to investigate complaints against the police. This body was abolished by the **Police Reform Act 2002** and replaced by the Independent Police Complaints Commission. Complaints may be made by anyone, in writing or in person.

Useful website

PACE Code of Practice: *www.homeoffice.gov.uk/docs/pacecodea.pdf*

BAIL

Earlier, it was indicated that a magistrate may endorse (make a note on) a warrant for arrest that the defendant may be released on bail. This means that the defendant will remain at liberty, and not in custody, between the arrest and the magistrates hearing, and between appearances in the magistrates' court and the Crown Court. While on bail, the defendant may carry out the normal functions of a free person.

Sureties

Bail is a security given by another person that the defendant will attend court on the appointed day and time. The persons who give this security are called sureties, and they usually promise to pay a sum of money into court if the defendant fails to attend the hearing. This promise is called a *recognisance*. It should be noted that sureties have the right to arrest if they consider that the defendant will not attend court as instructed.

Bail may be granted by

- the police
- magistrates
- the Crown Court.

The Bail Act 1976

The Bail Act 1976 provides that **there is a presumption that bail will be granted**, that is to say, that a defendant is entitled to bail unless a good reason can be shown why it should not be granted.

However, the **Criminal Justice and Public Order Act 1994** amended the 1976 Act by providing that this presumption be removed in cases where the defendant has committed an indictable offence, or one triable either way, while *already on bail* for a previous offence. In addition, the **Criminal Justice Act 2003** provides for presumption against bail in cases where a person arrested for an imprisonable offence tests positively for specified Class A drugs and refuses treatment.

This presumption against bail does not mean that bail may *never* be granted. There may be particular or exceptional circumstances under which the court may still decide to grant bail.

The 1994 Act, as amended by the **Crime and Disorder Act 1998**, also provides that bail shall be granted *only in exceptional circumstances* in the case of certain crimes. These are: murder, attempted murder, manslaughter, rape or attempted rape where the defendant has already served a custodial sentence for such an offence.

Although the Bail Act 1976 provides that, with the above exceptions, there shall be a presumption that bail will be granted, bail can be refused if there are reasonable grounds for believing that the defendant

- would fail to surrender to custody;

- would commit further offences;

- would interfere with witnesses.

It is also likely that bail would be refused if the court feels that the defendant should be kept in custody for his or her own protection. Other factors may be taken into account, such as the defendant's record where bail has been granted in previous cases, the nature and seriousness of the offence, the strength of evidence against the accused, whether he is likely to leave the country, and so on.

The **Bail (Amendment) Act 1993** provides that where a magistrate grants bail to a person who is charged with or has been convicted of

- an offence punishable by a term of five years imprisonment, or

- taking a conveyance without authority or aggravated vehicle taking,

the prosecutor may appeal to the Crown Court against the granting of bail, provided that the granting of bail had previously been opposed by the prosecution.

Police bail

In the case of police bail, the Police and Criminal Evidence Act 1984, as amended by the Criminal Justice and Public Order Act 1994, provides that the decision to grant bail is made by the custody officer. If it is suspected that the name and address given by the defendant cannot be discovered or may not be genuine, then the custody officer may refuse bail. Otherwise, the provisions of the Bail Act 1976 apply, as described above. The police have the power to arrest any person who fails to surrender to bail.

Under the Criminal Justice Act 2003 the police have been given the power to grant 'street bail'. This means that bail can be granted at the place of arrest. Instead of time-consuming paperwork at the police station, a form can be completed on the street at the time of arrest. It is then subsequently entered into the police records.

Conditions of bail

The police and the courts may make conditions for the granting of bail. These include:

- sureties, as described above;
- surrender of passport;
- reporting to a police station;
- curfew orders.

In addition, the courts may order that a condition of bail is to reside at a particular address, or at a bail hostel.

Problems in granting bail

People who are refused bail are remanded in custody. This means that there are people held in prison who are technically innocent, since their guilt has yet to be established in court. Some of these people may later be found to be innocent, but will not be entitled to any compensation for the time that they spent in custody. Others whose guilt is established in court may end up with a non-custodial sentence or receive such a short custodial sentences that they are released immediately.

It can be seen therefore that there is a conflict of interest between the right of the individual, who is assumed to be innocent until proved guilty, and the right of society to be protected from dangerous criminals. This problem was highlighted in the case of Andrew Hagans, who in 1992 raped and murdered a woman in Gloucester while on bail on another rape charge.

The Bail (Amendment) Act 1993 and the Criminal Justice and Public Order Act 1994 (see above) attempted to adjust the balance between these conflicting interests. Another way of solving the problem is the provision of bail hostels, where persons without a fixed address can be held with a certain amount of supervision. These hostels are run by the probation service, but unfortunately there are as yet insufficient places to meet demand. Another recent attempt to help the situation has been the introduction of electronic tagging.

Useful website

The criminal justice system: *www.cjsonline.gov.uk*

CRIMINAL SANCTIONS

As criminal offences are considered to be committed against the state, it is the state which provides and carries out the appropriate sanctions. In imposing these sanctions, society is expressing its disapproval and condemnation of criminal behaviour. There is a wide range of punishments available to the courts. Sentences, and the power to pass sentences, are now governed by the *consolidating act*, the **Powers of Criminal Courts (Sentencing) Act 2000** and the **Criminal justice Act 2003**.

There are various theories concerning the purposes behind the punishment of criminal offences. They may be briefly summarised as follows.

- **Retribution:** the criminal is getting the 'just deserts' of his activity.

- **Deterrence:** the individual criminal and would-be wrongdoers in general will be deterred from committing crimes in future.

- **Protection of the public:** a person in prison, for example, is prevented from further offending, and is no longer a threat to society. Similarly, a person while disqualified from driving cannot commit further motoring offences.

- **Rehabilitation:** criminal sanctions will serve to reform the offender, who will determine to 'go straight' in future. Good examples of appropriate sentences are those based on drug or alcohol rehabilitation.

- **Reparation:** an offender directly recompenses his victim financially through a compensation order, or to society generally by means of such sentences as community service orders.

It can be seen from the above that the first three of these theories of punishment can be said to be *authoritarian* in their approach, whereas the last two may be said to display a more *libertarian* outlook.

The Criminal Justice Act 2003 s.142 specifically states these purposes, which courts must take into account when sentencing an adult offender.

AVAILABLE SENTENCES

The following are sentences available to the courts. Sentences can be classified by division into a variety of options, according to the seriousness of the offence. The categories are, in ascending order of severity:

- discharges and fines;
- community sentences; and
- custodial sentences.

There are also other sentences available to the courts, (such as disqualification), which depend on the circumstances of the case.

Theses sentences are all provided for under the various sections of the Powers of Criminal Courts (Sentencing) Act 2000 and the Criminal Justice Act 2003, and are available to all courts unless otherwise stated.

Discharges and fines

Absolute discharge

The accused is found guilty of the offence, but the court does not consider that any punishment is justified. The accused is discharged absolutely.

Conditional discharge

Similar to the above, but the accused is discharged on condition that the convicted person does not commit any other offence. A condition may remain in force for up to a maximum of three years. If the accused commits another offence during that time, he or she may be sentenced in addition for the original offence.

Fines

Fines are sums of money which must be paid to the state. In many cases, the maximum amount of a fine is laid down by statute. Where an offence is punishable by a maximum prison sentence, (*e.g.* for theft, 7 years), the court can impose a fine at its discretion.

The Criminal Justice Act 2003 states that when a court imposes a fine, the amount must reflect the seriousness of the offence. The fine may also be increased or decreased, according to the offender's means.

Whereas the Crown Court can impose unlimited fines, magistrates' courts can only impose a maximum fine of £5000. Many offences triable by the magistrates carry a statutory fine at a certain level. For example, a person who does not leave an illegal rave when ordered to do so is liable to pay a level 4 fine. The current cash amounts (2005) for the different levels are:

Level 1: £200

Level 2: £500

Level 3: £1000

Level 4: £2500 (maximum for a summary offence)

Level 5: £5000 (maximum for an offence triable either way)

If an offender is under 18, the maximum fine that can be imposed by the magistrates is £1000. If the offender is under 14, the maximum is £250. Where an offender is under 18, a court can order the parent or guardian to pay the fine, unless it would be unreasonable to do so.

Fines are in theory payable immediately or within a set period, usually 14–28 days. In practice, fines are often paid off in weekly or monthly instalments, fixed by the court, and according to the offender's means. Non-payment of a fine is in itself an offence. The Criminal Justice Act 2003 provides for alternative ways of treating defaulting offenders other than prison. The court can impose unpaid work, curfews and driving bans.

The Courts Act 2003 provides for a new method of enforcing the payment of fines, whereby *fines officers* manage and collect fines on behalf of the courts. Discounts of up to

50 per cent will be available to prompt payers, and increases of up to 50 per cent of the fines of those who fail to pay promptly. This increase may be levied without the case having to go back to court. In addition, further steps may be taken, such as the removal of a defaulter's property, to recover the payment of the fine.

Spot fines

From November 1, 2004, the police have been given the discretion to impose spot fines for certain theft and criminal damage offences. The fines, of £80, will be for thefts under £200 and criminal damage up to the value of £500. No prosecution will follow, and therefore no criminal record will be incurred.

The reasoning behind this measure is that, since custodial sentences are unlikely to result from such offences as these anyway, there is no need to clog the courts up with them. Critics of this new policy say that if the offence is committed to feed a drug habit, for example, no help would be forthcoming by way of a court drug treatment and testing requirement (see below).

Referral order (Youth Court only)

Referral orders came into force on April 1, 2002, and are compulsory for first-time offenders aged between 10 and 17 years old who plead guilty. The order lasts from 3 to 12 months, at the court's discretion, depending on the seriousness of the offence. The local YOT (youth offending team) sets up a youth offending panel for the offender, which will then draw up a contract with the offender. The aim is to prevent future offending and make reparation to the victim.

Such orders are compulsory **unless** the offence is a serious crime, carrying a sentence of 14 years or more, and the court considers that a *custodial sentence* must be imposed.

Reparation order (Youth Court and Crown Court only)

This order is aimed at 10 to 17-year-old offenders. It is the 'standard' first punishment imposed by a criminal court after a referral order (see above). The court must impose this sentence unless some other order is made.

The order should be for a period lasting no more than **24 hours** and can involve reparation which is either **indirect** (to society) or **direct** (to the victim). Direct reparation requires the consent of the victim.

Community sentences

Following the Criminal Justice Act 2003, community sentences have, from April 2005, been replaced by a single community order. This is described on page. The various requirements which can be contained in such an order are in many cases based on the previous community sentences. For that reason, and the fact that some of these orders remain available, the old community sentences are described below.

Community rehabilitation order *(previously called* **probation order***)*

The object of this order is to secure the rehabilitation of the offender, to prevent the committing of further offences, or to protect the public from further harm from him. The offender must be aged **16 or over**. If the offender is aged 18 or over, he will be supervised by a probation officer. If the offender is under 18, supervision will either be by a probation officer or a member of the youth offending team.

   The minimum period of such an order is **6 months**, and the maximum is **3 years**.

Community punishment order *(formerly* **community service order***)*

The offender is punished by being put to work in the community. The work is unpaid, and is usually done at weekends. It must not be timed to interfere with the offender's job, education or religious observance. The work consists of a variety of jobs, such as repairing footpaths, hospital work, tending public gardens, etc., and is supervised by a probation officer, a member of the Youth Offending Team, or a social worker.

   The offender must be aged **16 or over**, and a pre-sentence report (PSR), is essential. The maximum sentence is **240 hours**, and the minimum is **40 hours**.

Community punishment and rehabilitation order *(previously called* **combination order***)*

This order combines elements of both the community rehabilitation order (12 months to 3 years) and the community punishment order (40 to 100 hours). This order is imposed where a custodial sentence might be the only other alternative.

   The offender must be aged **16 or over**, and a pre-sentence report is mandatory.

Curfew order

This sentence, having been tried in selected areas beforehand, became available throughout England and Wales from December 1, 1999. It requires the offender to remain at a specified place, usually at home, for a specified period of time. The order must not conflict with the offender's work, education or religious observance. The order is monitored by a 'responsible officer', and (under section 38 of the 2000 Act), by **electronic tagging**.

   The order is available for offenders aged **16 or over**, for between **2 to 12 hours** per day, for a maximum of **6 months**. For offenders **under 16**, the maximum is **3 months**.

Supervision order *(Youth and Crown Courts only)*

The effect of this order is similar to a community rehabilitation order, and can only be passed against a child or young person **under 18 years old**. This order is aimed at the younger and less mature offender, who is placed under the supervision of a member of the Youth Offending Team. The maximum length of such an order is **three years**, and must seek to balance the welfare of the offender and the 'just deserts' depending on the seriousness of the offence.

Attendance centre order

Under this order, an offender is required to attend a particular place at a specified time, and perform certain tasks, such as cleaning or decorating. This sentence was commonly used to keep, for example, football hooligans away from matches on Saturday afternoons.

Attendance centre orders are for offenders aged **between 10 and 21** (25 in the case of fine defaulters). The minimum sentence is usually **12 hours**, and the maximum **36 hours**, with a maximum of **3 hours on any day**. The order must not interfere with the offender's job, education or religious observance.

Drug treatment and testing order

This order can be passed if an offender is dependent on, or misuses drugs, and can be treated for, or requires treatment for this. The offender must submit to treatment which is designed to reduce or eliminate his dependency or tendency to misuse drugs, for example residence at a drug rehabilitation centre or embarking on a drug rehabilitation programme.

This sentence can be passed on an offender aged **16 or over**, and can be for a minimum of **6 months** and a maximum of **6 years**.

Action plan order (Youth and Crown Courts only)

By this order, an offender is required to comply with an action plan which may comprise a series of requirements. Examples of such requirements are: attendance centre, specified activities, reparation, exclusion from certain areas, educational courses, etc. The offender is placed under the supervision of a member of the local youth offending team, and the object is to prevent him from committing further offences and to secure his rehabilitation. A pre-sentence report is essential in order to achieve the appropriate balance of requirements.

The order is available for on offender aged **under 18**, and is for a maximum period of **3 months**.

New community sentence under the Criminal Justice Act 2003

As the result of provisions contained in the **Criminal Justice Act 2003**, all the above community orders are due to be replaced by a single community sentence. The new community order, due to be introduced in April 2005, is available to all offenders aged 16 or over, and can last for up to 3 years.

The new community order will have **requirements** attached to it in order to meet the seriousness of the offence and address the needs of the individual offender. In other words, there is a *menu* of requirements from which a selection can be made to suit each case. In the words of one JP overheard recently, "We shall mix and match".

The requirements upon which the new community order will be based are broadly similar to those community sentences described above. They are as detailed below.

- **Unpaid work requirement**, similar to the previous Community Punishment Order, but with an increase in maximum hours from 240 to 300.

- **Activity requirement**. This would include the previous probation requirement, attending anger management courses, the offender presenting him or herself at a specified place for specified activities.

- **Programme requirement**. The offender will take part in a programme of activity which has been accredited by the Secretary of State.

- **Prohibited activity requirement**. For example, a prohibition against driving.

- **Curfew requirement**, similar to the previous curfew order.

- **Exclusion requirement**. An offender must not enter a place or area specified in the order. This is to last for a maximum of two years, and will usually be electronically monitored.

- **Residence requirement**. The offender is to reside at a place specified in the order. Before imposing this order, the court is required to consider the offender's home circumstances.

- **Mental health treatment requirement**. The doctor or psychologist must be specified in the order. The offender must also agree to this order.

- **Drug rehabilitation requirement**. This order can only be imposed if the local Probation Board or Youth Offending Team recommends it. As with the previous DTTO (see above) this requirement can be reviewed by the court at regular intervals.

- **Alcohol treatment order**. The offender must agree to this order.

- **Supervision requirement**. This is similar to the Community Rehabilitation Order, described above.

- **Attendance centre requirement**. This is for offenders aged less than 25 years, and is similar to the previous Attendance Centre Order.

For **young offenders** (those aged under 16 years), the community sentences of curfew orders, supervision orders, attendance centre orders and action plan orders remain the same as previously described above. Referral orders are not affected by the 2003 Act.

Custodial sentences

Under section 79(2) of the 2000 Act, a custodial sentence should only be passed where the offence is so serious that:

- only a custodial sentence can be justified, or where

- the offence is of a violent or sexual nature and only a custodial sentence is adequate to protect the public from serious harm, or

- the offender refuses to consent to a community sentence, where such consent is required.

Imprisonment (Magistrates' and Crown Courts)

A convicted criminal **aged 21 or over** may be committed to one of Her Majesty's prisons. These prisons are of various kinds. Whitemoor and Dartmoor, for example are maximum security gaols. There are closed prisons, such as Wormwood Scrubs and Winson Green, and open prisons such as Littlehey.

Sentences of imprisonment are passed with reference to the statute under which the accused has been charged and convicted. Under the Murder (Abolition of the Death Penalty) Act 1965, for example, a conviction for murder must result in a *mandatory life sentence* (see Chapter 10). As will be seen later, other statutes such as the Offences Against the Person Act 1861 and the Theft Act 1968 lay down maximum sentences for specific offences. Examples are: Actual Bodily Harm, 5 years, and Theft, 7 years.

The Crown Court can pass any sentence of imprisonment from **one day** to **life**. The magistrates' courts can impose a maximum sentence of **six months** imprisonment for any one offence, and **12 months** for consecutive sentences for separate offences. Under the Criminal Justice Act 2003 the sentencing powers of magistrates is to be increased to a maximum of 12 months for any one offence. This provision is likely to take effect after December 2005. Time served on remand in custody is regarded as part of the sentence of imprisonment.

It should be noted that no person can be sent to prison if he is legally *unrepresented* (unless he refuses or does not apply for representation).

As a matter of policy, no convicted person, particularly under the age of 21, should be given a custodial sentence unless it seems to be the only reasonable way of dealing with the offender. Nevertheless, in 2004, the prison population in the United Kingdom reached a record figure of over 75,000, the highest *per capita* in Europe. One way of helping to reduce the prison population is through the system of **early release**. The following points show how the system operates.

- All prisoners must serve at least half their sentence.

- Those serving less than 12 months will be released after serving half their sentence, but the remaining portion can be re-activated if an imprisonable offence is committed before that portion would have expired.

- Those serving between 1 and 4 years will be released after half their sentence, but will remain on licence until the three-quarters point.

- Those serving over 4 years are eligible for discretionary release between half and two-thirds of their sentence. They must be released at the two-thirds point, but remain on licence until the three-quarter point.

- All prisoners in the last two months of their sentence can be released to **home detention curfew**, monitored by an electronic tag.

In the *Halliday Report 2001*, certain reforms in sentencing were proposed. One was the introduction of 'custody plus'. This was adopted, and the Criminal Justice Act 2003 provides that for all sentences of less than 12 months are to be replaced by custody plus. This means that after a maximum of three months of the sentence, the offender will be released and then spend at least six months under a community-type sentence. Failure to comply with the terms of the community sentence will result in a return to custody. For sentences of more than 12 months, the offender will spend half of the time in custody and the rest under supervision in the community.

Also introduced by the Criminal Justice Act 2003 was the concept of intermittent custody. Under this scheme, a prisoner will serve a custodial sentence intermittently, returning to prison at night or at the weekend. The object is to enable an offender to continue in employment or education, as well as retaining family ties, thus helping with rehabilitation.

In March 2002, the Home Secretary announced that prisoners convicted of non-violent crimes, (except sex offenders), would be released up to two months early in a further measure to deal with overcrowding in prisons. Those released are subject to electronic tagging. It is claimed that of over 44,000 prisoners released wearing tags in the previous three years, less than 2 per cent have re-offended during the remainder of their sentences.

Pilot scheme for satellite technology

One year later, in March 2003, the number of offenders to be tagged passed the 100 000 mark, and the re-offending rate, although slightly higher, still remained below 5 per cent. In 2004, the Home Secretary announced a pilot scheme for a more sophisticated method of electronic tagging. This involves satellite technology, and is aimed at hardcore career criminals, paedophiles and other sex offenders. By this system, the monitoring devices use satellites to pinpoint their position, unlike normal tags. Built-in electronic diaries can be downloaded at the end of each day by probation officers. In this way, a minute-by-minute record is provided of an offender's movements. The pilot scheme has been introduced in three areas of the country, and is intended to target prolific offenders for whom prison is ineffective.

Suspended sentence *(Magistrates' and Crown Courts only)*

Where an offender meets the criteria for imprisonment, as above, and there are **exceptional** circumstances which mitigate what would otherwise be an immediate custodial sentence, the court can consider a suspended sentence.

A prison sentence can be suspended provided the sentence does not exceed **two years** in total. The maximum period of suspension period is **two years**, and the minimum is **one year**. If the offender commits another imprisonable offence within the suspension period, he may be sentenced for that as well as for the previous offence.

Detention in a young offender institution *(Magistrates and Crown Courts only)*

Detention in a young offender institution comprises an element of training in accordance with the aim of rehabilitation, in addition to retribution. Home release can be granted, and the early release provisions are similar to those for adult offenders (see above).

This sentence applies to young offenders aged **18 to 20**. The criteria for sentencing them to a YOI are the same as for an adult offender. The minimum term is **21 days** and the maximum is limited to the **maximum for the offence** itself. Where the offender has reached the age of 21, and has not completed the sentence, the sentence becomes one of imprisonment and the offender is transferred to an adult prison.

A young offender must be legally represented before this sentence can be imposed, and a pre-sentence report is mandatory.

Detention and training order

This sentence is aimed at rehabilitating the young offender, and therefore training and education are its central aims. The offender is subject to a period of detention and training in secure accommodation, followed by a period of supervision. Secure accommodation includes secure training centres, young offenders' institutions, and accommodation provided by the local authority.

The sentence normally applies to offenders aged **12 to 18**, and is available to those **under 15** who are persistent offenders. The sentence is available to an offender **under 12** if necessary, to protect the public from his further offending. The sentence imposed must be of a fixed period varying from a minimum of **4 months** to a maximum of **24 months**. It is important to note that magistrates have the power to pass the maximum here, and are not limited to six months.

Detention during Her Majesty's pleasure (Crown Court only)

This sentence is passed where a person convicted of murder was under the age of 18 at the time of the offence. The sentence is also appropriate for offenders under 18 where

- the offence is one for which an adult could receive a prison sentence of 14 years or more;
- indecent assault has been committed;
- the conviction is for causing death by dangerous driving, or while under the influence of alcohol or drugs. In this case the offender must be aged **14 or above**.

The court can also pass this sentence if it feels that no other course of action is appropriate. The usual place of detention is local authority secure accommodation.

Other sentences

Binding over

This is when a person admits the offence, and is required by the court to enter into a contract *(recognisance)* with the court to keep the peace. If the offender commits another offence within the binding over period, the contract will have been broken, and the offender will have to pay over the amount specified in the recognisance. The courts can also bind over the parent or guardian of an offender under 18 to take proper care and control of the offender. The parent or guardian is bound to consent to this, or face a fine for refusing to do so.

The maximum length of a binding over order is **3 years**.

Disqualification

The most common use of this sentence is in connection with motoring offences. Driving while over the alcohol limit will mean disqualification, as will the attainment of 12 penalty points. The Crown Court has additional powers to disqualify an offender from driving under certain circumstances where a vehicle was used in the commission of an offence, or a non-fatal offence was committed by the offender while driving a vehicle.

Other statutory provisions authorise disqualification as a penalty. A person found guilty of cruelty to animals, for example, may be disqualified from keeping them in the future.

Compensation order

Where the commission of an offence has caused personal injury, loss or damage, the offender may be ordered to pay compensation to the victim of the crime.

The maximum amount of such an order is £5000 in the Magistrates Court, with no limit in the Crown Court.

Confiscation orders

In an attempt to tackle profits made from organised crime, the **Proceeds of Crime Act 2002** permits the use of civil procedures to recover money made from crime. Even if a conviction has not taken place, an individual may have to account for money the origin of which gives rise to suspicion. The Assets Recovery Agency has far-reaching powers to investigate such situations, and to bring proceedings to recover any property gained by unlawful means.

Hospital order *(Crown Court only, and magistrates' court in special circumstances)*

Where offenders are suffering from mental illness or severe abnormality of the mind, they may be detained with no specified release date at an appropriate institution, *e.g.* Broadmoor. In effect, this means that they will not be released until they make a complete recovery.

The person charged will have been found 'not guilty by reason of insanity' under the **M'Naghten Rules** (see page 265), or will have pleaded **diminished responsibility** (see page 248) under Section 2 of the Homicide Act 1957. Alternatively, the offender might have been found **unfit to plead** under the Mental Health Act 1983 (see page 266).

Anti-social behaviour orders

ASBOs, as they are popularly known, were introduced by the **Crime and Disorder Act, 1998**, and are not, strictly speaking, criminal sanctions. The police, or bodies such as local authorities, can apply for these to be made against any person who has behaved in an anti-social way. This sort of behaviour can take many forms, such as vandalism or the persistent intimidation of elderly people. The order prohibits the person involved from behaving in a particular way specified in the order for a minimum of two years. Typically, it might order a person not to enter a particular neighbourhood. By the end of 2004, over 2600 ASBOs had been made.

Although ASBOs are applied for using civil procedures, and are not strictly speaking criminal sanctions, they can be ordered as part of a criminal sentence. In addition, a person in breach of an ASBO can be fined or imprisoned (maximum five years), in the criminal court.

Opinions vary as to the effectiveness of these orders. Their supporters maintain that, for example, known drug dealers can be prohibited from entering a particular estate, or that older people who were previously afraid can now go about with safety. Critics of ASBOs say that because it is only necessary to show proof to the lowest civil standard, and because the normal rules of evidence do not apply (hearsay is acceptable, for example), the orders are too easily granted. Other critics maintain that a problem displaced merely goes somewhere else. It is also alleged that among the hooligan element the imposition of an ASBO is often seen as some sort of badge of prestige, to be worn with pride.

ASBOs are not imposed exclusively on young tearaways. In November 2004, an 88-year-old great-grandfather was fined by Liverpool Crown Court for breach of an anti-social behaviour order. He had been persistently abusing his neighbours.

FACTORS DETERMINING SENTENCING

When deciding what sentence is appropriate, the courts will consider the following:

What kind of sentence?

The court will consider what it hopes to achieve by passing the sentence. Is the main purpose retributive, rehabilitative, or for what other reason? This is now determined to a large extent by the age of the offender. In the **Youth Court** with a young offender, the sentence must reflect not only the **'just deserts'** of the offence, (retribution), but also the **'welfare'** of the offender, (rehabilitation). In the adult courts on the other hand, the greatest influence will be the **'just deserts'** element.

Jurisdictional factors

Some sentences, such as fines, community service, *etc*, are available to all courts. Others, such as imprisonment and supervision orders, are court-specific. In addition, magistrates' courts have limits on their sentencing powers, to a maximum of 6 months' imprisonment (12 months for consecutive sentences for separate offences) and/or a maximum fine of £5000. The Crown Court does not have these limits.

Summary offences carry lighter maximum sentences, whereas *indictable* offences are limited only by the maximum laid down for each offence.

If an accused **pleads guilty** to the offence, depending on the stage at which he pleads guilty, and the circumstances of the case, the court has the power to impose a less severe sentence. The usual reduction will be by **one third**, and applies to fines, imprisonment, hours of community service, etc.

The **facts** of the case are very important in deciding on the proper level of intrusiveness of sentence in relation to the **seriousness** of the offence.

In addition to the above, there are various **statutory provisions** which determine the sentence which may be passed for a particular offence. As will be seen in Chapter 10, many offences carry maximum sentences as laid down by statute. Under section 79 of the Powers of Criminal Courts (Sentencing) Act 2000, a *custodial* sentence should only be passed in the circumstances mentioned above under the heading 'Sentences Available'. Many offences have the limits of their sentences governed by Act of Parliament as follows:

- *Minimum sentences.* Examples of offences which carry a minimum sentence are drink-driving, (12 months' ban) and speeding, (3 penalty points). Under the 2000 Act, a third Class A drug trafficking offence attracts a minimum of 7 years' custodial sentence, and a third domestic burglary carries a minimum of 3 years.

- *Maximum sentences.* For example: theft, 7 years; robbery, life.

- *Discretionary sentences.* Manslaughter, for example, can be punished by anything from an absolute discharge to life imprisonment, according to circumstances.

- *Mandatory sentences.* Examples of these are murder (life imprisonment), and a person over 18 convicted of a second serious violent or sexual offence, (also life imprisonment).

Tariff for sentencing

Offences carry what is called a 'tariff', or 'going rate'. This is the sentence which would normally be passed for that offence in average circumstances for that particular case. The Court of Appeal and the Magistrates Association has laid down guidelines in this respect. These 'going rates' however can be varied according to whether there are **aggravating** factors (greater sentence) or **mitigating** factors, (lesser sentence). An example of an aggravating factor would be if there was a racial element in the offence, and a mitigating factor would be, for example, speeding in the course of a medical emergency.

Sentencing Guidelines

The Crime and Disorder Act 1988 provided for the setting up of the Sentencing Advisory Panel. This panel proposed guidelines for sentencing, which the Court of Appeal had to take into account. The Criminal Justice Act 2003 established a new body, the Sentencing Guidelines Council to produce a new set of guidelines for all criminal courts. The existing Sentencing Advisory Panel will now submit its advice on sentencing to the Council instead of to the Court of Appeal.

Personal factors

There are many other matters involving the defendant which will be taken into account when sentencing. The age of the offender is obviously important, both as to where the trial takes place (youth or magistrates' court), and whether imprisonment is an option (only available to defendants aged 21 or over). Some other factors may be summarised as follows:

- *Antecedents*. Under the 2000 Act, **any** previous *convictions* of the offender may be taken into account when deciding on the sentence. The court may look at any community sentences which may have been tried in the past, and how effective they were.

- *Pre-sentence Report*. This report is used as a basis for sentencing, and will indicate the suitability of different community sentences. The report is prepared by the Probation Service for offenders aged 16 or over, and by the local youth offender team for those aged 10 to 15. As has been seen above, sometimes a PSR is mandatory.

- *The relationship between offender and victim*. Examples are those between parent and child, teacher and pupil, doctor and patient, etc.

Other personal factors include previous good character, whether the defendant has a permanent address, the background of the offender, evidence of commitment to job, and family responsibilities.

RETRIAL FOLLOWING ACQUITTAL

Under the Criminal Justice Act 2003, the ancient rule of **double jeopardy** was abolished for a range of serious crimes. This rule previously provided that no person acquitted of a criminal charge could be tried again for the same offence. Under the 2003 Act, if *compelling new evidence* emerges which was not available at the time of the original trial, a previously acquitted defendant can be put on trial again for the same offence. As this change is intended to be retrospective, it is possible that cases may be reopened which date back many years.

The change was prompted by the case of Stephen Lawrence, a black teenager murdered from racist motives. It covers a large number of serious offences, including murder, manslaughter, rape, and arson which endangers life.

Before a suspect is re-investigated by the police, the consent of the Director of Public Prosecutions will be necessary. If a fair re-trial is unlikely because of, for example prejudicial media coverage, then a prosecution would not follow. There would be no possibility of repeated re-trials, as only one application for the quashing of an acquittal would be allowed.

Useful websites

The Halliday Review on sentencing: *www.homeoffice.gov.uk*

Youth justice: *www.youth-justice-board.gov.uk*

CIVIL REMEDIES

The purpose of civil remedies is not to punish but, for the most part, to compensate. Damages, (the payment of money), is the *common law* remedy, and the others are *equitable* remedies. (For an explanation of common law and equity, see *How the Law has Grown*, in Chapter 1). These civil remedies will be further touched on in subsequent chapters on contract and tort.

Damages (payment of money)

This is the remedy most often awarded, and is available in civil actions as of right. In tort, the aim of awarding damages may be to place the injured party in the financial position enjoyed before being wronged. In contract, it may be to place the injured party in the same financial position as if the contract had been completed.

Damages may be *nominal* (*e.g.* 1p), *substantial*, or *aggravated*. Nominal damages may be awarded where a person has a legal right, but has suffered no financial or other loss. Substantial damages are the actual amount needed to compensate the injured party. Aggravated damages are more than the actual loss, and are awarded where the injury suffered was aggravated by the malice or wrongful conduct of the defendant.

Specific performance

This equitable order is granted at the discretion of the judge. Its purpose is to force a party to carry out the terms of a contract which has been previously entered into. It is usually awarded in cases involving contracts for the sale of land. The law of contract is dealt with in Chapter 6.

Injunction

This equitable order is also granted at the discretion of the judge. The effect of such an order may be to make a party to carry out an act, such as knocking down a wall, for example. This kind of injunction is called a *mandatory injunction*.

A *prohibitory injunction* has the effect of preventing a person from acting in a certain way. An example of this might be to stop an actress under contract from making a film for another company.

An *interlocutory injunction* is sometimes granted to stop a person acting in a certain way pending a court action. An example might be to stop a newspaper from printing a possibly defamatory article.

Rescission

This is another equitable remedy, and is specific to the law of contract, (see Chapter 6). Its effect is to try to place the parties in the pre-contractual position by returning goods or money to the original owners.

SPECIMEN EXAMINATION QUESTIONS

1. Magistrates undertake a range of duties in court. Explain what is meant by:

   (i) granting bail;   (4 marks)
   (ii) issuing warrants;   (2 marks)
   (iii) the sentencing process.   (4 marks)

   AQA, Higher Tier, June 2004

2. In both of the following situations, **discuss** which **punishment(s)** the court may impose, giving **reasons** for your answer.

   (a) Fergus, aged 28, has been convicted of a dwelling house burglary. Fergus has a long history of offending behaviour, including burglary. However, he has not committed an offence for the last six years. The court has been told in mitigation that Fergus only reluctantly agreed to act as the "look-out" because he wanted to keep an eye on his younger brother, who was also involved. The pre-sentence report (PSR) indicates that Fergus is at low risk of re-offending and has a job and a family to support.   (6 marks)

   (b) Gretchen, aged 17, is before the court having pleaded guilty to a large number of shoplifting-type theft offences. She has a history of similar offences over the previous two years. Both the pre-sentence report and Gretchen's solicitor have indicated that Gretchen has a serious drug problem and is stealing to pay for her habit. The PSR also indicates that Gretchen is at high risk of re-offending and is currently unemployed.   (6 marks)

   AQA, Higher Tier, June 2003

3. Briefly describe any **two** community sentences. Discuss how effective you think these sentences are.

TALKING POINT

How far do you consider that "prison works" in controlling the crime rate?.

SUGGESTED COURSEWORK TITLES

Describe the main forms of criminal sanctions and their purpose. Consider how effective these sanctions are in punishing the guilty and protecting the public.

Explain what remedies are available to a claimant in the civil courts. How far are these remedies adequate in compensating an injured party?

What factors are taken into account when a decision is made to grant or refuse bail? What problems are likely to arise as a result of this process?

4 | Legal Personality

A legal system exists for the subjects or persons within the State. In English law there are two classes of person; human or natural beings, and corporate beings. The latter, called corporations, are artificial persons but they are recognised as having a legal status within the legal system. A corporation is comprised of human persons but has a legal existence separate from them.

All persons living in Britain have legal status. However, not everyone in the community has the same legal status. In many aspects of law, for example, children are treated differently from adults, and people who are mentally ill are treated differently from those who are not. These differences in treatment will be explained at greater length under the appropriate areas of law in subsequent chapters.

For most purposes, the legal status of a human being begins at birth and ends at death. An unborn child has certain rights, however, and the rights and intentions of a person (ensuring that the provisions of a will are carried out, for example), are protected after death.

CHILDREN

The age of majority is 18 when, generally, full legal status is acquired. Below 18 the age limit for legal responsibility and rights varies according to the particular section of law in question. The reason that young people do not have full legal status is not to prevent or curb their activities, but to protect them. Students will come across many names used to describe persons under 18, infants, minors, young persons, juveniles, children, etc., but in the main they all mean the same thing, a person who does not have full legal capacity.

Crime

A child under the age of 10 years is deemed to be incapable of committing a crime. A child aged 10 and over is liable for criminal prosecution, but special procedures are followed with regard to trial and punishment. Note that the old rule, the rebuttable presumption that a child between 10 and 14 was incapable of committing a crime (*doli incapax*), was abolished by the Crime and Disorder Act 1998.

Legality

Legitimate children

A child is legitimate if the parents were married at the time of conception or birth, even if the marriage was later declared void, provided that either of the parents reasonably believed the marriage to be valid.

Illegitimate children

A child born of parents who were not married to each other at the times stated above is illegitimate. If the mother is married, there is a presumption that her husband is the father, but this may be rebutted by evidence, such as the husband being out of the country for more than a year before the birth. An illegitimate child has the same rights as a legitimate child to an intestacy of either parents, and may claim as a dependant within the provisions of the Inheritance (Provision for Family and Dependants) Act 1975. Furthermore, if a will makes a bequest to "my children", illegitimate children are included. A legal disadvantage for illegitimate children is that they cannot succeed to a title or any property attached to the title.

Legitimation

An illegitimate child may be legitimated by the subsequent marriage of the parents and is then considered to be a legitimate child with the same rights.

Adoption

Children who have been legally adopted have all the legal rights as if the adopters were the natural parents.

Contract

A contract between an adult and a minor is binding on the adult, but not always on the minor. A minor is bound by a contract if it is for necessaries (food, clothing, etc.), or for the minor's benefit (training, education, etc.). A minor may make contracts to own moveable personal property (mobile phones, cars, etc.), but a minor cannot legally own land.

Tort

Minors are not so well protected in tort and the age of the person is not as important as the mental understanding of the specific individual. Obviously a young child cannot be expected to show the same standard of care in negligence as an adult, and conversely, an adult may have to show greater care with respect to children than with other adults.

Marriage

For a valid marriage to take place, both parties must be over the age of 16. If either of the parties is under 16, the marriage is void (non-existent at law). This is the case even if there was a genuine mistake which was not discovered until many years later. The effect would be that no marriage ever took place. This would be relevant, for example, in a situation where a party to the "marriage" dies intestate (see Chapter 12).

Litigation

A minor cannot personally bring a civil action, but may do so through a "next friend", who is usually a parent. A minor who is sued in civil law can defend the case through what is called a *guardian ad litem*, that is to say, an adult specially appointed to look after the minor's interests in court.

Minors may not apply for legal aid, although their parents or guardians may do so on their behalf.

Other Restrictions on the Rights of Minors

Voting and Jury Service

Young persons cannot vote at a local or parliamentary election, or be selected for jury service until they are 18 and their names appear on the *electoral roll*.

Wills

Generally, persons under 18 cannot make a valid formal will, although they may be competent to sign as a witness to a will (see Chapter 11).

Driving

A person must be 17 to obtain a licence to drive a car or motorcycle, although a person of 16 may obtain a licence to drive a moped.

Drinking

Persons under 14 are not allowed in bars of licensed premises, and persons over 14 and under 18, although allowed to enter a bar may not be served with, or drink, alcohol. Persons over 16 may consume certain drinks if served with a meal.

Gambling

Persons under 18 are not allowed in betting shops, gambling clubs or casinos, and they may not gamble in bars of licensed premises. A person under 18 may attend a club licensed to play "bingo" only, although they may not play or take part in the activity. A person under 16 may not buy a National Lottery ticket.

Cigarettes

Although it is not an offence for persons under 16 to smoke, shopkeepers may not sell cigarettes or tobacco to persons apparently under this age, whether or not they are for their own use.

Fireworks

A shopkeeper may not sell fireworks to persons under 18.

Tattooing

Persons under 18 may not be tattooed.

BANKRUPTS

A person who is unable to pay debts owing to others may be declared *bankrupt*. When a bankruptcy order is made, a trustee in bankruptcy or the official receiver will find out the total amount of the debts and the total amount of the assets of the bankrupt. Creditors are then paid in a strict order of preference. Unsecured creditors may only receive a proportion of what is left, and be paid perhaps only 10p or 15p for each pound owed. People who are declared bankrupt are disqualified from certain rights which they previously enjoyed. A bankrupt:

- cannot sit or vote in Parliament, either the House of Commons or House of Lords;

- cannot become a member of a local council or become a justice of the peace;

- may not be a director of a limited company or take part in its management;

- may not obtain a loan over a certain figure or make a contract without declaring their bankruptcy. It is a criminal offence to ignore this requirement.

Previously, some of these restrictions could last during a bankrupt's entire lifetime, but the Insolvency Acts 1985 and 1986 provided that anyone who has been a bankrupt for 10 years is automatically discharged. The bankruptcy courts may later review a bankrupt's position periodically, and make suggestions with the aim of restoring the bankrupt to full constitutional rights.

PERSONS OF UNSOUND MIND

The legal capacity of the mentally ill varies with the different branches of law and, in many ways, it is similar to the capacity of children.

Crime

Persons who can show that they did not understand the nature of their acts, or did not know that what they were doing was wrong, may plead *insanity* under the M'Naghten Rules. If the plea is successful, they will be found "not guilty by reason of insanity". A person accused of murder may plead the special defence of *diminished responsibility*. An explanation of this defence, and also of the M'Naghten Rules, will be found in Chapter 10.

Persons of unsound mind may also be found unfit to plead if they are deemed to be incapable of instructing lawyers, or following or giving evidence. In such cases, a second jury will consider whether the defendant "did the act as charged" in order for the court to determine a suitable order as to treatment or detention in hospital.

Contract

A person of unsound mind will be bound by a contract for the sale of necessaries like a minor (see above). Other contracts can be treated as void if it can be shown that the other party was aware of the mental illness.

Tort

The aim of the law of tort is to compensate an injured person, not to punish the person who committed the tort. A person of unsound mind therefore would be liable in tort *unless mental intent* needs to be shown.

Litigation

Actions on behalf of a person of unsound mind must be brought in the name of a "next friend", and defended by a *guardian ad litem*, as in the case of a minor (see above).

THE CROWN

The United Kingdom is a monarchy, and the Queen is the head of state. The Queen is a *constitutional monarch*, and the powers and duties conferred on her may only be exercised on the advice of her ministers.

The Queen has two distinct legal personalities. She is a *natural person* in her personal capacity, and she is a *corporation sole* in her public capacity.

- Because the Queen in a personal capacity "can do no wrong", she cannot be brought before a British court. The reason for this is that, technically, the courts are the Queen's courts and the judges are appointed by her. (Interestingly, during 2004, evidence provided from Buckingham Palace had a bearing on a criminal case involving a former royal butler, who was acquitted on a charge of theft).

- The Queen in her public capacity is usually referred to as *the Crown*. The legal person in this case is a corporation sole (see below), which evolves to each monarch in turn. When there is a change of king or queen, all Crown property is vested in the new monarch. Although the monarch in his or her personal capacity may not be sued in court, the Crown, as a corporation sole, and its agents may be sued. The Crown Proceedings Act 1947 permits the Crown to be sued for breach of contract, and for torts committed by Crown agents in the course of their employment.

CORPORATIONS

Corporations are artificial "persons" which have a corporate legal existence completely separate from the human beings who created and administer them. There are two types of corporation: the corporation sole, and the corporation aggregate.

- A **corporation sole** comprises a single human being at any one time. The legal person in this case is the *title* or *office*, and the human person who holds that title or office holds the property and carries out the required duties while in office. When the holder of the title or office dies, retires, is replaced, or resigns from office, the corporation sole continues and the property and powers are vested in the new holder. As seen above, the Monarch (Queen or King) is a corporation sole, as is also for example, the Bishop of Gloucester.

- A **corporation aggregate** comprises more than one person, usually called *members*. As in the case of a corporation sole, it is the corporation which has the legal existence, separate from the membership. The human membership may change from day to day, but the corporation remains unaffected. The Institute of Chartered Secretaries and Administrators, local councils and all limited companies are examples of corporations aggregate.

Ways in which corporations are created

By Royal Charter

The Monarch has the power to create corporations by Royal Charter, and in the past, trading companies such as the Hudson Bay Company and the East India Company were formed in this way. The British Broadcasting Corporation was granted its Charter in 1926. The power is used mostly these days to create professional bodies, which usually have the word "Chartered" in their title. For example, the Institute of Chartered Accountants, and the Chartered Insurance Institute.

By special statute

A specific Act of Parliament creates a specific or particular corporation. Most of the early railway companies were created in this way and it was used to create the nationalised industries, such as the National Coal Board and local government councils.

Corporations sole are now created by special statute, as are corporations aggregate which in the past would have been created by Royal Charter.

Unlike the BBC the Independent Television Authority was established in 1964 by the Television Act.

By registration under the Companies Acts

The Companies Acts provide the means for a group of people to create a corporation. This method is an alternative to those described above. Most registered corporations are trading companies wishing to acquire the advantages of limited liability, and the abbreviation "Ltd" following the name indicates this limited liability status. The Companies Act 1985 s.25 requires all new and existing limited companies to include after their names "public limited company", or the abbreviation p.l.c. A public company with its registered office in Wales may have the initials c.c.c indicating "cwmni cyfyngedig cyhoeddus".

It is not only trading companies which take advantage of this method of incorporation. Many charitable organisations and professional bodies not created by charter are registered under the Companies Acts in order to acquire perpetual existence.

Effects of incorporation

A corporation has a distinct existence separate from the people who are its members. In *Salomon v Salomon & Co Ltd* (1897), it was held that a company was a separate legal entity, different altogether from the members. Although after incorporation the business was exactly the same as before, the company was not the agent of its members.

A corporation may carry on business as an ordinary person, but its activities may be limited by charter or statute.

Chartered corporations have the rights and duties of ordinary persons, and may carry on any activities which are not specifically forbidden by, or against the spirit of, the charter.

Statutory corporations must limit their activities to the powers expressed in the creating statute. Any act outside the scope or beyond the powers of the statute is said to be *ultra vires* and void.

Registered companies are limited in their activities by two documents, the Memorandum of Association and the Articles of Association.

- The Memorandum of Association governs the company's external activities. Its main clauses provide information on the name and address of the company's registered office, the objects of the company (the purposes for which the company was formed, and its powers to attain them), the members' limited liability and the company's share or capital structure. Under the Companies Act 1989, s.110, the objects clause can be very wide, and may be amended by the company for any purpose.

- The Articles of Association govern the internal administration of the company on such matters as procedures at meetings and the appointment of directors.

A corporation has perpetual succession, which means that it continues to function until definite steps are taken to end its existence. Changing membership does not affect its existence and a corporation will remain in being despite members having died, resigned or transferred their interests to other people.

A corporation's liability for crime and tort

Although a corporation cannot physically commit a crime or act in a way which amounts to a tort, it may be liable for the acts of its human agents. A corporation therefore may be prosecuted for a breach of duty under the Health and Safety at Work Act 1974, or for allowing defective motor vehicles to be on the road. A company may also be *vicariously liable* for the torts of its agents or employees in the ordinary course of their employment (see *Vicarious Liability*, Chapter 9). In this way a company could be liable if its van driver was negligent while on company business and caused damage to another person's motor vehicle.

A corporation may sue, and be sued, in its own name.

Corporate killing

There has been growing pressure in recent years to introduce a new offence of corporate killing. In practice, it has been difficult in the past to identify individuals who could be prosecuted when corporations have been involved in fatalities. In the *Herald of Free Enterprise* disaster at Zeebrugge and the more recent rail accidents involving loss of life, prosecutions for manslaughter have failed despite obvious failure of duty on the part of the companies concerned. The new law would apply to any undertakings, including corporations, trades, businesses, schools, colleges, local authorities, charities, partnerships, trade unions and other organisations. Further consideration of this topic will be found under *Unlawful homicide*, in Chapter 10.

UNINCORPORATED ASSOCIATIONS

There are many forms of unincorporated bodies, *e.g.* cricket clubs, darts clubs, chess clubs. All sports and pastimes will probably have a club of some size, small or large. They consist of groups of people joined together to follow their common interest. Unincorporated associations differ from corporations in that they do not have a legal entity separate from their members, and the law regards the associations as a group of individuals who all share the legal responsibility.

When a member of a club makes a contract on behalf of the club, that individual is personally liable to the other party, although the whole committee who authorised the contract may be jointly liable. Generally, a member who commits a tort is personally liable, but a committee who authorised an act which leads to a tort may be liable.

In addition to sporting and social clubs, there are large professional associations which are treated legally in a similar way.

PARTNERSHIPS

The Partnership Act 1890, defines a partnership as a "relationship which subsists between persons carrying on a business in common with a view of profit". It is the aim of making a profit which is important, and it is this which distinguishes a partnership from the clubs and societies just mentioned.

A partnership has no separate legal entity and although the courts do allow a firm to sue and be sued in the name of the partnership, all partners are liable, both individually and collectively, for the legal liabilities of the firm.

Principal differences between partnerships and registered companies

Profit

A partnership must have the intention of making a profit. This is not necessary with a company, and many charitable organisations are registered companies.

Perpetual succession

A company, being a legal person, continues to exist regardless of its changing membership. A partnership may end with the death or resignation of a partner.

Membership

A partnership may not have more than 20 members (banking partnerships, only 10), although certain professions, such as accountants, solicitors and members of the Stock Exchange, may apply to the Department of Trade to have more than 20. A limited company must have a minimum of two members, but there is no maximum number.

Transfer of shares

Generally, shares in a company may be easily transferred to another person, but a partner may not introduce another partner in his place without permission of the other partner or partners.

Limited liability

A member of a company is liable for company debts only to the extent of the unpaid amount of the shares. If the shares are fully paid, the member has no further liability. A partner is personally liable for all partnership debts, and any private assets outside the partnership may be used to settle the partnership's liability.

As was noted in the previous chapter however, since 2001 solicitors have been able to form limited liability partnerships.

Termination or dissolution

A company is wound up either compulsorily, when creditors ask the courts to end the existence of the company because it may be the only way of recovering the debts; or voluntarily, when the company decides to discontinue its existence. A partnership may end by death or bankruptcy of a member, or by agreement, or at the end of an agreed period of time for which the partnership was created. The court may also terminate a partnership if it considers it "just and equitable" to do so.

TRADE UNIONS

A trade union is a group of persons who join together to better their working conditions by collective bargaining. Originally, trade unions were considered unlawful organisations in restraint of trade. In modern times they have legal recognition and are a necessary and powerful part of the country's labour force.

A union may be sued for contract in its own name, but the liability rests with the members, similar to other unincorporated associations. The Trade Union and Labour Relations Act 1974 provides that collective agreements are presumed not to be legally binding unless they are in writing and expressly provide for such an intention.

NATIONALITY

British nationality gives a person the right to vote; to be a Member of Parliament; to travel to and from the country and all other rights bestowed on a citizen. The British Nationality Act 1981 provided that United Kingdom citizenship may be acquired in a number of ways.

Acquisition by birth or adoption

A person born or adopted in the United Kingdom after the commencement of the Act shall be a British citizen if at the time of the birth or adoption the father or mother is:

- a British citizen, or

- settled in the United Kingdom.

Acquisition by descent

A person born outside the United Kingdom shall be a British citizen if at the time of the birth the father or mother is a British citizen (other than by descent).

Acquisition by registration

The following persons may apply to the Secretary of State to be registered as a British citizen:

- a minor whose mother or father was a British citizen by descent and that parent's mother or father was a British citizen other than by descent.

- a British Dependent Territories citizen or British Overseas citizen who has been in the United Kingdom for five years prior to the application for registration.

Acquisition by naturalisation

The Secretary of State may grant British citizenship to a person of full age and capacity if he is satisfied that he or she is of good character, has a sufficient knowledge of the English or Welsh or Scottish Gaelic language, has lived in the United Kingdom for more than five years and his home, after being granted British citizenship, will be in the United Kingdom.

Section 11 of the Act provides that a person who immediately before commencement of the Act was:

- a citizen of the United Kingdom and colonies, and

- had a right of abode in the United Kingdom under the Immigration Act 1971, as then in force,

shall at commencement of the Act become a British citizen.

It is normally the domicile (where a person permanently lives) that decides the jurisdiction of the civil law, regardless of nationality. Therefore, the laws of marriage, contract, tort, taxation, etc., depend, not on citizenship, but on domicile.

Useful websites

Company registration: *www.companieshouse.gov.uk*

Confederation of British Industries: *www.cbi.org.uk*

London Stock Exchange: *www.londonstockexchange.com*

SPECIMEN EXAMINATION QUESTIONS

1. Giving reasons, describe to what extent children are treated differently from adults in (a) crime and (b) tort? How far do you agree that these differences are necessary?

2. Giving examples, explain how a corporation can be:
   (a) sued in the law of tort;
   (b) prosecuted for a criminal offence.

TALKING POINT

In most European countries the age of criminal responsibility is 14. Do you think it should be the same in Britain?

SUGGESTED COURSEWORK TITLES

Describe how the law relating to minors generally differs from that relating to adults. Explain the reason for these differences, and whether you agree with the need for them.

Explain the law relating to corporate manslaughter. How far do you think that the law is adequate to deal with these cases?

5 | Civil Liberties

RIGHTS AND DUTIES OF THE INDIVIDUAL

It is often said that we live in a free society and that we enjoy freedom under the law. Individuals in the United Kingdom have freedom of speech, are free to choose where they shall live, may vote for whom they wish and may associate with whom they choose. This country has enjoyed these freedoms for many hundreds of years, but they are still denied to the citizens of some countries today.

It is important to note, however, that in the United Kingdom these rights are not absolute. Most freedoms of the individual are subject to some sort of modification or restriction, large or small. In addition, all rights of the individual have a corresponding duty. You have the right to the freedom of speech, and the rest of the community has a duty not to prevent you from exercising that right.

There are occasions when the freedoms or liberties of the individual may conflict with the needs of the community as a whole. In such cases, rights may be restricted by Parliament or by the courts. In recent years, the threat posed by international terrorism has resulted in tighter security and a consequent modification of some traditional freedoms. An example is the passing of the Anti-Terrorism, Crime and Security Act 2001 and the Prevention of Terrorism Act 2005.

It may be said that, in practice, our freedoms are what remain to us after the various restrictions have been taken into account.

FREEDOM OF THE PERSON

An individual's personal liberty is presumed to exist in this country unless a particular law dictates otherwise. A person is entitled to be free from arrest or detention unless there are justifiable reasons. Reasons justifying the loss of liberty include:

- arrest by warrant;
- imprisonment following conviction in court;
- detention of a person in need of care, such as a child or a person who is mentally ill.

Arrest without a warrant is also possible where it is reasonable to suspect that a person has committed an arrestable offence (see Chapter 3). In addition, the police have on occasions been given special powers by Parliament to intern people, as has happened in the past during the troubles in Northern Ireland. In more recent times the passing of the Anti-Terrorism Crime and Security Act (dealt with below), has introduced important measures restricting the liberty of the individual. Subject to such provisions, however, a person is arrested with the intention that he or she will be brought before the court to face trial. If this is denied, a person detained may apply for a writ of *habeas corpus* (see below, under Protection of Rights and Freedoms).

The Anti-Terrorism, Crime and Security Act 2001

This act was passed in December 2001 in response to anxiety following the terrorist atrocity of September 11th of that year which destroyed the World Trade Centre in New York. The act was aimed at protecting the United Kingdom from terrorist activity at a time of heightened threat to security by preventing terrorists from abusing immigration and asylum measures.

The act made provision for the indefinite detention without charge of non-British nationals suspected of involvement in terrorism. Detainees have the right to appeal to the Special Immigration Appeals Commission, (SIAC), and also the right to appeal on a point of law to the Court of Appeal. *Habeas corpus* and judicial review (see page 132), however, are not available. Detainees can leave the United Kingdom at any time if another safe country is prepared to take them. In introducing these powers of indefinite detention, the Government has had to "derogate" (opt out) from that part of the Convention on Human Rights, article 5, which protects the right to freedom. Of the 40 countries bound by the convention, Britain is the only one to suspend the operation of article 5.

The Anti-terrorism, Crime and Security Act is subject to a "sunset clause" which will cause it to lapse in November 2006

House of Lords ruling

SIAC had ruled in 2002 that the suspension of article 5 was unlawful, but the court of Appeal later overturned that ruling. In October 2004, the remaining detainees appealed to the House of Lords, sitting very unusually in a panel of nine law lords. This appeal challenged again the legality of Britain's opt-out from article 5. By a majority of eight to one the law lords judged that such indefinite detention was unlawful under the European convention on human rights. (The Human Rights Act 1998 has made the convention part of British law. This act is dealt with later in this chapter).

As a result of the House of Lords ruling, Parliament passed the Prevention of Terrorism Act 2005 (it was passed after the longest Parliamentary sitting—30 hours—since 1906). This Act gave the Home Secretary the power to impose control orders where necessary on any person suspected of terrorist activity. There is also a judicial role in the making of control orders. Control orders involve such measures as restrictions on association and communication, and in the most serious cases, house arrest. The remaining suspects who had been detained without charge under the 2001 Act were released under strict bail conditions. All those released on bail were made subject to control orders under the 2005 Act when the then-existing anti-terror powers lapsed.

FREEDOM OF SPEECH

This is perhaps the most familiar and frequently quoted of our freedoms. The right to freedom of speech covers all forms of communication, oral and written, and in all branches of the media. In many towns and cities there are special areas set apart where individuals can hold forth on all matters that engage their interest. An example of such a place is Speakers' Corner, in Hyde Park, London.

It is not only individuals who have the right to free speech. Newspapers, magazines and all forms of broadcasting also enjoy this freedom. In countries where the government controls the media, there cannot be said to be a "free press". The press in the United Kingdom is free to be politically biased, and frequently is. Broadcasting, however, must have no political bias, and must present a balanced outlook.

Like other rights, freedom of speech is restricted. Individuals and the media may say or write what they like, provided that they do not break the criminal or civil law. Examples of restrictions on free speech are explained below.

Defamation

An individual has the right to protect his or her reputation. The tort of defamation provides the legal means of stopping another individual from making damaging false statements to a third party. As well as being a tort, defamation may be a crime (criminal libel), if the statement is likely to cause or lead to a breach of the peace. Slander, which is defamation by the spoken word, may also be a crime if the statement would create an offence such as treason or sedition. Defamation is more fully dealt with in Chapter 9.

Censorship

Certain Acts of Parliament restrict the absolute right to perform plays and films. There is no censorship of plays, but the Theatres Act 1968 makes it a criminal offence to present an obscene play which is likely to corrupt or deprave any individual in the audience. The Attorney-General must consent to the prosecution, and defendants may claim as a defence that the play has artistic or literary merit.

There is no such protection for the showing of films, and at present anyone may start an action in respect of an alleged obscenity. Many people consider that the film industry should have the same rights as the theatre in this matter. Local authorities decide if a film is suitable for showing to the public, and they also have the responsibility of granting licences for premises used for showing films. A local authority may (but is not bound to) rely on the grading given by the British Board of Film Classification.

National security

The Official Secrets Acts

By the nature of their employment, certain persons may have acquired knowledge which, if made public, could jeopardise the safety of the State. Civil servants are obvious examples.

Such people are forbidden by the **Official Secrets Acts** of 1911 and 1920 from disclosing this information, and are subject to prosecution if such information is disclosed. The case of Clive Ponting is a well-known example of this (see under *The Jury* in Chapter 2).

'D' notices

The mass media (broadcasting and the press) are similarly liable for prosecution for publication of information in breach of the Official Secrets Acts. Although there is no direct censorship of the press, the issue of a "D" notice informs the press that the information in the notice should not be published.

In recent years the Government obtained an injunction to restrain the publication of *The Spy Catcher*, a book written by Peter Wright, formerly of MI5. An injunction was also granted restraining certain newspapers from publishing extracts from the book.

Obscenity

It is an offence to publish any obscene material which is likely to deprave or corrupt persons who have read, seen or heard the material. It is a good defence to show that the publication was for the public benefit, in the interests of science, literature, art or some other area of public interest.

Horror comics

The Children and Young Persons (Harmful Publications) Act 1955 makes it an offence to publish stories (in words or pictures) which show violence, crimes, cruelty, etc., which would be harmful to the minds of young readers.

Indecent photographs of children

It is an offence to take, distribute, possess or show indecent photographs of children. This includes pornography produced on videos, computers and other means of storing material electronically. The aim of the restrictions is to protect children against exploitation by the taking of indecent photographs, films, videos and indecent simulated photographs created on computers.

FREEDOM OF ASSOCIATION

As a general rule, an individual in the United Kingdom is free to associate with any other individuals. This can be for a variety of reasons, whether social, political, business or concerning trade unions. It is also the right of individuals to form associations which are in direct opposition to other associations. For example, employers in a particular industry or trade may join together for their common good, and their employees may form a trade union for the collective strength to bargain with the employers' organisation.

Similar to the other rights, this freedom only exists if an association's objectives and aims, and methods of achieving them, do not break the law. Examples of illegalities are:

- Employees have the right to withhold their labour (go on strike). Certain workers however are subject to acts of Parliament which make it an offence to take strike action. The police may not strike, nor may workers in other situations where to go on strike would cause danger to the public. From the 1980s legislation has been passed by Parliament which has placed further restrictions on the right to strike, such as the outlawing of secondary picketing.

- It would be a breach of contract to strike without giving the proper period of notice. Although technically an employer could sue employees for such a breach, in reality it is very unlikely.

- An association which is a secret society and has illegal objectives and administers unlawful oaths is not permitted.

It is possible for a change in the law to make previously legal membership of an association illegal. In 1984, for example, the Government decreed that civil servants at the Government Communications Headquarters at Cheltenham had to resign from their union. The stated purpose was to remove the possibility of strikes which could jeopardise national security. This restriction was later lifted, and GCHQ employees are again able to be members of a trade union.

FREEDOM TO WORSHIP

An individual in the United Kingdom may follow any religious creed, and it is generally illegal to discriminate against a person because of a religious belief. It is possible for some aspects of a religion to be opposed to the law. In some countries a Moslem man may have four wives (polygamy) but in this country a man, regardless of his religion, may only marry one (monogamy). A sikh is required by his religion to wear a turban, and the law of the United Kingdom requires a motorcyclist to wear a safety helmet; therefore it can be seen that a conflict between religion and law arose whenever a Sikh rode a motorcycle.

After many protests by the Sikh community in this country the law was changed to grant an exception from wearing a helmet to drivers who object on religious grounds.

An anomalous exception to the principle of freedom of worship is the Monarch, who must be a member of the Church of England.

The Anti-Terrorism, Crime and Security Act 2001 created a category of religiously aggravated offences, including *religiously aggravated harassment*.

FREEDOM OF MEETING AND PROCESSION

Members of the public are free to demonstrate, unless in doing so they break the law. The following are examples of illegal meetings:

- *A conspiracy to commit a crime* occurs when two or more people meet to perform an illegal act.

- *Riot* is committed when 12 or more persons present together use or threaten to use unlawful violence for a common purpose and cause a person of reasonable firmness present at the scene to fear for his personal safety.

- *Violent Disorder*. This offence is committed when three or more persons present together use or threaten to use unlawful violence and their joint conduct would cause a person of reasonable firmness to fear for his personal safety.

- *Affray*. One or more persons are guilty of affray if they use or threaten unlawful violence towards another and the conduct is such that would cause a person of reasonable firmness present at the scene to fear for his safety.

- It is unlawful for 50 or more persons to meet within one mile of Westminster when Parliament is in session.

- The Public Order Act 1986 provides that seven days' written notice must be given to hold a public procession, unless it is not practicable to give the advanced notice. The police may, if it is believed the procession may result in serious public disorder or cause serious damage to property, give directions to prevent the disorders, such as changing the route or prohibiting entry to any public place.

  A chief officer of police may apply to the council of the district for an order prohibiting the holding of a public procession in the district for a period up to three months.

- Unlawful meetings exist when torts are committed. If a meeting obstructed the highway it would be the tort of nuisance. Similarly a meeting on another person's land may be the tort of trespass.

PUBLIC ORDER RESTRICTIONS

Trespass to land is not generally a criminal offence and is usually treated in the civil courts under the law of tort (see p. 208). The Criminal Justice and Public Order Act 1994 introduced several new offences with regard to trespassers.

Trespass on land

The above Act provides that a senior police officer may "direct trespassers to leave land" if the trespassers are present with the intention of residing on the land and the occupier has taken reasonable steps to ask them to leave, and

- any of the trespassers has caused damage to the land or any property on the land; or

- any of them has been threatening, insulting or abusive; or

- they have at least six vehicles on the land.

Trespassers who fail to follow the direction to leave the land or who trespass on the land again within three months are subject to a maximum penalty of three months' imprisonment and/or a fine. In addition, the police may seize any vehicle that the trespasser has failed to remove under the direction.

Raves

The police have powers with regard to raves where:

- 100 or more persons gather on land in the open air (whether trespassers or not);
- amplified music is played with or without interruption during the night;
- the music, because of its volume, duration and timing, is likely to cause serious distress to the inhabitants of the locality.

The police have powers to "direct" peoples assembling on the land for a rave to leave and take any vehicles and property with them. Any person who fails to leave the land as soon as is reasonably practicable, or enters again within seven days, is liable for a maximum penalty of three months' imprisonment and/or a fine. The police also have powers to seize and remove any vehicles or sound equipment which has not been removed as directed.

Aggravated trespass

This offence takes place when a person trespasses on land and does anything intended to;

- intimidate people and deter them from engaging in lawful activity; or
- obstruct a lawful activity; or
- disrupt a lawful activity.

A lawful activity is defined as one which may be carried out without committing an offence or a trespass.

The police may remove people from the land who are committing aggravated trespass and the maximum penalty for the offence is three months' imprisonment and/or a fine.

Trespassory assemblies

This applies when at least 20 persons assemble as trespassers on land to which the public has limited or no right of access and takes place without the permission of the occupier of the land. If a chief officer of police believes that such an assembly is to be held and may result in either:

- serious disruption to the life of the community, or
- significant damage to land, buildings, or monuments of historical, architectural, archaeological or scientific importance,

an application may be made to the local district council for an order prohibiting all such assemblies for a maximum of four days.

Anyone who organises such an assembly is liable to three months' imprisonment and/or a fine. Anyone taking part in the assembly is liable to a fine.

An example of this offence could be an assembly at a site such as Stonehenge.

Unauthorised camping

A local authority may direct people living in vehicles:

- on local land forming part of the highway; or

- on unoccupied land or occupied land without the consent of the occupier,

to leave the land and remove their vehicles and property.

A magistrate's court may make an order requiring the removal of the offenders, their vehicles and property. Any person wilfully obstructing the eviction is liable to a fine.

PROTECTION OF RIGHTS AND FREEDOMS

The protection of an individual's rights is provided by many Acts of Parliament and by the courts. In addition, there are societies and agencies whose aims are to ensure that the individual's rights are maintained and preserved.

Habeas corpus

A person who is detained without being brought to court is entitled to apply for a writ of *habeas corpus*. This is one of the oldest of our civil rights remedies, and was enshrined in an Act of Parliament in 1679. The application is made to the divisional court of the High Court, and has priority over all other court business. The purpose is to challenge the legality of the detention. If it is not justified, the prisoner must be released immediately. Persons who are responsible for the wrongful detention are not punished, but will of course be liable in the tort of *trespass to the person* (see Chapter 9). They may have to pay compensation in the form of damages, or possibly face other charges and punishment.

Protection by Parliament

In the United Kingdom there is no guaranteed protection from Parliament, as any Act of Parliament can be repealed, and there is no safeguard that a law will not be changed. Some countries, such as the United States of America, have a written constitution where a Bill of Rights lays down the individual's rights, and which is difficult to change. Parliament is not bound by any such restriction and may legally change the law by passing an Act. In practice, however, it is very unlikely that any British government would repeal any law which protected an individual's rights if it did not have the support of the majority of the country. The writ of *habeas corpus* was created by Parliament in 1679, and it is inconceivable that this safeguard would be repealed unless replaced by another Act protecting the liberty of the individual.

While there is no Bill of Rights in the United Kingdom, the European Convention on Human Rights was signed by the United Kingdom in 1950, and this country is now bound by the rights provided in the Convention (see p. 126).

Protection by the courts

The decisions of judges in court have created precedents on constitutional matters and, unless they are overruled by a superior court or by Parliament, they are binding and protect the rights of individuals.

Judicial review

Judicial Review is a method by which freedoms are protected by the courts, and is an area of law which has grown rapidly in recent years. It is a system by which the High Court reviews the decisions of Government and other officials, inferior courts, public bodies, local councils and other bodies whose decisions effect the individual. During the 1990s, for example, there were several challenges to decisions by the Home Secretary on matters such as the treatment of asylum seekers, criminal injury compensation, parole, and immigration. The Foreign Secretary was also successfully challenged over the illegal funding of a dam in Malaysia.

Unlike an appeal to a higher court, judicial review does not consider the relative merits of a decision, but whether a particular body has the power to make it. If the public body concerned does not have the power to act in the way it did, it is said to be acting *ultra vires*, or "beyond its powers", as explained in Chapter 2 under Control of Delegated Legislation. This can be when:

- there has been a breach of natural justice (see below);

- where a public body has exceeded the powers granted to it by legislation (see p. 33);

- where a decision is so unreasonable as to amount to acting *ultra vires*.

The court cannot reverse a decision merely because it considers it to be wrong. It can only be if it was so unreasonable that no responsible official would have made it. This is sometimes referred to as "Wednesbury unreasonableness" after the case of *Associated Provincial Picture Houses Ltd v Wednesbury Corporation* (1948).

Application for judicial review is made to a judge of the High Court, and the hearing is usually before a single judge in the Queen's Bench Division.

Prerogative orders

These orders are available to the High Court and can be used where hearing of judicial review has been successful. A person's rights may also be protected by application to the High Court for a prerogative order.

The prerogative orders control courts and tribunals by compelling them to exercise their powers according to the law, or by restraining them from over-reaching their jurisdiction. The orders are:

Mandamus

This orders or commands a court or public body to carry out its duty. The order could, therefore, be to a court, a local council or Minister of the Crown. It should be noted that this order, unlike the following two, is not confined to judicial proceedings.

Certiorari

This requires the proceedings of an inferior court to be brought before the High Court, to consider whether the decision of the lower court should be quashed (made invalid). In *R. v Bolton Magistrates* (1991), defendants who had pleaded guilty before magistrates on evidence which later was discovered to be faulty, successfully applied for a judicial review to the Divisional Court to quash by *certiorari* their convictions.

Prohibition

This is an order to an inferior court or tribunal to stop proceedings which would be in excess of its jurisdiction.

Rule of Law

In addition to judicial precedent and the prerogative orders, a subject's rights are protected in the courts by the Rule of Law, which has been defined as "A principle or rule of conduct so established as to justify a prediction with reasonable certainty that it will be enforced by the courts if its authority is challenged".

The Rule of Law was first explained by A. V. Dicey in 1885. The phrase implies the following concepts which are essential and basic to the constitution of a free society.

- No person shall be punished unless he or she has been convicted in an ordinary court of law for a definite breach of law. This concept eliminates arbitrary arrest and conviction.

- All men and women are equal before the law, whatever their rank or station, and are subject to the ordinary law and procedures of the courts. For example, in 1977 the Princess Royal was fined for a motoring offence.

- If there has been a breach of law, there is a certainty of enforcement of justice.

- The constitution concerning the private rights of the individual exists as the result of judicial decisions made in the ordinary courts. It is the fact that every subject has a right to appear before the courts, which safeguards the liberties and freedoms of the individual.

Natural justice

In addition to the Rule of Law, the courts, tribunals and public authorities have a duty to act in a judicial way to ensure justice for all parties. This is achieved by following the rules of natural justice, which are, basically, that the judicial body shall not be biased, and that each party must have an opportunity to be heard.

Bias

The Latin maxim *"nemo judex in causa sua"* (no one can judge his own cause) means that a person in a judicial role must not have an interest in the result. In *R. v Sussex Justices* (1812), the following phrase was first used and has since been quoted over and over again, ". . . that justice should not only be done, but be manifestly and undoubtedly seen to be done". If only one member of a board or tribunal is "interested" the decision will be invalid, even if the financial interest is very small. In *Dimes v Grand Junction Canal Co* (1852), the Lord Chancellor awarded the decision to the company. He was a shareholder in the company, and the House of Lords later set aside his judgment.

However, in *R. v Mulvihill* (1990), M. was charged with conspiracy to rob a bank. The trial judge owned a small number of shares in the bank and did not disclose his shareholding during the trial, M. appealed on the grounds of bias. The Court of Appeal held that the trial proceedings were valid because the judge did not have a direct financial interest in the outcome of the case, which would have lead to a presumption of bias.

In local government, councillors and committee members must declare their financial interest on any item of an agenda, and will not take part in the discussion on the item.

Audi alteram partem

The principle of *audi alteram partem* (hear the other side) ensures that when a body is exercising a judicial function both parties must be allowed to explain their point of view.

THE OMBUDSMAN

The Parliamentary Commissioner Act 1967 created the post of Parliamentary Commissioner for Administration, commonly called the Ombudsman. The Ombudsman's responsibility is to investigate grievances referred to him or her by members of the House of Commons. These complaints come from the general public who claim to have suffered injustice through maladministration by central government departments. The Commissioner also has the responsibility of National Health Commissioner, and investigates complaints against all sections of the health service, hospitals, doctors, dentists, chemists, *etc.* Below are listed some examples of complaints brought before the Commissioner.

- A teacher from overseas complained that the Department of Education and Science refused to grant him qualified teaching status.

- A boy hurt at school and admitted to hospital was not examined by a senior doctor for four days.

- A man had to wait four-and-a-half years to have his tax problems sorted out.

- The request of a 60-year-old invalid for a supplementary heating allowance was dealt with by the Department of Health and Social Services in a manner ". . . far short of an acceptable standard".

In addition to the Parliamentary Commissioner, there is a local "Ombudsman". The Local Government Act 1974 established a Commission for Local Administration in England, and another for Wales, to investigate complaints about injustices suffered as a result of mal-administration in local government, or by a police or water authority.

The complaints of maladministration by local authorities are similar to the complaints that the Parliamentary Commissioner has to investigate, concerning such matters as neglect, bias, prejudice and delay. The Commissioner looks into the manner in which the authority has carried out its functions, not into the actual merits of the decision. It must be stressed that complaints must concern the maladministration of the authorities and not action taken by the authorities.

If a Commissioner decides to investigate a complaint, a report is presented to the authority which then opens it to inspection by the press and public. If the report indicates that a person has suffered an injustice, the authority must inform the Commissioner of the action it intends to take.

The Commissioner may not investigate complaints into:

- court proceedings,

- investigation or prevention of crime,

- matters dealing with the appointment, dismissal, etc., of personnel,

- certain educational matters.

England is divided into three areas with a local commissioner in charge of a particular area. Wales has a separate commissioner.

It is interesting to note that in recent years the commercial sector has followed along similar lines.

In January 1966, 19 banks, including all the big companies, established the Office of the Banking Ombudsman to investigate customers' complaints.

The Insurance Ombudsman was appointed in March 1986 to look into disputes where clients considered that the settlement of an insurance claim was too small or the claim was turned down completely, or where there has been undue delay in settling the claim. It should be noted that the ombudsman may only look into claims on companies within the scheme, and not all insurance companies are in the scheme.

A year later, in June 1987, the Building Societies Ombudsman was set up to delve into complaints from borrowers and savers. (The addresses of these officers are given in the appendix at p. 309).

INTERNATIONAL CONVENTIONS AND COURTS

There are organisations outside British jurisdiction which endeavour to attain human rights for all subjects regardless of a country's own laws. The United Nations has a Declaration of Human Rights which aims at a common standard of achievement for all peoples and all nations and lays down that:

". . . every individual and every organ of society . . . shall strive by teaching and education to promote respect for these rights and freedoms and by progressive measures, national and international, to secure their universal and effective recognition and observance."

The European Convention on Human Rights was signed in Rome in 1950. The document follows the United Nations in declaring the individual rights and freedoms which should be protected in all European countries. This convention has been incorporated into the law of many countries, including the United Kingdom (see under *The Human Rights Act 1998*, below). The European Court of Human Rights in Strasbourg has heard complaints against the United Kingdom from other nationals and British subjects. Below are some examples.

- The Irish government complained of British torture on prisoners in Northern Ireland.

- A prisoner in an English gaol was prevented by prison rules from bringing an action against a prison officer. He complained to the court that it was in contravention of his human rights, and when his claim was upheld the Home Office changed the prison rules to bring them in line with the Convention (*Golder's Case* (1975)).

- A man aged over 60 argued that the British Government's winter fuel allowance should be paid to men from the age of 60, the same as to women, instead of from the age of 65. The court found in his favour.

- In *Steel and Morris v United Kingdom* (2005), the applicants maintained that they were denied a fair trial because of the lack of legal aid (as we saw in Chapter 2, legal aid is not generally available in cases of defamation). They had been sued for libel by the fast-food chain McDonald's. The court held unanimously that there had been a breach of Article 6 of the European Convention on Human Rights, and that the applicants had been denied a fair trial. The court also held that given the lack of procedural fairness and the disproportionate award of damages, there had been an interference with their right to freedom of expression under Article 10. More details about this case will be found under *Defamation* in Chapter 9.

As a result, or in anticipation, of the findings of the Court, in these and other cases, our law has been changed accordingly.

The Court of Justice of the European Communities in Luxemburg, in the main deals with actions concerning the Community or its institutions. Recently the issue of protection of human rights was discussed and, while there is nothing in the Treaty of Rome on the matter, the court declared that "Fundamental rights form an integral part of the general principles of law the observance of which it ensures . . . "

THE HUMAN RIGHTS ACT 1998

In order to fall in line with the European Convention on Human Rights, The Human Rights Act 1998 gives citizens under English law the same rights and freedoms which are guaranteed under the European Convention. Those who consider that their rights have been contravened have the right to have their case heard in the United Kingdom, instead of Strasbourg.

The principal provisions of the Act are that:

- the courts try to interpret all legislation in a manner which is compatible with the European Convention;

- public authorities, such as courts, tribunals, police, etc., must act in a way which is compatible with the Convention;

- ministers must make a statement, when bringing new legislation, on the compatibility of the Bill with the Convention's rights.

The Human Rights Act came into operation in October 2000. Among the cases decided since that time, the following may be noted.

- In *Brown v Stott* (2000), a motorist refused to identify herself as the driver of a car involved in an accident. By statute it is a criminal offence not to disclose such information, but she maintained that this violated her right to a fair trial, contrary to the Convention. The court dismissed the claim on the grounds that a balance was needed between the right of the individual and the needs of the community.

- In *Regina (Robertson) v Wakefield Metropolitan District Council* the court ruled that the refusal by an electoral registration officer to allow an elector to have his name removed from an electoral register before that register was sold to a commercial concern for marketing purposes, was both a breach of his right to respect for his private and family life, and an invalid interference with his right to vote.

For the first time the European Court of Human Rights in Strasbourg had the chance to say whether our own judges had correctly heard a case which hung on the provisions of the convention. In February 2002, Mrs Diane Pretty was given "fast track" access to the Human Rights Court to determine whether her husband was to be allowed to help her to kill herself (see page 251). In April, however the Strasbourg Court ruled that the original decision had been correct, and dismissed her appeal.

Privacy law

The incorporation of the European Convention on Human Rights into the English legal system has meant that from time to time a conflict has arisen between the right to privacy under Article 8, and the right of free expression under Article 10. Following disclosures about the private life of the footballer David Beckham, a survey found that a majority of the public favoured a law which would protect celebrities from media intrusion. Although no privacy law as such exists in this country, as it does, for example, in France, there have been a number of cases brought under the Human Rights Act which come close to formulating such a law. The following may be noted.

- In *Douglas v Hello!* (2001), the court granted an injunction against the publication of unauthorised photographs of the wedding of the actors Michael Douglas and Catherine Zeta-Jones in advance of the authorised ones taken by *OK!* magazine. The court found for the claimants, but on the grounds of the confidentiality of trade secrets rather than the right to privacy.

- In *A. v B. & C. (No.2)* (2001), a married Premiership footballer obtained an injunction preventing one of the two women with whom he was having affairs from telling her story to a Sunday newspaper.

- In *Campbell v Mirror Group Newspapers* (2004), the House of Lords considered the balance that had to be achieved between an individual's right to privacy and the media's right to freedom of expression. In this case, the model Naomi Campbell complained that details of her treatment for drug addiction should not have been disclosed. One of the law lords described the case as "a prima donna celebrity against a celebrity-exploiting newspaper". The court held by a 3–2 majority that the risk of jeopardising the addict's recovery outweighed the press's right to publish. Campbell was awarded £3,500 in damages.

Derogation from the Convention

As has been previously noted, for the purposes of indefinitely detaining suspected terrorists, the Government had to derogate from (opt out of) those Articles of the Convention on Human Rights which protect the right to freedom.

Useful websites

National Council for Civil Liberties: *www.liberty-human-rights.org.uk*

Text of the Human Rights Act 1998: *www.hmso.gov.uk/acts/acts1998*

Parliamentary Ombudsman: *www.parliament.ombudsman.org.uk*

SPECIMEN EXAMINATION QUESTIONS

1.

> In the United Kingdom personal liberty is one of the basic freedoms. However, liberty can lawfully be denied to an individual in a number of situations. These include arrest, imprisonment, remand in custody and detention by court order.
>
> On occasions, a person's liberty may be unlawfully removed, giving that person a right to some form of remedy.

In **each** of the following situations, explain the legal basis under which the person's liberty has been removed, and also the legal basis of any action the individual may take to remedy the situation.

(a) Gavin appeared before his local Magistrates' Court charged with one offence of theft. He has a previous conviction for actual bodily harm and a number of previous road traffic offences on his record. He pleaded guilty to the theft offence. The magistrates sentenced him to six months imprisonment.

(b) Hamish appeared before his local Magistrates' Court charged with a serious assault on a minor, the daughter of his next-door neighbour. Hamish had no previous convictions. The magistrates remanded him in custody.

(c) Indira was shopping with her daughter, Jameila, in King's Department Store (KDS). They were approached by the store detective and arrested "on suspicion of shoplifting". The store detective's allegations were unfounded, but Indira and Jameila were held for over an hour in the manager's office while they were questioned and searched.   [*SEG* 1998]

2. (a) Briefly summarise the effect of incorporating the European Convention on Human Rights into English law.

   (b) Explain in what circumstances there may be a conflict between the right to privacy and the right to freedom of expression.

TALKING POINTS

Are our "freedoms" a confusing mixture of rights and restrictions? Is it time for it all to be codified in a new Bill of Rights?

How easy is it to introduce measures to counter the threat of international terrorism while still maintaining our basic freedoms?

SUGGESTED COURSEWORK TITLES

How far can the United Kingdom be said to be "a free country"? Discuss whether rights and freedoms should be enshrined in a Bill of Rights or similar convention.

Describe the main freedoms enjoyed by people in the United Kingdom. Discuss the need for restrictions on these freedoms, and how far you think they are all necessary.

6 | Contract

What is a contract?

A contract is

- an **agreement** between one or more parties who
- promise to give and receive something from each other, known as **consideration**, and who
- intend the agreement to be **legally binding**.

Whereas all contracts are agreements, not all agreements are necessarily legal contracts. If in return for the loan of a book, you promise a fellow-student a lift home from college, such an arrangement would not be intended to be legally binding. Your failure to turn up may result in a strained relationship, but it wouldn't result in your being sued in court for breach of contract. Our everyday lives are full of such informal promises and agreements, but they are not binding legal contracts.

On the other hand, every day we enter into legal contracts without perhaps realising it. Every time we buy a chocolate bar, buy a ticket for a concert, or take a vacation job behind a bar we perform an act with contractual legal implications. At the opposite end of the scale, international companies daily enter into multi-million pound contracts of trade which may have a significant economic effect.

In court cases involving the law of contract, the **claimant** brings the action against the **defendant**.

Which law?

In these days of global trading it is important to know which law applies to a contract. Is a contract between a British and a Japanese company, for example, governed by English or Japanese law? The general rule is that the law which governs the terms of a contract is the law of that place where the contract is carried out. Within the European Union, the Contracts (Applicable Law) Act 1990 makes it easier for businesses by providing that:

- the parties are free to choose which law shall govern the contract; and

- if no choice is made, the contract will be governed by the law of the country with which it is most closely connected.

ESSENTIALS OF A CONTRACT

The following elements are essential for the formation of a valid legal contract:

- **offer** by one side to the other;
- **acceptance** of that offer;
- **consideration**;
- **capacity** of the parties;
- **legal relations**;
- **legality** of the contract;
- **agreement** (*consensus ad idem*).

OFFER

Every contract must start by one person making an offer to another. The person making the offer is called the *offeror*, and the person who accepts the offer is called the *offeree*. When the offeror makes an offer, it is a declaration that he or she intends to be legally bound by the terms of the offer if the offeree accepts.

If Desmond offers to sell his car to Anne for £2000, and Anne accepts that offer, Desmond is then bound by the terms of his offer. He cannot later increase the price, nor change the agreed terms.

There are several matters which must be considered in relation to the making of an offer.

It may be made to an individual or to a large number of people

> In *Carlill v Carbolic Smoke Ball Co* (1892), the company, in an advertisement, promised to give £100 to anyone who, having purchased and used their smokeball remedy for influenza, caught the illness within 14 days. To show good faith, the company deposited £1000 with a bank to meet any claims. Mrs Carlill bought and used the remedy, caught influenza, and claimed the £100.

The court awarded Mrs. Carlill £100 and held that:

- an offer may be made to the world, it does not have to be to a specific person.
- although the general rule is that advertisements are not offers, the fact that £1,000 had been deposited with a bank showed it was a firm offer and legal relations were intended (see p. 156).

- communication of acceptance may be implied by the conduct of the acceptor (see below p. 146).

Carlill is an important case, which covers several aspects of the law of contract. Students are advised to note carefully the various legal implications which arise from it. They are discussed in the course of this chapter.

It may be made in writing, by words or by conduct

Many people think of a contract as a written document, because they read and hear of footballers or TV stars "signing a two-year contract". Although it is sometimes desirable to have written evidence of what was agreed, it is not essential for most contracts, and an oral contract is just as legal. On occasions the parties may not contract verbally, but may communicate their intentions by conduct. For example, a taxi may be hired by raising a hand; or a nod at an auction may make a bid for the item on sale.

Certain contracts, however, are required by statute to be in writing, in a particular form, to be enforceable. For example:

- consumer credit agreements;

- sale or disposition of land or interests in land;

- contracts of guarantee (see p. 171).

An offer must be communicated

It is possible for a person to accept the terms of an offer without being aware at the time that the offer existed. That person cannot later claim that the action taken was the acceptance of an offer of which he or she only later became aware.

Situations like this often arise where a reward is offered. Suppose, for example, Helen was to offer a reward of £100 for the return of her lost Burmese kitten, and a person unaware of the offer returned the animal to her. The finder would not be automatically able to claim the reward, because at the time of returning the kitten he or she did not know that there was an offer to be accepted. Helen of course might be so grateful to have her kitten back that she happily pays the reward, but she is not *legally* obliged to do so.

Revocation of an offer

Revocation means the withdrawal of an offer. An offer may be withdrawn at any time before it is accepted. However, such withdrawal must be communicated to the offeree. In *Dickinson v Dodds* (1976), the offeree was informed by a reliable third party that property which was the subject of the offer had already been sold. It was held that this communication, although made by an outside party, was good notice of the revocation of the offer.

If consideration (a sum of money, for example), has been paid to keep an offer open for a period of time, then the offer cannot be revoked before that time limit expires.

THE ILLUSTRATED LONDON NEWS

JAN. 30, 1892

155

CARBOLIC SMOKE BALL

WILL POSITIVELY CURE

COUGHS,	HOARSENESS,	THROAT DEAFNESS,	INFLUENZA,
COLD IN THE HEAD, CATARRH, ASTHMA,	LOSS OF VOICE,	SNORING,	HAY FEVER,
COLD ON THE CHEST, BRONCHITIS,	SORE THROAT,	SORE EYES,	HEADACHE,
			CROUP, WHOOPING COUGH, NEURALGIA.

As all the Diseases mentioned above proceed from one cause, they can be Cured by this Remedy.

£100 REWARD

WILL BE PAID BY THE

CARBOLIC SMOKE BALL CO.

to any Person who contracts the Increasing Epidemic,

INFLUENZA,

Colds, or any Diseases caused by taking Cold, after having used the **CARBOLIC SMOKE BALL** according to the printed directions supplied with each Ball.

£1000 IS DEPOSITED

with the ALLIANCE BANK, Regent Street, showing our sincerity in the matter.

During the last epidemic of **INFLUENZA** many thousand **CARBOLIC SMOKE BALLS** were sold as preventives against this disease, and in no ascertained case was the disease contracted by those using the **CARBOLIC SMOKE BALL.**

One **CARBOLIC SMOKE BALL** will last a family several months, making it the cheapest remedy in the world at the price—10s., post free.

The CARBOLIC SMOKE BALL can be refilled, when empty, at a cost of 5s., post free. Address:

CARBOLIC SMOKE BALL CO., 27, PRINCES ST., HANOVER SQ., LONDON, W.

Free Trials at our Consulting Rooms,

For Inhalation Only.

Invitations to Treat

It is very important to distinguish between an offer and an *invitation to treat*. In determining whether or not a valid legal contract exists, it is vital to know who is making an offer, and who is accepting it. In the case of goods displayed in a shop, it has been long established that it is the customer who makes the offer to buy, and the shopkeeper who accepts the offer. The price displayed on an item in a shop window is merely an invitation to the customer to make an offer, and the amount shown is only an indication of what price would be acceptable. This is what is known as an invitation to treat.

An important practical effect of this principle is that a shopkeeper does not have to sell an item for the price indicated on the label. Suppose, for example, a car for sale on a the forecourt of a garage has had one of the noughts blown away by the wind, the dealer would not be obliged to sell it for £500 instead of £5000.

The years following the Second World War saw the appearance of self-service shops. The routine of the customer taking individually-priced goods of the shelf and putting them in a basket, familiar is it is to us now, was quite novel at the time. There was therefore some doubt as to how the law of offer and acceptance would apply. When was the offer made, and when was it accepted?

In *Pharmaceutical Society of Great Britain v Boots Cash Chemists Ltd* (1953), it was held by the Court of Appeal that the customer makes the offer when the goods are presented for payment at the cash desk, and acceptance takes place when the cashier accepts the money. The law gives the cashier the right to accept or reject a customer's offer.

The difference between an offer and an invitation to treat has also implications in the matter of statutory interpretation (see Chapter 1).

In a criminal case, *Fisher v Bell* (1961), the defendant was charged with offering for sale an offensive weapon. He had displayed a flick knife with a price in his shop window. The court followed the law of contract and held that a priced article in a shop window is an invitation to treat and is not an offer for sale. The defendant, therefore, was not guilty of "offering for sale" the flick knife.

Advertisements

The rule relating to offers and invitations to treat has also been applied to advertisements. In *Harris v Nickerson* (1873) it was held that an advertisement giving details of a forthcoming auction was not an offer but an invitation to make an offer.

In *Partridge v Crittenden* (1968), Partridge was charged with offering for sale live wild birds. He had placed an advertisement in a paper offering birds for sale, but the court held that he had not made an offer for sale, as the advertisement was only an invitation to treat.

It should be noted that in *Carlill v Carbolic Smoke Ball Co* (see above), the court considered that the deposit of £1000 into a bank ("showing our sincerity in the matter") indicated that the advertisement was intended to be an offer. The wording of an advertisement is important in deciding whether it is an offer or an invitation to treat

Intention to make an offer

An offer must also be distinguished from an intention to make an offer.

> In *Harvey v Facey* (1893), Harvey sent a telegram asking Facey if he wished to sell a property called Bumper Hall Pen, and asked him to state his lowest price. Facey replied by telegram that his lowest price would be £900. Harvey accepted at that price but Facey refused to sell. The court held that there was no contract. Facey's telegram was not an offer but an invitation to treat, and £900 was the lowest price he would consider if he decided to sell in the future.

Note

The law as stated in the previous paragraphs is the result of decided cases. There are, however, other similar "offers" which remain to be subject to decisions by the courts. Is the wording on a vending machine an offer, or is it an invitation to treat? Does the customer make the offer when placing the coin in the slot? Is a bus making an offer when it stops, or is it inviting a passenger to make an offer which the driver or conductor accepts when the fare is handed over? It may be reasonable to assume that the customer in each case makes the offer, but until such cases are decided by the courts the law is not certain.

ACCEPTANCE

Once a valid acceptance of an offer has been made and all the other factors are present, a contract is in existence and neither party may escape from the terms expressed, unless both parties agree. As it is important to know when an offer is made, it is equally important to know the exact time an acceptance is made, because from that moment all the duties, obligations and liabilities of the contract are binding on the parties.

The following rules of acceptance have been decided by the courts over many years, but are still subject to change by the introduction of new techniques of communication.

Acceptance may only be made by the person to whom the offer was made

An offer made to a specific person may be accepted by that person only (*Boulton v Jones* (1857)). Otherwise there could be some odd situations, such as A offering C, a famous painter, £1,000 for a portrait, and D, a housepainter who was standing nearby, accepting the offer. The rule only applies when the offer is made to a specific person and not to the world at large, as in *Carlill's* Case.

Acceptance must be absolute and unqualified

The offeree must accept the offer as made, and not add any conditions or terms. **If a counter-offer is made the offer is terminated** and the offeror is under no obligation to honour the offer, even if at a later date the acceptor wishes to accept the original terms. In effect, when a counter-offer is made the acceptor is saying "I do not accept your offer, will you accept my offer?"

> In *Hyde v Wrench* (1840), the defendant offered to sell his land for £1,000. Hyde counter-offered to buy at £950 but after Wrench had refused this offer, Hyde "accepted" the original offer and sued for the land. It was held by the court that the counter-offer terminated the original offer.

Generally a seller would probably be prepared to sell at the price in the original offer but circumstances may change, for example another party may wish to buy at a higher price.

It must be noted, however, that a request for further information (*e.g.* an inquiry as to whether or not credit would be granted) is not a counter-offer (*Stevenson v McLean* (1880)).

Acceptance must be communicated to the offeror

Generally, this must be actual communication, either orally or in writing, but in *Carlill v Carbolic Smokeball Co* (see p. 142) the Court of Appeal considered that **acceptance may be implied from the conduct of the acceptor**. In this case, Mrs Carlill's action in buying the remedy implied her acceptance of the terms of the offer, and it was not necessary to actually communicate her acceptance.

A person making an offer may not stipulate in the offer that no communication will be taken to be an acceptance.

> In *Felthouse v Bindley* (1862), the plaintiff wrote to his nephew offering to buy a horse for £30, and "if I hear no more I consider the horse to be mine". The nephew did not reply but ordered Bindley, the auctioneer, to withdraw the horse from sale. In error the horse was auctioned and Felthouse sued for his loss. The court held that, as the nephew had not communicated his acceptance of the offer, no contract existed and Felthouse had no right of action.

Acceptance must generally be in the mode specified in the offer

If a particular method of acceptance is not specified in the offer, any reasonable method of communication may be used, but if the offeror stipulates a specific mode of acceptance, it must be carried out in this manner. In *Eliason v Henshaw* (1819), the plaintiff offered to buy flour from Henshaw. The offer stipulated that acceptance must be given to the waggoner who delivered the offer. The acceptance was sent by post and arrived after the return of the waggoner. It was held that as the specific mode of acceptance was not followed there was no contract.

This rule may be relaxed if it is shown that a different method of acceptance places the offeror in a no less advantageous position (*Manchester Diocesan Council of Education v Commercial & General Investments Ltd* (1970)).

This is particularly relevant with modern means of instantaneous communication. For example, if acceptance was specified to be by return of post and the offeree replied by fax.

Termination of an offer

There are several ways of ending an offer, as described below. When an offer has been ended in some way, it is then no longer capable of being accepted.

Refusal

When one party refuses the offer of the other, the offer is terminated.

Counter-offer

When the offeree does not accept the offer which was originally made, but makes another offer in return which changes the terms or conditions, then the original offer is ended. See *Hyde v Wrench*, above.

Revocation

As we noted earlier, an offer can also be ended by revocation (see page 143).

The offeror may revoke or withdraw the offer at any time before acceptance, unless consideration to keep the offer open has been given (*Dickinson v Dodds* (1876)).

Lapse of time

If no fixed time is allowed for acceptance, the offer is only effective for a reasonable time. What is a reasonable time depends on the circumstances of each case. Therefore, if a person made an offer to buy perishable goods, such as fresh tomatoes, it would be reasonable to expect an immediate or fairly prompt acceptance, but when more durable goods are the subject-matter of the offer, a longer period of time may be considered reasonable.

In *Ramsgate Victoria Hotel v Montefiore* (1866), M. offered to buy shares in the company. Nearly six months later the company accepted the offer but M. refused to take the shares. It was held that the period between the offer and acceptance was unreasonable and the offer had lapsed before the company's acceptance was made.

Death

Death by either party before acceptance terminates an offer, unless the acceptor does not know of the offeror's death and the dead person's personal representatives are capable of performing the contract. Obviously, this would not apply if the dead person's personal services were needed to perform the contract (*Bradbury v Morgan* (1862)).

Note

The *termination of an offer* must not be confused with the *discharge of a contract*. If an offer is ended or withdrawn, no contract comes into existence. Where a valid contract exists, it can be brought to an end (discharged) in a variety of ways. These are discussed under *Discharge of a Contract*, later in this chapter.

Offer and acceptance by post

In the past, the postal services were the most common means of communication, and many past cases in contract involve the use of letters or telegrams. In recent times, the use of e-mail, fax and other more or less instantaneous methods of communication have become widespread. Nevertheless, where the post is considered a reasonable means of communication between the parties, certain rules still apply.

- *An offer is only effective when it actually arrives*. An offer in a letter posted on July 1 and delivered on July 6 because of a postal delay becomes operative on July 6, and not when it would be expected to be delivered (*Adams v Lindsell* (1818)).

- *Acceptance* by post is also generally only effective when actually received by the offeror (*Holwell Securities v Hughes* (1974)). However, if it can be clearly and reasonably shown that the offeror intended that it be sufficient for the acceptance to be posted, acceptance is effective *as soon as it is placed in the post box*, provided that it is correctly stamped and addressed (*Henthorne v Fraser* (1892)). It would be considered good acceptance if the letter was lost in the post, and not delivered to the offeror.

> In *Household Fire Insurance Co v Grant* (1879), the defendant applied for shares in the company. The company accepted the offer and posted the letter of allotment, but it was never delivered to Grant. The Court of Appeal held that acceptance took place as soon as the letter was posted, because the post was considered the agent of the offeror. A possible reason for this reversal of the general rule is that it is easier to provide proof of posting than to prove actual receipt.

- *Revocation* (withdrawal) of an offer takes place only takes place when actually received by the offeree, not when it is posted (*Byrne v van Tienhoven* (1880))

Other methods of communication

When e-mail, Telex or fax is used as a means of communication, the rule established by the Court of Appeal in *Entores Ltd v Miles Far East Corporation* (1955) is that acceptance takes place when the information is received. Telex and fax is considered similar to using the telephone and not the post. However, in *Brinkibon Ltd v Stahag Stahl* (1982) the House of Lords held that this is not a universal rule and would not apply in every case. For example, if the telex was sent at night and was not read until next morning when the office staff arrived at work, the acceptance would not take place until it was read, i.e. communicated.

Revocation

Revocation (withdrawal) of an offer takes place when actually received by the offeree, not when posted (*Byrne v Van Tienhoven* (1880)).

CONSIDERATION

Unless stated otherwise, what follows in this chapter concerns the formation of a simple contract (for different forms of contract, see later in this chapter).

Consideration is merely the price in a bargain. The price does not have to be money, but it must have a monetary value. In a simple contract a party must promise to give consideration in return for a promise of consideration from the other party. A bookseller promises to give you sole ownership of a book, if you promise to pay him the cost of the book. The bookseller's consideration is the promise to give you the book, and your consideration is the promise to pay the price. The promise for a promise (*quid pro quo*) is essential, because in English law a promise by one party only is not enforceable (unless made by deed).

If a person promised to give you a £100 as a gift at the end of the month, the promise would not be enforceable, because it is a free gift. It has not been supported by a promise from you.

Consideration may, therefore, be defined as the price, although not necessarily a monetary one, which induces a party to enter into a contract.

The position of a third party

To bring a successful action in contract, the claimant must be the person who made the promise of consideration, not someone else. This is known as the *doctrine of privity*. It means that a person who is not a party to a contract cannot sue on it.

Suppose your father and your aunt promise each other to pay you £100 if you pass an examination. If your aunt refuses to pay following your success, you will not be able to enforce the contract. You gave no consideration for her promise. The contract was between your father and your aunt, and you were not a party to the agreement. Your father could however sue your aunt, because she provided the consideration.

In *Tweddle v Atkinson* (1861), William Guy and John Tweddle each promised the other to pay a sum of money to William Tweddle. Guy died before paying and William Tweddle sued Guy's executors. His action failed because he had not provided any consideration, nor had he made any promise to do so.

The Contract (Rights of Third Parties) Act 1999

This act has modified the rules relating to the law of privity of contract. It provides that a third party might be able to enforce a provision in a contract which purports to confer a benefit on that person if the contract:

* expressly provides that the person may enforce it, or
* it appears to give the third party an enforceable right.

Value and adequacy

Although consideration must have some value, it need not be adequate. Courts will not consider the merits or fairness of the bargain, so long as each party received what was promised. In *Chapple & Co Ltd v Nestles Co Ltd* (1960) the House of Lords held that wrappers from three bars of chocolate were good consideration.

The promise must be more than a duty

It would not be good consideration for a school teacher to promise a class that in return for extra money he would teach to the best of his ability, because it is his duty to teach in such a manner. It may, however, be good consideration if the teacher promised extra lessons after school hours, because this would be outside his duty.

In *Stilk v Myrick* (1809) two seamen deserted their ship, and the captain offered to share their wages between the rest of the crew if they brought the ship back to London. Stilk sued for his share, but the court held that he had not provided consideration as it was his duty to work the ship back to London (see *Atlas Express v Kafco Ltd* (1989), p. 163)

In a similar case, *Hartley v Ponsonby* (1857) the ship was in a dangerous situation, and because of this the court held that the promise to bring the ship home was good consideration because of the new danger.

This concept of consideration was discussed more recently in *Williams v Roffey Bros & Nicholls (Contractors) Ltd* (1990). Williams was subcontracted by the defendants to carry out refurbishing work on 27 flats for a fixed price. After completing only part of the work Williams found that he was in financial difficulties because the price was too low. The defendants were liable for a penalty clause if the work was not completed on time, so they offered to pay additional money if the plaintiff completed the work on time. The plaintiff completed the work on eight additional flats but when the defendants refused to pay the extra money he stopped work and claimed the total amount owing. The defendants argued that the plaintiff had not provided consideration for the promise of the additional payments as he was only carrying out work under the original agreement.

The Court of Appeal upheld the plaintiff's claim, and held that as the defendants were receiving a benefit in offering extra money if the work was completed on time, because they would have suffered under the penalty clause, it was good consideration for the promise to pay the extra money.

Promises involving debts

A promise to pay a smaller sum to be released from paying a larger sum already owing, is not good consideration.

A promise to pay £50 as payment in full settlement of a debt of £100, is not consideration, and the other party may sue for the balance. This is known as the Rule in *Pinnel's Case* (1602), and applies because in promising to pay £50 the debtor is doing nothing more than he is already legally obliged to do (*Foakes v Beer* (1884)).

In *Re Selectmove Ltd* (1995), the company agreed with the Inland Revenue to pay its tax arrears by instalments. At a later date the Inland Revenue demanded the arrears to be paid immediately. The House of Lords considered that the initial promise was not good consideration, and the Inland Revenue was entitled to the arrears, as the matter related to part payment of a debt.

Consideration must not be past

The promise must be to do something in the future. A party may not offer an act previously carried out as consideration for a future promise.

In *Roscorla v Thomas* (1842) a horse was bought at an auction. As the purchaser was leading the horse away, the previous owner promised that if the horse was vicious he would return the price. The horse was in fact vicious, but the court held that the promise by the original owner was not supported by consideration from the plaintiff. His action in paying the purchase price was before the second promise of the seller, and therefore his consideration was past.

In a more recent case, *Re McArdle* (1951), a widow had a life interest in a house and she repaired and decorated the property at a cost of £488. The person who would eventually become the owner of the property after the widow's death, later promised to pay the cost of the work. The Court of Appeal held that as the promise to pay was made after the work was completed the consideration was past and there was no legal obligation to pay.

If, however, a party acts at the request of another and it is inferred that payment is intended, the consideration may be good to support a later promise for payment. This is known as the Rule in *Lampleigh v Braithwaite* (1615). Braithwaite asked Lampleigh to obtain a King's Pardon for him, which he endeavoured to do, and later Braithwaite promised £100 for his efforts. The court held that there had been consideration for Braithwaite's promise because Lampleigh had acted on Braithwaite's request. Further exceptions to past consideration, are bills of exchange and the revival, in writing, of a statute-barred debt.

CAPACITY

Although in general any person may make a contract, the law places restrictions in certain circumstances. The reason for denying full contractual capacity is to protect rather than to prohibit. For this reason, minors, mental patients and people under the influence of drink or drugs may have less than full capacity to enter into a contract. For different reasons, corporations also may have restrictions placed on them in this respect.

Any difficulty in enforcing a contract entered into with a party of limited capacity is usually experienced by the party with full contractual ability.

Minors

The age of majority is reached on the first moment of the eighteenth birthday (Family Law Reform Act 1969). Until that moment arrives, a person is legally a minor. Of course, minors can enter into contracts, and do so on most days of the week. They buy sweets, chocolates, comics, magazines, pay to travel on buses and trains, pay to watch films and sporting events, and so on. The law does not stop persons under 18 from making contracts, but it does aim to protect them from certain types of contract.

Under the Minors' Contract Act 1987, minors' contracts fall into two types:

* binding contracts, where the minor must carry out the contract as agreed; and

* voidable contracts, which do not bind the minor, but are binding on the other party. The contract is voidable at the minor's option (see below).

Binding contracts

These are contracts for which the minor has full contractual capacity. They may be enforced against, as well as by, the minor. There are two types:

* contracts for **necessaries**, and

* **beneficial contracts of service**.

Necessaries

These may be defined as "goods suitable to the condition in life of such a minor, and his actual requirements at the time of sale and delivery".

It has been considered that a luxury cannot be a necessary, but it must be borne in mind that what might be considered a luxury for a person of small income might be a normally accepted part of life for the more wealthy.

In addition to the nature of the goods supplied, consideration must be given to the actual requirements at the time of sale. A pair of shoes would be necessaries if the minor was bare-footed, but they would not be necessaries if the minor had several pairs of shoes.

In *Nash v Inman* (1908), a Cambridge undergraduate, who was a minor, ordered 11 fancy waistcoats from a tailor, but refused to pay the bill. It was held by the court that the tailor's action failed because the minor already had a sufficient supply of clothing and therefore the waistcoats were not necessaries (see p. 144).

However, in *Chapple v Cooper* (1844), an infant widow contracted with an under-taker to arrange for the funeral of her deceased husband, and later refused to pay the cost. It was held she was liable, as the funeral was for her private benefit and a nec-essary service.

It is the responsibility of the party supplying the goods to prove that they are necessaries. Where goods are considered necessaries, a minor need not pay the contract price, but must pay a reasonable price.

Beneficial contracts of service

Included under this heading are contracts for training, education, apprenticeship and other similar contracts. They are binding if, taken as a whole, they are for the minor's benefit.

In *Doyle v White City Stadium* (1935) Doyle was a professional boxer and he entered into a contract which included a clause that if disqualified he would lose the prize money. He was disqualified, but claimed that as a minor the contract was not binding on him. It was held that although this particular clause appeared onerous, the contract taken as a whole was for his benefit.

This case must be contrasted with *De Francesco v Barnum* (1890), in which a minor became apprenticed as a dancer, on the terms that she would not marry, would receive no pay and would not dance professionally without the plaintiff's consent. When she made a contract to dance for the defendant, the plaintiff sued for damages and the court held the terms of her contract of apprenticeship to be unreasonably harsh and would not enforce the contract against the minor.

Voidable contracts

All contracts which are not binding on a minor are voidable at the minor's option. This means that the minor can repudiate the contract, that is to say, refuse to carry it out. A minor can force an adult to perform the terms of such a contract, but they cannot be enforced against the minor.

Partly-performed contracts

If a minor repudiates a contract which has been partly performed by the other party, the minor will have to pay for any benefit received. For example, a minor contracts to rent a flat for six months at £100 per month, and after three months wishes to end the contract. The minor is able to do this, but must pay £300 for the three months when he or she lived in the flat. A minor who pays a deposit on goods may not, after returning the goods, claim back the deposit unless there has been a total failure of consideration (*Steinberg v Scala (Leeds) Ltd* (1923)).

Consequences of repudiation

The Minors' Contract Act 1987 deals with situations where a minor refuses to carry out his or her part of a voidable contract. The act gives power to the courts, when "it is just and equitable", to allow the other party to recover from the minor any property acquired under the contract, or any property representing it.

If, for example, a minor receives goods under a contract (whether obtained by fraud or otherwise), and refuses to pay for them, the court may order the minor to return the goods to the claimant. If the minor has sold the goods, the court may order the return of the proceeds of sale to the claimant. If the minor has bought something else with the proceeds, the court may order the return of the goods bought. If the minor exchanges the goods obtained under a voidable contract for some other goods, then the court can order the return to the claimant of the goods received in exchange.

In the case of *Nash v Inman*, described earlier, the undergraduate would now have to return the waistcoats to the supplier, or pay for them, whether they were necessaries or not.

A minor might sell or exchange the property obtained under a voidable contract, and then consume or dissipate the proceeds. In such a case, the court may not order the minor to pay over a sum equal to the original price of the goods. For example, supposing a minor obtained a sports bag on credit and then sold it, using the proceeds of the sale to attend a performance of *Cats* in London. The seller would not be able to recover anything from the minor, because all the money was gone. However, if the minor had used the proceeds of sale to buy a DVD of *Cats*, instead of attending the musical, then the claimant could recover the DVD.

Long-term contracts

Long-term contracts concerning land, shares in companies and partnerships are voidable, and may be repudiated by a minor before reaching the age of 18, or within a reasonable time afterwards. If such contracts are not repudiated, then they are binding on both parties when the minor becomes 18.

Drunks and mental patients

Drunks and mental patients are liable on contracts for necessaries, and, like minors, must pay a reasonable price. Other contracts are voidable at the option of the drunks or mental patients if they can prove that at the time of making the contract:

- they were so drunk or ill that they did not know what they were doing; and

• the other party knew of their condition.

> In *Hart v O'Connor* (1985) the Privy Council decided, in a case where the other party did not know that the plaintiff was insane, that the validity of a contract made by a lunatic who appears sane is to be judged by the same standards as a contract made by a sane person.

Mental patients will be liable for a contract made during a lucid period, (a period of sanity). Contracts made while a person was of unsound mind can be ratified, or confirmed, during a lucid period. If the property belonging to a mentally ill person is under the control of the court, any contract made by that person in respect of it is void, that is to say, of no legal effect.

Corporations

The legal position of corporations is covered in Chapter 4. The limitations placed upon corporations to make contracts arise from the manner in which they are created.

• *Chartered Corporations* (*e.g.* the Institute of Chartered Secretaries and Administrators) are created by a Royal Charter, which lays down the purpose and objects of the corporation. The corporation is not restricted and may make any contract, but the Charter may be withdrawn if contracts are persistently made against the spirit of the Charter.

• *Statutory Corporations* are usually public bodies, created by Acts of Parliament. Contracts may only be made within the scope of the creating statute, and any contract outside of the Act is "*ultra vires*" (beyond the power of) and void.

• *Limited companies* are governed by the Companies Act 1985. Companies registered under the Companies Act have their powers specified in the objects clause of the Memorandum of Association, and contracts should not be made which go beyond these objects. If a person makes a contract with the company, knowing it to be outside the powers of the memorandum, the contract is "*ultra vires*" and void. The European Communities Act 1972 provides that if a person deals with the company in good faith (*i.e.* does not know the powers of the objects clause) any contract is valid, whether or not it is outside the powers of the objects clause. (See Chapter 4 for the provisions of the Companies Act 1989, s.110, which allow companies to carry on any trade or business.)

LEGAL RELATIONS

As we saw when considering offer and acceptance, it is essential to a contract that the parties intend to create legal relations. This means that the parties intend their contract to be subject to the law relating to contract, and that an action in the courts may follow any failure of one party to carry out the terms of the contract. This failure is called *breach of contract*. When determining whether parties intended to create legal relations, the courts will consider the kind of contract made, and the circumstances in which it was entered into.

Business contracts

The courts will always presume that with business contracts, the parties **intend legal relations**. If the parties intend otherwise, it must be clearly expressed.

In *Rose and Frank Co v Crompton* (1923) a written agreement between the parties stipulated that it was not a formal or legal agreement and should not be subject to the legal jurisdiction of the courts. The House of Lords held that the agreement had no legal effect.

The most common case of a contract in which legal relations are excluded occurs on football pools coupons. The contract is made "binding in honour only", and several court actions have been unsuccessful because the courts have held that the intention to create legal relations was expressly excluded (*Appleson v Littlewoods H Ltd* (1939)).

Social or domestic agreements

With social and domestic agreements, for example family arrangements, the courts are generally more likely to presume that legal relations were not intended. This presumption is rebuttable, and the courts will look at the relationship between the parties, and the facts and circumstances of the agreement before declaring their intention.

In *Balfour v Balfour* (1919) the husband went to work in Ceylon and agreed to pay his wife £30 per month. He did not pay the money and the wife sued. It was held that there was no contract because the parties did not intend to create a legal relationship.

However, in *Merritt v Merritt* (1970) a married couple separated and the husband agreed to make over the ownership of the house to the wife when she had completed paying all the mortgage repayments. The court held that there was an intention to be legally bound, because the parties were apart and consideration had been provided.

It is very common these days for people to join together in syndicates, both at work and in family situations for the purpose of entering the National Lottery. Clearly it is important in these situations to be clear as to whether a legal relationship is intended.

LEGALITY

If a contract requires either party to act in a way which is against the law, the courts will not help the guilty party. It is a rule of law that no court action will arise from an illegal act. A contract may be illegal because it is

- forbidden by statute, or
- against public policy.

An example of the first type would be if A makes a contract with B to pay him £50 to steal C's motorbike. The court would not award A a remedy if B later refused to carry out the contract.

With contracts of the second type, it is the courts which decide what is, or is not, in the public interest. The following are examples of contracts which the courts have considered to be against public policy, and therefore unenforceable.

Contracts resulting in the commission of a criminal offence

In *Alexander v Rayson* (1936) the rent for a flat was reduced to avoid paying rates, but the difference was charged as "services". The contract was illegal, because one of its purposes was to defraud the local council.

Contracts to corrupt public life

It is considered illegal for a person to make a contract to purchase a public honour. In *Parkinson v College of Ambulance* (1925), the plaintiff donated £2,000 on condition of obtaining a knighthood. When no honour was awarded Parkinson sued for the return of his money. The court held the contract was against public policy and illegal, and therefore no money was recoverable.

Immoral contracts

Contracts which are against public morals or against the sanctity of marriage are considered illegal.

In *Pearce v Brook* (1866), a prostitute hired a coach to help her acquire clients. The coach owner sued for the hire charge when she refused to pay, but the court held that the contract was illegal, and, as the coach owner knew the purpose of the contract, he could not recover the charge.

Contracts where damages are claimed following childbirth

An example of this kind of situation might follow a contract for a sterilisation operation. It has previously been considered that, as a matter of public policy, damages should not be awarded when, as the result of a breach of such a contract, a healthy child is born. However, the following case should be noted.

In *Thake v Maurice* (1986), a vasectomy operation was performed, but the operation was ineffective and a healthy child was later born to the parents. The surgeon did not warn the parents that there was a chance that a pregnancy could occur. The Court of Appeal held the defendant to be in breach of contract for not warning the plaintiff of the risk, and awarded damages for the cost of the birth, the upkeep of the child and for the discomfort of the normal pregnancy.

Contracts in restraint of trade

These contracts are aimed at preventing a person from carrying on a business or being employed in a particular trade. In general, the courts are reluctant to enforce such contracts, even if the restriction only relates to a limited period of time. However, the attitudes of the courts vary according to the nature of the contract, as the following situations show.

Contracts between employer and employee (contracts of employment)

An employer may make it a condition of employment that certain restrictions should be imposed when the employee leaves the job. An example might be that the employer should not work for competitor for a certain period of time. Alternatively, (or in addition), the employee should not work within a certain distance of his or her previous place of employment. Unless these agreements are intended to protect a proprietary interest, such as a trade secret, the courts will not enforce them on the grounds of public policy.

In *Attwood v Lamont* (1920), Attwood employed Lamont as a tailor on the condition that if he left, he would not work as a tailor within 10 miles. The court held the agreement to be illegal, because Attwood had no trade secrets to protect.

Fitch v Dewes (1921) was a contrasting case in that a solicitor in Tamworth employed his managing clerk on the agreement that if the clerk left his employment he would not practise as a solicitor within seven miles. The court held that this was reasonable and legal because it protected the interests of the master's clients.

The Court of Appeal, in *Oswald Hickson Collier and Co v Carter-Ruck* (1984), held that a partnership agreement which restrained a retiring partner from advising previous clients of the firm was, as a general rule, contrary to public policy, as it denied a client the right to choose his own solicitor.

However, in *Kerr v Morris* (1986) an agreement between medical practitioners provided that a partner who left the practice would not set up as a general practitioner within two miles of the partnership surgery for a period of two years. The defendant left the partnership and immediately started a practice a few doors away. The Court of Appeal granted an injunction to the plaintiff restraining the new practice, and held that it was not contrary to public policy to allow medical practitioners to be subject to reasonable covenants in restraint of trade.

In *Clarke v Newland* (1991), a case with similar facts, the Court of Appeal considered the restraint, "not to practise within the practise area" not too wide because, for example, the defendant could have worked in a hospital. The plaintiff was awarded damages and an injunction prohibiting the defendant from practising within this area.

Contracts for the sale of a business

A business may be sold on condition that the seller will not carry on a similar business within a fixed time and/or distance. The courts are more likely to uphold such agreements if they are considered reasonable between the parties.

In *Nordenfelt v Maxim Nordenfelt Guns & Ammunition Co* (1894), Nordenfelt was known throughout the world as an inventor, and a maker of machine guns and similar weapons. He sold his business on condition that he would not, for 25 years, engage in similar work anywhere in the world. It was held that because of his reputation, the restriction was reasonable.

It was held in *British Reinforced Concrete v Schelff* (1921) that a similar agreement was not binding on a small local company, because it was not reasonable between the parties.

Solus agreements

Traders may agree to be supplied by only one company. For example a garage may agree to be supplied for the next 21 years by only one particular petrol company. The courts consider such restraints as illegal unless reasonable. In *Esso Petroleum Co Ltd v Harpers Garage Ltd* (1967), the House of Lords held that an agreement for 21 years was too long, but an agreement for five years was reasonable. The Court of Appeal in *Alec Lobb (Garages) Ltd v Total Oil (GB) Ltd* (1985), held that an agreement to purchase the defendant's petrol exclusively for 21 years, with a provision for a mutual break after seven and 14 years, was a reasonable restriction on trading.

CONSENSUS AD IDEM (AGREEMENT)

If a party agreed to enter into a contract because of fraud, misrepresentation or mistake, the contract may be void or voidable. What may appear to be a valid contract, may be invalid because consent was affected by one of these elements. There is no *consensus ad idem*, no real agreement, if one party enters into a contract believing that certain facts, important to the contract, are different from those which actually exist.

Mistake

Mistake, as a general rule, does not make a contract void, unless the mistake was such that there never was a real agreement between the parties.

Raffles v Wichelhaus (1864). A contract was made for the sale of cotton aboard the SS. Peerless sailing from Bombay. Unknown to the parties, there were two ships of this name, one sailing in October and the other in December. The buyer thought he was buying cotton on the first ship, but the sale was for cotton on the second ship. The court held that there was no contract.

Mistake as to *quality* of goods will not make a contract void. Provided that all relevant facts are revealed, a mistake of judgment resulting in a bad bargain will not avoid a contract. The following, however, are instances where the courts have held that other kinds of mistake can make a contract void.

Mistake as to the subject-matter

Where one party sells goods, but the other party thinks he is buying something different (*Raffles v Wichelhaus*).

Mistake as to the existence of the subject-matter

Couturier v Hastie (1856). A contract was made for the sale of corn which was being shipped by sea. Unknown to the parties, the corn had begun to perish and had been sold at a port *en route*. The court held that at the time of making the contract the corn was not really in existence, having already been sold.

Mistake as to the nature of the contractual document

A contract will be avoided if it can be shown that the party who signed a document:

- thought the document to be of a completely different nature, and

- was not negligent in signing that document.

In *Foster v Mackinnon* (1869). An old man of feeble sight thought he was signing a guarantee, but a bill of exchange had been substituted. It was held that he was not liable on the bill.

In *Saunders v Anglia Building Society* (1971) an old lady signed a deed of gift of a house to her nephew. She had not read the document but a rogue had substituted his own name for that of her nephew, and later mortgaged the house to the building society. The House of Lords held that the contract was valid and the plea of "*non est factum*" "not my deed" could not be used because the lady had signed the kind of document she intended to sign: it was the contents which were different.

Mistake as to the identity of the other party

As a general rule, where parties are in a face-to-face position, the courts consider the identity of the parties unimportant, because it is presumed that the parties intended to contract with each other.

In *Phillips v Brooks* (1919) a rogue purchased jewellery and paid by cheque. The jeweller would not allow him to take the jewellery until the cheque was cleared by the bank, but when the rogue claimed he was "Sir George Bullough", he was allowed to take a ring from the shop. The rogue pawned the ring before the bank returned the cheque. It was held by the court that the contract was not void, because the jeweller's mistake was not the customer's identity, but his financial position. The pawnbroker thereby acquired a good title.

This decision was followed by the Court of Appeal in *Lewis v Averay* (1972). The facts were similar to the case above and the rogue, when buying a car, purported to be Richard Greene, a well-known film and TV actor, and signed a cheque for the price as agreed. The court held there was a presumption that the seller intended to deal with the person in his presence, although he was mistaken as to his identity. As a third party had acquired the car in good faith, the seller could not avoid the contract.

Where the parties do not meet, but negotiate at a distance, say by using the post or telephone, identity is important, and a contract is more likely to be avoided for mistake.

Cundy v Lindsay (1878). A person named Blenkarn ordered goods by post and signed his name on a letter-head so that it appeared that the order came from Blenkiron, a well-known and reputed company. The rogue also used a similar address. Goods were sent to Blenkarn and he resold them to Cundy. When the fraud was discovered, Lindsay (the supplier) sued Cundy in the tort of conversion, claiming that the goods were sent to Blenkarn by mistake. It was held that the contract was void for mistake, because the supplier never intended to deal with the rogue.

Unconscionable bargains

In cases where one party is able to exploit a weakness in the other party, the courts may grant an equitable relief.

In *Watkin v Watson-Smith* (1986) the plaintiff, a frail man of 80, agreed to sell his bungalow for £2,950. There was obviously a mistake, as a reasonable price would have been £29,500, and the court set aside the agreement as an unconscionable bargain.

Misrepresentation

A misrepresentation is a false statement of facts. As a result, a person may be induced to enter into a contract and in consequence suffers damage. The false statement may be made orally, in writing, or by conduct. Generally, silence will not be considered to be misrepresentation.

Misrepresentation must be a statement of *fact*, not of *opinion*. If a salesman, for example, categorically states that a car is "free of rust", it would be misrepresentation of the car turned out to be rusty. If, however, he merely claims to express the opinion that he "thinks it is free of rust", it would not be considered to be misrepresentation. There is a general rule of "buyer beware" (*caveat emptor*). In the case of the second statement, above, it would be the buyer's responsibility to have the car checked for rust.

Misrepresentation must also be distinguished from manufacturers' boasts, (known as "puffs"), which are found in advertisements. Claims such as "the best fish and chips in Yorkshire" or "the finest cheese in Gloucestershire" are merely the purveyors' opinions, and not to be made the basis of contracts.

Misrepresentation may be fraudulent, innocent or negligent.

Fraudulent

This is defined in *Derry v Peek* as a false statement made:

- knowingly, or

- without belief in its truth, or

- recklessly, not caring whether it is true or false.

Innocent

This is a false statement which the maker believed to be true.

Negligent

This is a false statement which the maker had no reasonable grounds for believing to be true.

As a result of the Misrepresentation Act 1967, remedies available to the injured party are rescission or damages. In cases of fraudulent misrepresentation the remedy may be rescission and damages (for the tort of deceit).

Rescission means that the parties are no longer bound by the contract and goods or money which changed hands are returned to the original owner. This is an equitable remedy, granted at the discretion of the court. It will not be awarded where:

- the injured party was aware of the misrepresentation and carried on with the contract;

- the parties cannot be returned to their original position (e.g. the goods which changed hands have been consumed);

- another party has acquired an interest in the goods; or

- the injured party waited too long before claiming this remedy.

Duress

Originally duress meant threats of, or actual physical violence to the person. A contract entered into by duress is voidable at the option of the threatened party. So a contract which resulted from a threat such as, "If you wish to walk again you'd better sign this contract", would be voidable.

In recent years the principle of duress has been extended to economic duress, where strong commercial pressure is applied.

In *Atlas Express v Kafco Ltd* (1989), the defendants were coerced into either entering a new contract or suffering serious financial loss. The plaintiffs had demanded an increased payment from that agreed in the original contract. The defendants agreed to pay the increased rate because they could not find another carrier and they were aware that if the goods were not delivered to their customer they would be sued for damages and lose the contract for future orders. When the plaintiffs presented the bill for work under the new contract the defendants refused to pay.

The court held that,

* economic duress may make a contract voidable if the coercion applied affects free consent, and therefore the defendants need not pay at the new rates because their agreement to do so was due to the economic duress exerted by the plaintiffs; and

* there had been no consideration for the promise to pay the new rate, and therefore the plaintiffs were merely performing an existing contractual duty (see p. 150).

Undue influence

Where a party makes a contract because of undue influence by another, the contract is voidable and may be set aside by the court, at the option of the party influenced.

Undue influence can arise where a "stronger" person has some special or fiduciary relationship over another, and uses this power to gain an advantage. (A fiduciary relationship is one relating to a trust or trustee).

In *Re Craig* (1971), an 84-year-old widower engaged a secretary until he died six years later. During this time he made gifts of large amounts of money to the secretary, which were later set aside by the court, because it was considered the relationship raised a presumption of undue influence.

This doctrine also applies to business contracts and in *Lloyds Bank Ltd v Bundy* (1975), the Court of Appeal set aside a guarantee which an old man had given to cover his son's bank balance. The son's business was in danger of failing and the court considered the bank had used undue influence to obtain the guarantee.

In *O'Sullivan v Management Agencies Ltd* (1985), Gilbert O'Sullivan, when young and unknown, entered into contracts to further his song-writing and singing career. He later applied to the court to have the contracts set aside. The Court of Appeal held that the contracts were unenforceable as a restraint of trade (see p. 159) and as the defendants had been in the position of a fiduciary relationship, the contracts had been obtained through undue influence.

In *Barclays Bank plc v O'Brien* (1993), a case which covers both misrepresentation (see p. 162) and undue influence, a husband persuaded his wife to sign a guarantee for a bank overdraft, using their jointly-owned house as security. The husband told her that the guarantee was limited to £60,000, but it was for £130,000. Before signing the documents the Bank's representative did not explain the transaction nor advise the wife that if in doubt she should take independent advice. When the Bank tried to enforce the security, Mrs O'Brien claimed, that at the most, she was only bound up to £60,000. The House of Lords held that the Bank should have had constructive notice of the risk of undue influence or misrepresentation. As Mrs O'Brien had been misled by her husband, and not received proper advice from the Bank, she was entitled to set aside the security on the matrimonial home.

DISCHARGE OF A CONTRACT

A contract is *discharged* when it places no further legal responsibilities upon the parties. A contract is discharged by:

- performance, or
- agreement, or
- breach, or
- frustration, (the impossibility of carrying out the contract).

Performance

A contract is discharged when the parties carry out their promises. If Jones Ltd agrees to paint Mrs. Smith's house for £550, the contract is performed when the house is painted and payment made.

Generally a party must do everything promised in the contract, and part-performance is no performance. If performance is not complete, payment for work done may not be recoverable, unless the other party was responsible for non-performance or accepted the work done. Time is not of the essence (that is, the date of performance is not important) unless it is a term of the contract, or becomes a term after agreement.

Agreement

The parties may agree to discharge the contract in the following ways, even though it has not been performed.

Discharge by deed or accord and satisfaction

When one party has performed the contract, the other party may be released from the promise to perform, either

- by deed, where no consideration for the release is given, or
- by accord and satisfaction. The parties agree to fresh consideration, by giving and accepting something outside the original contract.

Discharge when neither party has performed

Where neither party has performed, they may agree to waive their rights and release each other from their obligations.

Discharge on occurrence of specific events

The parties may agree beforehand that the occurrence of some specific event may discharge the contract. For example, a charterparty contract for the hire of a ship may contain a term that a dock strike will discharge the contract.

Breach

Breach of contract occurs when one party will not perform the contract as promised. If this happens, the other party may sue in the courts for breach of contract. Breach of contract may occur when one party fails to perform, or does not perform as agreed. An example of breach of the second kind might be when a manufacturer supplies sub-standard goods.

If a party gives notice of intention not to perform a contract at a future date, there is no need for the injured party to wait until the agreed time of performance before starting an action for breach. An action may be started immediately.

In *Hochster v de la Tour* (1853) a contract was made in January to start work as a hotel courier in six months' time. The employer informed the potential employee in February that the contract would not be honoured. The plaintiff was able to sue for breach of contract in February, and did not have to wait until July, the time that the contract was due to be performed.

Impossibility (frustration)

It may be no excuse that performance is impossible because of an event which occurred after the contract was made. The old common law view was that the parties should have foreseen all eventualities, and this rule to some extent still applies.

> In *Davis Contractors v Fareham UDC* (1956), the plaintiffs agreed to build 76 houses for a cost of £92,000. There were difficulties with labour and supplies, and when the houses were completed, the cost was £17,000 more than the agreed price. The builders contended that because of the difficulties, the contract was frustrated, and claimed the actual cost. It was held that the contract was not frustrated, as the events could have been foreseen and provided for.

The courts have however recognised some events as being enough to make performance impossible. In the following instances, the contract is automatically discharged, and the parties excused from further performance.

Subsequent statute

After a contract has been made, an Act of Parliament makes performance impossible or illegal.

> Re *Shipton, Anderson & Co* (1915). A contract for delivery of wheat was frustrated when, before delivery took place, an Act of Parliament was passed requisitioning all wheat for the Government.

Destruction of a thing necessary for performance

Taylor v Caldwell (1863). A contract for the hire of a music hall was frustrated when the hall was destroyed by fire before the time of performance.

> In *Gamerco v ICM Fair Warning (Agency) Ltd* (1995), the plaintiffs agreed to use the defendant's stadium for a concert. The stadium was later declared unsafe by engineers and the concert was cancelled. The court held that the contract was frustrated because the stadium was unsafe due to factors beyond the control of the defendants.

Personal incapacity in contracts for personal services

> In *Robinson v Davison* (1871), a piano player was ill on the day of a concert and the artist could not play as had been contracted. The court held that the contract was frustrated, as it was not the artist's fault that he was unable to perform.

Failure of some event which is the basis of the contract

If a contract is based on the happening of a specific event, the contract is frustrated if this event does not take place. The postponed coronation of Edward VII provided several interesting cases.

> In *Krell v Henry* (1903), the defendant hired a room which overlooked the route of the procession of King Edward VII's coronation. The King was ill and the coronation was cancelled. It was held that the contract was frustrated because the procession was the basis of the contract.
>
> This case must be contrasted with *Herne Bay Steamboat Co v Hutton* (1903). After the coronation the King was to travel to Spithead to review the fleet, which was assembled there. Hutton hired a boat to follow the royal barge, but because the King's illness prevented the royal review Hutton did not use the boat. It was held that the contract was not frustrated because the purpose of the contract was to review the fleet, and as it was still assembled at Spithead, the contract was possible. Hutton was liable to pay damages.

Effect or consequence of frustration

When a contract has been frustrated by an event, such as above, it is automatically discharged. Difficulty is sometimes experienced when money or property has been transferred beforehand, or where one party has worked on the contract before the frustrating event. The Law Reform (Frustrated Contract) Act 1943 provides that:

- money or property (other than specific goods which have perished) paid or passed over beforehand may be recovered;

- a party who has incurred expenses on the contract may claim out of the money paid beforehand or the amount payable;

- money due to be paid before frustration is no longer payable;

- where one party has gained a benefit from work done before frustration (e.g. a half-built house) the other party may be awarded an amount which the court considers fair and just.

The Act does not apply to (i) charterparties, (ii) carriage of goods by sea, (iii) insurance contracts.

REMEDIES FOR BREACH OF CONTRACT

When there has been a breach of contract, the injured party may treat the contract as being discharged. In addition, certain remedies may be claimed. The most common of these are damages, specific performance, injunctions and rescission.

Damages

The award of damages means the payment of a sum of money, and is a common law remedy. Damages are awarded to place the injured party in the same financial position as if the contract had been completed. For example, a contract was made for the sale of a diamond ring for £1,800 and the seller refused to transfer the ring. Another similar ring was bought at the market price of £2,000. The purchaser would claim £200 damages, the difference in price which had to be paid for the second ring and what the purchaser would have paid under the original contract.

Remoteness of damage

An injured party will not always receive damages for financial loss suffered as a result of a breach of contract if the court considers the damages too remote from the consequences of the breach.

In *Hadley v Baxendale* (1854), the plaintiff owned a mill and ordered a crankshaft to be delivered by a certain date. The carrier (Baxendale) delayed delivery and Hadley sued for loss of profits for the period during which the crankshaft was not working. The court held that the damages were too remote and the carrier was not liable, because he was unaware that his delay caused the mill to be idle.

Baron Alderson considered that damages should be awarded where:

- they arise naturally from the contract, or
- the damages were reasonably in the contemplation of both parties at the time they entered into the contract, as the probable result of the breach.

An excellent example of how these principles are followed came in *Victoria Laundry v Newman Industries Ltd* (1948). A boiler was ordered for the laundry to be delivered by a certain date. The boiler was delivered five months after the agreed date and the plaintiffs sued for:

- loss of normal profits;
- loss of profits from special dyeing contracts.

The court held (i) that the defendants were liable for normal profits, because they knew the laundry needed the boiler for ordinary production, (ii) the defendants were not liable for the special profits because they were unaware of the dyeing contracts and, therefore, had not contemplated the loss at the time of making the contract.

Liquidated and unliquidated damages

Damages may be either liquidated or unliquidated.

Liquidated damages are decided upon at the time the contract is made, and are a genuine pre-estimation of likely loss. The amount agreed as liquidated damages is payable whether the actual loss caused by the breach is more or less than agreed.

Unliquidated damages are not determined beforehand, but are left to the court to decide.

Liquidated damages and penalties

Liquidated damages must be contrasted with penalties. Penalty clauses in a contract are not estimates of potential loss, but are usually included to ensure that the contract is properly performed. If the courts decide that liquidated damages amounts to a penalty, it will be ignored. Unliquidated damages will be awarded to the claimant to cover the amount of the actual loss. A penalty will be held to exist:

- if the amount stipulated is extravagantly greater than could be reasonably expected;
- when the breach occurs because a sum of money has to be paid and the damages are greater than this amount;

• when the same amount of damages is payable on several occurrences, which would vary with regard to their effect on the financial loss.

Specific Performance

This is an equitable remedy, granted at the discretion of the court. Its effect is that the court orders one party to perform the contract as agreed. It is never awarded in the following cases.

- Where damages are an adequate remedy.
- Where either party is a minor.
- In moneylending contracts.
- Where the court would have to supervise the contract.
- In contracts for personal services.
- In contracts for sale of goods, unless the goods are unique.

It is usually awarded in contracts for sale of land or interests in land.

Injunction

This is an equitable remedy, granted at the discretion of the court. Its effect in contract is to stop a party from causing a breach of contract. It will not be awarded if damages are an adequate remedy, but will be awarded to restrain a breach of contract for personal services. It will, therefore, be used to stop a party under an exclusive contract from contracting with another third party. For example, a footballer under a two-year contract cannot join another football club until after the two years have elapsed, unless his club agrees to the move.

In *Warner Bros v Nelson* (1937), the defendant, a film actress better known as Bette Davies, agreed to make a film for another company although she had an exclusive contract with the plaintiffs. The court granted the injunction to the plaintiff and restrained the defendant from carrying out the contract with the third party.

Rescission

This is an equitable remedy, which endeavours to place the parties in the pre-contractual position by returning goods or money to the original owners.

THE FORM OF A CONTRACT

There are two classes of contract:

- *simple* contracts, and
- *specialty* contracts (made by deed).

The essential difference between these two types is that a simple contract may be made orally, by conduct, or in writing. A simple contract must be supported by consideration, as explained earlier. Specialty contracts on the other hand must be written and be "signed, witnessed and delivered". Such contracts do not require consideration.

Although the majority of simple contracts may be made informally by word of mouth or by implication, some contracts need to be made formally to be effective. The formality required might be either that the contract be in writing, or *be evidenced* in writing. These contracts are described below.

Contracts which must be in writing

Certain Acts of Parliament have laid down that the following contracts must be in writing:

- contracts of marine insurance;
- transfers of shares in a registered company;
- bills of exchange, cheques and promissory notes;
- hire-purchase contracts, and other regulated consumer credit agreements.

Contracts which must be evidenced in writing

The following contracts must be in writing if they are to be enforced in the courts. Technically, without writing they are good contracts but the courts will not enforce them unless the plaintiff has a memorandum in writing signed by the defendant.

Contracts of guarantee

These are governed by a very old act of Parliament, the Statute of Frauds (1677). A contract of guarantee is a promise to answer for the debt, default or financial miscarriage of another person. An example would be of a person obtaining an overdraft (or loan) from a bank on condition that his or her employer or parents give the bank a guarantee (a promise) to repay the loan if the borrower fails to do so.

Contracts for the sale of land

The Law of Property (Miscellaneous Provisions) Act 1989 provides that any contract for the sale or disposition of land, or of any interest in it, shall be in writing. All the terms expressly agreed by the parties must be incorporated into one document, (or two, where contracts are to be exchanged), and signed by, or on behalf of, all parties to the contract. The details in the contract would include:

- the parties (their names and description),
- the property (the subject-matter of the contract),
- the price (the consideration),
- any particular or special terms.

Contracts which must be made by deed

A deed is enforceable because of its form, regardless of the presence or absence of consideration. A deed must be:

- written,
- signed,
- witnessed,
- sealed, (where a corporation is involved), and
- delivered.

A document to convey or transfer a legal interest in land, (unless it is for a lease of three years or less), must be a deed. The creation of a legal mortgage of land must also be by deed. If in such cases the above requirements of a deed are not met by the parties, then the transaction will be of no legal effect. If for example the conveyance of a property was not witnessed, then no legal ownership of the land would pass.

The promise of a gift, unsupported by consideration, would have to be by deed to be enforceable.

LIMITATION ON BRINGING AN ACTION

The Limitation Acts provide that an action for damages in contract must be brought within a specified period of time. The Limitation Act 1980 provides that actions become "statute barred" and cannot be brought after the periods of time have expired, depending on the type of action as follows:

- an action based on a simple contract becomes "statute barred" and cannot be brought after six years from the date on which the right of action arose;

- an action for a specialty contract (a deed) cannot be brought after a period of 12 years;

- an action where damages for personal injuries are claimed cannot generally be brought after three years.

With cases involving fraud, mistake, misrepresentation and the like, the period of limitation does not start until the frauds etc. have been discovered or should have reasonably been discovered.

> In *Lynn v Bamber* (1930), the plaintiff bought plum trees in 1921, which were warranted as "Purple Pershores". In 1928, when the trees produced fruit, it was discovered that they were not that type of plum. The court held that the limitation period ran from the time that the fraudulent misrepresentation was discovered.

In addition, the period may start again if a defendant acknowledges in writing that a debt exists or makes a part payment of it.

No. [   ]

F.A. Copy	
League Copy	
Club Copy	
Player Copy	

F.A. PREMIER LEAGUE AND FOOTBALL LEAGUE CONTRACT

AN AGREEMENT made the.................................... day of...................................... 19 ....

between (name)..

of (address)...

acting pursuant to Resolution and Authority for and on behalf of ....

.... Football Club Limited (hereinafter referred to as "the Club") of the one part and

(name) ....

of (address)...

....

a Football Player (hereinafter referred to as "the Player") of the other part.

WHEREBY it is agreed as follows:–

1.   This Agreement shall remain in force until the 30th day of June 19.. unless it shall have previously been terminated by substitution of a revised agreement or as hereinafter provided.

2.   The Player agrees to play to the best of his ability in all football matches in which he is selected to play for the Club and to attend at any reasonable place for the purpose of training in accordance with instructions given by any duly authorised official of the Club.

3.   The Player agrees to attend all matches in which the Club is engaged when directed by any duly authorised official of the Club.

4.   The Player shall play football solely for the Club or as authorised by the Club or as required under the Rules of The Football Association and either the Rules of The F.A. Premier League or the Regulations of The Football League* dependent on the League in which the Club is in membership. The Player undertakes to adhere to the Laws of the Game of Association Football in all matches in which he participates.

5.   The Player agrees to observe the Rules of the Club at all times. The Club and the Player shall observe and be subject to the Rules of The Football Association and either the Rules of The F.A. Premier League or the Regulations of The Football League* as appropriate. In the case of conflict such Rules and Regulations shall take precedence over this Agreement and over Rules of the Club.

6.   The Club undertakes to provide the Player at the earliest opportunity with copies of all relevant Football Association Rules and F.A. Premier League Rules or Football League* Regulations as appropriate, the Club Rules for players and any relevant insurance policy applicable to the Player and to provide him with any subsequent amendments to all the above.

7.   (a)   The Player shall not without the written consent of the Club participate professionally in any other sporting or athletic activity. The Player shall at all times have due regard for the necessity of his maintaining a high standard of physical fitness and agrees not to indulge in any sport, activity or practice that might endanger such fitness. The Player shall not infringe any provision in this regard in any policy of insurance taken out for his benefit or for the benefit of the Club.

           (b)   The Player agrees to make himself available for community and public relations involvement as requested by the Club management, at reasonable times during the period of the contract (e.g. 2/3 hours per week).

8.   Any incapacity or sickness shall be reported by the Player to the Club immediately and the Club shall keep a record of any incapacity. The Player shall submit promptly to such medical and dental examinations as the Club may reasonably require and shall undergo, at no expense to himself, such treatment as may be prescribed by the medical or dental advisers of the Club in order to restore the Player to fitness. The Club shall arrange promptly such prescribed treatment and shall ensure that such treatment is undertaken and completed without expense to the Player notwithstanding that this Agreement expires after such treatment has been prescribed.

9.   Subject to the provisions of clause 10, in the event that the Player shall become incapacitated by reason of sickness or injury the Club shall, unless provision for the continuation of bonus payments be set out in the Schedule to this Agreement during the period of incapacity, pay to the Player for the first twenty-eight weeks of incapacity his basic wage as specified in the Schedule plus a sum equivalent to the amount of sickness benefit which the Club is able to recoup. After twenty-eight weeks of incapacity the Club shall, unless provision for the continuation of bonus payments be set out in the Schedule to this Agreement, pay to the Player his basic wage as specified in the Schedule without reduction for any state sickness or injury benefit that he may receive. The provisions of this Clause apply only to the playing season.

The Player agrees to notify the Club of any sickness benefit received after the end of the playing season in order for the Club to deduct the amount from the Player's gross wage.

10.   In the event that the Player shall suffer permanent incapacity the Club shall be entitled to serve a notice upon the Player terminating the Agreement. The Player's minimum entitlement shall be to receive 6 month's notice where the Agreement has not more than 3 years to run with an extra month's notice for each year or part year in excess of the said 3 years, provided that the parties shall be able to negotiate a longer period of notice if they so wish.

The notice may be served at any time after:–
(a)   the date on which the Player is declared permanently totally disabled in a case where the Player suffers incapacity within the terms of the Football League and/or F.A. Premier League Personal Accident Insurance Scheme; or
(b)   in any other case, the date on which the incapacity is established by independent medical examination.

Where the player is declared permanently totally disabled under the terms of The Football League and/or F.A. Premier League Personal Accident Insurance Scheme he will be entitled to receive a lump sum disability benefit in accordance with the terms of the relevant policy.

11.   (a)   The Player shall not reside at any place which the Club deems unsuitable for the performance of his duties under this Agreement.
(b)   The Player shall not without the previous consent of the Club be engaged either directly or indirectly in any trade, business or occupation other than his employment hereunder.

12.   The Player shall be given every opportunity compatible with his obligations under this Agreement to follow courses of further education or vocational training if he so desires. The Club agrees to give the Footballers' Further Education and Vocational Training Society particulars of any such courses undertaken by the Player.

13.   The Player shall permit the Club to photograph him as a member of the squad of players and staff of the Club provided that such photographs are for use only as the official photographs of the Club. The Player may, save as otherwise mutually agreed and subject to the overriding obligation contained in the Rules of The Football Association not to bring the game of Association Football into disrepute, contribute to the public media in a responsible manner. The Player shall, whenever circumstances permit, give to the Club reasonable notice of his intention to make such contributions to the public media in order to allow representations to be made to him on behalf of the Club if it so desires.

14.   (a)   The Player shall not induce or attempt to induce any other Player employed by or registered by the Club, or by any other Club, to leave that employment or cease to be so registered for any reason whatsoever.
(b)   The Club and the Player shall arrange all contracts of service and transfers of registration to any other Football Club between themselves and shall make no payment to any other person or agent in this respect.

15.   No payment shall be made or received by either the Player or the Club to or from any person or organisation whatsoever as an inducement to win, lose or draw a match except for such payments to be made by the Club to the Player as are specifically provided for in the Schedule to this Agreement.

16.   If the Player shall be guilty of serious or persistent misconduct or serious or persistent breach of the Rules of the Club or of the terms and conditions of this Agreement the Club may on giving fourteen days' written notice to the Player terminate this Agreement in accordance with the Rules of The Football Association and either the Rules of The F.A. Premier League or the Regulations of The Football League* as appropriate and the Club shall notify the Player in writing of the full reasons for the action taken. Such action shall be subject to the Player's right of appeal (exercisable within seven days of the receipt by the Player of such notice and notification of reasons from the Club) as follows:–
(a)   he may appeal to the Board of either The F.A. Premier League or The Football League, dependent on the League in which the Club is in membership, who shall hear the appeal within fourteen days of receipt of the notice of appeal.
(b)   either the Club or the Player may appeal against the decision of the Board to The Football League* Appeals Committee and such further appeal shall be made within seven days of the receipt of the Board's decision and shall be heard within fourteen days of receipt of the notice of the further appeal.

Any such termination shall be subject to the rights of the parties provided for in the Rules of The F.A. Premier League or the Regulations of The Football League* as appropriate. The Club may at its discretion waive its rights under this Clause and take action under the provisions of Clause 18.

17.   If the Club is guilty of serious or persistent breach of the terms and conditions of this Agreement the Player may on giving fourteen days' written notice to the Club terminate this agreement. The Player shall forward a copy of such notice to The Football Association and either The F.A. Premier League or The Football League* dependent on the League in which the Club is in membership. The Club shall have a right of appeal as set out in Clause 16(a) mutatis mutandis (exercisable within seven days of the receipt by the Club of such notice from the Player) and the Club or the Player as the case may be shall have a further right of appeal as set out in Clause 16(b).

18.   If the Player is guilty of misconduct or a breach of any of the training or disciplinary rules or lawful instructions of the Club or any of the provisions of this Agreement the Club may either impose a fine not exceeding two weeks' basic wages or order the Player not to attend at the Club for a period not exceeding fourteen days. The Club shall inform the Player in writing of the action taken and the full reasons for it and this information shall be recorded in a register held at the Club. The Player shall have a right of appeal as set out in Clause 16(a) (exercisable within seven days of the receipt by the Player of such written notification from the Club) and the Club or the Player as the case may be shall have a further right of appeal as set out in Clause 16(b) of this Agreement. Any penalty imposed by the Club upon the Player shall not become operative until the appeals procedures have been exhausted.

19.   In the event of any grievance in connection with his employment under this Agreement the following procedures shall be available to the Player in the order set out:-
(a)   the grievance shall be brought informally to the notice of the Manager of the Club in the first instance;
(b)   formal notice of the grievance may be given in writing to the Manager of the Club;
(c)   if the grievance is not settled to the Player's satisfaction within fourteen days thereafter formal notice of the grievance may be given in writing to the Secretary of the Club so that it may be considered by the Board of Directors or Committee of the Club or by any duly authorised committee or sub-committee thereof. The matter shall thereupon be dealt with by the Board or Committee at its next convenient meeting and in any event within four weeks of receipt of the notice;
(d)   if the grievance is not settled by the Club to the Player's satisfaction the Player shall have a right of appeal as set out in Clause 16(a) (exercisable within seven days of the Club notifying the Player of the decision of the Board or Committee) and the Club or the Player as the case may be shall have a further right of appeal as set out in Clause 16(b) of this Agreement.

20.   The Player may if he so desires be represented at any personal hearing of an appeal under this Agreement by an official or member of the Professional Footballers' Association.

21.   Upon the execution of this Agreement the Club shall effect the Registration of the Player with The Football Association and The F.A. Premier League or The Football League* as appropriate in accordance with   their Rules and Regulations. Such Registration may be transferred by mutual consent of the Club and the Player during the currency of this Agreement and this Agreement will be deemed to be terminated (but not so as to affect accrued rights) on the Registration by the The Football Association and by The F.A. Premier League or The Football League* as appropriate of such transfer.

22.   The Rules and Regulations of The F.A. Premier League and The Football League* as to the re-engagement and transfer of a registration shall apply to the Club and Player both during the currency and after the expiration of this Agreement.

23.   The remuneration of the Player shall be set out in a Schedule attached to this Agreement and signed by the parties. The Schedule shall include all remuneration to which the Player is or may be entitled. In the event of any dispute the remuneration set out in the Schedule shall be conclusively deemed to be the full entitlement of the Player.

24.   The Player shall be entitled to a minimum of four weeks' paid holiday per year, such holiday to be taken at a time which the Club shall determine. The Player shall not participate in professional football during his holiday.

25.   Reference herein to Rules, Regulations or Bye-laws of The Football Association; The F.A. Premier League, The Football League*, the Club and any other body shall be treated as a reference to those Rules, Regulations and Bye-laws as from time to time amended.

26.   If by the expiry of this Contract the Club has not made the Player an offer of re-engagement or the Player has been granted a Free Transfer under the provisions of The F.A. Premier League Rules or The Football League* Regulations then he shall continue to receive from his Club as severance payment his weekly basic wage for a period of one month from the expiry date of this Contract or until he signs for another Club whichever period is the shorter provided that where the Player signs for a Club within the month at a reduced basic wage then his old Club shall make up the shortfall in basic wage for the remainder of the month.

27.   The terms and conditions of this Contract shall continue to apply in the event of the Club losing Football League status to join The Football Conference except that the references to "Football League*" in Clauses 4, 5, 6, 16, 17, 21, 25 and 26 shall be deemed to read "The Football Conference" and in Clause 22 the words "The Regulations of The Football League" shall be altered to read "The Rules of The Football Association".

28.   All previous agreements between the Club and Player are hereby cancelled.

SCHEDULE

(a) The Player's employment with the Club began on the .... 19...................

(b) No employment with a previous employer shall count as part of the Player's continuous period of employment hereunder.

(c) The Player shall become or continue to be and during the continuance of his employment hereunder shall remain a member of the Football League Players' Benefit Scheme (and a member of the .... Pension Scheme) and as such (in the latter case shall be liable to make such contribution and in each case) shall be entitled to such benefits and subject to such conditions as are set out in the definitive Trust Deed or Rules of the Scheme.

(d) A contracting out certificate is not in force in respect of the Player's employment under this Agreement.

(e) Basic Wage.

£...per week from ....to ....

£...per week from ....to ....

£...per week from ....to ....

£...per week from ....to ....

(f) Any other provisions:–

Signed by the said ....
                                                                                                                                              (Player)

and ....

                                                                                               ....
in the presence of   (Club Signatory)

(Signature)..

                                                                                               ....
(Occupation)..   (Position)

(Address) ....

....

....

4

Useful website

For text of Acts of Parliament mentioned in this chapter: *www.hmso.gov.uk/acts*

SPECIMEN EXAMINATION QUESTIONS

The problem

Liverpool Car Sales Ltd (LCS) advertised an auction of classic cars to be held in its Anfield auction site at 2 pm on Saturday May 22, 2004. One car in particular, a rare 1950's Jaguar, was highlighted as being a particularly desirable vehicle. Various people decided to attend the auction.

Moshin arrived at the auction with the intention of bidding for the Jaguar and was very disappointed to find that the car had been withdrawn from the sale.

Neil was bidding for a 1965 Lotus sports car but got "carried away" and bid more than he could afford. He called out and withdrew his bid, but the auctioneer nevertheless sold the car to him.

Oliver was bidding by telephone for a 1950's Rolls Royce, but, at the precise moment he was entering his final bid, the telephone line went dead. Not realising the situation, the auctioneer then sold the car to Lady Penelope who had entered a lower bid in the auction room.

(a) In relation to the relevant law on offer and acceptance in a contract, **briefly** explain and illustrate what is meant by the following terms:

   (i)   an invitation to treat;
  (ii)   the postal rule;
 (iii)   rejection of an offer;
 (iv)   revocation of an offer;
  (v)   lapse of time.   (10 marks)

(b) Discuss whether or not Moshin would have a case for breach of contract against LCS following the withdrawal of the Jaguar from the sale.   (4 marks)

(c) Discuss whether or not Neil is legally obliged to pay for the Lotus.   (4 marks)

(d) Discuss whether or not Oliver has any legal rights in respect of the Rolls Royce.   (4 marks)

AQA Higher Tier, June 2004

TALKING POINT

"In the law of contract, minors should be treated the same as adults. If a child of 10 can be held responsible for a criminal act, or a tort, then liability should be extended to their entering into a binding legal contract".

SUGGESTED COURSEWORK TITLES

Distinguish "offers" from "invitations to treat". Comment on the legal implications of this distinction.

Explain the importance of consideration in the law of contract. Discuss the implications of allowing unsupported promises to be binding.

7 | Consumer Law

PROTECTING THE CONSUMER'S RIGHTS AND INTERESTS

A consumer is one who buys or uses goods or services. In the past, English law has tended to follow the doctrine of *caveat emptor* (let the buyer beware). We encountered this term in the last chapter when discussing misrepresentation. Under this doctrine, the buyer takes the goods as he or she finds them. Once the goods have been bought, the buyer has no rights to go to court if they prove to be unsuitable. To some extent *caveat emptor* still applies. If, for example you were to buy a second-hand electric lawn mower from a neighbour down the road, it would be in your own interests to check that it was in reasonable condition and worked properly before you bought it. However, in many ways this rather harsh doctrine has been modified and eroded by statute.

Most goods these days are purchased in shops, supermarkets, stores, through the internet and in a host of other ways. Many statutes have been passed to give consumers certain rights. In addition, many institutions and bodies have come into being to protect and inform the consumer. The aims of these statutes and bodies are to help the consumer to obtain value for money and to place the consumer on a more equal standing when dealing with more professional and experienced businessmen and with powerful commercial organisations.

A further reason for protecting the consumer is the increasingly complex technical development of many modern consumer goods. The ordinary customer cannot be expected to know if the goods are fit for the purpose for which they were bought, or whether they are of good or poor quality. *Caveat emptor* cannot reasonably be expected to apply, for example, when buying a heavily-packaged item of complex electrical equipment. The **Sale of Goods Act 1979** and other legislation now control the rights and interests of the consumer, and the protection they provide will be examined in this chapter.

SALE OF GOODS ACT 1979

Definition of a contract for the sale of goods

This act consolidates all the previous law relating to the sale of goods. Section 2 of the act states that "a contract for the sale of goods is a contract by which the seller transfers or agrees to transfer the property in goods to the buyer for a money consideration, called the price"

The act *only* deals with contracts for the sale of goods, and does not affect other contracts. Within the meaning of the act, goods are tangible things which can be physically possessed, like cars, hot-water bottles, DVD players, food, *etc*. It does not include land, legal rights such as debts, copyrights and trade marks. Nor does it include things obtained through barter, (the exchange of goods for other goods).

Implied terms

The act provides that there are certain *implied* conditions and warranties which apply in most contracts for the sale of goods. "Implied" means that they are assumed, or taken, to exist. They are to be read into such a contract without being expressly stated.

The aim of the act is to protect people who buy faulty or unsatisfactory goods. This protection may also apply to the sale of "seconds". A purchaser of unsatisfactory goods is entitled under the act to have the goods replaced. Alternatively, the goods can be returned and a refund made of the cost (for this reason it is wise to retain some proof of purchase, like a receipt or credit-card statement).

There is no right to return goods where:

- there is nothing wrong with the goods, but you decide that you don't like them (some large organisations will change goods which are not faulty, but they are not legally obliged to do so);

- you hold on to the goods for more than a reasonable amount of time, as it may be considered that you have accepted them; or

- you received the goods as a present (you were not a party to the contract; see the *doctrine of privity* referred to in Chapter 6).

Conditions

A condition is a term in a contract which goes to its very root. In a contract for the sale of a Jaguar car, for example, it is a condition of the contract that a Jaguar be delivered and not a BMW. Similarly, if a farmer buys cattle food, it is a condition of the contract that the food which is delivered shall not poison his cows.

If there is a breach of a condition, then there is no contract. The buyer may treat the contract as ended, and return the goods. If it is impossible to return the goods (in the example above, if the cows have eaten the food before it was discovered to be poisonous), the buyer may sue for damages.

Implied undertaking as to title (Section 12)

There is an implied condition that the seller has the right to sell the goods. In the case of an agreement to sell, the implied condition is that the seller will have the right to sell at the time the ownership is to pass. A person who steals goods generally would not have the right to pass on a good title to a buyer.

In *Rowland v Divall* (1923), the plaintiff bought a car from the defendant, who had stolen it from the true owner. The defendant did not therefore have a good title to the car. The car was later seized by the police for the true owner, and the plaintiff successfully sued the defendant for the return of the price paid.

However, exceptions to this general rule exist which enable a person who does not own goods to pass on a good title to someone else (see under *Nemo dat quod non habet*, later in this chapter).

Sales by Description (Section 13)

- Where there is a sale by description, the goods must correspond with the description.

- Where sale is by sample as well as by description, the goods must correspond with both.

In *Nichol v Godts* (1854) Nichol agreed to sell "foreign refined rape oil" as per sample. He delivered oil of similar quality, but it was not as described. It was held that Godts could refuse delivery.

- A sale of goods shall not be prevented from being a sale by description by reason only that, being exposed for sale or hire, the buyer selects the goods.

In *Beale v Taylor* (1967) the defendant advertised a car for sale as a "Triumph Herald 1200". The plaintiff inspected the car and bought it at the sale price. He later discovered that the rear of the car was a Triumph Herald 1200, but welded to the front was a Triumph Herald 948. The car was not roadworthy and the plaintiff sued for damages under section 13. The Court of Appeal awarded damages and considered that, as the plaintiff had relied on the advertisement, it was a sale by description, even though the plaintiff had inspected the car.

This subsection was originally introduced by the Supply of Goods (Implied Terms) Act 1973 to resolve the doubt as to whether or not self-service sales could be sales by description.

Undertakings as to quality or fitness (Section 14, 1979 Act, as amended by the Sale and Supply of Goods Act (1994))

Under section 14(2), where the seller sells goods **in the course of business** (*i.e.* the sale is not a private sale) there is an implied condition that the goods shall be *of satisfactory quality*. Goods are of satisfactory quality if they meet a standard that a reasonable person would regard as satisfactory, taking into account description, price and all other circumstances.
When deciding if goods are satisfactory, the following should be considered:

- their state and condition;

- the fitness for all the purposes the goods are usually supplied;

- appearance and finish;

- freedom from minor defects;

- safety and durability.

Section 14(2) does not apply if:

- defects are drawn to the buyer's attention before the contract is made;

- the buyer examines the goods before the sale;

- in contracts for sale by sample, a reasonable examination of the sample would show any defect.

In *Grant v Australian Knitting Mills Ltd* (1936) a doctor bought a pair of woollen under-pants and contracted dermatitis when they were worn. The wool contained a chemical which should have been removed before the sale. It was held that the sellers were liable because the buyer had made known the purpose for which the goods were required and they were neither fit for this purpose, nor of satisfactory quality.

In a more recent case, *Wormell v RHM Agricultural Ltd* (1987), the plaintiff discussed with the defendants a method of killing wild oats growing among his wheat crop. On the defendants' recommendation, the farmer used their spray but it had little effect on the wild oats. The court held that the goods were not reasonably fit for their purpose and the plaintiff was able to claim compensation for the cost of the goods and the cost of the labour used in spraying the wheat.

Sale by sample (Section 15)

Where sale is by sample, there is an implied condition that:

- the bulk shall correspond with the sample in quality;

- the buyer shall have reasonable opportunity of comparing bulk with sample;

- the goods shall be free from defects rendering them unmerchantable which would not be apparent on reasonable inspection.

Godley v Perry (1960) is an interesting case in that it involved sections 14 and 15. The plaintiff, aged six, bought a catapult which broke when used and injured his eye. The rubber of the catapult had a defect which was not apparent upon reasonable examin-ation. The shopkeeper was held liable in breach of section 14 because the catapult was not of satisfactory quality (it was bought by description) and, as a boy aged six relied on the seller's skill and judgment, it was not fit for the purpose for which it was required.

The shopkeeper claimed an indemnity from the wholesaler who supplied the goods and the court held that as the goods had been bought in bulk by sample the suppliers were in breach of section 15 and liable to indemnify the shopkeeper.

Warranties

Unlike a condition, a warranty is not a vital term of a contract. A breach of warranty does not end the contract, but it does give a buyer the right to sue for damages. An example of a breach of warranty might be if a car was delivered but the cigar lighter was not working properly.

A warranty in this context should not be confused with a guarantee (or warranty) given by manufacturers to repair faulty goods within a fixed period of time from their purchase.

Freedom from encumbrance and right to quiet possession

There is an implied warranty in section 12 that goods shall be free of any charge or encumbrance not disclosed to, or known by the buyer. This means that they shall not be subject to some financial burden, such as a mortgage.

Another implied warranty contained in section 12 is that a buyer will enjoy "quiet possession" of the goods. That enjoyment may only be interfered with by someone who has been disclosed under the contract as having a right or benefit from any charge or encumbrance.

Exclusion clauses

The **Unfair Contract Terms Act 1977** provides that none of the implied terms described above may be excluded by a seller *in a consumer sale*. A consumer sale is when a sale of goods is for private use or consumption, and not in the course of a business. With sales in the course of a business, for example a sale by a manufacturer to a retailer where the goods will be resold, sections 13, 14 and 15 may be excluded. However, an exclusion clause may not be enforced if it could be shown that reliance on it would not be fair and reasonable.

It should be noted that the implied condition in section 12 (as to title) may not be excluded or varied in any contract.

Passing the ownership of goods

If goods are damaged or destroyed between the time a contract is made and the time for delivery of the goods, one of the parties will have to suffer the loss. It is important, therefore, to know when ownership of the goods passes from one party to the other.

Unless it is agreed otherwise, ownership and responsibility for the goods (the risk) pass at the same time. If the buyer and seller do not clearly state the time they intended passing the ownership, the Act provides rules to help find the parties' intention. The rules depend on whether the goods are **specific** or **unascertained**.

Specific goods

Specific goods are ones which are identified and agreed upon at the time the contract is made. An example would be when a seller offers to sell a Ford car, registration number XZ 53 AHW, and the buyer accepts.

Under section 18 of the Sale of Goods Act, ownership of specific goods passes according to the following rules:

Rule 1. When goods are in a deliverable state, the ownership passes at the time of making the contract. It is immaterial if time of payment and/or delivery be at a later date.

Rule 2. When goods are not in a deliverable state and the seller is bound to do something to put the goods into a deliverable state the ownership does not pass until this thing has been done and the buyer has been informed.

Rule 3. When goods in a deliverable state have to be weighed, measured, tested or other such things by the seller to ascertain the price, the ownership does not pass until this has been done and the buyer has been informed.

Rule 4. When goods have been delivered on approval, or on a sale or return or other similar terms, the goods do not pass until:

- the buyer signifies his approval or keeps the goods beyond the agreed time, or beyond a reasonable time if no limit was agreed, or

- the buyer, by his conduct, adopts the goods (*e.g.* sells or pawns the goods, thereby acting as the owner).

Unascertained goods

Unascertained or future goods are sold by description. At the time of the contract, they have not been identified. A contract for the sale of 1000 litres of oil from a tanker containing 5000 litres would be an example of such a situation.

Rule 5 in section 18 of the Sale of Goods Act 1979 states when ownership of unascertained goods passes. It passes when goods of that description and in a deliverable state are unconditionally appropriated to the contract. This can be by the seller with the assent of the buyer, or the other way round. Such assent may be express or implied.

In the above example, when 1000 litres of oil have been pumped out and separated from the bulk, then that quantity has been ascertained and appropriated to the contract.

The Sale of Goods (Amendment) Act 1995

This act provides that where goods form part of an identifiable bulk, and the buyer has paid for the goods, the ownership of them would pass to the buyer at the time of payment. Again using the above example, the ownership of the 1000 litres of oil would pass to the buyer at the time of payment, and not at when the goods are ascertained.

The purpose of this act is to protect buyers of unascertained goods when a seller becomes insolvent.

SUPPLY OF GOODS AND SERVICES ACT 1982

The definition of a contract for the sale of goods, given at the beginning of this chapter, stated the need for a consideration of money (the price). The Sale of Goods Act does not cover transactions where money does not pass in the contract. Barter, or the exchange of goods for goods, was given as an example of such a transaction.

The **Supply of Goods and Services Act 1982** gives protection where contracts relate to the supply of goods and services, but are not covered by the 1979 Act. The 1982 Act gives similar protection as that provided by the implied terms contained in sections 12 to 15 of the Sale of Goods Act. It relates to the following contracts.

Contracts for the transfer of goods

Contracts under this heading would include barter, the offer of goods for tokens ("send 10 chocolate wrappers for a free poster of your favourite pop star"), and offers of goods for a service ("introduce a new customer and receive a free pocket calculator"). Goods received as a result of similar contracts to these would be covered by the implied terms.

Contracts of hire

Contracts of hire take place when a person has temporary possession of another person's goods. A fee is paid for the loan of the goods (*e.g.* cars, tools, camping equipment, etc.), which are later returned to the owner. While the goods are in the possession of the hirer, he or she has the benefit of rights similar to the implied terms in the 1979 Act.

Contracts of hire do not include hire-purchase contracts, where the goods will eventually become the property of the hirer.

Contracts for services

A contract for services (with or without the supply of goods) is subject to the following implied terms where the supplier of a service is acting in the course of a business.

- The service will be carried out with **reasonable care and skill.**

- Where a time for the service to be carried out is not agreed beforehand, the service will be carried out **within a reasonable time**.

- Where the consideration for the service has not been decided beforehand the supplier will receive a **reasonable charge**.

In these matters what is reasonable is a question of fact.

An example of how the above Act may work would be an electrician installing a new socket. The supplying of the socket would be subject to the implied terms of the Sale of Goods Act 1979, but supplying the service of installation would be covered by the Supply of Goods and Services Act 1982.

The Act does not cover the services of an advocate in court or tribunal, or the services of a director to the company for which he acts in that capacity. The Secretary of State has power to make other exceptions.

CONSUMER PROTECTION ACT 1987

This Act provides that it is the producer of defective goods who is primarily liable for damage caused by such defective goods.

The product and producer

The producer is strictly liable (see p. 208) for defective goods and the claimant need not prove negligence or fault, although the courts will consider the balance of probabilities.

The claimant must show that:

- the product contained the defect,
- the claimant suffered damage,
- the product caused the damage, and
- the defendant was the producer of the product.

The definition of the "product" is wide. It includes goods within the Sale of Goods Act, and also growing crops and things on land such as fences, although not the land itself. Intangible products such as electricity and gas are within the Act. Producers of fresh food, such as fish or vegetables which have not been processed in any way, are exempt from liability.

The "producer" means the manufacturer. This term covers any person who holds out as being the producer, for example, a person who puts a name or trade mark on goods supplied by another.

The defect

Defects are defined as:

- defects in design,
- defects in processing or manufacture, and
- an inherent defect without a warning being given.

There is a "defect in a product" if its safety is not that which a reasonable person might generally be entitled to expect. A producer would probably not be liable if the goods were badly misused by the claimant.

Defences

A producer may have a defence if it can be shown that the defect was caused by following a statutory requirement, or that the goods were not supplied in the course of business. For example, a person who donates a home-made cake at a local "bring and buy" would not be liable if a buyer ate the cake and was sick.

The burden of proof lies with the producer, although he may claim contributory negligence if the claimant fails to take reasonable care with a foreseeable risk.

Damage

Damage means death or personal injury or any loss of or damage to property.

The General Product Safety Regulations 1994, concerns all suppliers of products intended for consumers or likely to be used by consumers. It provides that no product shall be placed on the market unless it is "safe". A "safe" product is one which under normal use does not present any or only minimal risk, in keeping with an acceptable manner in which the product is used. Producers may avoid or lessen liability by displaying warning labels and the like, or presenting a defence that they took all reasonable steps and exercised all due diligence to avoid committing the offence. Breach of the regulations can incur a fine or a term of imprisonment.

The regulations do not apply to second-hand products that are antiques and those supplied for repair before use, provided that the supplier clearly informs the customer of this before the contract is made.

NEMO DAT QUOD NON HABET

This Latin rule of law can be translated as "no one gives what he does not have". When applied to sale of goods it means that a seller cannot give to the purchaser a better title than he has himself. If Tom owns a pen and sells it to Dick, Dick obtains a good title of ownership. But if the pen is then stolen and the thief sells it to Harry, Harry would not own the pen because the thief did not have a good title. The pen would still be owned by Dick and he could claim it back from Harry.

Exceptions to "nemo dat" rule

It can be seen from the above example that with such a sale, one innocent party will suffer; either the real owner or the purchaser. The Sale of Goods Act and other statutes provide exceptions to the general rule. In all the following cases the buyers receive a good title.

Estoppel (Section 21)

This provision applies where an owner is aware that his or her goods are being sold by a person who does not have a good title to them. An owner who does not inform the buyer of this will later be precluded or barred (estopped) from denying the seller's right to sell.

Sale by a person with voidable title (Section 23)

A sale by a person with a voidable title to goods will give the buyer a good title provided that:

- the seller's title had not been voided at the time of the sale, and
- the buyer had no knowledge of the seller's defect of title, and acted in good faith.

Seller or buyer in possession after sale (Sections 24 and 25)

If a seller allows a buyer to obtain goods (or document of title), before payment, a sale by that buyer gives a new purchaser a good title. In the same way, if a seller retains possession of goods after a sale and then sells the goods to another person, that second purchaser gets a good title in preference to the original buyer.

There is a moral to be learned from this exception to the *nemo dat* rule. Do not part with goods until you have been paid. If you have paid for goods, take possession of them as soon as possible.

Factors

Factors are mercantile agents, whose ordinary business is to sell goods in their possession. A sale by a factor, even without authority to sell, gives the buyer a good title provided that:

- the owner deposited the goods with the factor, and

- the buyer acted in good faith.

Motor vehicles subject to hire-purchase agreements

A private purchaser, (but *not* a person in the motor trade), can obtain a good title to a motor vehicle which is subject to a hire-purchase agreement or conditional sale agreement. However, to obtain a good title, the purchaser must have had no knowledge of such an agreement, and must have acted in good faith.

RIGHTS OF ACTION BY SELLER AND BUYER

Buyers and sellers have the usual remedies for breach of contract, as described in the previous chapter. The Sale of Goods Act 1979 specifies the following rights of action.

The seller's rights of action

- For the price.

  When the ownership in the goods has passed to a buyer who refuses to pay for the goods, the seller has a right of action for the price of the goods (s.49).

- Damages for non-acceptance.

  When the buyer wrongly refuses to accept and pay for the goods, the seller has a right of action for damages for non-acceptance (s.50).

The buyer's rights of action

- When the seller does not deliver the goods, there is a right of action against the seller for:
  - recovery of the price if paid beforehand;
  - damages for non-delivery of goods (s.51); and

- where the goods are unique, or for a special or specific purpose, a decree of specific performance.

- When there is a breach of warranty by the seller, there is a right of action for damages (s.53).

- When there is a breach of condition by the seller, there is a right of action for rescission and/or damages.

UNFAIR CONTRACT TERMS ACT 1977

This Act affects many of the terms and exclusion clauses used in contracts between businesses and consumers, and improves:

- a consumer's protection when buying goods or services, and

- the legal position of the consumer when entering or using business premises.

Protection provided by the Act

The Unfair Contract Terms Act provides the following protection to consumers.

- Generally, a business cannot exclude, by contract or by notice, liability for negligence resulting in a consumer's death or personal injury.

- A contract may not exclude or restrict a business's liability for breach of contract or claim that it may perform the contract in a way substantially different from what was agreed. As a result of this Act for example, a holidaymaker is entitled to be booked into the hotel and resort stipulated in the contract, and the travel company may not unreasonably exclude this right.

- A manufacturer's guarantee may not exclude or restrict liability for negligence to a consumer which results in loss or damage.

- The implied conditions in the Sale of Goods Act 1979 (with the exception of condition of title) are similarly available to consumers of goods obtained under hire, rental, and similar contracts, and under contracts for work and materials. Clauses excluding these conditions are subject to a test of reasonableness.

- A business may exclude or restrict liability for negligence (other than death or personal injury), but the clause must be reasonable as between the parties.

The effects of the Act

The effect of this Act is that it protects consumers, when buying goods or services, from unreasonable contractual exclusion clauses or terms, and it protects consumers from injury to their person or property by the unreasonable negligence of businessmen or their employees.

For example, a garage would be liable if its employees were unreasonably negligent and damaged your car. The garage may no longer exclude such liability.

THE UNFAIR TERMS IN CONSUMER CONTRACT REGULATIONS

The European Community Directive on unfair terms in consumer contracts became part of English law on July 1, 1995. Under these rules a consumer, acting outside of his/her business or trade, may challenge any contract made between the consumer and a seller of goods or a supplier of services, which is considered unfair and causes a significant imbalance to the detriment of the consumer. An action may be started in the courts or through the Office of Fair Trading.

Requirements of a consumer contract

Consumer contracts must be written in plain intelligible English. Contracts produced in small unreadable type, or expressed in impenetrable legal jargon would be regarded as unfair. This would be the case even if the content of the contract itself was fair.

The consumer should be given an opportunity to examine all the terms. If there is any doubt, the interpretation most favourable to the consumer should be used. Any contract which is considered to be unfairly weighted against a consumer could be judged as invalid.

Example

An example of how the regulations may be interpreted would be if a holiday insurance policy required any loss or theft to be reported to the police immediately, and you were camping in a remote area of a foreign country without a police station within a reasonable distance. If the insurance company refused compensation, because of failure to comply with this clause, it could be considered unreasonable and unfair, and invalid.

Further protection afforded to the consumer under European directives is given by the Consumer Protection (Distance Selling) Regulations (2000) and the Supply and Sale of Goods to Consumers Regulations (2002). These give to a consumer the right to the replacement or repair of goods which are faulty, and make guarantees legally enforceable.

CONSUMER CREDIT ACT 1974

This Act covers most aspects of buying and hiring on credit. Any provider of credit who does not comply with the Act will not be able to enforce the debt.

What is covered by the Act

The Consumer Credit Act concerns itself with *regulated agreements*. A regulated consumer credit agreement exists when credit not exceeding a prescribed amount is provided for an individual. The meaning of "credit" under the Act is very wide, and covers cash advances or loans, hire-purchase, credit sales, conditional sales, credit cards and the like. The agreement must not be one which is exempted from the Act, and it is important to know what agreements are not covered.

Exemptions from the Consumer Credit Act

There are five kinds of consumer credit agreements which are exempted from the Act.

- Traders who grant normal trade credit are exempt. It is normal for trade customers to pay all credit transactions of a particular period (usually a month) by one payment.

- Agreements involving low-cost credit are exempt. This is provided that no supplier is involved, and the agreement is solely between debtor and creditor. The charge for credit must not exceed a certain amount. An example of such an agreement would be between a bank and a customer, where the customer has the choice of how or where to spend the loan.

- Finance for foreign trade is exempt.

- Loans for land transactions which are settled in four instalments or fewer are exempt.

- Mortgages are exempt.

Cost of credit

The Act requires traders to show the true cost of credit, and all advertisements, whether in shop windows or in the mass media, must show the APR. This means the Annual Percentage Rate of the total charge for credit. Consumers can easily see which traders are giving the lowest terms of credit, as it includes all costs that the consumer will have to pay.

The agreement

A debtor must be made aware of all the regulations as required by the Act. An agreement would be unenforceable without this requirement, or if it was not made in the following way:

- in writing,
- containing all the express terms in legible form with no small print,
- complying with the provisions of the Act as to form and content,
- signed by the debtor and creditor, or their representatives.

A copy of the agreement must be given to the customer immediately if signed by the creditor, or, if not signed, it must be sent within seven days of the date of the agreement.

Default notice

If a debtor is in breach of the agreement, the creditor cannot exercise his rights unless a default notice has been given to the debtor. The notice gives details of the breach, the action the creditor intends to take and the time limit, which must not be less than seven days. Should the debtor not comply with the provisions of the notice, the creditor has the right to:

- end the agreement,
- demand earlier payment,
- consider that any right of the debtor is terminated,
- recover the property,
- enforce any security.

Regardless of the creditor's rights as above, a court order is needed if the goods are "protected". Protected goods are concerned with a regulated hire-purchase or conditional sale agreement, and the debtor has paid more than one-third of the price and has not terminated the agreement.

Credit card holders are liable for a charge if their cards are lost or stolen and used fraudulently. This liability ends once the credit company has been informed of the loss.

Termination

Section 99 provides that a debtor under a regulated hire-purchase or conditional sale agreement may terminate the agreement if he has paid:

- all sums due (including arrears), and
- one-half of the price, or less if the court so orders,
- compensation, if the debtor has not taken reasonable care of the property.

The debtor may pay off the whole debt before the date agreed, and will be entitled to a rebate of the interest or charges due to be paid.

Section 37 provides that a debtor may cancel a regulated agreement, if notice of the cancellation is given before the end of the fifth day following the day on which he received the copy of the agreement provided that:

- the agreement was signed at any place other than the place of business of the creditor or his associates;
- in negotiations before the agreement was signed, oral representations were made to the debtor by a person acting as a negotiator.

Further reforms

The Consumer Credit Act 1974 is a very complex piece of legislation, and the foregoing is only an outline of its provisions. Furthermore, difficulties encountered with it were compounded by the fact that it was introduced piecemeal, step by step. It has had a great effect on most people, because consumer credit is very much part of modern living. Recently there has arisen a strong body of opinion that the Act should be subjected to long-needed reform.

This was given a considerable boost in October 2004 by the case of a family in Merseyside. The family wished to borrow £2000 for a small home improvement, but were persuaded by a loan company to take out £5750. They struggled to keep up repayments, and ended up owing £384,000. They were faced with a court action to take away their home. The judge ruled that that the 34.9 per cent interest rate on their arrears was "extortionate", and cancelled the debt. The National Consumer Council commented that the case highlighted the irresponsible practices of many lenders who targeted people in financial difficulty. It said that daytime television and tabloid newspapers were important vehicles for this kind of advertising.

New regulations (which had been announced in June 2004), came into effect shortly after this case. The new regulations make it an offence to conceal the true cost of a loan in small print. In addition, they make it easier for a consumer to compare offers, introduce a standard way of calculating the annual percentage rate (the APR), and require the APR to be more prominently displayed than all the other financial information. Tighter rules on advertising and marketing, improved methods of checking borrowers' ability to pay, and a fairer way of treating people who are in arrears are also to be introduced.

Useful websites

The Office of Fair Trading: *www.oft.gov.uk*

National Consumer Council: *www.ncc.org.uk*

SPECIMEN EXAMINATION QUESTIONS

1. Jane bought a raincoat for £30 from Arthur's shop. The first time she wore the coat, it let in the rain and the buttons fell off because the stitching was faulty. Ashley would not refund the cost of the coat, although he offered a credit note. Advise Jane of her rights under the Sale of Goods Act. Should she approach the manufacturer?

2. Richard is shown a sample of some oranges at the local shop and places an order to be delivered to his home. When they are delivered they are:

    (a) a different type of orange, and
    (b) are bad and unfit for consumption.

    Explain Richard's rights under the implied conditions of the Sale of Goods Act 1979.

3. Lady Penelope bought a 1950's Rolls Royce car at the auction rooms of Liverpool Car Sales Ltd (LCS). She was delighted with her purchase, especially as the car had been described by LCS as being "in excellent order, reliable, and with low mileage". When she got the car home, she was dismayed to find the engine was damaged beyond repair, and that the car had done 250 000 miles and not 50 000 as she had been led to believe.

    Lady Penelope has been advised that she may have a case against LCS in respect of the Rolls Royce, under the Sale of Goods Act 1979 as amended.

(i)   Briefly explain the legal basis of this advice and whether an action brought by Lady Penelope would be likely to succeed.   (4 marks)
(ii) Comment on how well consumers are protected by consumer law.   (4 marks)

Adapted from AQA June 2004, Higher Tier

TALKING POINT

How clear is the law which protects consumers? What can be done to improve the law for their benefit? Have you ever had any problems with faulty goods for which the seller refused to admit liability?

SUGGESTED COURSEWORK TITLES

Describe the legislation aimed at protecting the consumer against the supply of shoddy goods and services. Do you think that consumers receive adequate protection from the present law?

Explain the implied conditions in contracts for sale of goods. Are the current laws sufficient to protect consumers from badly made and dangerous goods?

8 | Contracts of Employment

An employment contract is created when an employee agrees to work for an employer. The same essentials for a valid contract which we encountered in Chapter 6 apply to a contract of employment. There are two kinds of contract where people are employed to do work: the *contract of service* and the *contract for services.* There are important differences between the two, and they should be carefully distinguished.

Contracts of service

A contract of service is the usual form of contract between an employer and an employee. It is sometimes referred to, rather anachronistically, as a *master-servant* relationship. In such contracts, the employee (the "servant") is part of the employer's (the "master's") business, and certain duties are owed by one party to the other. The employer has control over what work the employee should carry out, and also where, when and how it should be done.

Contracts for services

A contract for services is the employment of an *independent contractor*. An employer who engages an independent contractor says what is to be done, but not how it is to be done. The independent contractor has full control over how the work is carried out, not the person who employs him or her.

The difference between the two might well be summed up to the effect that in a contract of service the employee is part of the employer's business. In contract for services, the independent contractor is outside the employer's business. An example of a contract for services would be when you hire an electrician to rewire your house. You say what is to be done, but not how. It may well be that the electricians who come to do the work are employed in a firm of electricians under contracts of service, but that is quite separate from your contract for services with the firm.

THE NATURE OF THE CONTRACT

Freedom to negotiate terms

In most ordinary contracts, both parties have the freedom to negotiate or bargain for terms and conditions. The same is true of employment contracts up to a point, but there is rather less freedom than might be expected.

There are occasions when an employer will stipulate the wages and conditions of work, and the potential employee has to "take it or leave it". If the employee does not accept the terms, he or she will not be employed. This is particularly the case in times of high unemployment. In times of full employment and a shortage of labour, the situation may well be reversed.

On the other side, trade unions and other bodies have agreed conditions with employers' organisations. These have to be followed by both employer and employee, and in such cases neither may be able to bargain for different conditions and wages.

Legislation

In comparatively recent years, a new factor has intervened to erode the principle of freedom of contract. Successive Acts of Parliament have been passed to regulate contracts of employment. These acts have for the most part been aimed at protecting the employee, giving new rights, greater job security and encouraging collective bargaining.

In employment contracts, the curtailment of freedom of contract probably now works largely to the benefit of the employee. An employer may not be able to dictate terms and conditions, but have to accept what has been collectively agreed.

FORM OF CONTRACT

As with other contracts, contracts of employment may be by word of mouth. However, the Employment Rights Act 1996, ss. 1–3, provides that employees must receive a written statement from their employers within **two months** of starting work. This statement must contain matters such as:

- the names of the employee and employer and when the employment started;

- the rates of pay, method of calculating payment and when paid (weekly or monthly, etc.);

- details of working hours and overtime payments;

- holidays and sick pay;

- pension schemes;

- notice required by the employee and employer to end employment, and length of a fixed term contract;

- disciplinary rules as applied to the employee.

DUTIES OF AN EMPLOYER

The duties owed by an employer to his employees are governed by common law and statute. The most usual duties are explained below.

To pay wages as agreed

If the rate of pay was not agreed beforehand, the parties may look at external conditions to reach an agreed wage, such as union rates of pay, or the usual rate for the particular type of work.

All employees, whether manual or non-manual workers and regardless of the method of payment, are entitled to receive from their employers an itemised pay statement, in writing. The statement must show:

- the gross amount of wages or salary,

- any fixed deductions (trade union subscriptions, savings, etc.),

- variable deductions (taxes, pensions),

- the net payment and the method of payment (cash, cheque or paid into bank account).

The national minimum wage

As a result of the National Minimum Wage Act 1998, an employer must pay an employee "not less than the national minimum wage". This applies to workers who are ordinarily working in the United Kingdom and are over the compulsory school age.

The amount of the national minimum wage is laid down by the secretary of state for employment, and is subject to regular review.

To indemnify against liability and loss

An employee who is properly performing duties of employment is entitled to be indemnified by the employer against any loss or injury incurred. "Indemnified" means freed or exempted from liability (see under *Vicarious Liability* in Chapter 9).

To provide a safe system of work

The common law and many statutes place a duty on an employer to provide a safe place to work and safe appliances to work with.

The Health and Safety at Work, etc., Act 1974, for example, places a duty on every employer to ensure, so far as is reasonably practicable, the health, safety and welfare of all employees. It is a comprehensive Act, covering all places of work. It protects not only most workers, but also the public against risks arising out of the activities of people at work.

> In *Dexter v Tenby Electrical Accessories Ltd* (1990), an employee of an independant contractor, while working on the defendant's roof, fell through the roof which was unsafe and suffered injuries. The Health and Safety Executive charged the defendants with a contravention under the Factories Act 1961. The Divisional Court held that an occupier of factory premises has a duty to make the premises as safe as is reasonably practical for all persons who may work there, even if they are not his employees. If a person is ordered by his employer, an independant contractor, to work on a factory roof, the occupier of the factory is liable under the Act if the roof is in an unsafe condition.

There is a Health and Safety Commission and an Executive, which are responsible for the administration and implementation of the Act. Inspectors visit places of work and give advice on the requirements of the Act; failure to comply with the provisions may lead to severe penalties, including imprisonment.

The Working Time Regulations SI 1998/1833 came into force on October 1, 1998 and provides workers with the rights to such things as health assessment for night workers, rest breaks at work, and paid annual leave up to four weeks from November 1999. Workers over the minimum school age but younger than 18 have rights with regard to health assessment for night work and rest breaks at work.

References

An employer does not have a legal duty to give a reference for a former employee. If one is given, however, the employer may be subject to an action in the torts of negligence or defamation (see Chapter 9). See also the case of *Gallear v J F Watson Ltd* (1979). Whereas a false statement may be actionable, a statement of opinion critical of an employee's ability **made without malice** would not be. The reason for this is that the employer has a duty to other employers, and in the absence of spite or malice, the employer has *qualified privilege* (see *Defamation*, Chapter 9), and would not be liable.

The practice of giving references "To whom it may concern" is now declining, and being replaced by confidential references from the current employer to the prospective employer. In such circumstances, however, the previous employer owes a duty of care to the employee not to give an unfair or inaccurate reference.

> In *Spring v Guardian Assurance plc* (1994), the House of Lords held that an employer owes a duty of care, in respect of a past or present employee, when providing a reference to a prospective employer.

DUTIES OF AN EMPLOYEE

Obedience

An employee has a duty to obey lawful orders. The refusal to do so may justify immediate dismissal. An isolated act of disobedience may not warrant dismissal without notice, but it would depend on the circumstances of the case. For example, when a gardener refused to plant some flowers, which then died as a result, it was held to be grounds for instant dismissal.

To show good faith

The employer's interests

An employee has a duty to work in the best interests of the employer. The employee's interests must not conflict with those of the employer. A company's buyer, for example, should purchase goods on behalf of the employer on the best terms available. Any profit or bribe received by the buyer from a salesman as an inducement to buy goods on less favourable terms is legally the property of the employer. Failure to disclose the bribe gives the employer the right to dismiss the employee.

Confidential information

It is a duty of an employee not to disclose confidential information gained from the employment, if it will cause damage to the employer. Where, however, an employee discloses the employer's *illegal* activities, the courts would consider the duty to the public to be more important than the duty to the employer.

Disclosure of misconduct

It is generally considered that an employee does not have a duty to disclose his or her *own* misconduct or breach of contract. In the case of *Sybron Corporation v Rochem Ltd* (1983), however, the Court of Appeal held that an employee with certain standing and authority may have the duty to disclose misconduct by *other employees*, of whatever standing in the company's staffing hierarchy.

TERMINATION OF EMPLOYMENT

If a contract of employment has provided for the employment to be for a fixed period, the contract terminates at the end of that period. The contracts of professional cricketers or footballers are generally of this kind. However, these contracts often give both parties the option of renewing them for a further period.

With notice

The usual contract of employment is terminated by **either party giving notice**. The length of time varies, and may be stated at the commencement of employment. For example, teachers agree to give two or three months' notice on specified dates so that replacements may be appointed in time for the start of the next term. If the period is not agreed beforehand, a reasonable period of notice has to be given, taking into consideration the nature of employment. In the past, the courts have considered that reasonable notice for a newspaper editor was one year, and for a theatrical manager, six months.

The Employment Protection (Consolidation) Act 1978 as amended by the Employment Act 1982 provides that most employees are entitled to receive minimum periods of notice as follows:

- after four weeks' continuous service—one week,

- after two years' continuous service—two weeks, and

- for every additional year's service—one week, up to a maximum of 12 weeks.

An employee is required to give at least one week's notice if employed continuously for one month or more. This notice is unaffected by longer service.

Without notice

Termination by either party without notice ends the contract of employment, and gives the injured party the right to bring an action for damages. It should be noted that this applies to both employee and employer. If an employee leaves without notice, the employer may sue if it can be shown that he suffered damage as a result of the employee's illegal termination of the contract of employment. In practice this rarely happens and it is usually the employee who brings an action for dismissal without notice.

Summary dismissal without notice may be considered lawful if the employee breaks the terms of the contract of employment. The terms may be implied in respect of acts of disobedience, dishonesty, incompetence or misbehaviour. In *Denco Ltd v Joinson* (1991), the Court of Appeal held that an employee's unlawful use of a computer password was gross misconduct.

A dismissed employee who has been continuously employed for 26 weeks or more has the right to request from the employer a written statement giving particulars of the reasons for dismissal.

Constructive dismissal

Constructive dismissal occurs when the conduct of the employer leaves the employee with no option but to resign. Where such a situation occurs, it is deemed that the employer, because of unacceptable conduct, actually dismissed the employee despite the fact that it was the employee who walked out of the job.

Unfair dismissal and employees' rights

Comprehensive procedures to enable employees who have been unfairly dismissed to complain to an employment tribunal are provided by the Acts. The Acts apply to most employees who work full-time or part-time and who have worked for more than 52 weeks continuously.

The main provisions are as follows.

- The right to complain applies to dismissals with or without notice, and where the employee is forced to resign because of the employer's conduct.

- The employee must make a complaint of unfair dismissal within three months of the effective date of termination.

- The employee has the opportunity of choosing, should the complaint be successful, to continue working for the employer or receiving financial compensation. Financial compensation, when unfair dismissal is proved, usually consists of a basic award of a number of weeks' pay plus a compensatory award, which the tribunal considers just and equitable. There are limits to amounts awarded.

- The following may be considered fair reasons for dismissal:

  (i)   the lack of capacity of qualification of the employee to carry on working,
  (i)   redundancy,
  (iii) the employee's conduct,
  (iv) where the continued employment of the employee would be illegal, or in breach of a statutory duty or requirement,
  (v)   some other substantial reason justifying dismissal.

- The following are considered unfair reasons for dismissal:

  (i)   trade union membership or activity,
  (ii) pregnancy,
  (iii) industrial dispute, when other employees involved are not dismissed.

Redundancy

The 1978 Employment Act provides for the payment of "redundancy pay" for employees who are dismissed because there is no work to do. This would occur:

- where the employer has ceased or intends to cease business at a particular place; or

- where the need for the particular work of the employee is no longer required. An employee is entitled to redundancy pay if he/she:

- works under a contract of employment;

- has been employed continuously by this employer for at least two years;

> The Act originally provided that employees who worked for less than 16 hours per week had to be employed for five years to qualify. In *Equal Opportunities Commission v Secretary of State for Employment* (1994), the House of Lords held that the provisions which enabled full-time workers to qualify for redundancy and unfair dismissal payments in a shorter time than part-time workers was incompatible with the EC Treaty and Council Directives on equal pay and equal treatment.

(the effect of this ruling is that part-time workers need to work only for two years to qualify for redundancy or unfair dismissal payments); and

- if the employee has been actually or constructively dismissed because of redundancy.

Redundancy pay

The amount of redundancy pay a dismissed employee receives is calculated on the basis of continuous service, age and the gross average wage. For each year of service an employee:

- aged 18–21 would receive half a week's pay,
- aged 22–40 would receive one week's pay, and
- aged 41–64 would receive one and a half week's pay.

The "weekly wage" for calculating redundancy pay is limited to a fixed maximum sum, which may change from year to year. This means that employees earning a wage in excess of the limit would only have their redundancy pay calculated on this lower amount, not at their actual average weekly wage. In addition, the maximum number of years which is taken into the calculation is 20 years. It should be noted that many employers give redundancy payments well in excess of the statutory requirements.

Maternity and parental rights

All employees who are pregnant have the right to take 26 weeks' maternity leave. The dismissal or making redundant of a woman on maternity-related grounds is deemed to be unfair.

Parliament has also introduced the right of unpaid parental leave for any employee of one year's service or more. This applies to men as well as women, and is set at 13 weeks for each child for whom the employee has responsibility. This right should normally be exercised before the child's fifth birthday.

SEX DISCRIMINATION

The Sex Discrimination Act 1975

The Sex Discrimination Act 1975, as amended by the Sex Discrimination Act 1986 and the Employment Act 1989, makes it illegal (with certain exceptions), for employers to discriminate on the grounds of sex. The Act applies to most kinds of employers, professions, and training and employment agencies. It implements the principle of equal treatment for men and women with regard to access to employment, vocational training, promotion, social benefits and working conditions.

The Act does not apply in cases where a particular sex is necessary for the job. A man would be required to play Superman in a film. Conversely, a woman would be required to play Wonderwoman.

In *R. v Birmingham City Council* (1989), the House of Lords held that there was unlawful sex discrimination when the Council provided 542 grammar school places for boys and only 360 places for girls, as the number of boys and girls starting secondary education each year was roughly equal.

It should be noted that sex discrimination does not apply only to women. Redress is also available to men who have been discriminated against on the grounds of sex.

In *James* v *Eastleigh Borough Council* (1990), the plaintiff and his wife were both aged 61. The Council provided free leisure facilities to persons who were of State pensionable age, which meant that the plaintiff had to pay but his wife did not. The House of Lords considered that as the statutory pensionable ages were discriminatory, the Council's provisions were equally discriminatory.

In *Smith v Safeways plc* (1994), a male employee was dismissed because he refused to have his long hair cut shorter. It was held to be discriminatory to treat men and women differently with respect to hair length, and was inconsistent with the 1975 Act.

In *Meade-Hill and National Union of Civil Servants v British Council* (1996), the plaintiff, a married woman, had a mobility clause in her contract of employment which meant that the company could send her to work at a place away from her home locality. The Court of Appeal held that the mobility clause was an indirect sexual discrimination and was unenforceable, unless it could be seen to be justified irrespective of sex.

Equal pay

The **Equal Pay Act 1970** provides that women should receive the same pay and benefits as men for similar or equivalent work. If an employer is in default of this requirement, a woman has the right of action to sue for breach of contract.

RACE DISCRIMINATION

The Race Relations Act 1976 makes it illegal for employers to discriminate on grounds of race, colour or nationality. This Act covers most forms of discrimination as shown above in sex discrimination, and relates to housing, education, training, membership of professions, trade unions and the right to public services and facilities. With relation to employment it does not apply:

- in private homes,

- when the discrimination can be shown to be a genuine occupational qualification.

The Courts and Legal Services Act 1990 amended the Race Relations Act 1976 and the Sex Discrimination Act 1975, by prohibiting discrimination in the legal profession, so that no barrister is unreasonably refused training or pupillage. The Act also prohibits discrimination in the giving or withholding instructions to a barrister or advocate.

Complaints against racial discrimination in employment are brought before certain county courts, or the employment tribunal.

In addition, the Public Order Act 1986 makes it an offence for any person to use words, or behaviour, or display written material, or to perform a play, record, video or television, which is intended or is likely to stir up racial hatred.

Racial hatred means hatred against a group of persons in Great Britain by reference to colour, race, nationality, or ethnic or national origins.

DISABILITY DISCRIMINATION

The Disability Discrimination Act 1995, makes it unlawful for an employer to deal with a disabled person differently from other employees. Employers have a duty to make reasonable changes to enable disabled workers to carry out the work. They should take steps to ensure that disabled persons are not at a disadvantage, such as making suitable arrangements for recruitment and by seeking specialist advice on equipment and the physical planning of the premises to assist disabled workers. Employers who fail to do so, must show that their refusal is justified.

HARASSMENT

The Criminal Justice and Public Order Act 1994 created a new offence of harassment, which could be applied to employment disputes. It is possible that the employer and/or an employee who harasses another could be liable for criminal sanctions. Employers could issue a warning to their staff against harassment, and this would probably be used as a good defence.

Protection from harassment

The Protection from Harassment Act 1997 provides protection for people from harassment and similar conduct.

Section 1 provides that a person must not pursue a course of conduct which that person knows, or ought to know, amounts to harassment of another person. The section does not apply where the actions were to prevent or detect a crime, or in the circumstances the actions were reasonable.

Section 2 provides that a person guilty of this offence is liable on summary conviction to imprisonment, or a fine, or both.

Section 3 provides a civil remedy for the victim in the form of damages or an injunction for any anxiety or financial loss caused by the harassment.

SEXUAL ORIENTATION DISCRIMINATION

In January 2005 the first successful case concerning discrimination on the grounds of sexual orientation was brought before a tribunal in Stratford, east London. Mr Rob Whitfield was awarded compensation for constructive unfair dismissal, harassment and discrimination. Mr Whitfield, a manager, had been forced out of his job by a sustained homophobic campaign by fellow-managers. It was held that the firm he had worked for had failed to act to eradicate anti-gay harassment on the part of its employees.

Useful websites

Commission for Racial Equality: *www.cre.gov.uk*

Equal Opportunities Commission: *www.eoc.org.uk*

Employment Tribunals (Central Office): *www.employmenttribunals.gov.uk*

SPECIMEN EXAMINATION QUESTIONS

1. In the following situation explain which area of **civil** law is involved and the likely outcome of the situation, and name the likely **venue** for the hearing of the case.

    Catherine, an Afro-Caribbean, is employed by Dukes plc, a large company. She works in the Accounts Department. Catherine has worked there for about five years and has acquired higher-level accountancy qualifications in her time at Dukes. Catherine applied for a promotion, but the post was given to Edgar who has only been with the company for about two years and is less well qualified.   (6 marks)

    Adapted from AQA Higher Tier, June 2004

2. Shelley worked as a clerk in the office of a large company. After working for a year she discovered that a male member of staff, appointed at the same time, was receiving a larger salary and one week's holiday more then her. They were both carrying out similar duties, and Shelley asked the employers for the same conditions of service.

   (a)   What law is concerned regarding Shelley's complaint?
   (b)   Will the question of pay be dealt with differently from the holidays complaint?
   (c)   If Shelley's request is turned down, does she have any recourse to a tribunal?

TALKING POINT

Should men be entitled to paid paternity leave?

SUGGESTED COURSEWORK TITLES

Describe the law relating to sex discrimination and racial discrimination in employment and education. Do you think it fair? Make some suggestions to improve the situation.

Describe the law relating to dismissal, and explain the procedure that a employee may take who considers that the dismissal was unfair. Do you consider the law to be adequate in this matter?

9 | The Law of Torts

Whereas a crime is a wrong committed against the community, punishable by the state, a **tort** is a **civil wrong**. A tort is a wrong (not arising out of contract or breach of trust) for which an action for compensation or damages may be brought by one individual against another. An action in tort can also be brought by or against a group of individuals, or corporations. In a case in tort, the action is brought by the **claimant** against the **defendant**.

In a contract, the parties agree the terms beforehand. If the terms are breached, one can sue the other for damages or other compensation, as we saw in Chapter 6. In tort, there is no prior agreement between two individuals not to wrong each other. The law fixes certain duties which affect everyone. For example, road users have a duty not to act negligently towards others. A pedestrian who jay-walks and causes injury to a motor-cyclist will be liable to compensate the motor-cyclist for any injury suffered. Similarly, a car driver who negligently damages another car will be liable for the cost of the damage.

In the same way, the law of torts decrees that a person shall have a duty not to say untrue and damaging things about another (*defamation*). There is a duty not to interfere with another's enjoyment of land (*nuisance*), or *trespass* on someone's person or land. These and other duties will be discussed in the course of this chapter.

The usual remedy for tort is damages. With certain torts, however, other remedies such as injunctions may be necessary because damages would not be an adequate compensation.

Multiple liability

It should be noted that it is possible for a single event to be a crime, a tort and a breach of contract. For example, Matthew hires Nick to drive Kate to the local railway station. Nick exceeds the speed limit, crashes and injures Kate. Nick could be liable for:

- an action by Matthew for breach of contract;
- an action by Kate in the tort of negligence; and
- a criminal prosecution for dangerous driving.

Malice

When deciding whether an action amounts to a tort (is *tortious*), motive or intention is generally unimportant. A wrongful or malicious intention will not necessarily make a lawful act unlawful.

In *Bradford Corporation v Pickles* (1895), the Corporation obtained water from springs fed by undefined channels through Pickles' land. In order to coerce the Corporation to buy the land at a high price, Pickles sank a shaft which interfered with the flow of water. The plaintiffs sought an injunction to restrain Pickles from collecting the underground water, but the court held that the defendant had the right to draw water from his own land. The motive behind his act was irrelevant.

There are some torts, however, where malice, or an improper motive, is an essential element. There are others where it may be an important factor.

- **Malicious prosecution** is committed when, *out of spite*, a person brings an unjust criminal prosecution against another.

- **Injurious falsehood** occurs when a party makes a deliberate false statement about another with the intention of causing loss or damage.

- **Conspiracy** is when two or more persons conspire together to injure another person.

- In **defamation**, the presence of malice can defeat certain defences.

- In **nuisance**, malice might turn a reasonable use of one's property into an illegal one.

STRICT LIABILITY

Generally, a person is liable in tort when an action is done *intentionally* or *negligently*. In some cases however a person may be liable where there is no deliberate intent or negligence. The law in these cases has imposed a strict limit on a person's activities. If this limit is exceeded, the defendant is strictly or absolutely liable. The most common example of this kind of liability is known as the rule in **Rylands v Fletcher** (1868). The rule applies under the following circumstances.

- **A person brings on to his land for his own purpose some dangerous thing, which is not naturally there** (water, wild animals, gas, fire).

In *Emanuel v Greater London Council* (1971), a contractor for the Council lit a fire on the Council's land and negligently allowed sparks to fly on to the plaintiff's land which caused damage to buildings. The court held that the Council was strictly liable under the rule in *Rylands v Fletcher* for the escape of the fire.

- **The dangerous thing escapes from the land** (strict liability does not apply if the injury occurs on your own land).

> In *Read v Lyons & Co Ltd* (1947), Read was working in a munitions factory and was injured by an explosion in the factory. She did not claim negligence, but brought an action based on the rule in *Rylands v Fletcher*. The House of Lords held that the rule did not apply because there had not been an escape from the land of the thing which caused the injury.

- **Damage is caused**.

If these three events occur the occupier of land is liable for the damage caused, but the following defences may be used:

- the untoward event was caused by the act of a stranger;
- it was the claimant's own fault;
- it was an act of God;
- there was statutory authority.

> In *Cambridge Water Co Ltd v Eastern Counties Leather plc* (1994), the House of Lords considered that strict liability only applies if the damage caused by the escape is foreseeable. Therefore, strict liability for things likely to do mischief only arises if the defendant knew, or should reasonably have foreseen, that those things might cause damage if they escaped.

The Consumer Protection Act 1987, is an example of a statute creating strict liability for producers of defective goods which cause damage to person or property (see p. 185).

NEGLIGENCE

To succeed in an action for negligence, a claimant must prove the following:

- that the defendant owed the claimant a **legal duty of care**;
- that there was a **breach** of that duty, and
- that the claimant suffered **damage** as a result of that breach.

Duty of care owed to the claimant

The following case is of considerable importance in the development of the principle of a duty of care (note that the Consumer Protection Act 1987 now provides for the strict liability of a producer of defective goods which cause damage to the consumer).

> In *Donoghue v Stevenson* (1932), the claimant was served with ginger beer in an opaque bottle. Having consumed some of it, she found that the bottle contained the remains of a decomposed snail. She was ill. The House of Lords held that the manufacturer of goods is liable if the goods are used by a consumer without an intermediate examination. The manufacturer owes the consumer a duty of care.

Probably the most important principle to emerge from the judgment came in the definition of Lord Atkin, of who is owed a duty of care. "You must take reasonable care to avoid acts or omissions which you can reasonably foresee would be likely to injure your neighbour". My neighbours are " . . . persons who are so directly affected by my act that I ought reasonably to have them in contemplation . . ."

The neighbour principle and "reasonable foreseeability" have been used in many different situations. For example, a duty of care has been held to be owed to:

- a lady locked in a public toilet (see p. 215);

- wearers of underpants who caught dermatitis from a chemical in the material (see p. 182);

- persons living in the neighbourhood of an open borstal;

- an opponent in a football game (see p. 236);

- a fireman attending a fire (see p. 237).

To succeed in an action for negligence a claimant must show that a duty of care was owed by the defendant.

- In *Bourhill v Young* (1943), a motor-cyclist crashed and was fatally injured. A pregnant fishwife, who was 15 yards away, later looked at the scene of the accident and the sight of the blood caused shock and, subsequently, a miscarriage. The House of Lords held that the lady was not owed a duty of care because it could not reasonably be foreseen that the accident would cause her to suffer such injuries.

- In *Smith v Littlewoods Organisation Ltd* (1987), vandals started a fire on the defendant's empty, derelict property, which also caused damage to the plaintiff's property. The House of Lords considered that as a general rule there was no duty of care to prevent a third party from causing damage to the plaintiff's property.

- In *Spring v Guardian Assurance plc* (1994), the House of Lords held that an employer owes a duty of care to a past or present employee, when providing a reference to a prospective future employer. The court considered the case should be dealt with under negligence, not defamation.

- In *King v Phillips* (1953) the Court of Appeal held that a mother was not owed a duty of care, when, after hearing her child scream and seeing the child's tricycle under a taxi, she suffered shock. In fact the child was not hurt.

- The defendant might be liable if aware that the plaintiff was nearby. In *Boardman v Sanderson* (1964) the defendant negligently backed his car and injured the plaintiff's son. The plaintiff, who was nearby, heard his son's screams and suffered shock. It was held that the plaintiff could recover damages because the defendant was aware the plaintiff was nearby and the consequence of the accident was reasonably foreseeable.

- In *Cotton v Derbyshire Dales DC* (1994) the Court of Appeal held that there is no duty of care upon the owner of a path, which was close to an **obviously** dangerous cliff, to erect a notice warning that the cliffs are dangerous.

In *Caparo Industries plc v Dickman* (1990), it was expressed that there are three separate steps to be considered in cases where a duty of care is an issue.

- *Proximity*.
  Are the parties near enough to each other for a duty of care to be created? A child playing in a driveway while a car was being driven out of a garage, for example, would be an obvious case of proximity.

- *Foreseeability of the damage*.
  Is there sufficient evidence that damage would likely be caused by the negligent act?

- *Would such a duty of care be just and reasonable*?
  For example, a duty of care was not owed to a serviceman by another serviceman in war conditions (*Mulcahy v Minister of Defence* (1996)).

Nervous shock

In *McLoughlin v O'Brian* (1983), a mother visited a hospital to see her husband and daughters, injured in a serious road accident, and as a result of what she saw and the account she heard from witnesses, she suffered severe nervous shock. The House of Lords held that although distance and time were factors to be considered they were not legal restrictions. The plaintiff was entitled to damages for nervous shock, even though she was not present at the accident, because it was a reasonably foreseeable consequence of the defendant's negligence.

The decision in *McLoughlin v O'Brian* has been followed by a spate of similar cases, particularly in the aftermath of the Hillsborough disaster where many spectators' lives were ost at a football match. In *Alcock v Chief Constable of South Yorkshire Police* (1991), after the judgement in *McLaughlin v O'Brian*, the House of Lords considered the following points.

- Other than in exceptional circumstances, only those within a parent/spouse relationship may obtain damages for nervous shock sustained. The exceptional circumstances would be relationships which could show the same criteria of love, affection and care, such as a fiancée or grandparent. These would be decided on a case by case basis.

- As a general rule, watching television is not generally regarded as the same as being present at the scene or its immediate aftermath, but simultaneous television may in certain circumstances be the equivalent as being within the sight and hearing of the event. In this case the House of Lords considered the position of ten claimants who had lost relatives at Hillsborough. The majority had witnessed the scenes on television. The claimants' appeals were dismissed because they did not have:

(i)   the close relationship required; or
(ii) had viewed the scenes on television, which did not show the suffering of any recognisable individual.

It was considered that relatives who attended the mortuary for the purpose of identification at least eight hours after the incident, were outside the immediate aftermath of the disaster.

This decision was followed in *McFarlane v E.E. Caledonia* (1994), where it was held that a mere bystander witnessing a disaster cannot claim damages for psychiatric harm unless able to show (i) sufficient degree of proximity to the place and (ii) a close relationship of love and affection with the victims or victim.

In the case of *Frost v Chief Constable of South Yorkshire Police* (1997), police officers, who endured long exposure to the horrific scenes at the Hillsborough disaster while acting as rescuers to the victims, later suffered mental injuries. It was held that they were owed a duty of care by their employers.

A breach of duty

Defendants will be in breach of duty if they have not acted reasonably. The standard of care varies with each situation, but as a general rule, the standard of care is that of a reasonable person who uses ordinary care and skill.

The courts will consider the risk involved. In *Paris v Stepney Borough Council* (1951), the plaintiff had only one eye and the defendants employed him on work that involved a certain risk to the eyes, although not sufficient to warrant ordinary workers to wear goggles.

Paris was blinded as a result of his work and the court held that the defendants were in breach of their duty to that particular worker.

A professional person must use the skill expected of the profession. In *Carmarthenshire CC v Lewis* (1955) a teacher was dressing young children before taking them out, when a four-year-old under her control left the school premises and ran into the road. A lorry driver was killed when swerving to avoid the child. The court held that the teacher was not negligent, but the county council had been negligent in allowing a situation to arise in which the child could leave the school.

As a matter of public policy, a duty of care is not owed by a participant in a crime to a partner in that crime.

In *Ashton v Turner and Another* (1980) the plaintiff and defendants had been drinking together and the second defendant allowed Turner to drive his car without insurance. Ashton and Turner later committed burglary and when driving away from the crime had an accident which injured Ashton (the passenger). Turner pleaded guilty to dangerous driving and driving while drunk. Ashton claimed damages against both defendants and the court held that as a matter of public policy the plaintiff was not owed a duty of care when injured during the commission of a crime. The court also held that Turner could successfully plead the defence of *volenti non fit injuria* (see p. 235).

In *Hill v Chief Constable of West Yorkshire* (1988), the mother of the last victim of the "Yorkshire Ripper" (Peter Sutcliffe) brought an action against the defendants, claiming negligence in failing to catch the killer before her daughter's murder. The House of Lords held that the police do not owe a duty of care to an individual member of the public in respect of an attack by a criminal.

However, in *Kirkham v Chief Constable of Greater Manchester Police* (1990), the Court of Appeal held that the defendant was in breach of a duty of care and awarded damages when the police did not pass information to the prison authorities that the plaintiff's husband had suicidal tendencies. Her husband was consequently treated as a normal prisoner and placed in a cell alone, where he hanged himself.

> In *White v Jones* (1995), solicitors delayed preparation of a new will by more than two months. The testator died before the will was prepared and the intended beneficiaries under the new will sued for the loss of their legacies. The House of Lords confirmed that the solicitors were in breach of a duty of care, as their negligence deprived the plaintiffs of their intended legacies under the new will.

Damage has been suffered

Although a claimant must prove damage, not all damage is actionable if it is too remote. The general rule is that a defendant is only liable for damages that a "reasonable man" should foresee.

> In *The Wagon Mound Case* (1961), oil was negligently spilt from a ship and floated across Sydney Harbour to a ship repairers, where sparks ignited the oil and caused damage to the wharf and to a ship. At that time it was not foreseeable that the oil would be set alight and cause the damage. The Judicial Committee of the Privy Council held that there was no liability.

This decision was followed in *Doughty v Turner Manufacturing Co* (1964). The claimant was injured when a fellow worker dropped an asbestos cement cover into molten liquid. An explosion followed and the claimant was injured. It was discovered later that a chemical reaction would be caused by the cement and molten liquid. The Court of Appeal held that the accident was unforeseeable and the defendants were not liable.

It is important to stress that the claimant must suffer damage. A person cannot be sued for negligence *purely* on the grounds of a negligent act. The negligent act must result in injury to the claimant's person or property.

Res ipsa loquitur (the facts speak for themselves)

As a general rule the burden of proof in an action for negligence is on the claimant. That is to say, it is for the claimant to prove that the defendant was negligent. There are however cases where, on the face of it, the act or omission seems to be so *obviously* negligent, that the burden of proof shifts to the defendant. In cases like this, it is for the defendant to try to prove that he or she was not negligent. This rule, known by the Latin phrase *res ipsa loquitur*, has been applied where:

- bags of sugar fell on the plaintiff from an upper floor of a warehouse (*Scott v London & St Katherine Docks Co* (1865))

- swabs were left in a patient after an operation. (*Mahon v Osborne* (1939))

- a customer slipped on yoghurt which had spilled on to the floor of a supermarket. (*Ward v Tesco Stores Ltd* (1976))

The application of the rule does not automatically mean that the defendant was negligent, but it is presumed that the act or omission was negligent, unless it can be shown otherwise.

In *Pearson v NW Gas Board* (1968), a gas explosion killed the plaintiff's husband and destroyed her home. The court applied the rule, but the defendants were able to show that severe frost caused the gas leak and, as there was no reasonable way in which the explosion could have been prevented, they were not negligent.

In *Widdowson v Newport Meat Corp* (1997), the claimant was injured in a road accident, and did not offer any evidence, relying on *res ipsa loquitur*. The defendant claimed there was no case to answer and gave no evidence. The court gave judgement for the claimant. The defendant appealed, and it was held that where the judge is unable to discover what actually happened, and where the defendant cannot explain what actually happened, *res ipsa loquitur* must apply.

Contributory negligence

The Law Reform (Contributory Negligence) Act 1945 as amended by the Civil Liability (Contribution) Act 1978 provides for situations where damage is caused partly by the claimant and partly by the defendant. In such cases, the injured party will be able to claim damages, but there will be a reduction in the amount recoverable. The amount is reduced to the extent that the court considers *just and equitable*, having regard to the claimant's responsibility for the damage. The court awards damages, and then reduces them by the percentage the claimant is considered to be responsible.

In *Capps v Miller* (1989), the plaintiff, a motor-cyclist, received head injuries as a result of the defendant's negligent driving. The plaintiff's crash helmet, which was unfastened, fell off before his head hit the road. The Court of Appeal held that although the sole responsibility of the accident lay with the defendant, the plaintiff's failure to secure his helmet had contributed to the injury. The Court held that the plaintiff's damages be reduced by 10 per cent.

It was also considered that the reduction would have been greater if a helmet had not been worn at all.

In *Sayers v Harlow UDC* (1958), the plaintiff entered a public toilet and, because of a faulty lock, could not open the door to get out. She was due to catch a bus, so in order to climb over the door she stepped on to the toilet-roll, slipped, and injured herself. The court held the defendants to be negligent, and although the plaintiff had acted reasonably in attempting to release herself, she had contributed to the injury by stepping on a revolving toilet-roll. The damages were reduced by 25 per cent.

In *Armstrong v Cottrell* (1993) a girl aged 12 ran into a busy road and was injured by a passing vehicle. The court considered that she was old enough to take care when crossing a road and her damages were reduced by 30 per cent.

It is generally considered that a young child is never guilty of contributory negligence.

Occupiers' liability for dangerous premises

The Occupiers' Liability Act 1957 provides that

* the **occupier** of premises, or
* the **landlord**, if responsible for repairs to the premises,
* has a **common duty of care** to see that
* all **lawful visitors** will be **reasonably safe** while visiting the premises.

Lawful visitors

A lawful visitor is a person who is expressly invited onto another person's property. The term also includes those who are impliedly invited, such as a milkman, postman or paper boy. People who enter premises under a contract, such as spectators at a rugby match, or rock concert, are also lawful visitors. Persons using a right of way, whether public or private, are not "lawful visitors" within the meaning of this Act. They have limited protection provided by the Occupier's Liability Act 1984 (see below for the 1984 Act, which deals with liability for visitors outside the scope of the 1957 Act).

The standard of care

The standard of care varies according to the visitor. Obviously the care shown for a child must be greater than for an adult. A notice "danger" would be of little use to a young child who could not read. Some dangers on premises may actually allure or attract children. In the case of allurements the occupier must take greater care to protect children. Occupiers have been held responsible for injuries to children caused by a railway turntable, red berries on trees, building sites, railway trucks, and threshing machines.

An occupier may not be liable for injuries to a very young child if it could be expected that the child would be accompanied by parents or other responsible persons.

Defences

In addition to the general defences available in tort (see later in this chapter), the occupier may show any of the following factors.

* Adequate notices or warnings of the danger were given (*e.g.* a "wet paint" sign or "dangerous cliff" notice).

In *Cotton v Derbyshire Dales DC* (1994) (see p. 211) it was held that the obligation of landowners to visitors "does not include an obligation of protection against dangers which are obvious".

---

* With visitors under contract, liability was excluded. For example it is usual for exclusion notices to be displayed at most sporting events, but it should be noted that the Unfair Contract Terms Act 1977 may limit exclusion clauses to a test of reasonableness (see p. 189).

* The injury was caused by the negligence of a competent independent contractor. For example, the occupier would escape liability if electrical fittings, erected by a qualified electrician, fell on a visitor. The occupier would be liable, however, if the fittings had been erected by a gardener. Independent contractors may be liable if they leave premises in a dangerous state and lawful visitors are injured as a result.

A.C. Billings & Sons Ltd v Riden (1958). Building contractors had to remove a ramp from the front of a house. Mrs. Riden left the house after dark and fell into a sunken area and suffered injury. It was held that the contractors were negligent as they had not taken reasonable care to ensure that visitors were not exposed to dangerous premises.

---

* The person injured was a trespasser and not a lawful visitor. The occupier is liable for trespassers for intentional dangers such as man-traps, and for injuries caused when all that a humane person should have done for the safety of a trespasser had not been done.

British Railways Board v Herrington (1972). A child trespasser was electrocuted and severely injured on the defendant's land. The fence guarding the line was broken. The House of Lords considered that there was a high degree of danger and as the defendants were aware of the possibility of such a trespass, and could easily have repaired the fence, they had not acted humanely and were liable.

The Occupiers' Liability Act 1984

This Act is concerned with the liability of occupiers towards people on their land who are not lawfully there. Such people are trespassers, and are outside the scope of the 1957 Act. The aim of the 1984 Act was to resolve doubts which followed the case of *British Railways Board v Herrington*, described above.

The duty of an occupier under the 1984 Act

Under this Act, an occupier has a duty to persons other than lawful visitors. This duty is owed in respect of any injury suffered on the occupier's premises because of some danger. The danger may be due to the state of the premises, or something done on them, or omitted to be done.

The duty is owed by an occupier who:

- is aware of the danger, or has reasonable grounds to believe that it exists,

- knows or has reasonable grounds to believe that there are others in the area where the danger is, or may come into that area, and

- the risk being such, may reasonably be expected to offer the other persons some protection.

There is only liability in respect of personal injury. There is no liability in respect of loss or damage to another person's property.

The duty is to take such care as is reasonable to see that others are not injured because of the danger on the premises. If warning of the danger is given, this duty will be discharged. The same is true when people are discouraged by the occupier from taking a risk. No duty is owed by the occupier to persons who willingly accept the risk.

> In *Revill v Newbery* (1995), the defendant slept in a shed in his allotment to protect valuable items stored in the shed. The plaintiff attempted to break into the shed and the defendant loaded his shotgun and fired through a small hole in the door, wounding the plaintiff. The plaintiff pleaded guilty to an offence and the defendant was aquitted of wounding. The plaintiff brought a civil action for negligence and a breach of duty of care owed to a trespasser under section 1 of the 1984 Act. The Court of Appeal held that under section 1, the duty of care owed to a trespasser was to take such care as was reasonable to see that the trespasser did not suffer injuries on the premises, even if he was on a criminal act. The plaintiff was awarded damages but the court found that he was liable for substantial contributory negligence.

Section 2 of the Act deals with visitors using premises for recreational or educational purposes. Occupiers of business premises may exempt themselves from provisions of the Unfair Contract Terms Act 1977, where access is granted for purposes not connected with the business. For example, a farmer allowing a football team to play on a field normally used for pasture.

SPECIMEN EXAMINATION QUESTION

William, a small boy, regularly uses the right of way across college grounds as a shortcut into town. He noticed some boys of his age playing football on the all-weather pitch, and joined them by climbing through a hole in the fence. The pitch had been closed to students because it was dangerous and notices saying "DANGER—KEEP OUT" had been erected on the fence. William fell on the pitch and broke his leg.

(i)   Identify the tort William could be committing when he leaves the right of way.

(1 mark)

(ii) Briefly discuss the legal effect of the notices erected by the college.   (2 marks)

(iii) Discuss whether an action in tort against the college, on behalf of William, could be successful.   (4 marks)

AQA Higher Tier, Summer 2001

TRESPASS

Trespass is probably the oldest tort, and many other torts owe their origin to the writ of trespass, which has been described as the "mother of actions". There are three forms of trespass:

* trespass to the person,
* trespass to chattels (goods), and
* trespass to land.

Each of these three forms of trespass is actionable *per se* ("by itself"). This means that a claimant does not have to show that the defendant caused any damage.

Trespass to the person

There are three separate actions in this tort. They are:

* assault,
* battery, and
* false imprisonment.

Assault

This tort is actionable when a person threatens or attempts physically to injure another, and the other person has reasonable fear that the threat will be carried out. Words are not sufficient by themselves, they must be accompanied by actions. If a person a hundred metres away shouted an abusive threat it would probably not be assault, because there would be no fear of immediate danger and no action to indicate an attack. However, if a knife or fist was raised close to a face, this would be assault as there would be good reason to be in fear of a physical attack.

Although words by themselves cannot constitute an assault, they can remove the fear of an attack. If for example a person raised a fist to strike another, but then said, "Because it's your birthday today, I won't hit you", the words would have the effect of removing the fear of being hit. There would therefore be no assault.

Battery

Battery takes place when an act goes beyond a threat, and a person is actually touched. Many instances of battery will take the form of a physical attack such as a punch or a kick. However, it should be noted that *any unauthorised touching* is actionable, regardless of its force or motive. Even a kiss, given with love and affection, is actionable if the recipient does not authorise it. It is unauthorised and intentional bodily contact, and a person may claim damages if he or she did not (for example), stand voluntarily under the mistletoe and accept the kiss.

In battery the attacker does not always have physically to touch the other person. An injury could be caused indirectly, such as by throwing a stone.

Assault and battery are usually joined in one action, and both are also criminal offences. Conviction in a criminal court may be used as evidence when claiming a remedy in a civil action.

In *Halford v Brookes* (1991), for the first time in English law a person was found liable in a civil court in respect of a murder for which he had not been prosecuted (see p. 238 for details).

False imprisonment

This tort is committed when a person's liberty is totally restrained by the intentional, but unjust, act of another. The imprisonment must be for an unreasonable length of time and be total. If a person has reasonable means of leaving the premises it is not actionable.

In *Bird v Jones* (1845) the public footpath over Hammersmith Bridge was closed. The plaintiff climbed over a fence and was stopped by the defendant from proceeding further along the footpath. The court held that it was not false imprisonment as the plaintiff could have left the bridge by the way he entered.

In *John Lewis & Co Ltd v Tims* (1952) Mrs Tims and her daughter were suspected of stealing and were kept in an office, against their will, until the store manager was informed. The House of Lords held that, as the detention had not been for an unreasonable period of time, there had not been false imprisonment.

A person may have a right of action even though he did not know at the time that he had been locked in a room while he slept (*Meering v Grahame-White Aviation Co* (1919)).

Specific defences to trespass to the person

• *Parental or quasi-parental authority*. Parents or guardians may use reasonable force to chastise or imprison children. A similar authority may be given to others who take the place of parents (*quasi* means "as if"). A teacher, therefore, would not be liable for keeping pupils in school after lessons provided good reason could be shown.

• *Self defence*. The force used must be reasonable, regarding the facts of the case. It may not be a good defence to shoot an attacker dead if the person was unarmed. In *Lane v Holloway* (1968), the plaintiff aged 64 hit a 24-year-old man on the shoulder, and in return received a blow to the eye which necessitated 19 stitches and a month in hospital. It was held that the blow received by the older man was out of all proportion to the provocation (the defendant had also been found guilty in the criminal courts.)

Further consideration of self defence will be found in the discussion of general defences to criminal offences in Chapter 10.

• *Statutory or judicial authority*. For example, lawful arrest by a police officer.

Trespass to chattels (goods)

Chattels are items of tangible moveable property, such as personal possessions (pens, books, desks, cars, records, etc., and money and cheques, etc.).

This tort is committed when a person

• intentionally interferes with goods in the possession of another, or

• carries out an unjustifiable act which denies a person of the legal right to possess the goods.

The merest touch of the goods without causing damage is sufficient, and it is not necessary for the defendant to disposses the goods.

Kirk v Gregory (1876). In order to place another person's jewellery in a safe place, the defendant removed the goods from one room to another. The jewellery was later stolen by an unknown party and the defendant was held liable in trespass to goods.

The tort may also be committed without touching the goods, *e.g.* opening a farm gate and driving cows or horses out of a field.

Possession is the basis of this tort, as it is the lawful possessor of the goods, not necessarily the owner, who may bring an action. For example, a hirer of a car, not the owner, would sue for damages from the defendant who had taken possession of the car.

Most actions under this tort are brought for the intentional dispossession of the possessor's rights to the goods.

Conversion arises when the defendant intentionally interferes with goods in a way that may be regarded as denying the plaintiff's rights of possession or use. If, for example, a car subject to a hire-purchase agreement is sold to a private person, the seller has given the buyer a good title (see p. 188) and denied the hire-purchase company the right of ownership of the car. The hire-purchase company could sue the seller for conversion. The usual remedies for conversion are damages and injunction.

Torts (Interference with Goods) Act 1977

Section 1 of this Act defines "wrongful interference with goods" to mean:

- conversion of goods,

- trespass to goods,

- negligence and other torts in so far as they result in damage to goods or interests in goods.

Uncollected Goods

If you take goods to a shop to be mended, repaired, cleaned, etc., you are the *bailor* and the trader is the *bailee*. After the goods have been mended, you have a duty to pay for, and collect your goods. The trader has a duty to return the goods. The situation often arises when you (the bailor) do not collect your goods.

Section 12 of this Act sets down the rights of the trader (the bailee) and the procedure to follow. In cases where the bailor has not collected the goods, the bailee has a right in certain circumstances to write to the bailor in a prescribed manner, giving notice of an intention to sell. If the goods have not been collected within the period stated in the notice, the bailee may sell the goods.

Trespass to land

This tort may be defined as

- the intentional entering onto another person's land without lawful permission, or

- remaining on the land after permission has been withdrawn.

The entering or interference with the land must be direct. Rubbish dumped on to another's land would be trespass, but if the rubbish was blown on to the land by gales, it would not be trespass because it was not the direct action of the defendant which caused the interference.

An invasion of air space may be a trespass of land, even though the land is not touched. The courts have held in *Kelsen v Imperial Tobacco Co* (1957) that a sign erected on a building, but which protruded over another person's land was trespass, as it was in *Woollerton and Wilson v Costain* (1970), where a crane swung over another person's land. In *Bernstein v Skyviews and General Ltd* (1978) it was held that an aircraft which took an aerial photograph would not be trespassing if it was at a height which did not affect the use of land.

Trespass is essentially a civil wrong, and a mere trespasser is not generally liable for criminal proceedings. The familiar sign "trespassers will be prosecuted" has therefore no legal effect, except in relation to certain government undertakings where an act of Parliament has provided for a fine for trespassing. See also Chapter 5, under *Public Order Restrictions*.

Specific defences to trespass to land

It is a defence to claim that entry on to land was justifiable. The following reasons may be used as a defence to show that entry was made:

- by leave or licence granted by the occupier of the land,
- by authority of law (such as a bailiff),
- involuntarily (such as landing in a parachute),
- where the highway was impassable, and
- to retake and retain possession of one's own property.

Remedies available to the claimant are:

- damages: if no real injury has been incurred the damages awarded may be nominal (*i.e.* 1p);
- injunction: this may be used to stop the defendant from repeating the trespass;
- forcible ejection: the occupier may only use reasonable force to move the trespasser after first requesting him to leave and giving him reasonable time to do so.

NUISANCE

There are two forms of nuisance which have quite different meanings and little in common. They are:

- public nuisance, and
- private nuisance.

Public Nuisance

This wrong arises when

- acts or omissions have caused annoyance, inconvenience or danger
- to a class or part of the general public.

Public nuisance includes such things as obstructing the public highway, throwing fireworks on to the road, smoke from chimneys causing damage to cars parked on the highway and quarry blasting which projects stones and dust on to the surrounding neighbourhood.

The crime of public nuisance

It should be noted that public nuisance is a crime. The offender is prosecuted, usually by the Attorney General.

In *R. v Shorrock* (1993), the defendant let a field on his farm for a weekend for £2,000. He did not know for what purpose the field was let and he went away for the weekend. The field was used for an "acid house party" which was attended by more than 3,000 people and created a great deal of noise. The police received nearly 300 complaints.

He was convicted of causing a public nuisance and fined. It was held by the Court of Appeal that it was not necessary for the Crown to prove that he had actual knowledge of the nuisance, merely that he was responsible for the nuisance as he ought to have known that there was a real risk that the consequences in letting the field would create this sort of nuisance.

In *R. v Johnson* (1996), the accused had made obscene telephone calls on several occasions to many different women. On appeal he argued that each separate call was an individual act and therefore could not be a criminal public nuisance. The Court held that his actions had reasonably affected a class of Her Majesty's subjects and, as the calls were so wide and random, it was not reasonable for the women to start individual proceedings.

Suing in tort

Although, as we have seen, public nuisance is a crime, it is possible for an individual to sue in tort. This happens when a person has suffered *special damage of a different kind* from that of the general public. An example might be where, in the case of blasting, an entire neighbourhood is covered in dust, but one individual is hit by falling stones.

Private nuisance

This tort is

- the unreasonable interference with the claimant's enjoyment or use of his or her land, or

- the disturbance of some legal interest over the land.

An example of interference with the enjoyment of land would be playing music very loudly in the middle of the night so that your neighbour's sleep is disturbed. Blocking your neighbour's access from the road to his house would be to disturb his legal right of way.

Unreasonable interference

The following factors have to be considered when establishing whether or not a nuisance exists.

Reasonableness

It is a good defence to claim the act was a reasonable use of one's own property. The courts take an attitude of "live and let live". What is reasonable is based on the conduct of the "ordinary man."

Sensitiveness

An act which would not disturb a normal person will not be a nuisance just because the claimant, or his property, is unduly sensitive.

> In *Robinson v Kilvert* (1884) the plaintiff stored brown paper in the defendant's premises. The heat from the defendant's boiler damaged the paper, which was extremely sensitive to heat. The court held the defendant was not liable in nuisance.

Locality

"What would be a nuisance in Belgrave Square would not necessarily be so in Bermondsey" said a judge in 1879. He was making the point that it is necessary to apply different standards to different areas. Thus it is possible that noise from a club in the city centre may be reasonable, but would be unreasonable in a residential area and would be a nuisance.

Continuity

The general rule is that a **single** event is not a nuisance and the plaintiff must show that there was some degree of **repetition** of the offending act.

> In *Bolton v Stone* (1950), a ball was hit out of a cricket ground and injured a lady. It was shown that a ball had been hit out of the ground only six times in 35 years. The court held that this was not often enough to be a nuisance.

Malice

The intention behind an act may be relevant in deciding whether a person's act was reasonable or not.

To shout, shriek, whistle and bang trays may be a reasonable use of your own property, but if it is done with the express purpose of spoiling your neighbour's musical evening, it may be a nuisance, because the acts would not be reasonable (*Christie v Davey* (1893)).

The parties to an action

The occupier of property has the right to bring an action but any other person injured on the property has no claim in nuisance. The person liable in an action for nuisance is likewise the occupier of the property from which the nuisance emanated.

In *Malone v Laskey* (1907), the plaintiff, the wife of a tenant was injured when a bracket on a lavatory cistern fell on her. The defendants who leased the property owned a generator which vibrated and caused the bracket to fall. The plaintiff sued in nuisance but the court held that, as she was only the wife of the tenant and not the tenant, she had no interest in the land. The House of Lords upheld this decision in *Hunter v Canary Wharf Ltd* (1997) and maintained that the only persons who could sue in private nuisance are those with an interest in the land.

Remedies

The usual remedies granted by the courts in an action for nuisance are **damages** and an **injunction**.

In *Kennaway v Thompson* (1981), the plaintiff lived near a lake used for motor boat racing. She was awarded damages by the High Court for nuisance already suffered and damages for future nuisance. The Court of Appeal varied the award and in the place of damages for future suffering, substituted an injunction which restricted the number of races that the defendants could hold.

With regard to the remedy of injunction, it must be stressed that it is awarded at the discretion of the court.

In *Miller v Jackson* (1977), the defendants, a cricket club, had played on a village ground since 1905. The plaintiffs, in 1972, moved into a house that adjoined the ground. A ball was hit into their house causing damage, and while a game was in progress there was always the danger of personal injury. The plaintiffs sought an injunction to restrain the club from playing cricket on the ground, as it interfered with their enjoyment of the land. It was held by the Court of Appeal that the interests of the public should prevail over the plaintiffs' individual suffering. The public had watched cricket for 70 years and their interest had to be guarded. The injunction was not granted.

There is a remedy which is available without recourse to the law. This is called **abatement**, and is available when the nuisance can be brought to an end without entering another person's land. It could be applied to overhanging trees or roots, for example, but it should be noted that any branches which are cut away still belong to the owner of the tree. If it is not possible to end the nuisance without entering the other person's land, permission must be first obtained unless there is immediate danger to person or property.

Statutory nuisance is noise from premises which causes a nuisance. In such incidents the local authority can issue an "abatement" notice requiring the noise to stop and to prohibit it from happening again. If this is ignored, fines of up to £5,000 can be made (£20,000 if the noise comes from commercial premises).

The Noise Act 1996 only affects districts where the Act has been adopted by the local authority. In these districts the local authority must inquire into any complaint that householders are being disturbed at night by excessive noise from a dwelling house, during the hours of 11.00pm until 7.00am The authority must issue a "warning notice" to the person responsible. If the warning is not heeded the guilty person is liable for a fine.

Defences

Statutory authority

It is a complete defence that a nuisance was expressly authorised by an Act of Parliament. However, in *Wheeler v J.J. Saunders* (1995), the defendant had planning permission for two pig weaning houses and contended that the smell emanating from the pigs could not be considered a nuisance. The Court of Appeal held that, although the nuisance originally came from the granting of the planning permission, this did not, in this case, provide immunity from liability for nuisance.

Prescription

When a nuisance has been in continuous existence for not less than 20 years, the right to carry on the act may be acquired.

Reasonable use of one's own property

That the damage caused was minute or minimal

N.B. It cannot be pleaded as a defence to an action in nuisance that the claimant came to it from elsewhere (See *Sturgess v Bridgman* (1879)).

Nuisance and trespass to land

These torts are sometimes confused. However, nuisance differs from trespass to land in two important respects.

- In nuisance, the interference must be **indirect**. The smell of a garden compost heap would be a nuisance to your neighbour; the throwing of garden rubbish onto your neighbour's garden would be trespass.

In *Esso Petroleum v Southport Corporation* (1956), a tanker ran aground and had to discharge its cargo at sea. The oil was carried by the tide and wind to the foreshore. The Court of Appeal held that the Corporation's action could not succeed in trespass, as the damage was not caused by the direct act of the defendants, but by the indirect act of the wind and tide.

- Trespass is actionable *per se*, whereas nuisance is only actionable by proof of special damage.

LIABILITY OF PARENTS FOR THE TORTS OF CHILDREN

It is a general rule that parents are not liable for the torts of their children. A parent will be liable, however, if he or she is negligent in allowing his or her child to be in a position to commit a tort.

In *Bebee v Sales* (1916), a father gave his 15-year-old son a shotgun, and the father was held to be liable when the son injured another boy.

However, the parent is not negligent if he has taken steps to lessen the risk of injury, as was the case in *Donaldson v McNiven* (1952). A father showed his son how to use an air-rifle, warned him of the dangers and told him not to use it outside the house. The father was held not to be liable when his son injured another child.

DEFAMATION

Defamation occurs when

- a false statement, made orally, in writing or by gestures
- is published to a third party, and
- attacks someone's reputation.

The statement, to be defamatory, must **lower a person in the estimation of right-thinking members of society**.

Although there is the public interest of freedom of speech, the tort of defamation protects an individual's private interest in his reputation. Two points from the definition must be noted.

The statement must be published to a third party

It is not defamation if the statement is published only to the claimant. It would be defamation if a third party heard the defamatory words, even by accident. Each time a defamatory statement is repeated, it is actionable even if the maker does not know the statement is defamatory. So, if Ellie made a statement to Jim about David, Jim would be liable (as would Ellie) if he repeated the statement to any other person.

Post cards are deemed to be published, even if the postal authorities have not actually read them.

The statement must lower the claimant's reputation in the minds of right-thinking members of society

A bank robber would not be liable for defamation if he informed other thieves that one of the gang had served a prison sentence for theft. This is because the gang would not disapprove, and they are not held to be right-thinking members of society.

In *Byrne v Deane* (1937) a golf club had some illegal gaming machines which the police removed. A verse was placed on the notice board, which inferred that Byrne had informed the police ("May he Byrne in hell and rue the day"). Byrne sued, but it was held that he had not been defamed, because right-thinking members of society would have approved of a person informing the police of an illegal practice.

In another case it was held that to depict a person as "hideous looking" was not libel, because it did not affect the person's reputation.

In addition to showing that the statement was defamatory and published to a third party, a claimant must prove that the third party understood that the statement referred to the claimant. It is for the judge to decide if the statement is likely to be understood as referring to the claimant and for the jury (if there is one) to decide if the third party actually did so.

Not all defamatory statements are actionable.

Consider the following statements and decide whether or not they are defamatory.

- "All students in class 1A cheated in their examination". (There were six students in the class.)

- "Half of the Maths 'A' level class (four students) cheated in the examination".

- "One or two of the law students (60 students) cheated in the examination".

The first statement would be defamatory because the class is small enough for all students to consider that they have been individually defamed.

The second statement would also be defamatory because, although it referred to only half of the class, it is small enough for any of the class to bring an action.

The last statement would not give a law student a right to sue because the class is too large for any one person to claim that it referred to him or her.

Innuendo

A statement may be defamatory **by implication**, even though the words are not defamatory in their ordinary sense, if it can be shown that another person's reputation has been affected.

> In *Cassidy v Daily Mirror Papers Ltd* (1929), the newspaper published a photograph of the plaintiff's husband and another lady, and the caption announced the engagement of the couple. The plaintiff alleged that the words implied that she had lived with the man without being married, and the court held that the picture and caption would lead a reasonable person to that conclusion.

It should be noted, however, that only a person defamed by innuendo may bring an action. If, for example, a student magazine wrongly stated a brother and sister to be illegitimate children (or words to that effect), the named persons would not be able to sue the editor, because they have not been defamed. Their parents would be able to sue, because the statement implies that they are not married.

Libel and Slander

Libel

This is defamation **in a permanent form**. It can be in writing, or broadcasting on radio or television. It could be in the form of a painting or cartoon, or on film, CD, DVD, video or audio tape. The placing of a wax figure of a person near similar figures of convicted murderers in a "chamber of horrors" was considered to be libel, in the case of *Monson v Tussauds Ltd* (1894)

Libel is actionable *per se*, which means that the claimant does not have to show that special damage was suffered.

Libel may also be a crime, if it tends to provoke a breach of the peace

Slander

This is defamation in a non-permanent form, such as by spoken words, or gestures.

Unlike libel, slander is not actionable *per se*, and a claimant must prove special damage. However, there are exceptions to this, and some slanderous statements are actionable without proof of special damage. They are those which:

- impute that a person has committed a crime punishable by imprisonment, or
- impute that a person is suffering from an infectious disease (for example, leprosy or AIDS), or
- impute the unchastity of a woman, or
- impute against the claimant in respect of his or her office, profession, calling, trade or business.

Defences

Justification

It is a defence to show that the statement was completely or substantially true. Defamation must be a false statement, and a true statement which damaged a person's reputation would not be actionable.

Fair comment on a matter of public interest

People in public life, such as politicians, film stars, TV personalities, footballers and so on, receive praise and adulation. They must also accept criticism. Provided that comments about them concern their public activities, and are not made spitefully or with malice, they are not actionable.

The Human Rights Act 1998

In recent years there have been several cases brought under the Human Rights Act 1998. The conflict between the right to privacy and the right to free expression was discussed in Chapter 5. It will be touched upon again later in this chapter.

Absolute privilege

The following carry complete protection from actions for defamation, regardless of the truth or motive behind the statement.

- *Parliamentary proceedings*
  This means any statement made by a Member of Parliament in either House, and officially authorised reports on parliamentary proceedings.

- *Judicial proceedings*
  This includes all statements made in court by judge, jury, counsel, witnesses, etc.

- *Statements between solicitor or barrister and client*

- *State communications*

- *Statements between husband and wife*

Qualified privilege

The following carry similar protection to absolute privilege, unless it can be shown that the maker of the statement acted from malice, such as an improper motive or out of spite.

- *Reports on Parliamentary and judicial proceedings*
  This covers newspaper and broadcasting reports and would also include reports on the proceedings of other public and international organisations (*e.g.* the United Nations).

- *Statements made to protect an interest*
  The interest may be to the benefit of the maker of the statement, the recipient or both, but the maker of the statement must have a duty, legal, moral or social, to protect the interest. An example would be a company director reporting to the chairman of the company about the misbehaviour of an employee.

The "Reynolds" defence

This version of the defence of qualified privilege emerged from the case when the former Irish Taoiseach, Albert Reynolds, sued the *Sunday Times* for libel in 1999. This case held that the media may have a defence to a defamation action even when stories are wrong or unprovable. It must be shown that they acted responsibly and in good faith. The reasoning behind this defence is that newspapers have a duty to communicate important information even if it cannot be proved. Having done all it can to authenticate its sources, a newspaper leaves its readers to form their own views.

The "Reynolds defence" failed, however, when the *Sun* newspaper was sued for libel by the former Liverpool goalkeeper Bruce Grobbelaar. Nevertheless it was reaffirmed in *Louchansky v Times Newspapers* (2001), only to be defeated again in *Galloway v Telegraph Newspapers* (2004). In this case, the MP George Galloway sued the *Daily Telegraph* for libel over allegations, based on disputed Iraqi documents found after the war, that the claimant had been in the secret pay of the dictator Saddam Hussein. Galloway was awarded the substantial sum of £150,000 in damages. This case is also of interest in that it was heard before a judge alone, without a jury.

Apology and amends

A newspaper or periodical may offer this defence if it can show that the libel was published without malice or gross negligence. An **apology** is published, and a sum of money is paid into court before the case is started. This payment is the **amends**. The Defamation Act 1952 provides that in the case of unintentional defamation, apology and amends is a good defence.

Apology and amends is only a defence for defamatory statements in newspapers, periodicals and the like. However, it might serve to reduce damages if offered by a private person.

The Defamation Act 1996 provides that a publisher of a defamatory statement may make an *offer* in writing to make amends by publishing *a correction* and *an apology*. The injured party would also be paid compensation. If the offer is accepted, the injured party may not continue the action. The Act also reduces the time limit within which an action may be taken to one year.

Responsibility for publication

The Defamation Act 1996 provides that a person has a defence if it can be shown that he or she:

- was not the author, editor or publisher of the statement complained of;
- took reasonable care in its publication; and
- had no reason to believe that his or her actions contributed to the publication of a defamatory statement.

Remedies

Damages are the usual remedy in defamation cases, and are awarded by the jury. Should a jury award excessive damages they may be set aside by the Court of Appeal and the claimant could be involved with the expense of a retrial. In *Sutcliffe v Pressdram Ltd* (1990), in an action against the satirical magazine *Private Eye*, the Court of Appeal considered the award to the plaintiff of £600,000 to be excessive and ordered a retrial on the question of damages only. The court was also of the opinion that in appropriate cases the judge should warn the jury of the consequences of an excessive award. The amount was subsequently reduced to £60,000.

In *John v MGN* (1996), the House of Lords, when assessing compensatory damages, declared that the jury could be referred to the scales used in personal injury cases, as well as early libel awards. As a result, the award of damages to Elton John was reduced from £350,000 to £125,000.

Defamation and the Human Rights Act 1998

As has been discussed earlier, in Chapter 5, a potential conflict exists between the right to privacy (Article 8) and the right to free expression (Article 10).

The law of defamation protects people from untrue and damaging statements being made about them. Whereas we have seen that newspapers, periodicals and the like have a duty not to be libellous, they do feel it their duty (and profit) to keep the public informed about the activities of those who enjoy a high public profile. These publications would consider such stories about film stars, footballers and so on, to be matters of public interest, and therefore fair comment. High-profile personalities set themselves up, and so, the argument goes, are considered to be "fair game".

On the other hand, even the most well-known people feel that they have a right to a certain degree of privacy. There is no privacy law as such in this country, as there is in others (like France), but recent cases show that such a law may now exist in all but name. Details of some of these cases, which were brought under the Human Rights Act, were covered in Chapter 5.

This is an area of law where there may well be further developments.

Legal aid in defamation cases

As we saw in Chapter 2, except in very exceptional cases, legal aid is not available in defamation cases. As a result of the case of *Steel and Morris v United Kingdom* (2005), heard before the European Court of Human Rights in Strasbourg, this situation may well change.

In the original trial the fast-food chain McDonald's had sued Steel and Morris for libel. The defendants had distributed pamphlets headed *What's wrong with McDonald's?* which alleged that McDonald's indulged in various unethical practises. Helen Steel and David Morris were penniless environmental campaigners, and because of the unavailability of legal aid, had to conduct their case themselves against an experienced and expensive team of barristers and solicitors acting for the claimants. Heard in the High Court between June 1994 and December 1996, it was the longest trial in English legal history, lasting 313 court days. The judge (sitting alone without a jury), found in favour of the claimants. He did however accept that some of the allegedly defamatory statements were true. The damages of £60,000 were later reduced to £40,000 by the Court of Appeal. The defendants refused to pay.

Steel and Morris subsequently took their case to Strasbourg, maintaining that as they had been denied legal aid, they had not had a fair trial, in contravention of Article 6 of the European Convention on Human Rights. There had also been a disproportionate interference with their right of freedom of expression, under Article 10. The court found unanimously in their favour on both counts. It awarded £13,750 to Ms Steel and £10,300 to Mr Morris.

VICARIOUS LIABILITY

This is the liability of a person for a tort committed not by him or her, but by someone else. This situation mainly arises in relationships between employer and employee ("master and servant" relationships).

The reasoning behind the liability of an employer for the tort of an employee is:

- to prevent an employer from hiring an employee to commit a tort;

- to encourage an employer to install and maintain safe systems of operation;

- as a general rule, an employer is in a better financial position to pay compensation to injured parties.

Employers are only liable for torts committed by employees **in the course of their employment**.

In *Lloyd v Grace, Smith & Co* (1912), L. asked the defendants, a firm of solicitors, for advice. All the negotiations were with a managing clerk and he persuaded L. to sign documents which conveyed property to him. The property was sold by the clerk and he kept the money. It was held that the firm was liable because the clerk was employed to give advice and convey property although in this case he did it for his own benefit.

An employer is liable if the employee commits a tort in the course of his employment, even though the latter performs his duty in a manner expressly forbidden by the employer.

In *Limpus v London General Omnibus Co* (1862) the defendants had expressly warned their drivers not to race against buses of another company. One of their drivers injured a third party while racing his bus and the court held that he was acting within the course of his employment.

A "frolic of his own"

An employer is not liable if an employee goes off on what is known as "a frolic of his own". This engaging but archaic term simply refers to an occasion when an employee leaves the duties of his or her employment to follow some personal pursuit. An example might be when a driver on his delivery round makes a detour to visit his girlfriend, and damages another vehicle while parking.

Unauthorised activities

If an employer, in the course of employment, does something for which he or she has no authority, the employer will not be liable.

> In *Beard v London General Omnibus* (1900) the conductor drove a bus and injured the plaintiff. The court held that the employer was not liable because the conductor was not acting within the scope of his employment.

In *Trotman v North Yorkshire County Council* (1998), a teacher was charged that, on a school holiday abroad, he committed sexual assaults on some children. It was held that the Council was not vicariously liable for the actions of the teacher, because his actions could not be described as an unauthorised way of carrying out a normal teacher's function. His actions were not in the course of his employment.

An employer will be liable, however, when the employee carries out an authorised task in an incorrect way, as in *Bayley v Manchester Sheffield and Lincolnshire Ry* (1873). A porter thought a passenger was on the wrong train and pulled the person off the train, causing him injuries. The company was liable because the porter acted within the scope of his employment.

In *Harrison v Michelin Tyre Co Ltd* (1985) S, an employee, whose duties included pushing a truck within a passage marked by chalk lines, deliberately moved the truck outside the lines as a practical joke and the plaintiff was injured. The plaintiff sued the company, arguing that S's negligence was within the course of his employment. The company contended that S was "on a frolic of his own". The court held that S's act could reasonably be regarded as incidental to the performance of his employment, regardless that the company had not authorised or condoned it. The company, therefore, was vicariously liable.

Independent contractors and vicarious liability

Employees must be distinguished from independent contractors. Employees are under the control of their employers, who tell them what to do and how it shall be done. Independent contractors, on the other hand, are hired to perform specific tasks, and choose their own methods of doing the work. An example would be that of a painter employed to paint your house.

People who employ independent contractors are not generally liable for torts committed by them, except in any of the following situations.

- They were expressly hired to commit a tort.
- In *Alcock v Wraith* (1991), the work involved a special risk of damage to an adjoining property, and the employer was liable for damage caused by the independent contractor.
- The work is bound to create a dangerous situation.
- The work obstructs the highway, thereby creating a public nuisance.
- The employer delegates a duty imposed by statute or common law.

GENERAL DEFENCES IN TORT

General defences must be distinguished from **specific** defences. As we have seen, specific defences apply only to particular torts. The defence of qualified privilege, for example, applies only to the tort of defamation. Prescription may only be a defence in an action for nuisance.

In many cases, the defence may be a straightforward denial of the alleged facts, as in a criminal case. There are general defences, however, which may apply to most actions in tort.

Statutory authority

An Act of Parliament may grant indemnity (no liability) for a particular act. In such a case, damages cannot be claimed unless the statute provides for compensation to be paid.

Consent *(volenti non fit injuria)*

The phrase *volenti non fit injuria* means literally "no injury is done to one who consents". In other words, where there is consent, there are no grounds to complain that an injury has taken place. As we have seen, the tort of battery involves physical contact, or touching, however slight. Clearly, when we visit the hairdresser, or dentist, we give our consent to inevitable physical contact and even a degree of discomfort. A rugby player consents to battery every time he plays for his club or takes part in a training session.

Consent may be express or implied. In the case of a medical operation, consent is expressly given by the signing of a form. In the case of the rugby player mentioned above, consent is usually implied (assumed to exist).

Volenti may also be a defence for a claim in negligence. There are many cases where an injured party has agreed to accept the risk of a breach of duty involved in an activity. Sport is an obvious example. Most sporting activities contain an element of risk, and it is common practice for organisers to make it a condition that spectators enter the ground at their own risk (next time you go to a football or cricket match, look for the notice as you enter the ground). In such cases, consent is expressly given.

Implied consent in sporting activities

It is usually implied that participants in sport have consented to the risk of injury. Most sports carry with them some risk of injury; it is part of the game It is generally accepted that participants have agreed to run the risk and therefore cannot bring an action for damages. However, in recent years the courts have recognised claims for serious injuries which happen on sports fields.

In *Condon v Basi* (1985), the defendant was found to be negligent when he broke the plaintiff's leg in a football match. The tackle had been executed in "a reckless and dangerous manner", although not with malicious intent. The Court of Appeal held that all players owed a general duty of care, but what was reasonable depended on the particular circumstances of each case.

In *Smalden v Whitworth* (1996), a young rugby player was seriously injured when a scrum collapsed. The referee was held to be liable because of the known dangers when a scrum collapses, and it was his duty to ensure that this did not happen. The player, who was 17 at the time of the incident, received a large out-of-court settlement from the Rugby Football Union.

In *McCord v Swansea* (1997), the court held that a deliberate foul in a football match which injured the plaintiff was negligent. This case was followed by *Watson v Gray* (1998), where the court awarded damages when the plaintiff's leg was broken by an unusually high tackle.

Knowledge of risk does not always imply consent

We have seen in the previous section that consent is usually implied when a sportsman (for example), knows that there may be a risk of injury. However, knowledge of the existence of a risk does not *necessarily* imply consent. If a worker knows that a crane passes dangerously overhead, he has not consented to the danger. If injured by a falling stone, he may sue for damages (*Smith v Baker & Sons* (1891)).

It is considered that, if a person has an alternative to riding with the drunk, the defence of *volenti* would be accepted, because the plaintiff has agreed to take the risk, rather than accept the alternative.

In *Dann v Hamilton* (1939), a young lady accepted a lift from a driver whom she knew had been drinking, and, as a result of his negligence, she was injured. The driver was not drunk when the outing began but became drunk later when it was difficult for the plaintiff to extricate herself. The court held that, although she knew of the risk, she had not consented to the driver's negligence.

In *Morris v Murray* (1990), Morris and Murray had been drinking together, during which time Murray had drunk the equivalent of 17 whiskies. Murray suggested that they should go for a joy-ride in his light aircraft. The plaintiff drove them to the airfield and assisted in the preparation for the take-off. Soon after take-off the plane crashed and Murray, who was the pilot, was killed. Morris was injured and sued Murray's estate. The Court of Appeal held that a passenger who agrees to travel in an aircraft when he knows the pilot is very drunk, has accepted the obvious risk of injury and has impliedly waived the right to claim damages for personal injuries caused by the pilot's negligence.

Trespass to goods

> In *Arthur v Anker* (1995), the plaintiff parked his car in a private car park. He saw that there was a notice which read "unauthorised cars will be clamped", and that there was a release charge of £40. His car was later clamped, and he claimed damages for wrongful interference with his vehicle. Arthur's action failed because, as he had read the notice, he had expressly consented to the defendant's action.

Rescue cases

A person might be hurt while attempting to rescue someone, or save property from damage. In that case the would-be rescuer may wish to sue the person who created the dangerous situation. The defendant in these circumstances might plead that the claimant (the rescuer) consented to the risk of injury while attempting the rescue. This defence may succeed *if there was no immediate danger to others*, as the courts may consider that the injured party did consent to take the risk. This is illustrated by the case of *Cutler v United Dairies Ltd* (1933). Cutler was injured while trying to stop a runaway horse on a quiet country road. It was held that he had consented to the risk.

> The claimant will not be a volunteer, however, if there was danger to others or if the claimant acted under a moral or legal duty, as in *Haynes v Harwood* (1935). A police officer was injured when he tried to stop a horse that had bolted in a town and was an immediate danger to women and children. It was held that, although the plaintiff knew of the danger, he had acted under a duty and had not consented to the risk.

In *Baker v T.E. Hopkins & Son Ltd* (1959), a similar decision was made, when a doctor went down a well to help men overcome by fumes. The doctor died as a result of the fumes and the court held that the defendants who created the dangerous situation were liable.

In a more recent case, *Ogwo v Taylor* (1988), the defendant negligently set fire to the roof of his house and a fireman was injured while attempting to put out a fire. The House of Lords considered that as the defendant had negligently caused the fire, it was reasonably foreseeable that a fireman would be at risk and, therefore, the defendant would be liable.

Inevitable accident

It is a good defence to show that the injury was caused by an accident which could not have been prevented through forethought or by taking ordinary precautions.

> In *Stanley v Powell* (1891) the plaintiff was injured during a shooting party when a pellet glanced off a tree. It was held that the defendant was not liable as his act was neither intentional nor negligent.

Necessity

It may be a defence to show that the damage was caused in trying to prevent a greater evil.

> In *Cope v Sharpe* (1912), fire broke out on the plaintiff's land and the defendant, who was a gamekeeper, set fire to other parts of the plaintiff's land with the intention of preventing the fire from spreading to his employer's land, where there were pheasants. The fire was extinguished by other means and the plaintiff sued for damages. The court held that the defendant had carried out a reasonably necessary act and was not liable.

Applying medical treatment in an emergency to a person unable to give consent, could come under this defence.

Act of God

This is an act of nature which could not have been reasonably foreseen.

> In *Nichols v Marsland* (1876), the defendant owned an artificial lake which overflowed as a result of a thunderstorm and caused damage to the plaintiff's land. The court held the defendant was not liable as the damage was caused by an act of God.

Lapse of time

Although not technically a defence, a defendant may claim that the claimant's right of action is "statute barred". If after a specified period of time an action has not started the right of action is no longer enforceable. The Limitation Act 1980 provides that the right to bring an action in tort will expire after the following periods:

- generally, six years from the date when the cause of the claim arose;

- three years in cases for claims of personal injuries and in cases where both personal injuries and damage to property are claimed.

The period of time usually runs from the date when the accident, libel, assault, etc. occurs, although section 33 of the Limitation Act 1980 gives the courts power to ignore, or disapply, these periods if it appears to the court that it is equitable to do so.

In *Halford v Brookes* (1991) the Court of Appeal exercised this discretion. The plaintiff's daughter was murdered in 1978 and the second defendant was tried and acquitted of the murder, after accusing the first defendant of committing the crime. In 1985 the plaintiff was informed that a civil action might be brought in the tort of battery, and in 1987 a writ was issued against the defendants. The defendants alleged that the claim was statute barred as the cause of the action arose more than three years before the issue of the writ. In considering the discretion under section 33, the Court of Appeal held that the plaintiff did not know her legal rights until 1985 and had acted promptly from then on. Any prejudice to the plaintiff in preventing an action far outweighed any prejudice to the defendants in disapplying the limitation period. This was the first case in English legal history of a civil court upholding a claim against an alleged murderer who had not been convicted of the crime.

Self defence

An individual may use such reasonable force as is necessary to protect person, family or property. Such force may also be used to prevent the entry of, or to eject, a trespasser from one's land.

The force used must be reasonable in the circumstances. In *Cresswell v Sirl* (1948), the defendant shot the plaintiff's dog, which he considered was to attack the livestock. The court held that it was reasonable to assume that the shooting was necessary and was a good defence.

Act of State

No action may be brought against the Crown or against servants of the Crown for any acts within their duties.

Illegality

It is a defence to prove that the claimant had acted illegally. A claimant can not succeed in an action if it is necessary to depend on his own illegal acts or is contrary to public policy. If, for example, in attempting to open a safe, a burglar negligently passed explosives to his accomplice which causes an injury, his partner would have no cause of action.

Useful websites

For cases in the law of tort: *www.lawreports.co.uk/index.htm and www.courtservice.gov.uk*

For statutes concerning tort: *www.hmso.gov.uk/acts*

SPECIMEN EXAMINATION QUESTIONS

1. The problem

Nigel was employed by Ogden's plc as a delivery driver between Ogden's factory in Birmingham and various retail outlets in Manchester. Nigel's job therefore was spent driving in and around and between these two cities. One day Nigel was driving on the M6 between Birmingham and Manchester and was involved in a collision with a car driven by Paul. Nigel was tired from too little sleep the night before and fell asleep at the wheel, drifting into the fast lane of the motorway. Paul was driving at over 100 mph and was therefore unable to prevent the collision.

On a separate occasion Nigel, having finished his deliveries early in Manchester, was driving during work hours in Sheffield in Ogden's van. Nigel had decided to drive over to Sheffield to watch his football team. Whilst driving in Sheffield, Nigel was involved in a minor collision with Queenie, a pedestrian. The accident was entirely Nigel's fault because he was rushing to the match so as not to miss the kick-off.

(a) Paul is considering suing in the tort of negligence.
     Explain what he will have to prove in court in order to succeed in this action.

                                                                            (8 marks)

(b) Paul's solicitor has advised him that, although the case is likely to be successful, full damages may **not** be awarded by the judge.
     Explain why this may be so.   (4 marks)

(c) In the context of a negligence case, explain what is meant by the term *res ipsa loquitur*, and its legal significance.   (4 marks)

(d) (i) Queenie is also considering suing for negligence.
          Advise Queenie whether she should be suing Nigel or Ogden's plc.

     (ii) What advice would you give to Paul in answer to the same question?   (6 marks)

(e) Identify any **other two** possible legal implications of Nigel's actions and the two incidents in the problem.   (2 marks)

                                                         AQA Higher Tier, Summer 2003

2. The problem

Quentin is a well-respected politician with a prominent position in his party. He has a reputation for being honest and straightforward and has in the past been associated with the promotion of family values. His wife Rachel is a solicitor who has been involved in a number of well-publicised cases. Quentin and Rachel have three children, the oldest of whom, Stephen, is 17 years old.

Rachel has recently been professionally involved in a property deal to purchase a holiday home abroad. Unfortunately, the client, whom Rachel has never met, is a drug dealer.

This fact has been discovered by Terry, a journalist working for a tabloid newspaper, the *Planet*.

Armed with this story, Terry decides to investigate further. He has discovered that Stephen was arrested by the police for being drunk and disorderly, but was not charged following an intervention by his parents.

In addition, Terry has heard rumours that Quentin has been having an affair with a female MP, Veronica, and that they were seen leaving a hotel together late one evening. In fact, the rumours are completely untrue and Quentin and Veronica were leaving the hotel following a perfectly proper political meeting.

The *Planet* has now published what it promises to be the first of a series of stories about Quentin and his family. The published story directly accuses Rachel of being involved with a drug dealer and hints about further revelations concerning Quentin's secret love life. The story also ridicules Quentin's views on family values, using Stephen's night out as the basis of the story.

(a) There are **two** types of defamation, libel and slander. Explain the differences between them.   (4 marks)

(b) Rachel is considering suing Terry and the *Planet* for defamation.

    (i)   Explain to her what she will have to prove.   (6 marks)
    (ii) Briefly explain why Rachel would be more likely to sue the newspaper rather than sue Terry, and state the legal basis of the newspaper's liability.   (2 marks)

(c) Quentin believes that he may have been defamed by **innuendo**. Explain what is meant by this term, and why Quentin thinks he may have been defamed in this way.

                                                                            (4 marks)

(d) Explain, in outline, how the Human Rights Act 1998 could be relevant in this case, especially in relation to the allegation involving Stephen and his parents.   (4 marks)

(e) Identify and explain any of the special defences to defamation that the *Planet* may wish to plead.   (4 marks)

                                                                         AQA Higher Tier, Summer 2004

TALKING POINT

Is it time for a new statute clearly setting out the law relating to privacy?

SUGGESTED COURSEWORK TITLES

Distinguish between criminal and tortious liability. As some torts are also criminal acts, is there any justification for considering them separately?

Explain the law of libel. What balance do you think should there be between the amount of damages awarded in defamation cases, and those awarded for personal injury in negligence cases?

10 | Criminal Law

DEFINITION

There are as many definitions of crime as there are books on criminal law. The reason for this is that it is difficult to attach a definition to something which has so many different aspects. Crimes vary from parking offences to murder; from theft of a chocolate bar to treason; from bigamy to blackmail and so on. From this brief selection it is possible to see their great variety, and how widely they differ in seriousness.

In Chapter 1, criminal law was classified as **public law**. This is because a crime is an offence against the state and is punished by the state. A definition of a crime therefore might be that

- it is an offence against the public at large (even though only one person might be affected), and

- the person who committed it (by positive act or omission of a legal duty) will be punished in some manner laid down by the state.

In a case before the House of Lords, *Board of Trade v Owen* (1957), Lord Tucker quoted this definition from *Halsbury's Laws of England*:

"A crime is an unlawful act or default which is an offence against the public and renders the person guilty of the act or default liable to legal punishment".

CLASSIFICATION OF OFFENCES

Crimes can be classified in several different ways. A common way of classifying crimes is that based on the method of trial for particular offences. Crimes can also be categorised according to whether they are arrestable or non-arrestable. Arrestable offences are those defined in Chapter 3.

Method of trial

In order to establish the method of trial, offences are classed as:

Indictable offences

These are serious offences, triable by judge and jury, for which a Bill of Indictment sets out the charges alleged to have been committed by the person(s) sent to the Crown Court for the trial. They include such crimes as murder, rape and robbery.

Summary offences

These are the less serious offences, and are always tried in the magistrates' courts. They include such offences as common assault, minor acts of criminal damage, and a wide range of motoring offences.

Offences which are triable either way

These are offences which may be tried either summarily or on indictment. They comprise a wide variety of offences, and include theft, burglary and assault causing actual bodily harm.

Power to arrest

A classification of offences was introduced by the Criminal Law Act 1967, which is important with respect to the power to arrest without a warrant (see Chapter 3).

Arrestable offences

These are offences established by The Criminal Law Act 1967, ". . . for which the sentence is fixed by law or for which a person (not previously convicted) may . . . be sentenced to imprisonment for a term of five years". The Police and Criminal Evidence Act 1984 extended the list by including certain offences under Customs and Excise law, Official Secrets Act, Sexual Offences Act, Theft Acts and offences of corruption in office. This classification is important in that arrestable offences are subject to the power to arrest without a warrant.

Non-arrestable offences

Although this class is not defined by the Act, it relates to all other offences which are not arrestable offences.

Other ways of classifying crimes

There are other ways of classifying crimes.

- According to their nature: for example crimes against the person, crimes against property, motoring offences, and so on.

- According to their origin or source, for example whether they are statutory or common law offences.

- According to whether they are incomplete *(inchoate)* crimes such as attempts, incitement or conspiracies, or actually carried out (are *substantive*).

ELEMENTS OF A CRIME

As a general rule, in order that a person be found guilty of a crime, two elements must be shown to be present:

- A **wrongful act** (or omission) which amounts to a crime. This is called the *actus reus*.
- The **intention** to do the wrongful act, knowing it to be a crime. This is known as the *mens rea*.

In most crimes therefore, there must be both a physical element, the wrongful act, or *actus reus*, and a mental element, the guilty mind or intention, the *mens rea*. If one or other of the elements is missing in a situation where both must be proved, there is no crime.

There are some crimes however where it is sufficient merely to commit the wrongful act or omission. In such crimes it is not necessary to prove the intention to commit them. They are known as **crimes of strict or absolute liability** (see below).

Mens rea

Mens rea means **guilty mind**, or **wrongful intention**. Of course it differs from crime to crime. The wrongful intention of a person committing theft is quite different from that of a person committing treason. With certain exceptions (see below), to be criminally liable, a person must have *intended* to do wrong. Alternatively, that person must have acted in such a reckless and negligent way that a reasonable person must have realised that a crime would inevitably be committed.

What constitutes the *mens rea* for a particular crime will be explained when each crime is dealt with in the course of this chapter.

Crimes of strict or absolute liability

Certain offences have **strict or absolute liability**, and *mens rea* is not essential. For example, the Health and Safety at Work, etc., Act provides that certain machines must have safety covers, and if these covers are not fixed, the employers are strictly liable. In one case, the employers asked an outside contractor to supervise the safety regulations but the employers were still liable when the contractors did not comply with the statutory requirements. Strict liability arises when the crime consists of performing a forbidden act or not performing a statutory duty (the *actus reus*); the wrongful intention (the *mens rea*) is irrelevant here.

In *Meah v Roberts* (1977) two children were served with glasses of caustic soda instead of lemonade. Meah was found guilty of selling food unfit for human consumption, contrary to the Food and Drugs Act 1955, even though another person was responsible for the cleaning fluid being in the lemonade bottle.

When interpreting statutes, there is a general presumption that *mens rea* is necessary in all crimes. This rule can only be replaced if an Act of Parliament expressly or impliedly excludes the necessity of *mens rea* (*Sweet v Parsley* (1970)).

Actus reus

This element includes all the circumstances relating to a crime other that the *mens rea*. It is the wrongful conduct which results in the commission of a crime. It can be an act, such as punching someone in the face, or a failure to act, such as not taxing your car. The act must be unlawful, and (usually) voluntary. Thus in theft, for example, the *actus reus* (put simply) is taking over someone else's property unlawfully, and the *mens rea* is the dishonesty involved in the taking and the intention never to return it.

SPECIFIC CRIMES

Unlawful Homicide

Homicide is the killing of one human being by another, and may not always be unlawful. To kill as a means of lawful self-defence is not unlawful homicide and is not a crime. During a war, a soldier is not acting unlawfully when he kills the enemy: as the traditional phrase has it, that enemy is not "under the Queen's peace".

Murder

Murder can be defined as the **unlawful killing** of a human being **with malice aforethought**. The *actus reus* (the wrongful act) of murder is of course the killing of another person. This normally does not present too many problems, except perhaps in the case of a body never being found. "Malice aforethought" is the *mens rea* of murder, the guilty mind, or wrongful intention. This is more difficult to prove, as it is not always easy to appreciate what goes on in the mind of another person.

For murder to occur, the victim must be *in being*, that is, a living human being with an independent existence. Thus to kill a child while it is still in the womb would not be classed as murder. Moreover, a mother who kills her child during the first year of its life would often be more likely to face a charge of *infanticide* rather than murder (see below).

The intention need not be to kill or injure a specific person. If a killer intends to kill one person, but instead kills another, it would still be murder. A person who kills while committing a crime or resisting arrest would only be guilty of murder if the intention described below was present.

The old rule of death having to occur within a year and a day was abolished in 1996. However if death occurs more than three years after the injury, the consent of the Attorney-General is required to prosecute for murder. The same is true where a person has already been found guilty of an offence which was connected to the circumstances of the death.

Mens rea in murder

The House of Lords has ruled that in order to establish the necessary *mens rea* for murder, there must be the **intention either to kill**, or **to inflict serious injury**. It is for the jury to decide whether the necessary intent is present for murder in any particular case. This is never an easy task, but following three important cases in the 1980s, the courts attempted to clarify the situation, as described below.

The mere foresight of the probable consequences of the act does not *necessarily* mean that the consequences were intended. If it is *overwhelmingly* likely that death or serious injury would result from the actions of the accused, then it may be assumed that the accused must have intended such a result.

In *R. v Maloney* (1985) the accused accepted a friendly challenge by his stepfather to see who was "quicker on the draw" with shotguns. The two men were good friends, and both were drunk. Maloney shot and killed his stepfather. He claimed that he had no intention to do so, and did not appreciate that the gun was aimed at the victim. The House of Lords ruled that Maloney was not guilty of murder, because a person only intends the result of an act if the purpose is to bring about that result. Because Maloney did not *intend* to kill his stepfather, he was not guilty of murder. He was, however, guilty of manslaughter.

In *R. v Hancock and Shankland* (1986) the defendants were striking miners. From a bridge over a road, they pushed blocks of concrete which landed on the windscreen of a taxi taking a miner to work. The driver of the taxi was killed and the defendants were charged with murder. They claimed that they had not intended to kill or injure anyone, but merely to block the road. The House of Lords ruled that in such cases the *probability* of death or injury resulting from the act is of great importance. "If the likelihood that death or serious injury will result is high, the probability of that result may be seen as overwhelming evidence of the existence of the intent to kill or injure". During the miners' strike at that time, there was great animosity between striking and non-striking miners and feelings were running very high. The two men were found not guilty of murder, but guilty of manslaughter.

This decision was followed by the Court of Appeal in *R. v Nedrick* (1986). In this case the jury was to ask itself two questions:

- was death or serious injury the *virtually certain* result of the accused's voluntary act? and

- did the accused *foresee* that death or serious injury was the virtually certain result of his act?

If the answer to both questions was "yes", then the jury could reasonably *infer* that the accused *intended* the consequences of his act.

In *R. v Woollin* (1998), the defendant lost his temper while feeding his baby son. He threw the baby against a wall, and the child died of the injuries sustained. In Woollin's appeal against a conviction for murder, the House of Lords approved the direction given in *R. v Nedrick*, above, provided that the word *find* was substituted for *infer*. Woollin's conviction for murder was changed to one of manslaughter.

In *R. v Matthews and Alleyne* (2003) the defendants threw their victim from a bridge into a river. They knew that he could not swim, and left the scene before he could reach safety. The victim drowned.

In *R. v Woollin*, it would seem that the House of Lords saw foresight of the consequences of an act to be the same as intention. In *R. v Matthews and Alleyne*, on the other hand, the Court of Appeal regarded this more as a rule of evidence. A jury in such cases is entitled to find the existence of intention, but does not necessarily have to. Despite what the Court of Appeal may have considered to be a technical misdirection to the jury, the court decided that it would not have made any difference to the jury's decision. The conviction of Matthews and Alleyne was therefore upheld.

The punishment for murder

The punishment for murder is life imprisonment. If a person is found guilty of murder, the judge has **no alternative** but to pass this sentence. It is known as a **mandatory life sentence**. This can mean prison literally for life, but more usually persons whom it is felt are no longer a threat to society are released after an average of about 12 years. When sentencing, a judge can recommend that a minimum number of years are to be served.

Criticism of mandatory life sentences

The mandatory life sentence for murder was laid down in the Murder (Abolition of the Death Penalty) Act 1965, and it has come in for much criticism in recent years. It is felt that it does not enable a judge to differentiate between murders of differing degrees of seriousness. For example, a cold-blooded serial killer and a person who from motives of love performs what is called a "mercy killing" both receive a life sentence. Another objection to the mandatory life sentence is that so as to avoid it, inappropriate verdicts of *manslaughter* (see below) are sometimes returned. Attempts have been made to do away with the mandatory life sentence, and give judges the discretion to impose sentences of fixed terms of imprisonment up to and including life. Nothing has come of these efforts so far, and the mandatory life sentence for murder remains.

Specific defences to murder

Diminished responsibility

The defence of diminished responsibility was introduced by the Homicide Act 1957. The defence is that the killer was suffering from an **abnormality of the mind** at the time of the crime, which **impaired the mental responsibility** for committing the act. If this defence is accepted, then the charge is reduced from murder to manslaughter. In the "Yorkshire Ripper" case, the jury did not accept this defence, and Sutcliffe was found guilty of murder.

In *R. v Byrne* (1960), the defendant was a sexual psychopath who strangled and muti-lated a young woman. He was convicted of murder, but the Court of Appeal substituted a conviction for manslaughter. The court held that the abnormality of mind covered the inability to control irresistible impulses. According to medical evidence, Byrne's condi-tion was such that he was unable to resist his perverted desires. (Despite the conviction of manslaughter substituted for one of murder, Byrne was nevertheless still sentenced to life imprisonment).

Provocation

This defence was also introduced by the Homicide Act 1957. To plead this defence success-fully, a defendant must show that the actions or taunts of the victim were such that any rea-sonable person would **lose control** of the mind. This loss of control must be shown to be **sudden and temporary**. The defence is not available to a defendant who, after the provocative acts or assaults, has time to think and reflect before carrying out the killing. As with the suc-cessful plea of diminished responsibility, the successful plea of provocation will result in a verdict of manslaughter.

The "reasonable man" test is applied when determining whether provocation is enough to cause a loss of self control. In applying this test, the jury must take into account such matters as the age and sex of the defendant (*R. v Camplin* (1978)), and any other relevant charac-teristics (*R. v Smith (Morgan James)* (2000)).

"Slow fuse" cases

The requirement of the defence of provocation, that loss of control must be sudden and tem-porary, has been subject to some criticism in recent years. In cases where women have been abused for a long time, and then suddenly "snapped", the defence has not been available because some time had elapsed between the last act of provocation and the subsequent killing.

In *R. v Ahluwalia* (1992), the defendant Kiranjit Ahluwalia had been physically abused by her husband over many years. One night before he went to sleep, her husband threat-ened her with violence the next day. When he was asleep, she poured petrol over him and set him alight. She was convicted of murder. The Court of Appeal disallowed her appeal on the grounds of provocation, holding that where there is a delay, the act of killing is more likely to be deliberate. The court did however uphold her appeal on the grounds of diminished responsibility.

In *R. v Thornton* (1992), the defendant had received a series of serious domestic violence and abuse from her husband. After one such incident she went to the kitchen to calm down, looked for a weapon and took a carving knife, sharpened it and returned to the living room where she stabbed her husband to death. The Court of Appeal confirmed her conviction of murder, holding that there had not been a sudden loss of control. This case has raised the question whether this defence makes allowances for such victims of domestic violence, and for the different temperaments and characteristics of men and women. In Mrs Thornton's retrial in 1996 for the murder of her husband, it was shown that she was mentally unbalanced, and the jury returned a verdict of manslaughter based on diminished responsibility.

In *R. v Richens* (1993), the accused's girlfriend was allegedly raped. He confronted the culprit, who contended that the woman had consented and been a willing partner. The accused became enraged and stabbed him to death. In his defence, the accused pleaded provocation. The Court of Appeal, accepting the defence, held that the defence of provocation does not require the accused to have such a loss of control that he did not know what he was doing, but simply suffered such a loss of control that he was unable to restrain himself from doing what he did.

The effect of these defences

Diminished responsibility and provocation are defences which are specific to murder. As has been seen, the effect of successfully pleading one or other of these defences reduces the charge of murder to one of manslaughter. The effect of this is that a conviction for murder carries an automatic life sentence, whereas manslaughter does not. In the case of a manslaughter verdict, the judge has the discretion to impose whatever sentence is suitable, given the facts of the case. This could mean a sentence of anything from a conditional discharge to a maximum of life imprisonment.

Manslaughter

Manslaughter is unlawful homicide **without** malice aforethought. It is where there is an unlawful killing, but the necessary *mens rea* for murder does not exist. Manslaughter is either voluntary or involuntary.

Voluntary manslaughter

Where diminished responsibility, provocation or suicide pact (see below) is successfully pleaded, the manslaughter is classed as voluntary. The reason is that the crime would have been murder but for these defences.

Gross negligence manslaughter

This is where a person who, as a result of **gross negligence**, kills another person. It is classed as involuntary manslaughter.

In *R. v Adomako* (1994), the House of Lords stated that for gross negligence manslaughter there must be the killing of a human being (as with all homicide), plus a risk of death, and a duty of care which is breached as a result of gross negligence. Mr Adomako was an anaesthetist whose patient had died as the result of lack of oxygen when the tube into his mouth had become detached. Mr Adomako had not realised sufficiently quickly why his patient was turning blue.

In *R. v Misra and Srivastava* (2003) the Court of Appeal held that the ingredients of the offence of manslaughter by gross negligence, as identified by the House of Lords in *Adomako*, were sufficiently clearly defined and did not offend against the retrospective provisions of the European Convention on Human Rights (see Chapter 5).

Other examples of involuntary manslaughter

• Where a person kills another while carrying out an unlawful act which would not normally kill or seriously hurt that other person. This was sometimes known as **constructive**, or **unlawful act** manslaughter. An example might be where one person hits another intending no more than to commit an assault causing actual bodily harm, but the victim falls and sustains fatal injuries to the head.

• Where a person is directly the cause of another's death, although the actual killing was the act of a third party. An example of such a situation might be where a person involved in a shooting incident with police uses the victim as a shield as protection from police bullets.

The maximum punishment for manslaughter is imprisonment for life.

As we saw in Chapter 4, it is possible for corporations to be prosecuted for manslaughter. In February 2005 the trial opened against two companies, Railtrack and Balfour Beatty, both being charged with corporate manslaughter. Five individuals, all railway managers who were responsible for maintenance of the east coast main line, were also charged with manslaughter. The case arose from the Hatfield train crash in October 2000, in which four people died and over a hundred were injured.

Useful website

The Government's consultation paper on the reform of the law relating to involuntary manslaughter: *www.homeoffice.gov.uk/docs/invmans.html*

Suicide

Suicide and attempted suicide are not in themselves crimes. The Suicide Act 1961, s.2, however, states that it is a crime to aid, abet, counsel or procure the suicide of another person. When two or more people agree that they shall be killed by some means, a *suicide pact* occurs. The survivor of such a pact is charged with manslaughter, regardless of which one did the actual killing.

In 2001, Mrs Dianne Pretty, who was suffering from motor neurone disease, was refused an undertaking from the director of Public Prosecutions that her husband would not be prosecuted under the Suicide Act for helping her to end her life. She took her case to the Divisional Court of the High Court to challenge this decision, on the grounds that it denied her the right to die with dignity, a right which is afforded under the Human Rights Act 1998. The court ruled against her.

Infanticide

Infanticide is committed when a child under the age of 12 months is killed:

- by its mother, and
- at the time of the killing, the mother was mentally disturbed as a result of not fully recovering from the effects of the child's birth.

The maximum punishment is the same as for manslaughter.

Causing death by dangerous driving

This offence is committed when a motorist drives in such a negligent or dangerous fashion that the death of another person results. It is punishable by imprisonment of up to 10 years and/or a fine.

An example of such a case is that of Gary Hart (2001) who after having been awake all night, undertook a lengthy drive with a Land Rover and trailer. He fell asleep at the wheel, the vehicle left the motorway, and crashed onto the east coast main railway line. Two trains were involved in the resulting collision, and 10 people died. He was convicted of causing death by dangerous driving.

Assault and Battery

It is common to hear these two charges joined as one. They are, however, separate offences.

Assault

This is an act which causes another person to be in immediate fear of an unlawful physical attack. It is generally considered that mere words are not sufficient but that they must be accompanied by some positive action. An action which arouses fear, although there was no intention to harm, would still be an assault.

Battery

This is the actual unlawful force on another person, without lawful reason or just cause. The force may be the merest touch which caused no physical harm or injury.

It is usual for both offences to occur at the same time, but assault is not committed if the person is unaware that the battery is to take place. For example, if an attack takes place behind a person's back.

Defences include lawful consent, parental or quasi-parental authority and reasonable self-defence.

The Criminal Justice Act 1988 provides that assault and battery are both summary offences, each punishable upon conviction by a maximum of six months' imprisonment or a fine.

Statutory offences (Offences against the Person Act 1861)

In addition to the common law offences described above, the Offences Against the Person Act 1861 provides for various statutory offences involving the infliction of actual or grievous bodily harm, or malicious wounding.

Actual Bodily Harm (Section 47)

The prosecution must prove that the accused was guilty of an assault or battery that caused actual bodily harm to another. **Actual** bodily harm would be less than **grievous** bodily harm (see below), and probably any degree of bodily harm would suffice. In *R. v Chan-Fook* (1994), it was held that while psychiatric injury could be included within the definition of actual bodily harm, it did not include mere emotions such as fear, distress or panic.

> However, in *R. v Ireland* (1997) the defendant made a large number of unwanted telephone calls to three women. He never spoke to the women and repeated the calls over a short period of time. In each case the women suffered psychological symptoms such as palpitations, dizziness, inability to sleep and stress. The defendant was convicted of assault occasioning actual bodily harm, because when a victim answered the phone followed by silence she was in immediate fear and this amounted to an assault under section 47.

Wounding without intent (Section 20)

This offence consists of the unlawful and malicious wounding or inflicting any grievous bodily harm upon any person, either with or without any weapon or instrument. This offence does not require **intent**. It is only possible to make this charge if there has been serious bodily harm or wounding by a breaking of the skin.

A bruise, burn or scratching of the skin is not wounding in this sense, nor would the breaking of a bone be so if the skin was not broken. It would appear, therefore, that bleeding from the wound is necessary for this offence. In *C. v Eisenhower* (1983) a pellet from an airgun did not break the skin, but caused internal bleeding. The court held the defendant to be not guilty of unlawful wounding as there had not been a breaking of the skin.

In *R. v Burstow* (1997), the defendant, over a six month period, made silent phone calls to a previous lady friend, and also performed such acts as following her to work, stealing clothes from her clothes line and sending hate mail, with the intention of preying on her mind. The Court of Appeal held that "grievous bodily harm" could include psychiatric injury, and the offence can be committed without personal violence being applied to the victim's body, either directly or indirectly.

Inflicting GBH by having sex

In *R. v Dica* (2003), the defendant was convicted of inflicting grievous bodily harm through consensual sexual intercourse. He knew that he was suffering from a serious sexual disease (HIV), and recklessly transmitted that disease to two women who did not know of it and did not consent to the risk of infection. He was sentenced to 8 years imprisonment. In 2004 the Court of appeal allowed Dica's appeal against conviction on the grounds that the trial judge should not have removed from the jury the question of consent to the risk. A retrial was ordered, but the principle remains as established.

Wounding with intent (Section 18)

This offence consists of the unlawful and malicious wounding, or causing any grievous bodily harm to any person

- with **intent** to do grievous bodily harm to such person, or
- with **intent** to resist or prevent the lawful apprehension or detention (*i.e.* arrest), of any person.

This is the most serious of these statutory offences against the person, and carries a maximum of life imprisonment.

Consent as a defence to offences against the person

As we saw in Chapter 9 under the heading *Volenti non fit injuria*, consent is implied in the case of battery resulting in minor injuries. The examples given were mainly from sporting activities. The same is true in battery as a crime as well as a tort. However, in *Attorney-General's Reference (No. 6 of 1980)* (1981) it was held that it was **against the public interest** when two men agreed to have a fight in the street to settle a quarrel. It would seem therefore that where an activity is against the public interest, consent is not a defence to an offence under the Offences Against the Person Act.

This was confirmed in the case of *R. v Brown and others* (1993). In this case a group of homosexual men had indulged in a series of sado-masochistic activities involving the infliction of bodily harm and wounding. All were adults, and all consented to everything which took place. The House of Lords upheld their convictions under the Offences Against the Person Act. Although the acts were entirely consensual, and the injuries were "transitory and trifling", it was against the public interest to allow consent as a defence.

Time for a new Act?

The Offences Against the Person Act 1861 has given rise to some confusion. It was passed nearly a century and a half ago, and much of the language tends to be rather archaic. Terms such as "occasioning", "inflicting" and "causing" for example, together with other complexities, have caused problems of interpretation.

There have been various proposals for new legislation, and in 1993 the Law Commission issued a report suggesting reforms. The Government issued a draft bill in 1998 based on these proposals. As yet, there has been no new legislation.

Useful website

Consultation paper and draft bill for a new OAP Act: *www.homeoffice.gov.uk/docs*

Rape

This offence occurs when a man has unlawful sexual intercourse with a woman or man without consent. It would still be rape if consent was given by a trick, such as a man pretending to be the woman's husband.

The House of Lords, in *R. v R.* (1991) held that a husband who rapes his wife can be prosecuted, as all rapes (even in marriage) are unlawful.

A woman who forces a male to have unlawful sexual intercourse would be liable to the charge of indecent assault.

The maximum penalty for rape is life imprisonment.

The law relating to sexual offences, including rape, was comprehensively overhauled by the Sexual Offences Act 2003.

Offences against property

The Theft Acts 1968 and 1978 provide for a wide variety of offences against property.

THE THEFT ACT 1968

Theft

The offence of theft covers any case of stealing, whether it be of property worth many millions of pounds, or a chocolate bar from a corner shop. Contrary to popular belief, there is no such offence as "shoplifting": the offence is theft. Theft is triable either way, either summarily in the magistrates court, or on indictment in the crown court. The maximum sentence for theft is seven years' imprisonment.

Section 1(1) of the Theft Act 1968 defines theft as follows:

"A person is guilty of theft if he dishonestly appropriates property belonging to another with the intention of permanently depriving the other of it."

It is immaterial whether the appropriation is made with a view to gain, or is made for the thief's own benefit (s.1(2)).

The definition contained in s.1(1) above, contains words and phrases which are amplified for the purpose of interpretation in sections 2 to 6.

Dishonestly (Section 2)

This could be considered the *mens rea* of stealing, so that if a person did not intend to be dishonest, there would be no theft. For example, if I took another person's coat from a rack, thinking it was my own, there would be no theft, but if I took it knowing it was not my coat, it would be dishonest. If I took the coat thinking it was mine, but later discovered it belonged to another person, it would be theft if I decided to keep it.

The Act does not define "dishonestly" but gives examples of when the appropriation of another's property would not be dishonest.

- If a person believes in law that he has the right to deprive the other person of the property.
- If a person believes he would have the owner's consent. For example, borrowing £5 from a friend's locker.
- If a person (other than a trustee) believes that, after taking reasonable steps, the owner of the property which he holds cannot be found. This example would apply to the finding of lost property.

Clearly, if a person finds a £2 coin in the street, if would not be likely that the owner could be traced. If on the other hand the property was unique and of great value, or was a purse with credit cards in it, for example, the presumption would be that the owner could be, and should be, found.

Appropriates (Section 3)

Appropriation takes place when a person assumes or takes over the rights of an owner.

In *R. v Morris* (1983) the defendant took articles from shelves in a supermarket and substituted the price labels with labels from lower priced goods. The House of Lords held that there had been a dishonest appropriation.

In *R. v Adams* (1993), a motor cyclist brought some spare parts for cash. He did not know at the time they had been stolen. It was held that the person who buys property in good faith does not commit theft when he subsequently learns that he is not the owner.

Property (Section 4)

The term includes all things which can be owned, money, goods, rights of action and, in certain circumstances, land. As a general rule, it is not theft to pick mushrooms, flowers, fruit or foliage from a plant or trees growing wild, provided that the picking is not done for sale or other commercial purposes. It would not be stealing to pick flowers growing wild and give them to a friend, but it would be stealing to sell them for gain. Electricity is not "property" under the Theft Act and cannot be stolen (see p. 259).

Belonging to another (Section 5)

Property belongs to anyone who has possession or control of it. This clearly means property owned by someone at the time of the theft. But the definition is broader that that, and includes property which in the possession or under the control of someone who does not actually own it. If a thief steals a television set obtained by hire purchase before the last payment is made, it is clearly stolen from the hirer, not the legal owner.

In *R. v Turner* (1971) the defendant had left his car to be repaired at a garage. He later took it from outside the garage after it had been repaired, intending not to pay the repair bill. It was held that, despite the fact that the car belonged to Turner, the garage had possession and control over it within the meaning of the Act. Turner was found guilty of theft; in effect of stealing his own property.

The intention of permanently depriving (Section 6)

This element is fundamental to the crime of theft. If property belonging to another is dishonestly appropriated, but there is the *intention to return it*, then theft is not committed. There must be the intention to deprive the owner permanently of that property. If, unauthorised, you take a book from a fellow-student, intending to read it and then return it the following week, you have not stolen that book within the meaning of the 1968 Act. However, if you (legitimately) borrow a book and then, while it is in your possession decide to keep it, you have then stolen that book. The act of theft occurred at the time when you decided to keep the book permanently.

In *R. v Lloyd* (1985) a cinema projectionist took films from his employer's cinema and made pirate video copies for sale. The films were returned to the cinema within an hour or two. The Court of Appeal held that there was no intention to deprive the owner permanently of the property.

Section 6(1) provides that in certain cases borrowing goods would be theft, even if there was *no* intention permanently to deprive. Theft would occur in the following circumstances, for example:

- a person steals a train ticket from a railway company with the intention of returning it on arrival at the station of destination;

- a person steals a football club season ticket and returns it to the owner at the end of the football season;

- a person steals a sack of potatoes from a farmer and sells it back to him, pretending to be the owner of the potatoes.

In these cases the owners are not permanently deprived of their property. All three instances are cases of theft, however, because there is the intention by the borrowers to treat the property as their own, and to deprive the owners of their rights to the property. In the first two cases, the period of time is important, because it amounts to an outright taking of the goods.

> In *R v Marshall* (1998), the defendant obtained unexpired underground rail tickets from passengers who no longer needed them, and then sold them to other passengers travelling on the railway. The Court of Appeal held that he intended to treat the tickets as his own when he sold them, and had the intention to permanently deprive the rail company of their rights.

Robbery

Robbery is **theft** with the use or threat of **force**. Section 8(1) provides that: "A person is guilty of robbery if he steals and immediately before or at the time of doing so, and in order to do so, he uses force on any person or puts or seeks to put any person in fear of being then and there subjected to force". The maximum punishment is imprisonment for life.

The principal elements of this offence are:

- stealing;
- using force; or
- fear, on the victim's part, of force being used.

A person does not commit robbery if there is no theft. The force used must be more than a gentle push, or more than is needed to take the property from a passive victim. It has been considered that merely snatching a handbag from a woman who did not resist would not be using force as required by the Act.

What constitutes force in any particular set of circumstances is for the jury to decide.

Burglary

Burglary is defined by Section 9 of the Theft Act 1968.

Section 9(1)(a) provides that burglary is committed when a person enters a building or any part of a building **as a trespasser** with **intent** to commit any of the following offences:

- theft,
- inflicting grievous bodily harm,
- rape, or
- unlawful damage.

Section 9(1)(b) provides that burglary is also committed when a person **having entered** the building or any part of it **as a trespasser**

- **steals** or attempts to steal anything in the building, or

- inflicts or attempts to inflict **grievous bodily harm** on any person in it.

The essential requirement of burglary in both subsections is that the person **enters as a trespasser**.

In s.9(1)(a) the additional essential element is the **intent** to commit one of the four offences specified. No actual offence needs to be committed, so long as the intention to steal, etc. was present at the time of entry as a trespasser. A person who is apprehended by the householder before any offence can take place has still committed burglary, so long as the necessary intent was there.

In s.9(1)(b) a person may have entered *without* the intention of committing any offence. If however that person **having entered** as a trespasser then commits theft or GBH, that person is a burglar. An example might be where a person, having entered a house (uninvited, *i.e.* as a trespasser) for no other reason than to shelter from the rain, sees a gold watch lying on a table and steals it. That person has then committed burglary.

The maximum punishment for burglary is 10 years' imprisonment for burglary of commercial premises, and 14 years for the burglary of domestic premises.

Aggravated burglary

Section 10 of the Theft Act 1968 defines the offence of aggravated burglary. This is where, while committing burglary as described above, a person is carrying

- a firearm, or

- an imitation firearm, or

- any offensive weapon, or

- explosive.

The maximum penalty for aggravated burglary is life imprisonment.

Other Offences

The Theft Act 1968 provides for many other offences against property. The following are of interest.

Section 12—Taking a vehicle without consent

It is an offence to take a conveyance without the consent of the owner, or to drive or travel in the conveyance knowing that it has been taken without the owner's consent. This offence is popularly known as "twocking". It is not an offence if the person thought that he or she had the owner's consent, or would have had consent if the owner knew that the conveyance was being taken. The offence is not committed where permission to use the conveyance is obtained by fraud.

In *Whittaker v Campbell* (1983), W., who did not have a driving licence, hired a van by showing someone else's licence. The court held that he was not guilty of an offence under s.12 because he had the consent of the owner to take the van, despite the fact that the consent was obtained by fraud.

Within the meaning of the Act, a *conveyance* includes anything which will carry a person by land, sea or air. This section does not apply to the taking of a pedal cycle without the owner's consent. This is a separate offence, albeit a less serious one.

Aggravated vehicle-taking

The more serious offence of **aggravated vehicle-taking** is committed when a vehicle is taken without the owner's consent, as above, and then is driven dangerously, or is involved in an accident which causes damage to any property or injury to any person.

Note: in these cases involving the taking of vehicles, both the driver *and any passenger* in the vehicle are guilty.

Section 13—Dishonest abstraction of electricity

This section provides for the unauthorised and dishonest abstraction of electricity. It is an offence to dishonestly use, divert or waste electricity and any person convicted is liable to imprisonment for a term not exceeding five years.

In *Low v Blease* (1975), the defendant entered a building as a trespasser and made a telephone call. He was charged with burglary, but it was held that as electricity is not property within the meaning of section 4, Theft Act 1968, he was not guilty.

He should have been charged under section 13.

Section 15—Obtaining property by deception

This provides that it is an offence to dishonestly obtain *property* belonging to another by deception. It carries a maximum of ten years' imprisonment. For example, it would be an offence to obtain a TV set on rental by showing the owner a means of identity which belonged to another person.

It essential that "property" is obtained. In *R. v Preddy* (1996) it was held that section 15 is not an appropriate charge for a fraud using electronic means to transfer money from one account to another, as no indentifiable "property" passed in the transaction.

As a result of this case, the Theft Acts of 1968 and 1978 were amended by the **Theft (Amendment) Act 1996**. This Act created two new offences.

- Section 1 provides for the offence of *obtaining a money transfer by deception*. It is committed regardless of whether the transfer takes effect on the presentation of a cheque or another method.

- Under Section 2 it is an offence to retain credits from dishonest sources, in particular where a credit is made in the circumstances of an offence committed under Section 1.

Section 16—Obtaining financial advantage by deception

This provides that it is an offence for a person to dishonestly obtain a pecuniary *financial advantage* by deception. The maximum penalty is five years' imprisonment. Examples of pecuniary advantages would be obtaining an overdraft, or insurance policy, or obtaining employment or advancement at work, or winning money by betting. The deception may be by words or conduct. This offence would be committed, for example, if a person applying for a job falsely claimed to have certain qualifications and was employed as a result of the deception.

In *R. v Callender* (1992), the Court of Appeal held that the defendant, who obtained employment and earned remuneration by the deception that on his curriculum vitae he falsely claimed to have professional qualifications, had dishonestly obtained a pecuniary advantage by deception, contrary to section 16.

However, in *R. v Rozeik* (1996), it was held that if the company had not been deceived by the false representation the accused could not be guilty of this offence.

Section 21—Blackmail

This section provides that the offence of blackmail is committed when a person *with a view to profit* makes an *unwarranted demand with menaces*. Menaces may be expressed threats of violence, or threats of some action which would be detrimental or unpleasant to the person addressed. Alternatively, the conduct of the accused may justify the opinion that a demand with menaces has been made. The maximum punishment for blackmail is 14 years' imprisonment.

Section 22—Handling stolen goods

This offence occurs when a person, knowing or believing goods to have been stolen, dishonestly receives the goods or helps or arranges for them to be removed or sold. The maximum sentence for this offence is 14 years' imprisonment.

Section 24a—Retaining a wrongful credit

This offence was created by the Theft (Amendment) Act 1996. It occurs when a person, knowing that his or her account has been wrongfully credited, fails to take reasonable steps to cancel that credit. A credit is wrongful if it has been obtained by theft, blackmail or other similar offence.

Section 25—"Going equipped for stealing"

It is an offence for a person, *while not at his or her place of abode*, to have any article for use in the course of, or in connection with, any theft, burglary or threat. Any person may arrest without warrant anybody whom he or she reasonably suspects to be committing this offence. The maximum penalty for this offence is 3 years' imprisonment.

In the following case, the court had to decide if the car of the accused was a "place of abode".

In *R. v Bundy* (1977) the police stopped the appellant's car and found articles for use in the course of theft. Bundy claimed that his car was his place of abode and therefore he had not committed a crime under section 25 of the Theft Act 1968. The Court of Appeal held that "a place of abode" meant a place in which the occupier intended to stay, and as a car was a means of transport, it was not a place of abode within the meaning of the Act.

THE THEFT ACT 1978

The Theft Act 1978 introduced three new offences.

Obtaining services by deception

Section 1 of the Theft Act 1978 makes it an offence dishonestly to obtain *services* by *deception*. It applies when services are obtained and the other person is induced to provide some benefit on the understanding that it has been, or will be, paid for.

An example would be where a person pays for a service by cheque, knowing the cheque to be worthless. It would also apply where, by a dishonest deception, a person is induced to make a loan on the understanding that interest or some other relevant compensation will be paid.

The evasion of liability by deception

Section 2 provides for the offences of *evasion of liability* by deception. It applies where a person by any deception:

- dishonestly secures the remission of the whole or part of any existing liability to make a payment, whether his own liability or another's; or

- with intent to make permanent default in whole or in part on any existing liability to make a payment, or with intent to let another do so, dishonestly induces the creditor or any person claiming payment on behalf of the creditor to wait for payment (whether or not the due date for payment is deferred) or to forgo payment; or

- dishonestly obtains any exemption from or abatement or liability to make a payment.

Examples of the above offences are:

(a) Jones owed the butcher £100 and falsely informed him that he was out of work and, as a result, the butcher reduced the debt.

(b) Smith had a car on hire and owed the rental for one month. Robinson, the owner of the car, demanded payment of the arrears or the immediate return of the car. If Smith needed the car for another day and gave Robinson a cheque for the overdue rental, knowing that she was leaving the country in two days and had closed her bank account, it would be an offence under this section because she had intended to permanently default the payment of an existing liability by deceiving Robinson into thinking the cheque was good.

(c) Barclay had a period contract on the railways and his friend Lloyd borrowed the contract and used it to obtain a free journey, although the contract was not transferable.

In *R. v Coady* (1996), the accused obtained petrol at a self-service station, and then told the cashier to charge the cost to his former employer, which he had no right to do. The Court of Appeal held that he was not guilty of obtaining the petrol by deception, because he got the petrol legally before the deception. He should have been charged under section 3 (see below).

Making off without payment

This offence is covered by **section 3** of the Act. It applies where a person knows that *payment on the spot* is required for any goods supplies or services rendered. Such a person who then makes off without paying, with the intention of avoiding payment, is guilty under this section. Making off without payment is made by the Act an arrestable offence.

This offence would be committed in cases such as leaving a café or a filling station or bus or train without paying. In *R v Allen* (1985) the defendant left a hotel without paying the bill. He claimed that he genuinely intended to pay at a later date. The House of Lords held that in order to be guilty under this section, a person must act dishonestly and intend to evade payment altogether. The defendant was therefore not guilty.

However, in *R. v Aziz* (1993), the defendant and another person hired a taxi. When they arrived at their destination they disputed the fare and refused to pay, telling various lies. The driver decided to take them back to their hotel, but when he pulled into a petrol station they ran away. The driver caught the defendant, who was later convicted of making off without payment. The Court of Appeal held that in this case, (i) "on the spot" means in the taxi or just outside it and, (ii) "making off" involves a departure from this place.

Payment had been requested while they were in the taxi and the subsequent drive back to their hotel did not alter the situation.

Section 3 does not apply when the payment cannot be legally enforced. For example, if a man makes use of the services of a prostitute, and then leaves without paying, he would not be guilty under this section (if he had no intention of paying from the outset, he may be guilty of obtaining services by deception, since section 1 makes no mention of legally unenforceable payments).

Useful website

Law Commission report on fraud: *www.lawcomm.gov.uk/files*

Criminal damage

Criminal damage includes all kinds of damage to property, from daubing graffiti or scratching the paintwork of a car to burning a school or factory to ashes. The **Criminal Damage Act 1970** provides for the essential elements of this crime.

Section 1(1) provides that it is an offence to unlawfully destroy or damage any property *belonging to another*, either intentionally or recklessly.

Section 1(2) provides that it is an aggravated offence to unlawfully destroy or damage property *with the intention of endangering the life of another*, whether the property belongs to *the offender or another person*. Note that under this subsection, when the intention to endanger life is present, the property can be the offender's own or someone else's. Intent means either the specific intention of endangering life, or recklessness as to whether life is endangered.

Arson takes place when the damage to, or destruction of property is caused by fire (*Section 2*).

The maximum penalty for Section 1(2) and Section 2 offences is life imprisonment.

Misleading trade descriptions

The Trade Descriptions Acts of 1968 and 1972 provide that it is a criminal offence for a person to provide a false or misleading trade description.

The Trade Descriptions Act 1968

Under this act, an offence is committed when*, in the course of a business*, a person makes a false description of goods with regard to such matters as price, size, quantity or method or place of manufacture.

In *Wings Ltd v Ellis* (1984), a holiday brochure was published with false information. The brochure was later amended but a customer booked a holiday relying on the original brochure. The House of Lords held that it is no defence that the defendant did not know at the time of publication that the statement was false. In *R. v Nash* (1991), the Court of Appeal upheld a sentence of imprisonment on the defendant who, when selling a car, described it as being in excellent condition when it was in fact a potential death trap.

There have been many prosecutions under the 1968 Act. A typical example would be selling a motor car with the meter showing a mileage far less that the car has actually travelled (it should be noted that as a result of this Act, many garages now expressly state that they do not guarantee the mileage shown to be correct).

Section 24 provides that it would be a defence to show that the misleading or false description was made:

- in circumstances over which the defendant had no control; or

- where the defendant could not have known that the description was false; or

- where the defendant took all reasonable precautions to ensure that an offence was not being committed.

The Trade Descriptions Act 1972

The *Trade Descriptions Act 1972* makes it an offence not to indicate the origin of goods which bear certain United Kingdom names and trade marks and have been produced or manufactured outside the United Kingdom.

Note: These Acts do not give buyers the right to enforce contracts. The Acts only provide for criminal sanctions.

SENTENCING IN CRIMINAL CASES

There are many types of punishment in criminal law which are common and well-known (imprisonment, community order, fines, etc.). For a comprehensive treatment of criminal sanctions, refer back to Chapter 3. With many crimes, it is left to the judge to decide the appropriate punishment for the crime, subject to the maximum stipulated for a particular offence.

The Crime (Sentences) Act 1997 provides for minimum and mandatory custodial sentences. When the court decides on a minimum sentence (the length of sentence a convicted person must serve before release) it must consider the circumstances of the offence, the offender, and any circumstances which would make the sentence unjust. When considering a life sentence for certain offences, the court must look at the circumstances of the offence or the offender.

When persons over 18 are convicted for the second time of a serious offence, such as manslaughter, rape, or robbery with a firearm, a mandatory life sentence will be imposed unless there are exceptional circumstances.

GENERAL DEFENCES

When faced with a charge of committing a crime, a defendant may well simply deny responsibility for it: "It wasn't me", or "I was somewhere else at the time", and so on.

Alternatively a defendant might plead a defence which is specific to the crime of which he or she is accused. In the case of theft, for example, dishonest appropriation of someone's property might be admitted, but the accused might plead that there was no intention permanently to deprive the owner of it, but merely to borrow it for a while. Similarly, a person might be accused of murder. The killing might be admitted, but the specific defence of provocation, or diminished responsibility might be pleaded.

There are also defences which are general to all, or most, crimes. A defendant may admit performing the actions which resulted in a crime being committed. That defendant might plead however that there were certain circumstances by reason of which he or she is not guilty. These general defences are discussed below.

Insanity

The defence of insanity in criminal cases is based on the M'Naghten Rules. In 1843, Daniel M'Naghten, motivated by an insane delusion of persecution by Sir Robert Peel, killed Edward Drummond who was Peel's secretary. M'Naghten was acquitted on the grounds of insanity, and the House of Lords, in its Parliamentary role, produced the following rules which still apply today.

- Every person is presumed sane until the contrary is proved.

- The defence must show that the accused was labouring under a **defect of reason** caused by a **disease of the mind**, and that he did not know the nature and quality of his act, or, if he did know it, he did not know that he was doing wrong.

- Where a person commits a crime under an insane delusion, he is considered to have the responsibility that he would have had if the facts as he imagined were real.

If a man had insane delusions that another man was about to kill him, and in self-defence he killed the other man, there would be no criminal liability. If, however, his delusions were that the man was making friendly advances to his girl friend, and he killed him, he would be liable for punishment, because his delusion did not warrant the action he took.

The defence of insanity may only be raised when *mens rea* is an essential element of the offence. Therefore, if a defendant commits a strict liability offence, such as driving with excess alcohol, where *mens rea* is not an issue, the defence of insanity is not available.

In relation to the defence of insanity, the following points should be noted.

- It is for the defence to prove the insanity of the accused, not for the prosecution to prove that the accused is sane.

- If insanity is proved, the verdict is "not guilty by reason of insanity".

The general defence of insanity is not the same as diminished responsibility, which is a defence specific to murder.

Unfitness to plead

Although this is not strictly a defence, a defendant may be found to be suffering from such an abnormality of mind as to be considered to be unfit to plead. Unfitness to plead is assumed when an accused is deemed to be incapable of instructing lawyers, or following or giving evidence. In such cases, a second jury will consider whether the defendant "did the act as charged" in order for the court to determine a suitable order as to treatment or detention in hospital.

Automatism

This is an act done by the muscles of the body without any control of the mind. It could be a reflex action, a blackout, an act done when sleepwalking, or any other involuntary movement, provided the person's physical and mental state was not caused by his own negligence.

The defence is based on a general rule that an offence is not punishable if the action of the defendant was involuntary. Drivers experiencing the condition known as "driving without awareness", when drivers on long motorway journeys experience a trance-like state, cannot use automatism as a defence, because there has not been a total destruction of voluntary control.

Similarly, a defendant cannot plead this defence if he or she knows that, because of an illness, an attack is likely to occur while driving, resulting in loss of control of the car. Driving in this condition is obviously dangerous, and the offence of dangerous driving will already have been committed. The defence of automatism will not be available.

Self-defence or the prevention of crime

This can be a defence to most crimes (even theft, for example), but is applicable mainly to fatal and non-fatal offences against the person. It covers not only action taken to protect oneself from an attack, but also any action taken to protect another person or prevent the commission of a crime.

The Criminal Law Act 1967 s.3 states that a person may use "such force as is reasonable in the circumstances" to prevent a crime being committed. What is reasonable in the circumstances depends on what the defendant honestly and instinctively thought the needs of the moment to be. Clearly, the use of excessive or disproportionate force cannot be a defence. The use of force by way of retribution or revenge when the danger to person or property has passed also cannot be used as a defence.

The defence of self-defence to a charge of murder raises particular problems. If the degree of force used is found to be reasonable in the circumstances, then an acquittal will result. If on the other hand the force used is deemed to be unreasonable, then the verdict will be one of guilty of murder, with the consequent sentence of life imprisonment. There may be a fine line dividing what is reasonable from what is unreasonable, but the result is either an innocent person or a convicted murderer, with nothing in between. Unease has been felt by many people recently about the apparent injustice in some such cases. It was highlighted in the case of *R. v Martin (Anthony)* (2001).

Tony Martin, a reclusive farmer, lived in an isolated farmhouse in East Anglia, and he had been burgled in the past. On the occasion which resulted in his trial, he heard the sound of intruders, took a shotgun, and fired in the darkness without warning. One of the intruders, 16-year-old Fred Barras, was shot in the back and killed. Martin was found guilty of murder. On appeal, his plea of self-defence was rejected on the grounds that the force he had used was unreasonable. His conviction was reduced to manslaughter however on the grounds of diminished responsibility and he was freed in 2003.

In February 2005 the Crown Prosecution Service and the Association of Chief Police Officers jointly issued new guidelines aimed at reassuring householders that they would not necessarily end up in prison if they tackled burglars in their homes. Householders are unlikely to end up in court provided that they do what they "honestly and instinctively believe is necessary in the heat of the moment". This is the case even if they use a weapon and seriously injure or kill an intruder. The law does not expect a householder to be attacked before using defensive force. The leaflet reminds householders that they must not use force maliciously, or by way of retribution or revenge.

The leaflet, entitled *Householders and the Use of Force against Intruders*, is available at Citizens' Advice Bureaux. It states that, "As a general rule, the more extreme the circumstances and the fear felt, the more force you can lawfully use in self-defence".

Mistake

Mistake as to the *law* is not a defence. However, a person may claim that, had the true *facts* been known, the crime would not have been committed.

In *R. v Tolson* (1889), a woman remarried during the lifetime of her husband. It was shown that she honestly believed her husband to be dead, and she was acquitted of a charge of bigamy.

The mistake pleaded as a defence must be reasonable. In Tolson's case, the plea was accepted because her husband had been reported drowned at sea and had been missing for five years.

Intoxication (by drugs or alcohol)

Although it is not a defence in itself, and in some cases it is an offence, the plea may be used to show that the *mens rea* required for the offence was not present.

In *R. v Hardie* (1985) the defendant was under the influence of valium, which had not been prescribed for him, and he set fire to a friend's flat, endangering lives. The Court of Appeal held that he did not have the *mens rea*, and considered that while intoxication cannot usually be pleaded as a defence to offences of recklessness, the rule will not generally apply to drugs which are merely sedative. Obviously, this defence could not be used in cases such as dangerous driving.

It may also be a defence to show that intoxication produced insanity and that the M'Naghten Rules are relevant.

A person who forms the intention of committing a crime whilst sober and becomes drunk to acquire "Dutch courage" will not be able to use this defence. In *Att-Gen for Northern Ireland v Gallagher* (1963) a man planned to kill his wife and drank a bottle of whisky before committing the crime. His defence of drunkenness was refused by the House of Lords. In *R. v Fotheringham* (1989), a husband and wife expected to be returning late and told the baby-sitter to sleep in their bed. When the couple returned home the husband, who was drunk, got into the bed and raped the baby-sitter. His defence was that he was drunk and thought he was in bed with his wife. The Court of Appeal held that intoxication which is self-induced is no defence to rape.

In *R. v Kingston* (1994), a 15-year-old boy had been drugged unconscious by another person, who invited the accused to sexually abuse the boy. When charged with indecent assault, the accused claimed that he had no recollection of the assault, as his drink had also "been laced" with drugs by the other person, who photographed the indecent act. The House of Lords held that involuntary intoxication is not a defence to a defendant who is proved to have the necessary criminal intent when he committed the offence.

Necessity

There is no general defence of necessity. It can, however, be claimed as a defence if by committing a crime a greater harm is prevented, such as charge of careless driving in a case of emergency, as in *R. v Backshall* (1998). It would appear that the defence cannot be used for the murder of an innocent person.

In *R. v Dudley & Stephens* (1884) two seamen who had been shipwrecked for nearly three weeks killed and ate the cabin boy, who was the only other survivor. The defence of necessity was rejected and they were found guilty of murder, even though the jury considered that they would have died from starvation had they not killed the boy. (Though sentenced to death by hanging, they were reprieved and served only a short period in prison).

In *Cichon v DPP* (1994) the defendant claimed that he allowed his pit bull terrier to be in a public place without a muzzle (contrary to the Dangerous Dogs Act 1991), because the dog was ill and it would be cruel to keep it muzzled. The Court held that the aim of the Act was to protect the public, not the dog.

Duress

Duress may be raised as a defence when a person is threatened that, unless he commits a certain crime, he or another person may be killed or suffer serious personal injury. Threats may also arise from circumstances, such as, for example being chased by a rioting mob and driving the wrong way down a one way street.

The House of Lords in *R. v Howe* (1987) ruled that duress is not a defence in murder. In *R. v Gotts* (1992), a 17-year-old man caused serious injuries when he stabbed his mother with intent to kill her. He was charged with attempted murder but alleged that his father told him to do so and threatened to kill him if he did not carry out his wishes. The House of Lords, following the decision in *R. v Howe*, held that as duress is no defence to murder, it would be illogical to apply this defence to attempted murder.

In *R. v Cole* (1994), the accused was charged with robbery. His defence was that he owed money to moneylenders who threatened him and his family with physical violence if he did not repay the debt. The defence did not succeed because, (i) the moneylenders had not stipulated that the accused must commit robbery, and (ii) there was no threat of "immediate peril".

Coercion

If a wife commits a crime, other than murder or treason, under the coercion of, and *in the presence of* her husband, she may plead this defence. Marital coercion might take the form of threats of physical injury, or mental anguish (caused, for example, by a threat to leave the family).

Duress of circumstances

This defence was recognised by the Court of Appeal in the case of *R. v Conway* (1988). Conway had been found guilty of reckless driving. He had honestly believed that his passenger, who had been previously involved in a shooting incident, was about to be killed. On his appeal, the court held that necessity was only available in cases of reckless driving where it amounted to duress of circumstances.

In *R. v Martin (Colin)* (1989) the Court of Appeal again recognised this defence when the defendant, while disqualified from driving, drove his stepson to work. He claimed that his wife, who had suicidal tendencies, had threatened to kill herself if he did not take her son to work.

In *R. v Biezanek* (1993) a doctor was acquitted of supplying cannabis to her daughter. She had deemed it to be necessary as a treatment for her daughter's illness, and successfully pleaded duress of circumstances. Other cases of a similar kind are presently (2005) under consideration by the Court of Appeal.

This type of defence can be said to have taken the place of necessity (see above). It would clearly not be available in cases of murder.

SPECIMEN EXAMINATION QUESTIONS

1. The Problem

Norman escaped from prison and was 'on the run' and desperate for money. He was hoping to be able to leave the country and start a new life abroad.

During his time 'on the run', Norman committed a number of offences.

Near the prison from which Norman escaped, he broke into the unoccupied house of Lady Olivia. He took and ate some food and also removed a gun from a cabinet. He then took a car from the garage and drove to a nearby town where he set fire to the vehicle and then ran away.

While in town, Norman entered a bank and, having threatened the staff with the gun, left with a large quantity of cash.

On leaving the bank, Norman forced Penny to drive him to the airport, where he hoped to catch a flight to South America using a false passport.

In a scuffle at passport control, Norman hit Quentin with the handle of the gun, leaving him with bruising and mild concussion.

Ron, an armed security guard, seeing the gun, fired two shots at Norman as Norman was running towards him. Both shots missed. Ron fired one more shot, after Norman had passed him, which hit Norman in the leg. Now disabled, Norman was arrested shortly afterwards.

(a) Discuss Norman's criminal liability **as he entered** Lady Olivia's house.   (4 marks)

(b) Discuss Norman's criminal liability in respect of:

    (i)   the food he took from the house;   (4 marks)
    (ii) Lady Olivia's car.   (4 marks)

(c) Discuss Norman's criminal liability for any offences he committed in the bank.

                                                                              (8 marks)

(d) **Briefly** discuss Norman's criminal liability with respect to Quentin's injuries.

                                                                              (2 marks)

(e) Penny has been questioned by the police, who suspect her of assisting Norman in his escape, and Ron has been questioned about the shooting of Norman.

    (i)   Name the defence Penny may be able to plead.   (1 mark)
    (ii) **Briefly** explain the offence with which Ron could be charged.   (2 marks)
    (iii) Name the defence which Ron may be able to plead.   (1 mark)

(f) Choose **one** of the defences you have identified in (e) above.

    Comment critically on the law in relation to this offence.   (4 marks)

AQA Higher Tier, Summer 2000

2. The Problem

Yvonne and Zak have been married for 10 years. Their relationship had been very stormy. Zak had been a very heavy drinker and had beaten his wife on several occasions when he was drunk.

Yvonne had been diagnosed as suffering from severe depression and had been prescribed anti-depressants which she had been taking for several months.

One night, Zak returned home drunk and attacked Yvonne, breaking her nose and cutting her cheek with the ring he always wore. He then fell asleep in the armchair.

Yvonne waited until he was asleep and then, in a furious rage, stabbed him to death with a kitchen knife.

Yvonne was arrested and charged with murder. She said, in her interview with the police, that she could not remember much about what had happened that evening.

(a) If Zak had lived, he could have faced criminal charges for the attack on Yvonne.

    (i)   Consider Zak's criminal liability for this attack.   (3 marks)
    (ii) To what extent could Zak's drunken state have provided him with a defence?

                                                            (3 marks)

(b) In relation to the crime of murder, explain what is meant by the following:

    (i)   "malice aforethought, express or implied";   (4 marks)
    (ii) "a mandatory life sentence"   (2 marks)

(c) Yvonne is likely to defend herself on a charge of murder by pleading some sort of defence.

    Discuss how the following defences could apply in her case:

    (i)   provocation   (4 marks)
    (ii)   insanity   (3 marks)
    (iii) diminished responsibility   (4 marks)

(d) (i)   Identify the court that would try Yvonne for murder.   (1 mark)
    (ii)   Assuming Yvonne was convicted of manslaughter rather than
        murder, identify **two** possible sentences the judge could impose.   (2 marks)
    (iii) How well does the criminal law deal with the issue of domestic violence?

                                                            (4 marks)

AQA Higher Tier, Summer 2001

TALKING POINTS

Is it time for a new Offences Against the Person Act?

"Women react quite differently from men in the face of provocation. They have a longer fuse: abuse and ill-treatment build up resentment over a longer period, until an eventual breaking point arrives". Is this true, and should the defence of provocation be applied differently in the case of women?

SUGGESTED COURSEWORK TITLES

Explain the concepts of "means rea" and "actus reus", and strict liability. Do you think that there should be strict liability for a crime where there was no prior intention to commit the offence?

Explain the law relating to the defence of self-defence and the prevention of crime. Comment on the effectiveness of this defence, and how far you think it might be in need of reform.

11 | Family Law

MARRIAGE

The standard definition of a marriage is that taken from the case of *Hyde v Hyde* (1866). It is "the voluntary union of one man and one woman to the exclusion of all others".

In this country, marriage is monogamous, that is to say as the definition above indicates, between one man and one woman. Polygamous marriages, where a person may have several spouses, are allowed in some countries.

In a marriage, the parties must be respectively male and female. A person's sex is fixed at birth and the registration of birth is an historical record. In *R. v Registrar General of England and Wales* (1996), the court held that a birth certificate cannot be changed for persons who have undergone surgery for a sex change.

Homosexual couples may, and frequently do, enter into loving and committed unions for life. As things stand, these unions are not 'marriages' in the legal sense, although they may result in some legal consequences. From late 2005 gay and lesbian couples will be able to register their unions as civil partnerships, giving them many of the rights conferred by marriage.

The obligations and duties which follow from a valid legal marriage are examined in this chapter. It may be helpful also to look at the legal consequences of such matters as an engagement to be married, and cohabitation.

Engagement

Engagements are usually formalised by the man giving the woman an "engagement" ring. The ring remains the property of the woman should the engagement be broken, unless at the time it was given the man made it clear that in the event of the marriage not taking place the ring was to be returned.

Cohabitation

The legal status of an unmarried couple living together as man and wife is very complex, as the law does not recognise such an arrangement as being a "marriage". Parliament has recognised, however, that in certain matters these partners have similar duties and problems as legally married partners and has provided appropriate legislation.

An example of such legislation is the Inheritance (Provision for Family and Dependents) Act 1975, and the Law Reform (Succession) Act 1995. These Acts provide for a cohabitee to receive financial provision from a deceased partner's estate in certain circumstances (see under *Family Provision* in the next chapter).

As things stand at the moment, heterosexual couples who cohabit without being married are left with almost no legal redress when the relationship comes to an end. However, the Law Commission has been asked to produce proposals for legislation at a later date, to give such couples new rights similar to those following divorce, to make claims for financial support and a share in the other party's property.

Requirements of a valid marriage

Both parties must be 16 years of age or older

For a valid marriage to take place, both parties must be over the age of 16. If either of the parties is under 16, the marriage is void (non-existent at law). This is the case even if there was a genuine mistake which was not discovered until many years later. The effect would be that no marriage ever took place

If either of the parties is between 16 and 18, he or she can marry, but must have the consent of both parents, if alive. Should a parent unreasonably refuse consent, a minor may apply to the magistrates for permission to marry. The magistrates will make a decision based on the best interests of the minor. If a marriage takes place where one or both of the parties is 16 or 17, and there is no parental or court consent, then the marriage is nonetheless *still valid* (however, in such a case there may be criminal consequences, as it follows that there must have been fraud or deception involved).

The prohibited degrees

People who are too closely related to each other cannot marry. Apart from the matter of public policy, there is also the genetic risk of undesirable side-effects in a child born to parents who are blood relatives.

The Marriage Act 1949, as amended by the Marriage (Enabling) Act 1960, provides two complete lists of the *prohibited degrees*. These are lists of the relationships which are so close as to prohibit marriage. Obvious examples are brother-sister, parent-child, and grandparent-grandchild. Generally, uncles may not marry their nieces, nor aunts their nephews. Marriages between people within the prohibited degrees are **void.**

First cousins however may marry each other. A woman may wed her husband's brother, uncle or nephew if her marriage has been ended by death or divorce. A man has similar rights to marry his former wife's sister, niece or aunt.

The Marriage (Prohibited Degrees of Relationship) Act 1986 makes further provision for the marriage of persons related by affinity (or marriage). For example, a man can now marry a woman who is the daughter of his former spouse (though obviously not his daughter), provided that they are both 21 or over, and the younger party had not been a child of his family at any time before attaining the age of 18.

Neither party must be in an existing marriage

It is not possible for a person who is already married to 'marry' again. If a person who is in an existing legal marriage to another goes through a ceremony of marriage to a third person, that second 'marriage' is void and of no effect.

Furthermore, a person who 'marries' for a second time while his or her first marriage is still in existence, may be committing the crime of *bigamy*. However, it is possible to plead one or more of the following defences to bigamy:

* that in good faith and on reasonable grounds, it was believed the spouse was dead;

* that in good faith and on reasonable grounds, it was believed that the first marriage was annulled or dissolved;

* that the first spouse had been missing continuously for seven years, and there was no reason for supposing that partner to be alive.

The formalities required by statute

A marriage ceremony must be performed and solemnised as provided by the Marriage Acts 1949 and 1983.

Void and voidable marriages

A **void** marriage means one which, as far as the law is concerned, does not exist. It is as if the marriage had never taken place, and the parties are still in a single state. A marriage is void if there is some defect which is so fundamental that it is considered that no marriage ever existed.

A **voidable** marriage, on the other hand, is regarded as legally valid until a relevant court declares it to be void, or of no effect (a *nullity*). A voidable marriage is valid, but because of certain circumstances after, or at the time of the wedding, it may be annulled by the courts.

Void marriages

The Nullity of Marriage Act 1971, as now consolidated in the Matrimonial Causes Act 1973, provides that marriages shall be void for the reason that a valid marriage had not taken place because:

* one or both of the parties—
  were under 16 years old (see p. 273)
  were within the prohibited degrees (see p. 273)
  were already married (see above)
  had entered a polygamous marriage whilst being domiciled in England or Wales (see p. 273)

* there was a basic defect in the marriage ceremony (see p. 275).

* the parties were not respectively male or female (see p. 273).

Voidable marriages

Section 2 of the Nullity of Marriage Act 1971, as consolidated in the Matrimonial Causes Act 1973, provides that marriages are voidable for any of the following reasons.

- The marriage had not been consummated, owing to incapacity or the wilful refusal to consummate, by either party. This means that one party was incapable of having sexual intercourse or refused to do so.

- There was no valid consent to the marriage on the part of one or both of the parties because of duress, mistake, unsoundness of mind, or some other reason. Parties to a marriage must freely consent to it. An insane person cannot give valid consent because of failure to realise the consequences of what is being said or done. A similar situation may arise where one (or both) of the parties is drunk or under the influence of drugs.

- Either party, at the time of the marriage, was suffering from a mental disorder within the Mental Health Act 1983 making him or her unfitted for marriage.

- At the time of the marriage, one of the parties was suffering from a venereal disease in a communicable form, and the other party did not know.

- At the time of the marriage, the bride was pregnant by a man other than her husband, and her husband did not know of this.

A petition for nullity of a marriage may be made to the court immediately. There is no need, as with divorce, to wait for a period of time. Petitions for the last three reasons above, must be made within three years but this period may be extended if the petitioner has been suffering from a mental disorder. The court has the discretion to refuse to grant a decree if it considers it would be unjust to do so.

Children of void and voidable marriages

Children born of a voidable marriage are legitimate, even if the marriage is later declared void by the court. Children born of a void marriage are legitimate if, at the time of conception (or the marriage, if later), the parties reasonably believed the marriage to be valid.

The formalities of a valid marriage

A marriage may be solemnised by a ceremony of the Church of England, by ceremonies of other religions, in a Registrar's Office, or on some other approved premises. The formalities may differ according to the place where the marriage is solemnised.

Church of England

- Banns have to be published. Banns are a public announcement that the marriage is to take place and they must be published on three Sundays in the churches of either or both of the parties.

- A common licence has to be issued by a Bishop for the marriage to take place within the parish of one of the parties, or the Archbishop of Canterbury has to issue a special licence which permits the parties to marry anywhere.

- A superintendent registrar's certificate has to be issued, which authorises the church to solemnise the marriage.

- The wedding must take place between the hours of 8 am and 6 pm within three months of the banns being published, and there must be two or more witnesses.

Marriages solemnised by a Superintendent Registrar's certificate

The certificate authorises a marriage to take place:

- in the superintendent registrar's office, or

- in a registered building (usually a church of a non-Anglican religion) except in marriages between two professing Jews or between members of the Society of Friends (Quakers);

- between the hours of 8 am and 6 pm before open doors and witnessed by at least two persons (except Jewish or Quaker marriages);

- within three months of the issue of the certificate.

- The Marriage Act 1983 enables marriages of house-bound and detained persons to be solemnised at the place where they reside.

The Marriage Act 1994 enables civil marriages to take place on "approved premises"

Premises are approved by the local authority, and must have provision for members of the public to attend. The marriage must have two witnesses, a superintendent registrar and a registrar of the registration district in which the premises are situated. A religious service may not be used.

The aim of the Act, which came into force on April 1, 1995, is to maintain the sanctity of marriage and the ceremony may be held in a fixed building, in a dignified setting in a specified room or area of the premises licensed by the local authority.

The change has resulted in many applications from a variety of "buildings" including football clubs, The Royal Pavilion at Brighton, Blackpool Tower and other similar attractions.

Such marriages must take place between the hours of 8 am and 6 pm.

Other places

In 2002 it was proposed that some 15,000 local authority registration officers should be licensed as 'celebrants'. They would have the power to conduct marriages in *any safe location with public access*. This would mean that marriages could take place more or less anywhere provided that there was safe access for the public, such as beaches, private homes, and so on. The system was to be introduced in 2004.

The duties of husband and wife

The legal consequence of marriage is that certain duties fall upon the parties. Some of the duties are laid down by statute, while others are provided by the common law.

The principal duties are as follows.

- A spouse has a duty to maintain his or her partner, but this right is lost if a partner commits adultery or desertion. A husband has a common law duty to maintain his wife, but a wife will have to maintain a husband who is ill and incapable of earning an income. Although the old rule by which a deserted wife had authority to obtain credit against her husband's account, as an "agent of necessity", was abolished in 1970, a wife who lives with her husband has the implied authority to pledge the husband's credit (buying goods on credit on his account) for necessary household goods. This authority is based on the presumed, implied consent of the husband that she is his agent. This presumption may be rebutted by the husband informing the trader not to give credit to his wife, or by showing the court that the wife had a sufficient supply of the goods in question, or that she had a sufficient allowance to pay for them herself.

- Both parents normally have custody of their children until they are 18, although it can be lost earlier if the children marry or leave home. Parents may lose the right of custody should the marriage end in divorce, or if the children are taken into care because they are considered to be in danger.

- Both parents have a duty, depending on the age of the children, to;

  financially support and maintain their children;
  educate their children, and this usually means sending them to school;
  protect them from dangers in the home (*e.g.* unguarded fires);
  protect them from many other dangers likely to harm their health and moral welfare (*e.g.* introduction alcohol or prostitution).

THE CHILDREN ACT 1989

The aim of this Act was to bring together all public and private law relating to children into a single Act of Parliament. It is very detailed and wide-ranging, and brought about radical changes and improvements to the law relating to the care, upbringing and protection of children. It provides a single and consistent statement of the law in this area.

The Act considers that children are generally better looked after within the context of a family. Both parents should play a full part in this without resorting to legal proceedings. However, the Act provides for general principles which courts should observe, and details orders which the court may make.

General principles

Section 1 of the Children Act provides for three main principles to guide courts when making decisions under the Act. These principles, described below, are of general application.

The welfare principle

The child's welfare shall be the paramount consideration of the court when it decides any question with respect to:

- the upbringing of the child, or
- the administration of the child's property, or
- the application of any income arising from that property.

Presumption of no order

Where the court is considering whether or not to make an order under this Act, it will *only* do so if it considers that it would be better for the child than making no order at all.

Delay

As a general principle, any delay in determining the upbringing of a child is likely to prejudice the child's welfare. Therefore the court must draw up a schedule, or timetable, for deciding such matters without delay. Any delay can only be justified if it safeguards or enhances the welfare of the child concerned.

Orders available to the courts

Section 8 of the Children Act provides for the following orders (known as Section 8 orders). They are available for all proceedings relating to children. The courts of course must consider the above principles when making an order.

Contact order

This order requires the person with whom the child lives (or is to live), to allow the child to visit, stay with, or otherwise have contact with another person who is named in the order.

Prohibition order

This is where an order specifies some step which could be taken by a parent in meeting his or her parental responsibilities. The order provides that no such step may be taken without the consent of the court.

Residence order

This order settles arrangements as to the person with whom a child is to live. It is an important order, and replaces orders for custody, care and control.

A specific issue order

This order gives directions for the purpose of deciding a specific question which has arisen, or which may arise, in connection with any aspect of parental responsibility for a child.

DIVORCE

Either party may petition for divorce (apply to have the marriage legally ended), after one year of marriage. This is provided for in the **Matrimonial and Family Proceedings Act 1984**. Divorce cannot take place after less than a year of marriage, and the courts have no discretion to shorten this period. In divorce, the person seeking the dissolution of the marriage is called the *petitioner*, and the person from whom the divorce is sought is called the *respondent*.

Grounds for divorce

The **only** reason for petitioning for divorce is that **the marriage has broken down irretrievably**.
  The basis of the law on divorce is the **Matrimonial Causes Act 1973**. A petitioner for divorce must show that because of any one of five factors, the marriage has irretrievably broken down. The five "facts" are not in themselves grounds for divorce, but proof of one of them may establish the breakdown of the marriage. These five facts are discussed below. (It should be noted that, even if one or more of these facts are established, the court will not grant a divorce unless it is convinced that the marriage has actually broken down).

Adultery

Adultery is voluntary sexual intercourse between two persons, one or both of whom are married, but not to each other. The petitioner must prove that the other spouse committed adultery and that this act makes it *intolerable* to continue living with the respondent.

Unreasonable behaviour

The petitioner must show that the respondent's behaviour was such that the petitioner could not reasonably be expected to live with the respondent.
  It is a question of fact in each case, but the court would obviously expect to see evidence of very unreasonable behaviour, such as violence, extreme bad temper, drunkenness, obsessive jealousy and so on.

Desertion

It must be shown that the respondent deserted the petitioner for a period of two years or more. Generally desertion means living apart, but if the parties live in the same house, not as man and wife but following completely separate lives, this might be considered sufficient to prove desertion. It would be desertion if the respondent acted in such a way that the petitioner had to leave the family home.

Living apart for two years

The petitioner must show that the parties have lived apart continuously for more than two years immediately before presentation of the petition and that the respondent consents to the decree being granted.

Living apart for five years

It is sufficient under this heading to show that the marriage has broken down and the consent or otherwise of the other party is irrelevant to a spouse's right to petition.

Divorce decrees

When a petition for divorce is successful, the court grants a *decree nisi* (this literally means 'a decree unless . . .'). This decree does not dissolve the marriage immediately. It will, however, be dissolved unless good reason can be shown to the court, within six weeks, why the decree should not be made absolute. There may be special circumstances where the court might grant the decree absolute earlier, but the period is generally one of six weeks.

Six weeks after the *decree nisi*, the petitioner may apply to the court for a *decree absolute*. Until the decree absolute has been granted, the parties are not divorced. They may not therefore remarry until after the decree absolute. To do so would be committing the crime of bigamy.

Undefended divorces

Well over 90 per cent of divorce petitions are undefended. This means that the respondent does not contest the divorce, but agrees to its being granted. The procedure for such cases had been made simpler, and neither the parties nor their lawyers need attend the hearing. Divorces in these cases are often called 'postal divorces'.

JUDICIAL SEPARATION

A decree of judicial separation may be sought when one or both parties to a marriage no longer wish to live together as man and wife, but do not wish to be divorced. The reasons for making such petitions are usually religious, or because children are involved.

The petition may be brought at any time, and it is based on the grounds for divorce as outlined above. After a decree of judicial separation has been granted the parties are still legally married. The main effect is to release the parties from their obligation to cohabit.

There are fewer than a thousand petitions each year for decrees of judicial separation.

THE FAMILY LAW ACT 1996

Part I

Part I of the Act sets out a number of 'basic principles' underlying Parts II and III. These principles should be followed in matters relating to divorce, separation and legal aid for mediation in family matters. The basic principles are:

(a) the institution of marriage is to be supported;

(b) the parties to a marriage which has broken down are to be encouraged to take all practical steps to save the marriage; and

(c) a marriage which has irretrievably broken down should be brought to an end:

- with minimum stress to the parties and any children affected;
- with questions dealt with in a manner designed to promote as good a continuing relationship between the parties and any children affected as is possible, and
- without costs being unreasonably incurred in connection with the procedures mentioned above, and
- that any risk to one of the parties or the children, of violence from the other party should, as is reasonably possible, be removed or diminished.

Parts II and III

The Act introduced a "no fault" divorce, although the principle remained that the only grounds for divorce was to be the irretrievable breakdown of the marriage. This part of the Act still remains to be implemented, as the result of difficulties relating to the provision of counselling, which was to be an integral part of the proceedings. As things stand at the moment (2005), the position concerning divorce and separation is much the same as outlined in the previous pages.

Mediation, however, is an important factor in matrimonial proceedings. This involves arranging meetings with marriage guidance counsellors or other impartial persons. The reasons for such meetings cover a wide spectrum of concerns, from (at best) attempting to save the marriage, to details relating to the care of children, financial provisions, the future of the matrimonial home, and so on, where it is obvious that the marriage has irretrievably broken down and divorce is inevitable.

The judge can suggest that parties enter into arrangements for mediation, but in most cases this will have been done, either in private meetings involving "Relate", round-table conferences between the parties and their solicitors, or in some other context. Such meetings result in arrangements which can subsequently be accepted by the court as a settlement in the divorce. The court has the power, however, to set aside such arrangements if it considers them to be grossly unfair or contrary to public policy.

Useful websites

Marriage guidance counselling: *www.relate.org.uk*

Mediation: *www.mediation.org.uk*

MAINTENANCE

A wife whose husband neglects to maintain her or the children of the marriage, may apply to the courts for a matrimonial order for maintenance. Maintenance is a financial payment or settlement from a husband to maintain a wife and family. An order for maintenance may be obtained from the magistrates' court, county court or High Court. It is possible for a man to apply for maintenance from his wife, but, because it is more common, the text that follows refers to wives claiming from husbands, although it would apply to the reverse situation.

Maintenance is usually claimed when the married parties do not live together because of a breakdown in the marriage. A party may claim as a result of a judicial separation or divorce, or when the parties are separated but no legal action has been taken.

Maintenance claims made before or after divorce or legal separation

- *Before the divorce or legal separation*, the courts may award periodical cash payments to be paid by the spouse. The amount payable is what the court considers reasonable in the circumstances. It is provided to enable the claimant to maintain herself until the court action. Maintenance for children may also be claimed at this time.

- *After legal proceedings*, the courts may award in addition to a periodical cash payment:

  a lump sum for the wife and children, or
  a part of the husband's capital (usually no more than one-third) to be secured for the benefit of the wife and children, or
  a transfer of property belonging to the husband or which was owned jointly.

The court has discretion as to the size and nature of an award. Where the court makes an award of a periodical payment order, however, the Matrimonial and Family Proceedings Act 1984, provides power to the courts to implement "the clean break principle". The court should consider whether it would be appropriate to either award a lump sum payment or to limit the duration of the periodic payments for a time considered sufficient to enable the recipient to adjust to the end of financial dependance on the other party.

The court should consider:

- the income, earning capacity and financial resources of both parties;

- the financial needs and obligations the parties have or are likely to have;

- the standard of living enjoyed by the family before the breakdown of the marriage;

- the age of the parties, and the length of the marriage;

- any disability of either of the parties, physical or mental;

- the contribution each party made to the welfare of the family. (In *Gojkovic v Gojkovic* (1990), the Court of Appeal considered that the wife's share should not only be calculated on the wife's reasonable needs, but that her contribution to the family should also be taken into consideration);

- after a divorce or nullity, the value of the loss of some benefit (such as a pension) which cannot be acquired because of the termination of the marriage.

In addition, the Matrimonial and Family Proceedings Act 1984, requires:

- that first consideration should be given to any child of the family under the age of 18, and

- the court should consider whether it may exercise its power so that the financial obligations of each party to the other might be ended as soon as is just and reasonable after the decree of divorce.

The courts have power to vary the awards on the application of either party. The amounts may be increased or reduced or the method of payment varied or the payment stopped. For example, in *Cann v Cann* (1977) a wife obtained a matrimonial order from the magistrates' court and a year later, in 1961, the couple were divorced. In 1974, the wife successfully applied for a variation and the order was increased to £7 per week. Two years later the husband retired and applied for a reduction. His weekly income was £23 and the wife's income was £13. The court reduced the order to £5 per week, and considered that the one-third rule was inappropriate in this case. The result of the variation was that both the husband and wife had weekly incomes of £18.

In *Clutton v Clutton* (1991), the parties' sole capital asset after divorce was the family home, in which the wife and their daughter lived and which was in the husband's name. When considering an order to transfer the house to the wife as a "clean break", the Court of Appeal held that the transfer of the house would be unfair to the husband and ordered that the sale of the house be postponed until the wife remarried or cohabited with another man. The proceeds of the sale should then be divided on the basis of two-thirds to the wife and one-third to the husband.

Maintenance claims when there are no judicial proceedings for divorce or separation

A wife may apply to the courts (magistrates or superior courts) for maintenance on the grounds that her husband has neglected to provide maintenance for her and her children (if any). The claim may also be made on the grounds that, because of the husband's desertion or behaviour, the wife could not reasonably be expected to live with him. This behaviour could include such acts as adultery, cruelty, violence, drunkenness, and the like.

Maintenance paid to claimants is a weekly sum and is loosely based on one third of the gross total income of the parties. For example, if a husband earned £300 and the wife had no income, the wife would receive £100 a week. However, if the husband earned £160 and the wife earned £160 per week, the wife would receive nothing because she earned more than one-third of the total income. A county court or High Court may award a lump sum.

An important factor when assessing maintenance is the payment of income support. Anyone receiving income support will have the payments reduced by the amount of maintenance received.

SPECIMEN EXAMINATION QUESTION

The problem

Una and Victor have been married for 30 years and have three children, William, Alistair and Bernard, aged 26, 21 and 16 respectively.

William is planning to marry his cousin Cheryl. They were hoping to get married quietly one evening without telling either set of parents because they do not approve of William and Cheryl's relationship.

Alistair is also planning to marry despite the fact that six years ago, when he was 15 years old, he went through a marriage ceremony with his then childhood sweetheart, Donna. Neither Alistair nor Donna has taken any steps to dissolve their "marriage" in the last six years.

Bernard has been seeing his girlfriend Erica for the last year and recently discovered that she is pregnant. Erica's father has insisted that Bernard should "do the right thing" and marry his daughter. Reluctantly, Bernard has agreed. Bernard is too frightened to tell his parents as he does not want them to find out about the pregnancy. Bernard, Erica and Erica's family are organising a ceremony in secret. Unknown to Bernard, he is not the father of Erica's baby.

Una and Victor have recently been going through some difficulties in their marriage. Una is always complaining that Victor never gives her enough housekeeping money. Victor has, in fact, been spending his money on Fiona, his lover, whom he has been seeing for over a year.

(a) A marriage can either be **valid**, **void** or **voidable**.

   Explain the meaning of these terms.   (4 marks)

(b) Discuss the legal status of William's intended marriage to Cheryl.   (3 marks)

(c) Discuss the legal status of Alistair's intended marriage, in the light of his earlier "marriage" to Donna.   (3 marks)

(d) Discuss the legal status of Bernard's planned marriage to Erica.   (6 marks)

(e) Una has approached you for legal advice in respect of her marriage to Victor.

   Advise her as to the differences between divorce and judicial separation.   (4 marks)

(f) In the context of the divorce process, explain the meaning of the terms *decree nisi* and *decree absolute*.   (4 marks)

(g) (i) Identify the **two** civil courts where divorce cases can be heard.   (2 marks)

(ii) If Una and Victor were to divorce, they would almost certainly go through a process of **mediation.**

Briefly explain what this term means and comment on whether or not mediation is a beneficial process in the context of a divorce.   (4 marks)

AQA Higher Tier, Summer 2004

TALKING POINT

What are the relative merits and drawbacks of the institution of marriage? With the growing fashion of cohabitation, and the ever-increasing divorce rate, is marriage now outdated?

SUGGESTED COURSEWORK TITLES

Explain the present situation in English law with regard to marriage for people under the age of 18 years. Argue for and/or against the position that minors below this age should be able to marry without consent of adults.

Describe fully the grounds upon which a divorce will be granted. How far do you think it is now time for 'no-fault' divorces?

12 | Law of Succession and Property

The law of succession determines how, and to whom, a deceased person's goods will be transferred to new owners. In other words, this branch of the law deals with the question of what happens to a person's property after his or her death.

In general, the destination of a person's property will be determined by whether or not that person left a **will**. A will is a document in which a person indicates what shall happen to his or her property after death. Whether or not a person leaves a will, the duty of transferring property falls to other people who are known as the *personal representatives*.

Where a person dies leaving a **will**, the personal representatives are called **executors**.

A person who dies *without* leaving a will is said to die **intestate**. In these cases, the personal representatives are called **administrators**.

PROPERTY

Before looking at wills and intestacy in detail, it might be helpful to examine what is meant by a person's property. Property is anything which can be owned. It is either **real property** (freehold land), or **personal property** ('chattels': all moveable things, such as clothes, furniture, jewellery, as well as leasehold property, and legal rights over things, such as copyrights). Real and personal property can all be sold or otherwise disposed of and can also be left to others in a person's will.

A house or flat is very often the most valuable part of a dead person's estate. Home ownership falls under the headings of either **freehold** or **leasehold**.

Freehold land

A person who owns freehold land owns *real property*, as indicated above. The technical name for the ownership of freehold land is *fee simple absolute* in *possession*. 'Fee simple' means that the property is an estate of inheritance, and it may be left in a will to whomever the owner wishes, without any restriction. 'Absolute' means that it is not subject to any condition of length or period of time. 'In possession' means that the owner has immediate right of possession of the land or the right to receive rents for it from someone else who might reside in it.

Leasehold land

This is not complete ownership of land. It gives the holder the right to enjoy 'ownership' of the land for a specific period of time. This period is determined by the length of the *lease*. Its technical name is *term of years absolute*, and the term can vary between a very short period (a week), to 999 years.

Like freehold land, leasehold land may be sold or inherited during the term of the lease. At the end of the term of the lease, however, the land reverts to the freeholder, together with any house or other buildings which might have been erected on the land. There is statutory provision for leaseholders to purchase the freehold under certain conditions and within the period of the lease.

Mortgages

The majority of house buyers do not have the money to purchase a house or flat outright. They have to borrow the necessary money from various institutions. A loan is made on the security of the property and a *mortgage* is created.

A mortgage is a conveyance of freehold or leasehold property as security for the repayment of the sum of money which has been borrowed. If the borrower of the money (the **mortgagor**) fails to repay the loan, the lender (the **mortgagee**) may take possession of the property. The borrower usually (but not always), provides a proportion of the cost of the house purchase, and the balance is repaid, with interest, over a period of time. This period varies, but may typically be 25 years.

Building societies are the most common lenders of money for house purchase. Insurance companies, banks and local councils will also assist home buyers by providing mortgages. An insurance company may make the loan on the security of a life assurance policy: the borrower pays the interest plus the premiums of the life assurance policy, and in some cases, the loan.

Covenants and other restrictions

It may be noted here that home ownership does not necessarily give unrestricted rights over the property. It may be subject to a variety of restrictions contained in covenants, local bye-laws or government statutes. There may be, for example, a covenant in a conveyance of a house in a residential area that the owner shall not keep poultry on the land, or use the premises for the purposes of a commercial business.

WILLS

A will is a declaration concerning the distribution of real and personal property after death. A man who makes a will is called a **testator**; a woman who makes a will is called a **testatrix**. For the sake of simplicity, the term 'testator' will be generally used in this chapter.

Anyone who is aged 18 or over and who is of sound mind may make a will. For a will to have legal effect, however, it must comply with the requirements of the **Wills Act**

1837 and the **Administration of Justice Act 1982**. Theses requirements are examined below.

It is on the whole desirable for a person with a large or complex estate to leave a will, although for those who have little property the need is not so great. A will is necessary however where there is the intention to leave property to persons who are not members of the testator's immediate family. There may even be the intention that a specific or near relation should not inherit anything. A wife whose husband has deserted her, for example, might not wish him to inherit her property. In such a case, she may wish to make a will leaving the property to someone else.

Drawing up a will

Solicitors are traditionally used for the drawing up of wills. The use of their professional expertise is commonly relied upon, and in many cases one of the executors named might be the family solicitor involved. It is not absolutely necessary, however, for a solicitor to be used: wills in blank form can be bought from most stationers and may be used without difficulty provided that the testator's intentions are straightforward. It is also common for banks and other institutions to draw up wills.

It is impossible to know how many people make wills. It has been estimated however that less than 25 per cent of those entitled do so.

When a will takes effect

A will does not come into operation, and has no legal effect, until the death of the testator. A person named in a will has therefore no claim or right to any property until the testator's death. The testator or testatrix, while alive, may do whatever he or she likes with the property. It may be sold, destroyed or given away to someone else not named in the will.

Requirements of a valid will

A will must comply with the requirements of the Wills Act 1837 and the Administration of Justice Act 1982. If any of the necessary formalities or requirements is absent, then the will is invalid. This means that the intentions of the testator are ignored by the law, and the property is distributed as on intestacy. A will must be

- made by a person over 18 years of age;
- made by a person of sound mind;
- in writing;
- signed by the testator or testatrix;
- witnessed by at least two witnesses who are present at the same time.

Persons over 18

A valid will may only be made by a person who is 18 years of age or older. There are certain limited circumstances where this rule may be relaxed (see under *Soldiers' wills*, below), but for most purposes, a will made by anyone under 18 is invalid and of no effect.

Persons of unsound mind

If it can be shown that a person was of unsound mind when making the will, then it will be invalid. It is important that a testator is aware of, and understands the nature and contents of the will. Capacity to make a will may be affected by other factors, such as some disability.

> In *Buckenham v Dickinson* (1997), the testator who was aged 93, was deaf and had poor sight, changed his will to exclude his son and include members of his wife's family. A solicitor read the will out loud and asked the testator if he confirmed the changes. The testator's hand was placed on the will and he signed. His son contested the changes, claiming that his father did not have the capacity to make a will. The court agreed with the challenge, stating that a doctor should be present when capacity is in doubt and it was doubtful if the testator had heard or understood the contents of the will.

A will must be in writing

The writing of a will can be on any kind of paper or parchment (there was one famous occasion when a will written on an egg shell was apparently accepted as being valid). A will may refer to several other documents, provided that they can be identified and were in existence at the time when the will was made.

The requirement of a written will may be waived in the case of a 'soldier's will'.

Signature of the testator or testatrix

The will must be signed by the person making it. The signature should normally be at the end of the writing. However, if the signature was at the top of the document, it would still be effective if the testator intended that signature to validate the will.

In *Wood v Smith* (1992), a testator made a handwritten will which was headed "My will, by Percy Winterbone". It was contended that there had to be a will in existence when the signature was made, but the Court of Appeal held that the signature could precede the contents of the will provided the signature and preparation of the will were all part of one operation.

If the testator cannot write, a "mark", usually a cross, or an ink thumb-print will suffice provided that the "mark" can be identified as the testator's. If, for reasons of infirmity for example, a testator cannot sign the will, another person may sign on his behalf. This must be done in the presence of the testator, who must acknowledge to the witnesses that the other person signs on his behalf.

Witnesses

The testator's signature must be witnesses by at least **two** witnesses who are **present at the same time**. The witnesses do not need to be present when the testator's signature is made, provided that the testator acknowledges the signature to be his. The witnesses must sign the will, testifying that the signature of the testator was made or acknowledged in their presence.

If the witnesses are not present together at the time of the signature or the acknowledgment of it, the will is generally void. However, the Administration of Justice Act 1982 provides that if only one witness is present when a testator signs a will, both the testator and witness may acknowledge their signatures at a later date when a second witness is present and adds a second signature. This provision would not apply when an *attestation clause* is used, see below under *Specimen form of a draft will*. It is not strictly necessary to include an attestation clause when making a will, although it is the usual practice.

Witnesses may sign, or make their marks, immediately below the testator's signature.

Capacity of witnesses

Witnesses must reasonably understand that they are witnessing a signature, but it is not necessary for them to know the nature or contents of the document. A competent witness can be a person under 18, of extreme old age or illiterate, provided that he or she has sufficient understanding that a signature is being witnessed. A blind person would not be a competent witness because observation of the testator's signature would not be possible.

Witnesses as beneficiaries

Witnesses or their spouses generally cannot benefit under a will. If there are other beneficiaries named in the will however, the will would remain valid, and only the gift to the particular witness (or spouse) would be void.

In *Re Bravda* (1968), a will had four witnesses, although a valid will only requires two. The last two witnesses were to benefit under the terms of the will, and the testator only wished them to be aware of the existence of the will and its contents. Because the Wills Act 1837 provided that witnesses cannot benefit from the will of which they are witnesses, the court ruled that they could not receive their inheritance.

It was because of the injustice caused by this case that Parliament passed the Wills Act 1968, which now provides that if there are **at least two non-benefiting witnesses**, gifts to any additional interested witnesses will be valid (unfortunately, this legislation came too late to help the two persons concerned in the *Bravda* case).

Dating the will

It is usual to date a will, although failure to do so would not invalidate it. If there is more than one will, however, a date would be valuable evidence when deciding which would be the later, and therefore valid, one.

Survivorship clauses

It is common practice to have a survivorship clause included in a will. This provides that a beneficiary must survive the testator by a given period of time. If the beneficiary does not survive this period, the gift would go to another person.

Soldiers' wills

In times of emergency or war it may not be possible to comply with the strict rules for making a valid will. A sailor whose ship is sinking, for example, may have difficulty in finding witnesses to attest his signature.

The strict rules for making a will as described above are therefore relaxed for

- soldiers, sailors and airmen on actual military service, and

- any seaman at sea.

An informal will may be made by the above persons if they are **aged 14 and over**. If a will made in these circumstances is in writing, it need not be witnessed. An informal (or *nuncupative*) will may be made orally, but in such a case there would obviously have to be witnesses.

In *Rapley v Rapley* (1983) a 15-year-old sailor wrote an unwitnessed will while on shore leave. When he died more than 40 years later the court held that as he was not at sea when the will was made, it had no effect and he died intestate (see p. 298).

Whether or not the forces are on actual military service depends on the nature and activities of the force to which they are attached.

In *Re Jones* (1981), Jones was a soldier stationed in Northern Ireland. In 1978 he was shot and on the way to the hospital and before two officers said "If I do not make it, make sure Anne gets all my stuff" (Anne was his fiancee). Jones died on the following day. It was held by the court that this statement be accepted as his last will even though he had previously made a formal will in favour of his mother. The court considered that he was on actual military service at the time of making the statement although there was no state of war and the forces to which he belonged were not engaged against a regular or uniformed enemy.

An informal will remains valid even after the hostilities or emergencies have ended.

Revocation

A testator may change, vary or *revoke* a will. To revoke a will means to cancel it completely. Revocation may be express (deliberate, intentional) or implied from the conduct of the testator.

By expressly revoking the will

An express revocation has to be made in exactly the same way as making a will, *i.e.* in writing, signed and witnessed.

By making a new will or codicil

A new or later will revokes all previous wills which are not inconsistent or different. It is usual to start a new will with a statement revoking all previous wills, thereby making an express revocation. If this statement is not made, any gifts in a previous will would still be effective if not accounted for in the subsequent will.

For example, a will may direct "my money in the bank to Matthew, my car to Kate and my dog to Sarah". If a subsequent will provides "my money in the bank to Peter, my car to Nicholas and my boat to Jonathan", and there is no clause revoking previous wills, Sarah would be entitled to the dog. The reason for this is that the second will made no provision for this property, and it is presumed that the first will expressed the testator's wishes in this respect. Without the express exclusion clause, it would be necessary to study all previous wills to find the testator's intentions.

Codicils

A *codicil* is a later addition to a will, which varies or amends it. A codicil, which is inserted in or attached to the will, has to be signed and witnessed in the same way as the will itself.

In *Re White (Deceased)* (1990), the testator dictated amendments to his original will, which were handwritten on to the original will. At the foot of the last page of the will the testator wrote, "Alterations to will dated 14.12.84. Witnessed", and two witnesses duly signed below, although neither the testator nor the witnesses signed or initialled the alterations. It was held that the original will, without the amendments, was the valid will, because neither the testator nor the witnesses of the alterations had signed in the prescribed manner.

By destroying a will

A will is only revoked if it is **intentionally** destroyed. This may be done by the testator, or by someone else in the testator's presence and as instructed by the testator. Destruction may be by burning, tearing or any other means, but it must be done with the intention of destroying the will.

A will destroyed *accidentally* would still be valid. In such a case, the personal representative would refer to other material, such as a copy of the will or oral evidence, to try to find the testator's intentions.

> In *Re Adams (Deceased)* (1990), the testatrix instructed her solicitors to destroy her will. The will was returned to her with the advice that she should destroy it herself. When after her death the will was found, it had been heavily scribbled on with a ballpoint pen. It was impossible to read the signatures on the will, but other parts of the will could still be read. It was held that, as the signatures had been destroyed with the testatrix's clear intention that the will should be revoked, the whole will had in fact been revoked.

By subsequent divorce

When a marriage ends in divorce, a will made before the divorce or annulment is affected as follows:

* any gift to the former spouse is revoked, and

* the appointment of the former spouse as executor or executrix is also revoked.

If any other person is named as a beneficiary in the will, it would remain valid. Only gifts to the former spouse would be invalid.

If the former spouse was the only beneficiary, the dead person's estate would be distributed under the rules of intestacy (see page 298).

The Law Reform (Succession) Act 1995 provides that if a testator's marriage is ended by divorce or is dissolved after the date when the will was made, any gifts in the will to the former spouse shall pass as if the former spouse had died on the day of the divorce.

By subsequent marriage

If a person marries, any will made before that marriage is revoked. If however the will is made *in contemplation of marriage*, that is to say, with a particular marriage in mind, it will not be revoked provided that

* the name of the intended spouse is stated in the will, and

* the testator intended that the will should not be revoked by the marriage.

Family Provision

Before 1938 a man could leave his property to whomsoever he wished, and there was no requirement to provide for his family. A man could give his entire estates to charity and leave his wife penniless. The **Inheritance (Family Provision) Act 1938** gave the court power to make a financial provision out of the husband's estate to a wife and certain other dependants if they had not been provided for in the will. Further and more extensive powers were given to the courts by the **Inheritance (Provision for Family and Dependants) Act 1975.** This Act provides that the court has a discretion to make an award out of the dead person's estate to dependants who have not received "reasonable financial provision", from a will or intestacy, or from both. The following persons may apply to the court for family provision.

Spouses

The husband or wife of the dead person may apply for family provision under the Act. Former spouses who have not remarried may also apply.

Children

Children of the deceased may apply under the Act. It makes no difference if a child is illegitimate, adopted or merely treated as a child of the family. There are no restrictions as to age, incapacity, sex, or whether married or not.

> In *Re Callaghan (Deceased)* (1984), a married man, over 40, made a successful claim to be treated as a child of the family and was awarded a lump sum because the deceased, who died intestate, had treated him as a son from the age of 12.
>
> In *Re Pearce (Deceased)* (1998), a farmer left his estate to his second wife. His son, who had worked for years on the farm for no pay, on the promise that the farm would be left to him, successfully made a claim for an award from his father's estate.

Other persons

Any other persons who immediately before the death of the deceased were being maintained, either wholly or partly, by the deceased can apply under the Act. This heading covers other relatives, such as sisters, brothers, mothers and fathers. It also includes friends who were receiving substantial financial support before the deceased's death.

Cohabitees

The **Law Reform (Succession) Act 1995** provides that a cohabitee can apply under the 1975 Act without the need to show dependency. The parties must have lived together for two years or more to qualify, otherwise dependency must be shown.

Reasonable financial provision

"Reasonable financial provision" means:

- in the case of a spouse, financial provision as would be reasonable in all the circumstances, whether or not that provision is needed for maintenance,

• in the case of other persons, such financial provision, as would be reasonable in all the circumstances, needed for their maintenance.

The applications must be made within six months of grant of probate or letters of administration being taken out. The court would consider the value of the estate and the provision already made to the applicant. In the case of a spouse, consideration would be given to age, duration of marriage and the contribution made by the applicant to the family and its welfare.

With regard to young children, educational needs would be considered and with older children, the ability reasonably to maintain themselves. The court would also take into consideration statements made by the deceased as to the reasons why certain provisions were made or were not made.

The court may award lump sums or periodical payments, transfer certain property, such as the family house, and make settlements of other property.

Legacies

Gifts named in a will have different names in law according to the nature of the property. A transfer of real property (freehold land) is called a *devise*. Gifts of personal property (chattels) are called *legacies* or *bequests*. Legacies (bequests) are of different types.

General legacies

A general legacy is a gift where no specific thing is named. Examples might be, "I leave a painting to my daughter Catherine", or "I give a chair to my son-in-law Adrian"

Specific legacies

A specific legacy is when a thing is named or otherwise identified. "I leave my painting of the Matterhorn by Fred Elwell to . . .", or "I give my black leather Parker-Knoll reclining chair to . . ."

Residuary legacies

After all outstanding debts have been paid from the estate, and the general and specific devises and legacies distributed to the beneficiaries, the *residue* is what is left.

If a general or specific gift is no longer owned by the testator at the time of death, then that gift cannot be passed on. It is said to be *adeemed*, and there is no inheritance.

If a person named in a will as a beneficiary should die before the testator, then whatever gift is due to that beneficiary will lapse and go into the residue. If the beneficiary is a child of the testator and dies leaving children, however, the position will be different (see below). Sometimes the will might provide for another person to receive that gift. It is quite common, for example, for a gift to be left to X, but if X dies before the testator, then it will go to Y.

Children of the testator

As indicated in the previous paragraph, where a testator leaves property to children who pre-decease him, the gift does not lapse if they themselves die leaving children (the usual term for this is *leaving issue*). If a son or daughter has one or more children alive at the time of the testator's death, then the property passes to those children. This is through the process known as *per stirpes* ('by way of descendents'). This means that those children would take, in equal shares, the gift intended for their father or mother. If any of those children were under 18 at the time of the testator's death, then the property would be held *in trust* for them until they reached the age of 18.

A trust is where property is held by one person (called the trustee) on behalf of, or for the benefit of, another person. It is often the case when a person is under the age of majority, as above. When the minor reaches the age of 18 then the property is passed to him or her outright.

If a gift is made in a will to a son or daughter who dies *childless* before the testator dies, then the gift will lapse and become part of the residue.

Personal representatives

The persons who take control of the property of a deceased person are known as the deceased's *personal representatives*. The legal expression is that the property *vests* in the personal representatives. They have a duty to collect all money and property owned by, or due to, the deceased. They pay all debts owed by the deceased, including funeral expenses, and sell or convert property as necessary. They then have the duty to distribute the remainder according to the relevant circumstances.

Where the deceased has left a will, these personal representatives are named in it. They are called *executors*. Where there is no will, or where an executor is unwilling to act, the personal representatives are called *administrators*.

Executors

Executors, frequently more than one, are usually named in the will. A beneficiary in the will can be appointed as executor. It is also common for solicitors or banks to act as executors.

Before an executor may deal with the estate of the deceased, it is necessary to apply for a *grant of probate*. This is normally a formal exercise in presenting the will and giving details of the property and value of the deceased's estate. Probate is normally granted in a short time, provided that there are no complications.

As soon as probate has been granted, the executors can pay off debts and then distribute the estate according to the terms of the will.

Administrators

Administrators are appointed where the deceased does not leave a will. In such a case the deceased is said to die *intestate*.

Administrators are appointed by the court, and are usually the spouse or children of the deceased. Administrators apply for *letters of administration* in the same way as an executor applies for a grant of probate. Administrators distribute the estate of a person who dies intestate according to the *rules of intestacy*. These rules are dealt with below.

An administrator is also appointed if an executor is unwilling or unable to act, or is not named in the will. In this case, after the grant of letters of administration, the administrator will distribute the estate according to the terms of the will.

Form of a Draft Will

This is the last will and testament of Homer Doe of 69 Amherst Street, Tewkesbury.

1. I HEREBY REVOKE all former wills made by me and declare this to be my last will.

2. I APPOINT MY SON BARTHOLOMEW DOE as the executor of my will.

3. I BEQUEATH to my son Bartholomew Doe my car and £5,000.

4. I DEVISE AND BEQUEATH all the residue of my estate both real and personal whatsoever and wheresoever to my wife Marjorie Doe absolutely, PROVIDED that she survives me by 28 days. In the event that she predeceases me or fails to survive me by 28 days, I give the residue of my estate to the said Bartholomew Doe absolutely.

IN WITNESS whereof I have set my hand this twenty-ninth day of March Two Thousand and Five.

Signed by the above named Homer Doe
as his Last Will and Testament in the
presence of us both present at the same
time who at his request in his presence   HOMER DOE
and in the presence of each other have   *(Signature)*
hereunto subscribed our names as witnesses.

Uriah Heap – *(Signature)*
Solicitor,
Cheltenham.

Ebenezer Scrooge – *(Signature)*
Vickery Street,
Gloucester,
Company Director.

Note: the writing opposite the signature of Homer Doe is called the *attestation clause*. The witnesses sign as being "present at the same time" (see above under *Witnesses*).

Intestacy

When a person dies without making a valid will, he or she is said to die intestate, and the property is distributed according to the rules laid down by the Administration of Estates Act 1925, as amended by other Acts. These rules also apply to a partial intestacy which occurs when all the testator's property has not been disposed of by a will.

For convenience, the following rules assume that it is a man that has died, but the rules are similarly applied when a woman is deceased.

A surviving wife only

If there are no children to the marriage and the deceased has no living parents, brothers or sisters, or their issue—the wife receives the whole estate.

A surviving wife and children

The wife receives

- all the personal chattels, (such as furniture, the car, etc.), and

- the first £125,000 of the estate plus interest at 7 per cent from the date of her husband's death to the time of payment

The balance of the estate is then halved. Then

- the wife receives interest on one half for life, and

- the children immediately share equally in the other half, and in the mother's half after her death.

The share for children **under the age of 18** is kept in trust for them until they reach that age. A grandchild of the testator would inherit its parent's share if that parent died before the testator.

An illegitimate child has full rights of inheritance and may claim against the estates of both his or her parents on the same basis as legitimate children.

A surviving wife with no children, but a surviving parent, brother or sister, or their issue

The wife would receive the chattels, the first £200,000 with interest at seven per cent as above, and the absolute ownership of half of the remaining balance. Surviving parents would equally share the other half, but if there were no surviving parents, the deceased's brothers or sisters (or their issue if they predeceased the intestator) would share this half of the residue.

The Law Reform (Succession) Act 1995, provides that in an intestacy or partial intestacy the spouse of the deceased person only benefits under the intestacy rules if the spouse has survived the deceased by 28 days.

Surviving children but no wife

The children take absolutely all the estate in equal shares. If under 18 the property would be held on trust. They take the estate regardless of all other relatives.

Surviving parents, but no wife or children

The parents share absolutely the whole estate.

No surviving wife, children or parents

The following relations will be entitled to the estate in the following order:

- brothers and sisters of the whole blood,
- brothers and sisters of the half blood,
- grandparents,
- uncles and aunts of the whole blood,
- uncles and aunts of the half blood.

If none of these relations survive the intestate, the estate passes to the Crown *as bona vacantia*. The property which comes the way of *bona vacantia* is disposed of and the proceeds paid into the Exchequer. It is possible to recover the proceeds at a later date if an unknown relative makes a belated claim.

Forfeiture rule

It is a general rule of law that a person who unlawfully kills another is stopped from benefitting as a consequence of the killing. The "forfeiture rule" arises from public policy. Obviously, a person named in a will cannot benefit from the will if he murders the testator.

The Forfeiture Act 1982 was created to enable certain persons found guilty of unlawful killing (other than murder),

- to obtain relief from forfeiture of inheritance,
- to enable such persons to claim for financial provision out of the deceased person's estate, and
- to receive certain pensions and social security benefits.

The Act allows persons convicted of unlawful killing (manslaughter, death caused by dangerous driving, suicide pacts, infanticide, etc.) to make a claim, within three months of conviction, to the court to modify the "forfeiture rule". The court will only do so if the justice of the case requires it to do so. It must be stressed that convicted murderers do not come within this Act.

> In *Re K. (Deceased)* (1985) (the first case under this Act) a wife, during a quarrel, killed her husband with a shotgun. She pleaded guilty to manslaughter, and as she had been subject to unprovoked violent attacks by the husband, she received a two year probation order. The court held that although the "forfeiture rule" applied on the facts of the case it would be unjust if she was stopped from receiving benefit under the will, and ordered that the effect of the "rule" should be modified accordingly.

In *Dunbar v Plant* (1997), the parties had a suicide pact. Dunbar killed himself but the defendant survived. The defendant was entitled to certain benefits upon the death of her fiance but it was argued that under the Forfeiture Act she could not benefit. The Court of Appeal, while affirming that aiding and abetting a suicide would normally mean that the survivor would not benefit, considered that in this case the public interest would not be served by forfeiture.

However, in *Jones v Roberts* (1995), the applicant killed his parents while suffering from paranoid schizophrenia. He pleaded guilty of manslaughter, on grounds of diminished responsibility. His parents died intestate, but it was held that he was not entitled to benefit from his crime as he was subject to the forfeiture rule.

Useful websites

Wills and intestacy: *www.wills-direct.co.uk and www.family-solicitors.co.uk/Wills_section.htm*

Probate and letters of administration: *www.probate.org.uk*

SPECIMEN EXAMINATION QUESTIONS

The problem

Angus made a will 18 months ago leaving his entire estate to a children's charity. He made no provision in his will for his wife Bonnie, or his three children, Charlie, Donal and Eleanor, aged 24, 18 and 15 respectively. Charlie has not been seen by the rest of his family for the last six years, having left home to join a religious group when he was 18. Angus has also not made any provision for his life-long friend, Fergal, to whom he had promised a valuable gold watch.

Angus drafted his will at the end of his 2002 diary but, because of lack of space, had to sign it at the top of the next page.

Having drafted his will, Angus asked his next-door neighbour, Gus, to sign as witness. Angus then went round to Fergal's house to ask him to be a witness as well. Fergal, thinking he might be a beneficiary, refused to sign. Angus then went to see another friend, Hamish, and both Hamish and his granddaughter, Isla, aged 16, signed as witnesses.

Angus died suddenly last week, leaving an estate worth £245,000. There is a suspicion that he may have committed suicide. Angus's doctor has indicated that he had been treating Angus for severe depression for the last three years.

(a) Discuss the validity of Gus and Isla as witnesses to Angus's will.   (4 marks)

(b) Discuss the validity of Angus's will, taking into account all the relevant issues raised in the situation.   (7 marks)

(c) If Angus's will were to be declared invalid, he would die intestate. Explain how Angus's estate would be distributed under the intestacy rules.   (7 marks)

(d) If Angus's will were to be declared valid, it would almost certainly be contested.

   (i)   Name an Act of Parliament under which a will can be contested.   (1 mark)
   (ii) Identify **three** groups of people who are entitled to contest a will under this Act.
                                                                              (3 marks)

   (iii) In this particular situation, discuss who may choose to contest Angus's will and who may have the best chances of success.   (4 marks)

(e) Choose your answer to **either** (c) **or** (d)(iii). Comment how well the intestacy rules **or** the rules on family provision have dealt with Angus's estate.   (4marks)

AQA Higher Tier, Summer 2004

TALKING POINT

Approximately only a quarter of those people entitled to make a will bother to do so. What is the reason for this? Does it matter?

SUGGESTED COURSEWORK TITLES

Explain the requirements to make a valid will. Consider whether or not the present position of witnesses is suitable for today's methods of recording data.

Describe the method of distribution of a person's estate under the rules of intestacy. Could you suggest a fairer method of distribution?

13 | Examination Technique

REVISION

Remember that it is never too early to start revising for your exam. There are many ways of approaching revision, and there are also many favourite techniques. Here are a few suggestions.

- Revise systematically, topic by topic, by carefully reading through your notes and any other materials that you have accumulated during your course. If there is any concept with which you have difficulty, go over it again, consult other books, ask fellow students, or in some other way make sure that you understand it.

- Law is constantly changing. Although you are not expected to be absolutely up-to-date with legal matters, it is good practice to be aware of current developments. Keep your eye on the media for high-profile cases relevant to your course, or proposals for radical changes to the law.

- Be sure that you cover the whole syllabus. It is sometimes tempting to leave out some part which you find difficult or uninteresting. There will of course be choices of question, but a topic which you have ignored might appear in a compulsory section of the examination, and then you would be seriously disadvantaged.

- In each area of law, make a list of relevant cases and the *ratio decidendi* (the principle for the decision), for each. Make sure that you learn as many of these as you can, as well as the names of relevant Acts of Parliament. The dates of cases and statutes are not vital, although it might be useful to be able to distinguish between, for example, the Theft Act 1968 and the Theft Act 1978.

- Engage the help of somebody else, preferably a fellow-student, in your revision. Test each other, by, for example, one reading out a general principle, and the other responding with the name of a case which illustrates it. Try it the other way round: name a case, explain the principle.

- Look at past papers. Familiarise yourself thoroughly with what will be required of you. Note the form of the questions, the time available, which questions are compulsory, and where you have a choice.

Use these past papers and the specimen questions given in this book to practice written answers. Check your response against your text book or your notes. Estimate how many marks you might have scored out of those available.

Try not to leave revision to the last moment. Burning the midnight oil the night before the exam is not a good idea, and is bound to be counter-productive. It is far better to have a good night's sleep, and arrive early and clear-headed at the examination centre. Make sure, too, that you have with you whatever may be required for the examination, especially at least two serviceable pens.

THE EXAMINATION

Read the instructions carefully. Note how many questions need to be answered, which ones are compulsory, and which ones offer a choice. This is very important. If you are asked to answer any **one** question from a choice of four, for example, and you answer them all, you would only get credit for one of them, and would have wasted a great deal of valuable time. When you start writing your answers, bear the following things in mind.

- Different questions carry different numbers of marks. It follows therefore that the length of your answer will be approximately proportional to the number of marks available. A question carrying only one mark will clearly require only a single word or short phrase by way of response, not several sentences. Conversely, an eight–mark question may require a paragraph of several sentences. A useful rule of thumb is that you should spend approximately *one minute per mark* when writing your answer.

- Avoid the "scatter gun" or "shopping basket" approach. If the question requires you to name, say, three types of judge who sit in the crown court and you name every kind of judge you can think of in the hope of getting three of them right, you will almost certainly lose marks if you get any of them wrong.

- Always, where possible and relevant, illustrate your answer by quoting suitable authorities in the way of cases, statutes, etc. As indicated earlier, dates are not vital, although they might sometimes be helpful. If you cannot remember the name of a case, try to give a very brief description of the circumstances. If, for example you couldn't remember the name *Sayers v Harlow UDC* (1958), when discussing contributory negligence, it would be better to say, "as in the case of the lady locked in a lavatory . . .", than not to mention any case at all.

- Use suitable language in your answers, and avoid colloquialisms and slang expressions. Law uses a wide range of specialist terms, and you should always use these where possible. A glossary to help you in this respect follows this chapter. Never say, for example, *"He could be done for GBH"*, or *"She hasn't got a leg to stand on"*, but instead say "He could be prosecuted for", or "She does not seem to have a defence in this case". Credit will be given for the accurate use of specialist terms. Remember also that you are sitting a *law* examination, and therefore your answer must deal with *legal* issues, not moral or political ones.

- Where a question asks you to argue the case for or against some aspect of the legal system, try as far as possible to state both sides of the argument, even if you come down heavily on one side or the other. A one-sided answer, well argued, can score high marks but rarely the maximum, and it is better to show that you are aware of a contrary view.

- When answering a problem question, that is to say, one which outlines a series of incidents and asks you to state the probable legal consequences, work from the general to the particular. This means that you should start by discussing the general principles of law raised by the question, supporting your discussion by quoting authorities where you can, and then apply these to the facts you have been given, coming to some sort of reasoned conclusion. It does not necessarily have to be the "correct" conclusion (it could go either way). It is enough to show that you understand the issues, can illustrate the law, and attempt to apply it to a given set of facts.

- Be aware always of time constraints. Keep an eye on the clock, and allocate your time carefully, according to the requirements of each question. It is very important to finish each question, as most of the heaviest scoring tends to be nearer the end than the beginning. Do not rush; write with care, but do finish the paper.

- There is usually a small percentage of the overall mark awarded for quality of written expression. Try to write as far as possible in intelligible English, using appropriate legal terms as mentioned above. No marks are awarded for standard of handwriting, but it is as well not to antagonise a marker who has to spend a lot of time trying to decipher your script!

- If time allows, read over your paper when you have finished to check what you have written.

COURSEWORK

Coursework is work written by you in the course of your studies. It is marked by your centre, and submitted to the examination board by the required date. It may be in your own handwriting, typed, or word-processed, but it must be your own work. Coursework allows candidates to select, interpret and use information relating to the law, and then analyse and evaluate this information by means of systematic and well-reasoned arguments. Whereas there is some scope for exercising these skills within the written examination, coursework provides a freer and wider opportunity to do so.

The particular requirements for coursework will be set out by the relevant examinations board. These requirements should be carefully noted and followed. Your centre should give you guidance in this respect. Whatever these requirements may be, it is important to bear in mind the following points.

- The topics dealt with in your coursework **must** deal with topics of law included in the subject content of your syllabus. Controversial matters of contemporary interest, such as "Hunting with Hounds", however compelling, should not be chosen. Suggestions for coursework titles appear in the course of this book. Other suggestions may well be found in the relevant section of your G.C.S.E Law syllabus, and in addition your teacher or lecturer may be able to help. Such lists are not exhaustive, however. If you produce more than one piece of coursework, the subject matter of the one must not overlap with that of the other.

- Coursework is your own work, and the result of your own research. There is plenty of scope for finding material for your coursework from a wide range of sources. These include a variety of text books, case reports, reports of visits you have made to the courts, newspaper reports and material from other branches of the media. Many helpful leaflets are available from places like public libraries and Citizens Advice Bureaux.

- Information which you use must be presented in your own words, and not be merely unprocessed material. You will get very little credit for simply copying out of books or cutting out pictures and reports from papers and other sources and sticking them onto the page. Of course, your coursework may be judicially illustrated in this way where necessary, but the input must be essentially your own. Remember also that you must always try to maintain the relevance of your selected material to your title.

- Try to keep as nearly as you can to the number of words stipulated for each piece of coursework. If you fall too far short, you may not be able to do justice to your topic. If you go well over the limit, you may become repetitive or irrelevant.

You will notice that the coursework titles suggested in the body of the text are invariably in two-part form. This pattern gives you the opportunity to exhibit your skills of selection, presentation and use of information in the first part, and analysis and evaluation in the second.

Appendix

GLOSSARY

Below is a list of some of the more common specialist legal terms to be found in the body of the text. Latin tags are given as nearly as possible their literal translation. Words expressed in italics in the explanation of these legal terms are themselves separately defined. Many words, such as plaintiff and writ are still in common use, although they have in recent years been replaced by alternative expressions.

Accused, The	One accused of a crime. Now called *defendant*.
Acquit, acquittal	Find not guilty of a crime. The process of finding not guilty.
Act of Parliament	A formal document which enacts laws made by Parliament. See *statute*.
actus reus	"Guilty act". That element of a crime which involves the commission of a wrongful act. See *mens rea*.
Administration, letters of	Granted to administrators to enable property to be distributed when a person dies *intestate*.
Advocacy, advocate	The putting forward, or pleading of, a person's case in court. One who does this.
Anarchy	Where there is no law. A state of lawlessness.
Annulment	The process of making something, e.g. amarriage, *void*.
Antecedents	An accused person's previous record.
Appellate court	A court which can hear appeals from a lower court.
Appropriation	Treating property as if it were one's own.
audi alteram partem	"Hear the other side". A rule of natural justice that each side shall be given the opportunity to state its case.
Beneficiary	One who is to receive, or who receives, a gift in a will.
Bequest	A gift of property of any kind in a will.
Bill	A draft of proposed law which is submitted to Parliament.
Binding	Must be followed. Applies to laws, rulings, precedents, etc.
bona vaccantia	Property which belongs to no-one.
Breach	A breaking, as of a duty of care, or a contract, etc.
caveat emptor	"Let the buyer beware". A purchaser should take care when entering into a contract of sale where statutory protection may not apply.
certorari	"Be contended". A *prerogative order* requiring the proceeding so an inferior court to be brought before the High Court.
Chattels	Items of all kinds of personal property which are moveable.
Claimant	One who brings a case in the civil court. Previously called the *plaintiff*.

consensus ad idem	"Agreement to the same thing". Genuine agreement: an essential element in a valid contract.
Consideration	The price paid, or something of value, which passes from one party to another in a contract. An essential element in a valid contract.
Consolidation, consolidating Act	All the previous provisions of several *Acts of Parliament dealing* with a common topic are brought together into one *Consolidating Act*
Conditional fee	A fee for a court case which will be paid only on the event of the case being won. "No win, no fee".
Contributory negligence	Where a party in a negligence case is partly responsible for the injuries, damage, etc. sustained. *Damages* are proportionally reduced.
Conveyancer	A person who is qualified to act in the transfer of land. One who draws up a conveyance of such property.
Convict, conviction	To find guilty of a crime. An instance of having been found guilty.
Curfew	A restriction of movement, particularly between certain hours. Usually at night.
Custodial sentence	A sentence which involves loss of freedom, *e.g.* imprisonment.
Damages	The sum awarded to be paid by one party to the other in a civil case by way of compensation.
Defendant	One who defends an action in either a criminal or civil court.
Delegated legislation	The power to make laws passed on by Parliament to some other person or authority, *e.g.* Minister of the Crown, local authority, etc.
Devise	A gift of freehold land, real property, in a will.
doli incapax	"Incapable of deceit". The assumption that a child below a certain age is incapable of committing a crime.
ejusdem generis	"Of the same kind". A guideline in the interpretation of statutes.
Electoral roll	Register of all those entitled to vote in elections. Used in the selection of juries.
Enabling act	An act of Parliament which gives powers to a minister, local authority, etc., to pass *delegated legislation*.
Equity	A system of justice which evolved to relieve any hardship caused by the common law.
Executive	The branch of government responsible for carrying out laws. The Cabinet.
Executor, executrix	Man, woman, who is appointed by a person making a will to carry out the provisions of that will.
First instance, court of	A court where a case is heard for the first time.
Frustration	The impossibility of carrying out the terms of a contract because of some intervening event.
Fusion	The concept of merging together the two branches of the legal profession.
guardian ad litem	One who looks after the interests in court of a person who is incapacitated in some way, *e.g.* an infant or person of unsound mind.
habeas corpus	"That you may have the body". A writ which requires a person who is being detained without apparent reason to be released, or justification to be shown for such detention.
Hereditary	By right of birth, *e.g.* peerage passed down from one generation to another.
ignorantia juris haud excusat	"Ignorance of the law in no way excuses". Not knowing the law is no defence to a criminal charge.
Implied	Taken to exist in the context. *E.g.* implied terms in a contract, though not expressed, apply by the provisions of the Sale of Goods Act.
Indictment	A formal written charge of crime. Used in crown court proceedings.
Ineligible	Does not qualify because of some state of affairs.

Injunction	An instruction or order by the court to one party to refrain from doing something, *e.g.* committing a nuisance.
Intestate	Not having made a will.
Judicature	The administration of justice; the functions or powers of a judge.
Judicial precedent	Judge made law. Where the decisions of judges in higher courts are *binding* upon inferior courts.
Judiciary	The judges.
Jurisdiction	The area or extent of law which can be heard in a particular court, etc.
Legacy	A gift in a will, especially of money or personal property.
Legislation	The process of making law.
Legislature	The branch of government responsible for making laws. Parliament.
Liable, liability	Legally responsible, particularly in a civil case. Legal responsibility. Do not confuse with *libel* (below).
Libel	False and damaging statement (defamation) made in permanent form, *e.g.* writing.
Litigation	The act or process of bringing or contesting a lawsuit.
mandamus	"We order". A *prerogative order* commanding a court or public body to carry out its duty.
Mandatory	Compulsory, essential. Cannot be avoided.
mens rea	"Guilty mind". The intention, or mental element in the commission of a crime.
nemo dat quod non habet	"No-one gives that which they do not possess". A person with no entitlement to something cannot pass the title to someone else.
nemo judex in causa sua	"No-one is judge in his own cause". A rule of natural justice. A judge must not act in a case in which he has an interest.
Null, nullity	*Void*, of no legal effect. Something which has no legal effect.
obiter dicta	"Incidental words". Thing said by the way, and not forming part of the ratio *decidendi.* May have *persuasive* effect.
per incuriam	"By mistake". Where a court makes a decision in error.
per se	"By itself". Actionable *per se* means actionable without the need to prove damage.
Persuasive	Of a *judicial precedent,* not *binding,* but of sufficient authority to be taken into consideration when coming to a decision.
per stirpes	"by way of descendants".
Petitioner	The traditional term for a person seeking a divorce. See *respondent.*
Plaintiff	A person bringing an action in the civil courts. Now known as the *claimant.*
Prerogative orders	Orders which control courts and tribunals by compelling them to exercise their powers according to the law.
prima facie	"At first appearance". On the face of it.
Probate, Grant of	Obtained by *executors* to enable them to carry out the terms of a will.
Prosecute	Bring criminal proceedings against.
Puisne judge	(Pronounced "puny"). An alternative term for High Court judge.
ratio decidendi	"The reason for deciding". That part of a judgement which contains the main reason for coming to a particular decision. It forms the *binding* precedent.
Rebut, rebuttal	Show to the contrary. The offering of an alternative.
Rescission	The act of cancelling or annulling a contract.
Remedy	Method of righting a wrong in a civil case, by, *e.g., awarding damages,* or an *injunction* to the successful party.
Recognisance	Promise by a person standing bail to pay a sum of money into court if the accused fails to respond.
Representation	Acting as an *advocate* in court on behalf of one of the parties.
res ipsa loquitur	"The thing itself speaks". Where from the circumstances it is obvious that *e.g.* negligence has taken place. It is then for the *defendant* to *rebut* this.

Respondent	The traditional term for one against whom a petition of divorce is brought.
Sanctions	Method by which the law is enforced; penalties by way of punishment, *e.g.* fines or imprisonment in a criminal case.
Slander	An untrue and damaging statement (defamation) in spoken form. See *libel*.
Solus agreement	A contract in which it is agreed that one party shall be the sole supplier. *E.g.* of fuel to a filling station.
Specific performance	A *remedy* in civil law where by the courts order one party to carry out its side of an agreement.
stare decisis	"The standing of a decision". The relative importance, according to the hierarchy of courts, of *judicial precedents*.
Statute	Document enacting a law. See *Act of Parliament*.
Stipendiary magistrate	Full-time, legally qualified and salaried magistrate. Now called District Judge. (Magistrates Court).
Sue	Bring an action against a person in the civil courts.
Summary trial	Trial of a minor offence which takes place at a magistrates' court.
Testator, testatrix	Man, woman, who makes a will.
Tortfeasor	Person who performs an act amounting to a civil wrong, and is potentially liable in tort.
ultra vires	"Beyond the powers". Where a body has acted in excess of the powers granted to it.
Vicarious liability	The *liability* of a third party for the tort of someone else .*E.g.* a company, for the tort of one of its employees.
Void	Of no legal effect. Null. As if it had never existed at law.
Voidable	Capable of being made void, but having effect until nullified.
volenti non fit injuria	"There is no injury to one who consents". One who willingly accepts the risk of injury cannot then complain of damage.
Writ	A document starting an action in the civil court. Now called statement of claim.

LIST OF ADDRESSES WHERE INFORMATION MAY BE OBTAINED

Consumer Matters

National Associations of Citizens Advice Bureaux
115–123 Pentonville Road, London N1 9LZ
www.citizensadvice.org.uk

The Office of Fair Trading
Fleetbank House, 2–6 Salisbury Square, London EC4Y 8JX
www.oft.gov.uk

National Consumer Council
20 Grosvenor Gardens, London SW1V 0DH
www.ncc.org.uk

Consumers' Association
2 Marylebone Road, London NW1 4DF
www.which.net

British Standards Institution
389 Chiswick High Road, London W4 4A
www.bsi-global.com

Design Council
34 Bow Street, London WC2E 7DL
www.design-council.org.uk

Professional Associations

The British Insurance Brokers' Association
BIBA House, 14 Bevis Marks, London EC3A 7NT
www.biba.org.uk

The Law Society Consumer Complaint Service
Victona Court, 8 Dormer Piace, Leamington Spa CV325AE
www.lawsociety.org.uk

General Business

London Stock Exchange
10 Palernoster Square, London, EC4M 7LS
www.londonstockexchange.com

The Financial Ombudsman Service
South Quay Plaza, 183 Marsh Wall, London E14 9SR
www.financial-ombudsman.org.uk

Building Societies Association
3 Saville Row, London W1S 3PB
www.bsa.org.uk

Confederation of British Industries
Centre Point, 103 New Oxford Street, London WC1A 1DU
www.cbi.org.uk

Chambers of Commerce, Industry & Trade
See local directories

Companies Registration Office
21 Bloomsbury Street, London WC1B 3XD
www.companieshouse.gov.uk

Other Useful Addresses

General UK Government Website:
www.direct.gov.uk

The Parliamentary and Health service Ombudsman
Millbank Tower, Millbank, London SW1P 4QP
www.ombudsman.org.uk

Commission for Local Administration in England
21 Queen Anne's Gate, London SW1H 9BU
www.lgo.org.uk

Commission for Local Administration in Wales
Court Road, Bridgend, Mid Glamorgan CF31 1BN
www.ombudsman-wales.org

Office of the Health Service Commissioner for Wales
Greyfriars Road, Cardiff CF1 3AG

Police Complaints Authority
10 Great George Street, London SW1P 3AE
www.pca.gov.uk

Commission for Racial Equality
10–12 Allington Street, London SW1E 5EH
www.cre.gov.uk

National Council for Civil Liberties
21 Tabard Street, London SE1 4LA
www.liberty-human-rights.org.uk

Rights of Women
52 Featherstone Street, London EC1Y 8RT
www.rightsofwomen.org.uk

Equal Opportunities Commission
Arndale House, Arndale Centre, Manchester M4 3EQ
www.eoc.org.uk

Advisory, Conciliation and Arbitration Service (ACAS)
Brandon House, 180 Borough High Street,London SE1 1LW
www.acas.org.uk

Employment Tribunals (Central Office)
Ground Floor, Victory House, 30–34 Kingway London WC2B 6EX
www.employmenttribunals.gov.uk

SUGGESTED BOOKLIST

The following list consists of books that may help students who require additional reading for a piece of coursework on a particular topic, and sources, where other material may be found, which will update students with recent changes in the law and current legal issues.

Most of this material should be obtained from the public libraries, if it is not available in school or college. It must be stressed that students should obtain the latest edition available.

Book	Author/s	Publisher
General Introduction		
Williams: Learning the Law	Smith	Sweet & Maxwell (12th ed. 2002)
Understanding Law	Adams & Brownsword	Sweet & Maxwell (2nd ed. 1999)
Business, Consumer & Contract Law		
Davies on Contract	Upex	Sweet & Maxwell (8th ed. 1999)
Charlesworth's Business Law	Dobson et al.	Sweet & Maxwell (16th ed. 1997)
Sales of Goods & Consumer Credit	Dobson	Sweet & Maxwell (6th ed. 2000)
Textbook on Contract	Downes	Blackstone Press (6th ed. 2001)
Law of Contract	Poole	Sweet & Maxwell (4th ed. 2002)
Contract Law	Elliot & Quinn	Addison Wesley Longman (2nd ed. 1999)
Understanding Contract Law	Adams & Brownsword	Sweet & Maxwell (3rd ed. 2000)
Applebey: Contract Law	Applebey	Sweet & Maxwell (1st ed. 2001)
Civil Liberties & Human Rights		
Human Rights Law in the UK	Shorts & de Than	Sweet & Maxwell (2nd ed. 2001)

Criminal Law

Criminal Law	Reed & Seago	Sweet & Maxwell (2nd ed. 2002)
Textbook on Criminal Law	Allen	Blackstone Press (6th ed. 2001)
Criminal Law	Elliot & Quinn	Longman (4th ed. 2002)
Understanding Criminal Law	Clarkson	Sweet & Maxwell (3rd ed. 2001)

Employment Law

Employment Law	Pitt	Sweet & Maxwell (4th ed. 2000)
Textbook on Labour Law	Bowers & Honeyball	Blackstone Press (6th ed. 2000)

English Legal System

The English Legal System	Walker & Walker	Butterworths (8th ed. 1998)
The English Legal Process	Ingman	Blackstone Press (8th ed. 2000)
Eddey & Darbyshire on the English Legal System	Darbyshire	Sweet & Maxwell (7th ed. 2001)
English Legal System	Elliot & Quinn	Longman (4th ed. 2002)

Family and Social Welfare Law

Family Law	Cretney	Sweet & Maxwell (4th ed. 2000)
Social Work and the Law	Vernon	Butterworths (3rd ed. 1998)

Law of Tort

Textbook on Torts	Jones	Blackstone Press (8th ed. 2002)
Torts	Mullis & Oliphant	Palgrave (2nd ed. 1997)
Tort	Elliot & Quinn	Longman (3rd ed. 2001)

| Tort | Giliker & Beckwith | Sweet & Maxwell (1st ed. 2000) |

Updating Materials

Law Quarterly Review		Sweet & Maxwell
Student Law Review		Cavendish Publishing
Modern Law Review		Blackwell Publishing
Law Reports and columns in newspapers		The Times, The Guardian, The Daily Telegraph, The Independent, etc.
Law in Action		BBC Radio 4

Examination Technique

| The Students' Guide to Exam Success | | Open University Press |

Index

LEGAL TAXONOMY
FROM SWEET & MAXWELL

This index has been prepared using Sweet and Maxwell's Legal Taxonomy. Main index entries conform to keywords provided by the Legal Taxonomy except where references to specific documents or non-standard terms (denoted by quotation marks) have been included. These keywords provide a means of identifying similar concepts in other Sweet & Maxwell publications and online services to which keywords from the Legal Taxonomy have been applied. Readers may find some minor differences between terms used in the text and those which appear in the index. Suggestions to taxonomy@sweetandmaxwell.co.uk.

SANCTIONS—*contd*
  Police Complaints Authority, 95
  powers of arrest
    introduction, 91
    summons, by, 91
    warrant, by, 92
    without warrant, 92–93
  powers of entry, 95
  probation orders, 101
  process, 91
  programme requirements, 103
  prohibited activity requirements, 103
  rationale, 98
  referral orders, 100
  reparation orders, 100
  residence requirements, 103
  retrials, 110
  search and seizure, 93
  sentencing
    categories, 98
    community sentences, 100–103
    custodial sentences, 103–106
    determining factors, 108–110
    discharges, 99
    fines, 99–100
    introduction, 97–98
    rationale, 98
    referral orders, 100
    reparation orders, 100
    spot fines, 100
    supervision orders, 101–102
  sentencing guidelines, 109
  sentencing tariff, 109
  sentencing (young offenders)
    action plan orders, 102
    community orders, 103
    custodial sentences, 105–106
    referral order, 100
    reparation order, 100
    supervision orders, 101–102
  seriousness of offence, 109
  spot fines, 100
  stop and search, 93–94
  supervision orders, 101–102
  supervision requirements, 103
  suspended sentences, 105
  tariff, 109
  unpaid work requirements, 103
SATISFACTORY QUALITY
  conditions of sale, 181–182

SEARCH AND SEIZURE
  police powers, 93
SECOND READING
  legislation, 18
SELF DEFENCE
  criminal offences, 266–267
  torts, 239
  trespass to the person, 220
"SELLER IN POSSESSION"
  transfer of title, 187–188
SENDING FOR TRIAL
  generally, 52
SENTENCING
  categories, 98
  community sentences, 100–103
  custodial sentences, 103–106
  determining factors, 108–110
  discharges, 99
  fines, 99–100
  generally, 264
  introduction, 97–98
  manslaughter, 250
  murder, 247
  rape, 254
  rationale, 98
  referral orders, 100
  reparation orders, 100
  spot fines, 100
  supervision orders, 101–102
SENTENCING GUIDELINES
  generally, 109
SENTENCING TARIFF
  generally, 109
SENTENCING (YOUNG OFFENDERS)
  action plan orders, 102
  community orders, 103
  custodial sentences, 105–106
  referral order, 100
  reparation order, 100
  supervision orders, 101–102
SEPARATION
  divorce, 280
SERIOUSNESS OF OFFENCE
  sentencing, 109
SERVICE PERSONNEL
  wills, 291
SEX DISCRIMINATION
  contracts of employment, 203
SEXUAL ORIENTATION DISCRIMINATION
  contracts of employment, 205